SPAIN IN ARMS

SPAIN IN ARMS

A Military History of the Spanish Civil War 1936–1939

E. R. HOOTON

CASEMATE
Philadelphia & Oxford

Published in the United States of America and Great Britain in 2019 by
CASEMATE PUBLISHERS
1950 Lawrence Road, Havertown, PA 19083, USA
and
The Old Music Hall, 106–108 Cowley Road, Oxford OX4 1JE, UK

Hardback Edition: ISBN 978-1-61200-637-6
Digital Edition: ISBN 978-1-61200-638-3 (ePub)

A CIP record for this book is available from the British Library

Printed and bound in the United States of America

Typeset in India by Versatile PreMedia Services. www.versatilepremedia.com

For a complete list of Casemate titles, please contact:

CASEMATE PUBLISHERS (US)
Telephone (610) 853-9131
Fax (610) 853-9146
Email: casemate@casematepublishers.com
www.casematepublishers.com

CASEMATE PUBLISHERS (UK)
Telephone (01865) 241249
Fax (01865) 794449
Email: casemate-uk@casematepublishers.co.uk
www.casematepublishers.co.uk

Front cover: Bottom image: Building of the Diputación Provincial of Madrid in ruins after the Battle of Madrid, with Republican soldiers in the streets of Teruel above. (Wikimedia) Top image: A Condor Legion Heinkel He III drops bombs. (Robert Forsyth)

Contents

List of Maps

Preface

The Spanish Civil War ended 80 years ago yet retains an extraordinary fascination for the Spanish and for foreigners alike while continuing to influence contemporary events, most recently the struggle for Catalonian independence. It also arouses great passions: as this manuscript was being completed the Spanish government decided to exhume former Nationalist leader Generalissimo Francisco Franco's body from his mausoleum and convert the Valley of the Fallen into a memorial for victims of the conflict.

Whole libraries are devoted to almost every aspect of the war, with the notable exception of its military history, which has produced more garbage than a landfill site. Legend has the gallant Republican troops, denied weaponry by the western democracies, overwhelmed on the battlefield by an army of largely Italian, Moorish, and German troops with numerical superiority in armor, aviation, and artillery to achieve a Nationalist victory. There is an element of truth in this claim, but Nationalist success relied upon Spanish troops and was due more to their application of muscle to produce a succession of victories which made them stronger by providing new men and material. But their greatest and most profoundly underestimated success was in mobilizing resources.

The reason why the legend has remained unchallenged may be found in human psychology, in which the defeated console themselves with tales of gallantry against overwhelming odds, tales which, if unchallenged, become accepted as history. This is true of the South in the American Civil War, of Germany in two world wars, of the western European campaign of 1940, and of the Republic in the Spanish Civil War. In the last, the legend was partly accepted by the victors who could argue that they snatched victory against overwhelming odds.

The paean to Republican heroism was sung loudly by the Communist Party's propaganda chorus during the war to drown out questions about the military effort on both sides. Consequently too many foreign historians have unquestioningly followed this line, less as an ideological choice and more a professional one. Most historians focus upon diplomatic, economic, and social events, for they have little interest in, or knowledge of, military history which many seem to disdain. This lack of battlefield knowledge means that descriptions of military events are high on rhetoric and short on detail, while parroting the term "Blitzkrieg" to describe combined armored and air operations makes, by extrapolation, Henri Pétain and Sir Douglas Haig pioneers of mechanized warfare!

This is the first attempt in English to redress the balance and to produce a purely military history of the conflict from December 1936, when the two armies emerged, until the Republic's surrender in 1939. It is based upon numerous published Spanish works, themselves the result of thousands of hours in the scattered Spanish archives, augmented by Italian and Russian books as well as German and British records, the latter including intercepted Italian communications. Some will question this reliance upon published sources, but since these are based upon well-mined archives in Spain, Italy, and Russia, the author sees no reason to reinvent the wheel, especially as many foreign writers on the subject have followed this precedent.

The book is an attempt to counteract simplistic views reminiscent of contemporary Wild West movies in which the hero and villain wore white and black hats respectively. The weakness of such views was brought home to the author during a tour of Castile with a Catalonian guide. The young lady mentioned that her parents had always spoken Catalan within their home even when it was officially banned during the Franco era and their children had followed suit. She also said that her father had served as an officer during the Civil War, not with the Catalonian or Republican governments but with Franco!

The simplistic approach to Spain's military struggle extends to issues such as the bombing of Guernica (see Chapter 3), to "prove" this was a German terror attack, and the "failure" of the western democracies to arm the Republic, which is always ascribed to distaste for the Republic's left-wing stance when it was actually due to a scarcity of resources. Indeed the much despised non-intervention was less of a political statement than an admission of military weakness.

This demonstrates that the military struggle in Spain should not be seen in isolation. There are echoes of World War I and omens of World War II, while the conflict must be examined against these influences as well as against both contemporary European military doctrine and the issue of rearmament. Doctrine is a very narrow field of interest and for this reason it is ignored by historians studying the Iberian conflict. What is less understandable is the failure to exploit Spanish sources which are a deep mine of information; indeed the author was astonished to find that even when foreign writers referred to works available for 40 years there was little attempt to determine the background to military events such as the Teruel campaign or Nationalist military decision-making.

A major frustration for any attempt to write about the military events of this conflict is the question of statistics, especially relating to logistics and casualties. The Spanish sometimes took a casual attitude to record keeping, and indeed the author has yet to see any source providing detailed figures on air sorties, apart from a total for the Ebro campaign. Spanish historians have done their best, especially with casualties, but it is evidently a difficult task and sometimes met only by a best estimate. Generally the author has accepted the scholarship of the distinguished historian José Manuel Martinez Bande, but it is interesting to note that he provides no indication of Nationalist casualties in his account of the 1938 Levante campaign.

However, the British politician George Canning once observed, "Statistics can tell you everything you wish to know, except the truth," and one area of the conflict where this applies is in artillery. The enumeration of ordnance is usually divided into four areas; light (30–74mm), field (75–89mm), medium (90–159mm), and heavy (160mm and above). Neither side possessed the huge artillery trains of the Western Front; indeed in contrast to the conventional European table of organization and equipment, which called for at least four guns per battery (six in the British Army), Spanish batteries usually had three or, in the heaviest batteries, only two. Most "barrel-counting" in the conflict includes light ordnance, such as the 65mm "Tiger" Italian mountain guns which were a significant part of the Nationalist artillery train, but antitank and heavy antiaircraft guns (75–88mm) are often included. I have included light artillery, but not antitank ordnance, in statistics of artillery support. Statistics on air strength are more complete and it is worth comparing the figures for both sides.

While this account is primarily for those interested in military history, the author hopes it will also prove valuable for these whose knowledge of that subject is limited. Some explanation of terminology would, therefore, not go amiss.

The terms Tactical, Operational, and Strategic may well cause some bewilderment. In the past the terms Tactical and Strategic were the norm but during the 19th century the German and Russian armies felt they lacked precision. They introduced the concept of the Operational Level which entered general military usage during the 1880s. At its most simplistic the Tactical Level are operations conducted within army corps while the Operational Level involve armies or army groups, the Strategic Level being above that. As the Spanish Civil War involved smaller forces, the author has applied the term Tactical to divisional level and Operational to formations and commands above this and retains Strategic for overall war direction.

Some technical terms also require explanation. Mortars, which were used extensively, were usually operated by infantry and most were of the Stokes pattern with a smoothbore metal tube incorporating a firing pin. The bomb, with propellant and primer in the rear, was dropped down the barrel and initiated by the firing pin. Both sides also received heavy and cumbersome Great War German *minenwerfer* which were rifled-barreled weapons with a recuperator system.

Automatic weapons consisted of "automatic rifles" and machine guns. The automatic rifles, later called light machine guns or squad automatic weapons, supported rifle platoons and were usually bipod-mounted, air-cooled weapons to provide short bursts of fire from 30/50-round box magazines although the Lewis Gun and Degtyrarev DP 28 used drum magazines. The machine gun was usually a tripod-mounted, water-cooled weapon fed with a 250-round belt to provide sustained fire in support of rifle company and battalion operations, although the Spanish Army used the air-cooled Hotchkiss Model 1907 fed with 24-round strips. Light water- and air-cooled machine guns based upon Maxim designs, often on bipod mounting, also appeared in Spain, notably the German MG 08/15 and the Russian Maksim-Tokarev PMT, the last using 100-round belts.

Purists may be unhappy with my anglicization of place names: Aragón becomes Aragon, Cataluña becomes Catalonia, Extremadura becomes Estremadura, Navarra become Navarre, and Zaragoza becomes Saragossa. However, I have tried to provide Spanish names as they are in the original.

No work on this scale can be accomplished solely by an individual and I have been extremely lucky to have been aided by advice, information, illustrations, and translations. One of the joys of a preface is acknowledging the assistance I have received, although all errors of fact and interpretation are mine alone. From Casemate Publishing I would like to thank Clare Litt, Ruth Sheppard, Isobel Nettleton, Samuel M. Caggiula and Connor Reason. I would also like to thank Defense Attaché's office of the Spanish Embassy in London (and especially Warrant Officer Antonio Puerto), my colleagues in the British Commission for Military History, the staff at the Bodleian Library, the British Library, the Marx Memorial Library, Uxbridge Library and above all Señor José Antonio Fernández Demaría of Campúa. The two great forums on the Spanish

Civil War are El Gran Capitan and the Spanish Civil War section of the Axis History Forum, and within the latter especially "Iron Machine." Individually I would like to express my thanks and appreciation to the following: Robert Forsyth, Will Fowler, Dr J. P. Harris, Dr Jennifer Hooton, Professor Geoffrey R. Jensen, Christophe Pommier, Klaus Schmider, and Juan Carlos Selgado Rodriguez. All errors of fact or interpretation are mine alone.

E. R. Hooton

Comparative Ranks

Spanish*	Italian	German	Russian	British/U.S.
General de Ejército	Generale	Generaloberst	Komandarm	General (Colonel General)****
Teniente General	Generale di Corpo Armata	Generaleutnant	Komkorps***	Lieutenant General
General de Division	Generale di Divisione	Generalmajor	Komdiv***	Major General
General de Brigada	Generale di Brigata**	Generalmajor	Kombrig***	Brigadier/ Brigadier General
Coronel	Colonnello	Oberst	Polkovnik	Colonel
Teniente Coronel	Tenente Colonnello	Oberstleutnant	Podpolkovnik	Lieutenant Colonel
Comandante	Maggiore	Major	Major	Major
Capitan	Capitano	Hauptmann	Kapitan	Captain
Teniente	Tenente	Leutnant	Leytenant	Lieutenant/First Lieutenant
Alferez	Sottotenente	Fahnenjunker	Starshii Leytenant	Second Lieutenant

**The Republican Army had only the rank of General and not General de Division or Brigada until October 24, 1938. It then added the ranks of General de Division and Teniente General.*

*** The MSVN equivalent of the Generale di Brigata was Console Generale.*

**** The military commissar equivalent ranks were Korpskomm, Divkomm, and Brigkomm respectively.*

***** The British and U.S. armies do not have a rank of Colonel General but the German term has been included for comparison.*

CHAPTER I

Testing the Blades: The Madrid Front

With the loss of its empire at the end of the 19th century, Spain's social, economic, and political problems grew like boils. In a vain attempt to lance them a military coup d'état was staged from July 17, 1936 but led to the three-year Civil War that proved traumatic not only for the Iberian Peninsula but also for Europe. Its effects are still being felt.

By the end of July the rebels, who came to be called Nationalists, held much of northern Spain around Galicia, Leon, and Old Castile under Brigadier General Emilio Mola, leaving the government controlling eastern Spain and much of Andalusia in the south and a pro-government enclave along the Biscay coast.[1] Of the army's 113,800 troops, nearly 74,000 sided with the rebels, including 36,000 from the Army of Africa, the Iberian forces being split evenly, while of the 60,400 paramilitary troops (Civil Guard, Carabinieros, Asaltos) only 23,250 sided with the rebels.[2] In reality the government's writ barely extended beyond the ministers' doors as a social revolution enveloped what became Republican territory, directed by a myriad of self-appointed committees, while in some places anarchy literally reigned. As in Nationalist territory, much effort was expended arresting and often murdering opponents both real and imagined.

Each side hastily formed columns to extend their territory and in the north the Nationalists reached the French frontier to isolate the northern enclave. But the understrength conscript garrisons that had participated in the rising and were augmented by enthusiastic militias were too weak to achieve much more. The strategic scale was tipped only by military professionals, the battle-hardened Army of Africa under Brigadier General Francisco Franco. The Africanistas, based upon Foreign Legion and Moorish troops, were initially isolated in Morocco because most of the Fleet opposed the rebellion, but an airlift brought 13,900 men into the Nationalist bridgehead of Seville

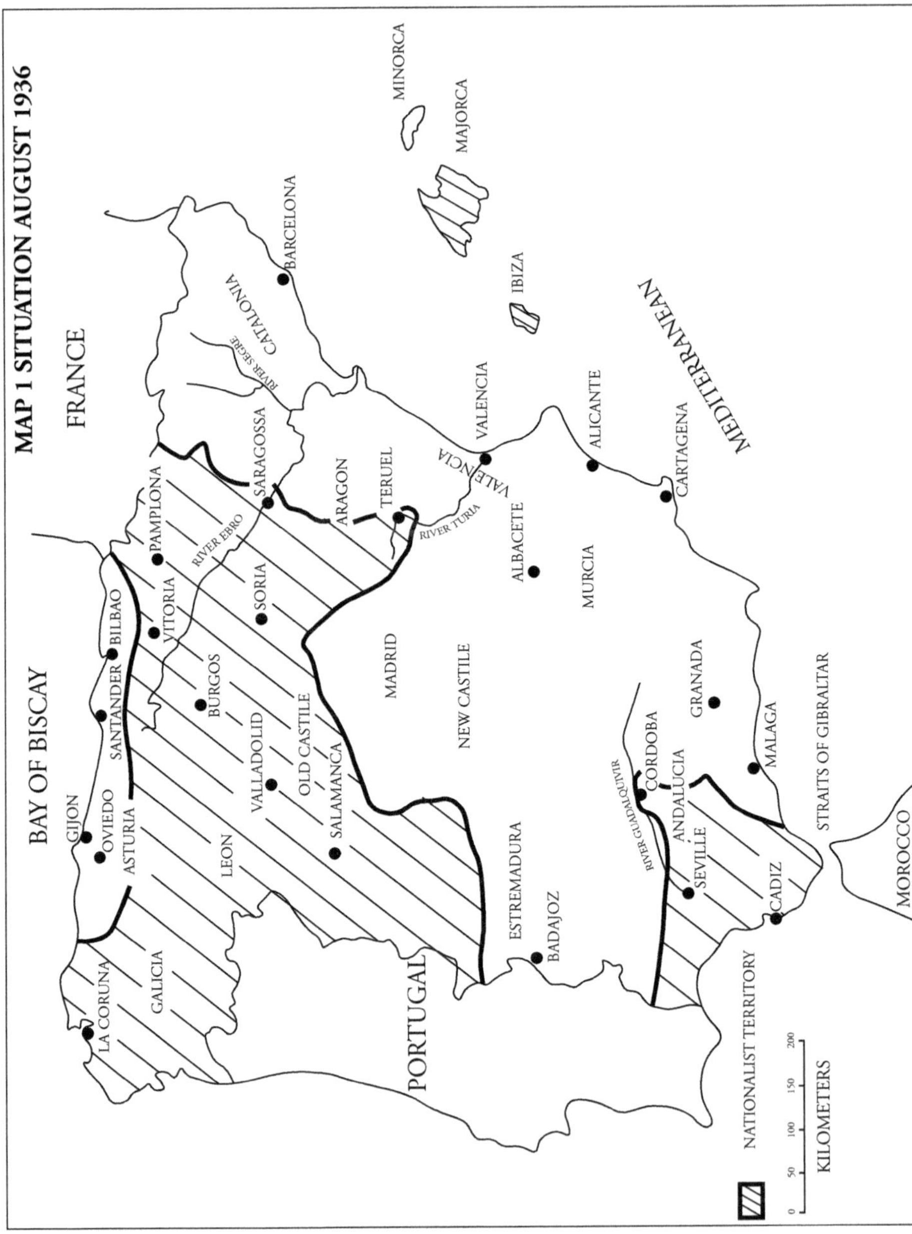

MAP 1 SITUATION AUGUST 1936
FRANCE
BAY OF BISCAY
MINORCA
MAJORCA
IBIZA
BARCELONA
CATALONIA
RIVER SEGRE
MEDITERRANEAN
VALENCIA
ALICANTE
CARTAGENA
SARAGOSSA
ARAGON
TERUEL
VALENCIA
RIVER TURIA
PAMPLONA
RIVER EBRO
ALBACETE
MURCIA
BILBAO
VITORIA
SORIA
MADRID
NEW CASTILE
SANTANDER
BURGOS
OLD CASTILE
GRANADA
GIJON
OVIEDO
ASTURIA
VALLADOLID
SALAMANCA
CORDOBA
RIVER GUADALQUIVIR
ANDALUCIA
MALAGA
STRAITS OF GIBRALTAR
LEON
ESTREMADURA
SEVILLE
CADIZ
MOROCCO
GALICIA
LA CORUNA
BADAJOZ
PORTUGAL
NATIONALIST TERRITORY
0 50 100 150 200
KILOMETERS

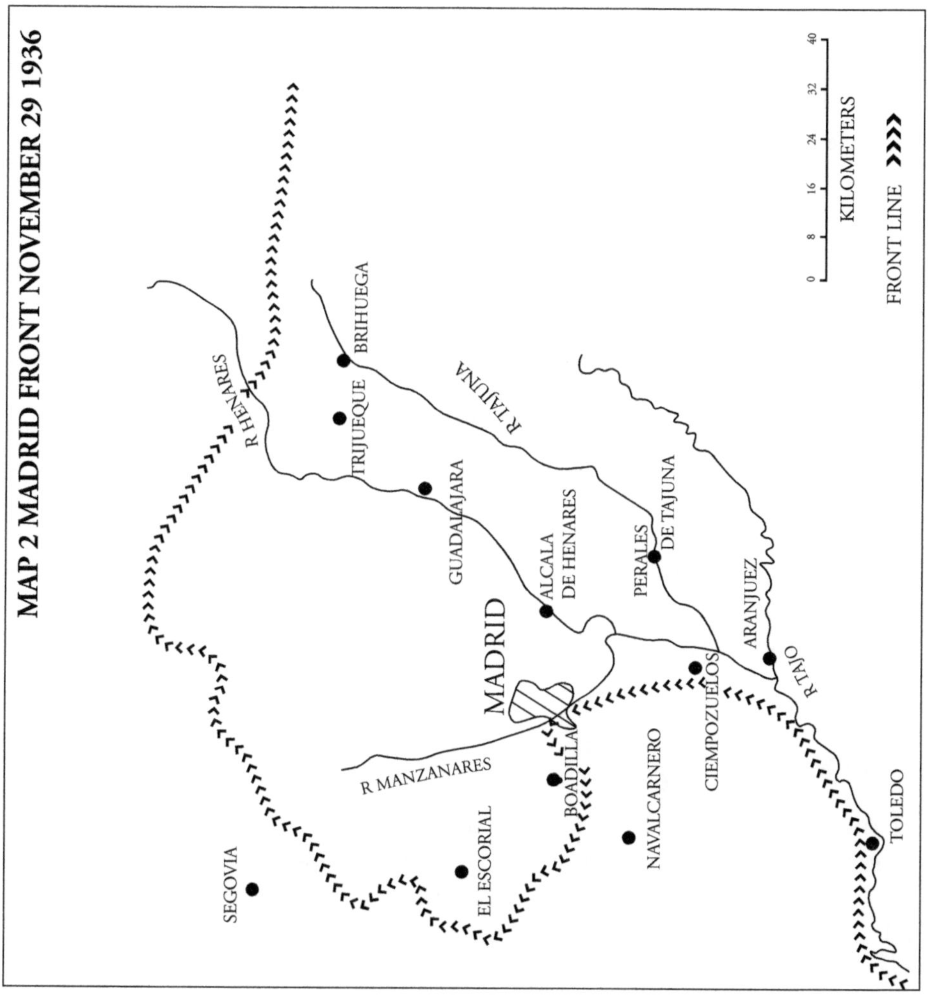
MAP 2 MADRID FRONT NOVEMBER 29 1936
MADRID
SEGOVIA
EL ESCORIAL
BOADILLA
NAVALCARNERO
CIEMPOZUELOS
TOLEDO
ARANJUEZ
PERALES
DE TAJUNA
ALCALA
DE HENARES
GUADALAJARA
TRIJUEQUE
BRIHUEGA
R HENARES
R TAJUNA
R MANZANARES
R TAJO
0 8 16 24 32 40
KILOMETERS
FRONT LINE

from where they spread out during August to establish a major bridgehead in Andalusia.[3]

The Nationalists established a National Defense Council (Junta de Defense Nacional), then an administrative council to control their territory while Franco's successes in the south ensured he received supreme command at a meeting near Salamanca on September 21, and this was proclaimed at Caceres on September 28.[4] In mid-August Franco's troops drove nearly 500km northward through Estremadura to take Talavera de la Reina and link up with Mola. Then, rather than advance upon Madrid, Franco made a diversion to relieve a beleaguered outpost in the Alcazar of Toledo under Colonel José Moscardó. This cost him time but cemented his prestige, and on October 1 he was appointed Generalissimo and *de facto* head of state while the Nationalist general headquarters (GHQ) was established in Salamanca.

The Nationalists now advanced upon Madrid from the west and by the end of October were in the outskirts, but the government, which fled to Valencia, was now receiving Russian military support, notably armor and modern aircraft which helped to halt the enemy. In open country the Army of Africa could out-maneuver the militia masses but the urban environment restricted movement condemning them to a battle of attrition.[5] There was a brief moment of hope when the Africanistas exploited their skills in the open spaces of Madrid's great northwestern park, the Casa de Campo, to cross the River Manzanares at the Frenchmen's (rail) Bridge (Puente de los Franceses) and establish a bridgehead in the University City complex, but then were stopped. Yet as the battle raged in Madrid the troops began a gradual metamorphosis into new armies that would ultimately decide the fate of Spain.

The Corunna Highway

At the end of November Franco, Mola, and Colonel José Varela, the field commander on the Madrid front, held a two-day conference at Varela's headquarters in Leganes where Franco accepted Mola's suggestion to abandon a direct advance on the capital. He agreed to envelop the city which dovetailed with Varela's concerns about the security of the University City bridgehead at the tip of a salient 7km long but less than 4km wide at its broadest point.[6]

West of the Manzanares, the exposed salient cut the Corunna Highway and railroad, then ran south into the Casa de Campo to the Estremadura Highway but it had few internal roads. The Estremadura Highway was the Nationalists' prime supply line to the Madrid front with the enemy barely a kilometer away from it at the base of the salient. All agreed it was vital to secure the highway and on November 28 Varela was ordered to do so by advancing to a line from Pozuelo del Alarcon (Pozuelo) to Aravaca.

The battlefield was marked at its northern edge by the Corunna Highway, which curved around Aravaca and continued for nearly 20km to Las Rozas, then went northwest into the Sierra de Guadarrama. The western boundary was the River Perales, which with the River Guadarrama to the east and its tributary the Aulencia, ran roughly north to south through a rolling plain cut by deep gullies from streams feeding the waterways which created frequent winter mists. Apart from the gullies the only defensive features on the landscape were numerous olive groves and orchards, notably north of Brunete, along the banks of the Guadarrama, east of Boadilla del Monte (Boadilla), west of Majadahonda, and around Pozuelo. The area was dotted with thick-walled summer villas called *castellos*, whose walled gardens and olive groves or orchards helped to make them excellent strongpoints.

East of the Guadarrama the ground slowly rises with a few hills, notably west of a road which ran from the Corunna Highway at Las Rozas through Majadahonda, Boadilla, Villaviciosa de Odon (Vilaviciosa) to the Estramadura Highway. Boadilla was the key road junction with an important road west–east from Brunete through Retamares to the Estremadura Highway and a side road north through Pozuelo and Aravaca to the Corunna Highway. Southeast of Pozuelo was Humera from which the enemy could threaten the Nationalist salient, while to the north the Corunna railroad diverted around Aravaca to Pozuelo station, a kilometer northeast of the town, then ran parallel with the highway. Between the Perales and the Guadarrama was another road which ran north from the Estramadura Highway at Navalcarnero through Nationalist-held Brunete, Villanueva de la Cañada, and Valdemorillo to the Corunna Highway at San Lorenzo del Escorial (Escorial) with a side road north of Villanueva de la Cañada eastward through Villanueva del Pardillo to Majadahonda.

Varela organized three regimental-size columns with 7,000 men under the overall command of Colonel Francisco García-Escámez. On the left was Lieutenant Colonel Marcelino Gavilán's Cavalry column based upon seven squadrons, in the center was Lieutenant Colonel Siro (Félix) Alonso with four light/field batteries, and on the right was Lieutenant Colonel Maximiano Bartoméu who would strike west from the Casa de Campo Col with two batteries, Varela providing five batteries of mostly heavy artillery in support.[7]

They faced the Central Army created on October 24 under 60-year-old cavalryman Major General Sebastián Pozas, a former Director General of the

Civil Guard and Interior Minister, whose brother Gabriel was Mola's aide. A fervent Republican despite being born into a conservative Monarchist family, he distinguished himself like many in the Moroccan Rif War.[8] Despite being court-martialed in 1934 for refusing to prevent the declaration of the Catalan state in 1936, he became Director General of the Civil Guards and was briefly Interior Minister.[9] On October 5 he became commander of 1 Division District and President of the Madrid Defense Council (Junta de Defensa de Madrid) but on October 23 General José Miaja took over the division, leaving Pozas nominally in charge of the Defense Council and, from New Year's Eve, commander of the Central Army responsible for the sector from the Sierra Guadarrama down to the Tajo river.

He had 35,800 men and 134 guns by the end of November, but the Madrid Defense Council, which remained the fiefdom of the Communists, was determined to retain its autonomy, as was Miaja. The 58-year-old owl-like Miaja was a conservative infantry officer and despite service in Morocco and membership of the right-wing Unión Militar Española (UME) was never fully trusted by the right and his Madrid-based brigade remained loyal when the uprising began, possibly by accident rather than design. He was an affable man, a competent "plodder," brave but vain and slightly deaf.[10]

On November 20 he reorganized the defense of Madrid between the Guadarrama and the Jarama in the south into four sectors, of which the 1st (or Right) between the Perales and the University City north of the Nationalist salient was under a Rumanian-born Russian advisor, Manfred or Moishe Stern who had the *nom de guerre* of Kléber.[11] Kléber had led the 11 International Brigade (BI) into battle in Madrid and was a competent soldier as well as a member of Soviet Military Intelligence (Glavnoye Razvedyvatel'noye Upravleniye or GRU) since 1924 serving in the United States before being transferred to China. He had 10,400 men and ten guns, six heavy, organized into Column Colonel (Luís) Barceló, Lieutenant Colonel Francisco Galán's 3 Mixed Brigade (BM), medical Major Miguel Palacios's Brigade "X," which was being activated from his column and that of Colonel Julián Fernández-Cavada, as well as Captain Fernando Sabio's 5 BM, later reinforced by 12 BI.[12]

Varela's attack on November 29 struck Galán, whose men, caught in the open having failed to dig, broke and fled being rallied only at Pozuelo where their pursuers took the town's cemetery. The arrival of 12 BI regained the cemetery and prevented Alonso from taking the town, and while Gavilán advanced 3km Bartoméu made little progress. However, the Nationalists had succeeded in protecting the Estremadura Highway which they secured by repulsing Kléber's counterattack on December 3.

In a surfeit of optimism Franco and Mola decided to exploit their success to seize Escorial and isolate Republican forces in the Sierra Guadarrama, the mountain chain shielding Madrid in the north, while simultaneously cutting the capital's water and electricity supplies. On December 7 Franco ordered "a sudden and surprise attack" to isolate Madrid from Pozas's troops in the Sierra de Guadarrama. Two days earlier the Nationalist *ad hoc* command arrangements on the Madrid front were regularized with the creation of what was usually abbreviated to the Madrid Reinforced Division under 55-year-old Brigadier General Luis Orgaz, a Monarchist who had opposed the Republic from its birth.[13] A friend of Mola, he was described as "resolute and irascible" and as an ardent coup supporter he was scheduled to lead the rising in Madrid. But the suspicious government exiled him to the Canaries where he worked closely with Franco. With Nationalist air chief, Brigadier General Alfredo Kindélan, he became one of Franco's most trusted confidantes and it was he who proposed Franco as supreme military leader.[14] Orgaz's command was split into three brigade sectors of which I Brigade was north of the Estramadura Highway under Varela who had 10,000 men in 15 battalions, nine squadrons and two tank companies supported by 13 batteries with 52 guns.

Columns under Colonels Fernando Barrón and Eduardo Sáenz de Buruaga would advance from Villaviciosa to take Boadilla while Colonel José Monasterio's column would advance north from Brunete to take Villanueva de la Cañada. Given the Nationalist superiority in open country, Varela hoped he could stampede the enemy and reach the Corunna Highway. They faced Kléber with 12,100 men and six guns and, having relieved 3 BM, he now had Barceló's column in the Guadarrama Valley, Lieutenant Colonel Juan Perea's Anarchist column on his right holding the line to Pozuelo station and Palacios around Aravaca, with Major Alejandro Gallo's 6 BM holding the line down to the Nationalist salient. In reserve was 5 BM, now under Carabinero Captain Hilario Fernández after Sabio fled his command post during the first attack.

Thick fog disrupted Varela's planned attack on December 13 and when it began the following afternoon dense vapors returned and quickly brought it to a halt. Only when visibility improved by dawn of December 16 did the attack begin in earnest. The thin-faced, graying Barrón from the west and Alonso from the east isolated Boadilla, held by Barceló's men and elements of 11 BI who failed to prevent Buruaga taking the town. Yet Kléber contained the threat by sending in tanks to disrupt the advance while bringing 11 BI down the Guadarrama Valley and 12 BI to cover the highway to the east.

Monasterio managed to take Villanueva de la Cañada but fog again blanketed the battlefield and lifted only on December 19 by which time Varela

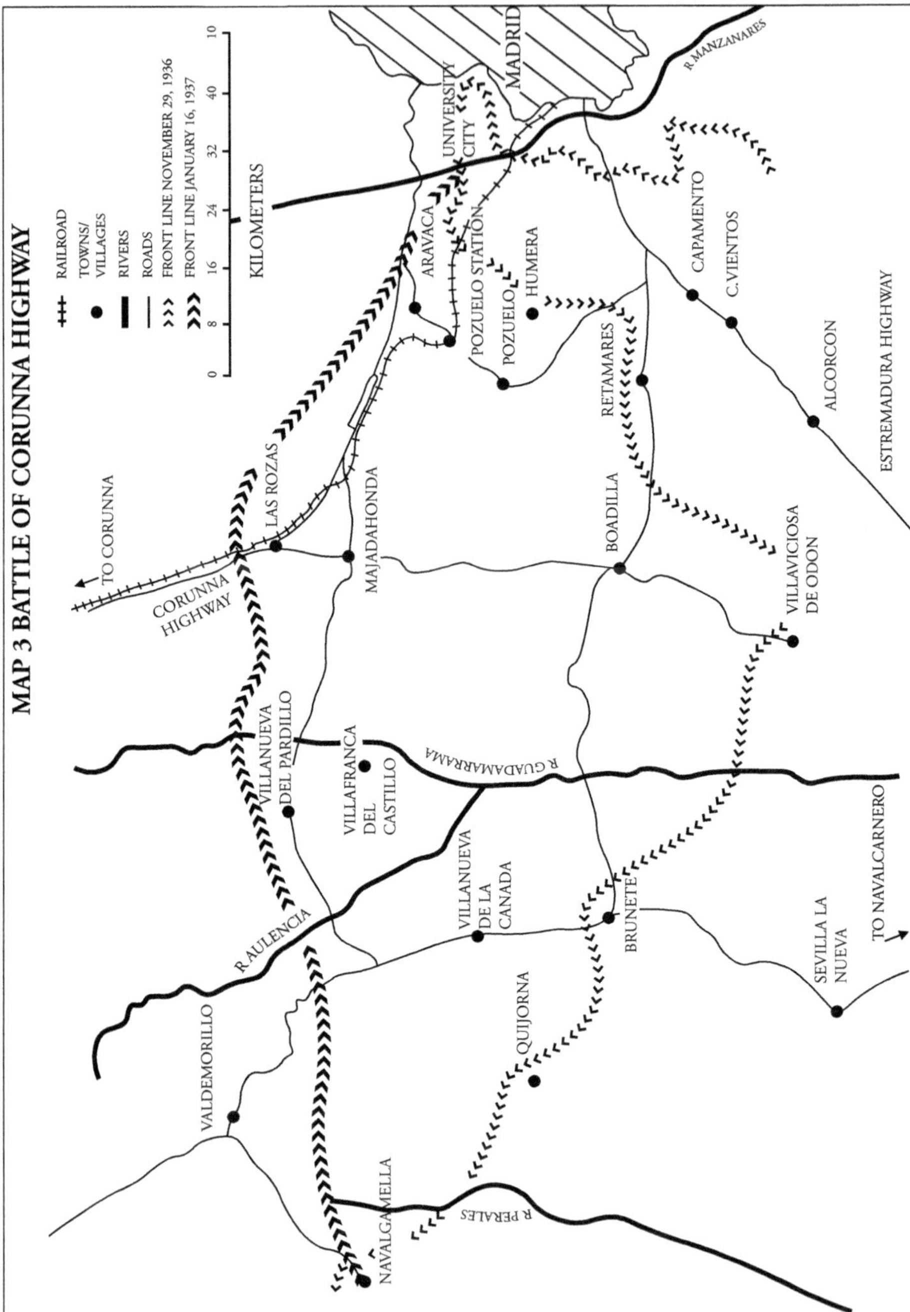

MAP 3 BATTLE OF CORUNNA HIGHWAY

realized he was outnumbered and had lost the element of surprise. Cannily he withdrew from his more exposed positions while retaining Boadilla and Villanueva de la Cañada. He planned to renew the assault after Christmas but was wounded on that day causing a delay.

From December 20 through January 2 the 12 BI under Hungarian Communist Lukàcs's (Mate Zalka) vainly struck along the Guadarrama Valley toward Brunete but gained time for Miaja to reorganize his forces again on December 31; the former 1st Sector becoming the 8 Infantry Division (DI) with 35, 37, 44 BM under Major Eduardo Cuevas. Kléber had irritated both the Socialist Spanish Premier and War Minister Largo Caballero, once dubbed the "Spanish Lenin," and the Madrid Defense Council leadership by disparaging the Spanish troops and demanding the international brigades be concentrated as a spearhead for an offensive on the Madrid front. He reportedly told Perea, who was leading an Anarchist column, that Spain needed a leader like the Soviet Union's Defense Minister Marshal Kliment Voroshilov to control the war effort and suggested Perea as a potential candidate.[15] The paranoid Anarchists perceived this as the start of a Communist coup while the equally paranoid Communist organizer of the international brigades, André Marty, who was jealous of Kléber, also dismissed the idea. Kléber was relieved and sent to live in a small hotel in Valencia until the crisis blew over, whereupon he returned to command a new division.[16] Barceló's column was redesignated 35 BM but on New Year's Day he was shot in the face by a battalion commander in a row over the relief of two companies and replaced by the Italian Communist Nino Nanetti.[17]

Nanetti shielded Valdemorillo with 11 BI under "Hans" to the east.[18] On his right was 5 DI (formerly 2nd Sector) under Perea from December 31, with 5, 38, 39 and Z BM, while Captain Joaquin Zulueta's 38 BM held Pozuelo with Palacios's 39 BM on its left. Being activated in the rear were 37 BM (Fernandez-Cavada) and 44 BM (Major José Enciso) and the defenders had a total of 20,300 men.[19]

On December 19 Franco demanded that Madrid be encircled from the north as soon as possible, and on New Year's Day Orgaz ordered a new advance upon the Corunna Highway with 12,000 men supported by 40 tanks and 80 guns swinging the Nationalist line northward like a closing door hinged upon Pozuelo. A new column under Colonel José Iruretagoyena, with 4½ battalions and six squadrons, had relieved Monasterio at Villanueva de la Cañada and was to strike northeast toward Villanueva del Pardillo and Las Rozas covering the left. The main blow would be from Villaviciosa by Barrón's and Colonel José Asensio's columns with a combined strength equivalent to nine battalions.

A quartet of CTV CV-33/35 tankettes assemble to spearhead the CTV advance during the Santander campaign. With their twin machine guns and thin armor these vehicles were no match for the Russian T-26. (Photo by José Demaría "Campúa")

A Condor Legion Heinkel He 111 drops bombs while the gunners, one in a "dustbin turret" below the aircraft, keep a watchful eye for enemy fighters.

A formation of Nationalist Air Force tri-motor Junkers Ju 52/3m bombers. Many of these aircraft had served with the Condor Legion and some had been used to fly in troops from Morocco at the beginning of the war.

Republican infantry prepare to meet an attack. While there was much rhetoric about "Spanish Trenches," as this picture illustrates neither side liked digging so that trenches were often shallow. (Courtesy of Marx Memorial Library, London)

Buruaga, advancing from Boadilla, would cover their right with 4½ battalions and together they would strike northward in the direction of Majadahonda then swing eastwards and advance to the highway north of the La Pozuelo station. García-Escámez, who was south of Pozuelo would first mask, then envelop the town with his 3½ battalions and occupy the highway south of the railroad. Each column had four batteries, one heavy, and most had a tank company. Only one battalion was in reserve and there was additional support from eight heavy batteries south of Pozuelo.

The 14km-front attack on January 3 saw Iruretagoyena cross the Aulencia and approach Villanueva del Pardillo but Barrón and Asensio made slow progress against Cuevas who committed Hans's 11 BI. The command was expanded to Group Cuevas (Agrupación Cuervas) which received Brigade "E" under Communist Valentine González, better known as El Campesino (the Peasant), some International Brigade cavalry and three tank companies. But the reinforcements failed to prevent Iruretagoyena taking Villanueva del Pardillo the following day as Barrón isolated Majadahonda from the north, allowing Asensio to take the town before fog and resistance from the castillos slowed the Nationalist advance. Cuevas now created a divisional-sized reserve from Hans's, Nanetti's and Campesino's brigades augmented by a couple of battalions from other brigades.

The Nationalist offensive's next phase began on January 5 when Barrón, Asensio, and Buruaga turned east, shielded by Iruretagoyena, to strike the brigades of Nanetti, Campesino, and the Anarchist Cipriano Mera. The defenders' resolve was shaken by heavy artillery fire and the brigades lost contact with each other to fight private wars as they withdrew. The sense of isolation led to panic due to rumors of Moorish cavalry in the rear, a side effect of Republican propaganda emphasizing the brutality of the North African troops. At Pozuelo six Soviet armored cars knocked out a dozen PzKpfw I as Barrón and Asensio bypassed the town to reach the Corunna Highway near Las Rozas smashing Hans's Thaelmann Battalion which attempted to hold the town unsupported.[20]

The defenders ran short of ammunition, reportedly forcing Miaja to send up blanks so that the men had the illusion of resisting while his reserves had only 20 rounds each when the official requirement was 300. He took personal command of the sector and conducted a mock execution of deserters from Campesino's and Mera's units, while, ominously, scarce machine guns were set up behind the lines. Miaja also ordered the transfer of Enrique Lister's 1 BM from the southern suburbs to shield the Corunna Highway and also brought up 12 and 14 BI. Meanwhile the defenders rallied and fought stubbornly until the arrival of Lukàcs's 12 BI and Lister supported by Russian tanks, but an overnight counterattack failed.

The Nationalist waves lapped up to the Corunna Highway on January 6 when Barrón and Asensio cut the Corunna railroad west of Pozuelo Station but the newly arrived 69 BM under Major Gustavo Durán thwarted Buruaga's attempts to take the station as Campesino shielded Las Rozas.[21] The defenders were also displaying greater spirit with numerous bayonet charges which bought time during the day but at great cost.[22] But despite this the following day saw García-Escámez take both Pozuelo and Humera while Barrón added another 2km of the highway. García-Escámez's well-timed assault upon Pozuelo almost trapped the French battalion of 11 BI with a tank company and while they escaped it was at great cost, their escape aided by a diversionary attack from 6 BM. Hans's Thaelmann Battalion was not so lucky, being isolated when it was sent forward to plug a gap near Las Rozas then almost annihilated.

The Nationalist advance was slowing. During the evening of January 8 they took Aravaca but the following day Asensio and Buruaga failed to take the hills on the other side of the highway. This left the Nationalists with a line from Las Rozas to the outskirts of Madrid, including 10km of the Corunna Road but Varela could advance no further.

The arrival of 12 and 14 BI and six fresh Spanish battalions gave Miaja the opportunity to plan a counteroffensive against Las Rozas and Majadahonda respectively. Cuevas had Hans's, Campesino and Duran in line with Galán's brigade in reserve while Perea's division had along the highway 6 and 39 BM with a reserve of Lister's 1 BM with 21 and 38 BM and Brigadier General Dimiti Pavlov's tanks.[23] On the other flank Lieutenant Colonel Ricardo Burillo, the 9 DI commander, was sent from the Jarama front with some of his battalions to command a division-sized group with Lukàcs, Nanetti, and 14 BI augmented by 2 and 3 DI battalions.

As the attack began on January 11 the temperature dropped to freezing as a thick mist again arose to disrupt both sides' preparations. Nanetti's failure near Majadahonda exposed the neighboring 12 BI but the largely French 14 BI, under the Polish Karol Swierczewski, a former Moscow Military School professor known as "General Walter," managed to take Las Rozas with the aid of Russian tanks. But when they withdrew to refuel the Frenchmen followed, believing there had been an order to withdraw and their attempt to retake the town the next day saw them cut to pieces.

The Russian tank performance was poor, with vehicles driving around firing wildly because they had new leaders. The experienced Major Paul Arman and Brigadier General Semon Krivoshein had been recalled to Moscow for debriefing and been replaced by Pavlov, who had assumed command of the Tank Brigade on December 6 with 56 tanks and 68 armored cars reduced to 47 tanks a month later. Both his predecessors had recognized the difficulties of coordinating tank, infantry, and artillery into what are termed "combined arms operations." This led to a Catch-22 situation where the tanks easily outpaced the infantry, the former then being exposed to antitank guns and the latter to automatic weapons. To square the circle Krivoshein ordered the tanks to provide direct support to the infantry and stray no more than 500m ahead. With the departure of Arman and Krivoshein together with many veterans, Pavlov had to relearn these lessons, as tanks were used either for infantry support or as cavalry acting as fire brigades to plug gaps.

The clashes confirmed the inferior firepower of the Nationalist tanks, armed only with a pair of rifle-caliber machine guns. The German tank advisor Lieutenant Colonel Wilhelm Ritter von Thoma ordered his advisors to avoid engaging enemy tanks whenever possible. Attempts to up-gun the German and Italian tanks proved futile but the Spanish followed Thoma's advice to support their armor with 37mm antitank guns which often proved deadly against the T-26.

Meanwhile, the fighting continued for another three days with ever-decreasing success, and as ammunition ran low combat evaporated. Some advanced Republican detachments remained in the Nationalist line until Iruretagoyena and Asensio straightened it out on January 16. Orgaz had advanced some 20km but it was claimed he had suffered 15,000 casualties, a figure which was clearly exaggerated, but certainly the inexperience of the new units was reflected in their heavier casualties and was probably about 1,500. Republican casualties were also exaggerated at 15,000; the actual figure was 6,775 with a further 4,100 reporting sick, but a third of the International troops became casualties. The success, with Communist propaganda support, cemented Miaja's reputation, and while never a Communist himself he did hold membership cards for every political party in Madrid, including the joint youth movement even though he was 58!

Jarama

Despite the failure of the Corunna Highway operation, Franco was determined to continue the encirclement of Madrid, this time through the Jarama Valley, some 20km southeast of the capital, to cut the Valencia Highway.

The road, running northwest to southeast, marked the battle's northern boundary through Vaciamadrid, Arganda, and down to Perales de Tajuna. It crossed the River Jarama at the Arganda Bridge just east of Vaciamadrid which is a couple of kilometers north of the confluence of the rivers Manzanares and Jarama overlooked by the Corbertas Heights. The Jarama runs southward and southwest of Titulcia and is joined by the River Tajuna, which the Valencia Highway crosses near Perales de Tajuña, with both valleys dominated by Mount Pingarron.

The Nationalist line passed west of Perales del Rio (Perales) to a point east of Valdemoro running parallel with the Madrid–Alicante railroad. The railroad ran southeast past Ciempozuelos, 5km northwest of Titulcia on the other side of the Jarama, before running down the valley and splitting west of Aranjuez to go to Andalusia. South of Ciempozuelos it ran parallel to the 17th-century Jarama Canal which ran to the River Tagus.

The communications hub on the western bank was San Martin de la Vega (San Martin), through which ran a road from Perales down to Ciempozuelos, skirting the 697m La Maranosa which dominated the confluence of the Manzanares and Jarama. The Jarama here ran swiftly and on the opposite bank was a range of hills through which ran a narrow-gauge branch line, built in 1922, between a sugar refinery on the Madrid–Valencia line to Ciempozuelos, crossing the river at the Pindoque Bridge. Whereas much of the western battlefield was an open, sandy plain, this was an area of rolling hills dotted with olive groves with the prime height being Pingarron (693m) north of the San Martin–Morata de Tajuna (Morata) Road.

Orgaz planned to strike across the Jarama on a 40km front between the rivers Tajuna and Henares to cut the Valencia Highway, then link at Alcala de Henares (Alcala) with Nationalist troops who would push down the Saragossa Highway from Brihuega. From January 15 he assembled 18,600 men in five brigades, three under a recovered Varela as Task Force North (Destacamento Norte) and two under García-Escámez as Task Force South (Destacamento Sur) with 24 battalions and 15 squadrons. There were 42 tanks scattered among the brigades, each of which had five batteries, and there were six heavy batteries—a total of 101 guns, half of them heavy but the only reserves consisted of 2½ battalions.[24]

On the afternoon of January 22 Orgaz issued orders for Phase One, a 10km advance to the Jarama and the canal to secure the line of the Manzanares. In Phase Two the Jarama would be crossed between Vaciamadrid and San Martin using the Pindoque bridge and one near San Martin, followed by an advance northeast to seize the high ground between the Jarama and the Tajuna to establish a bridgehead bounded in the north by the Valencia Highway. Phase Three involved a 25km advance to Alcala.[25] The offensive was scheduled to

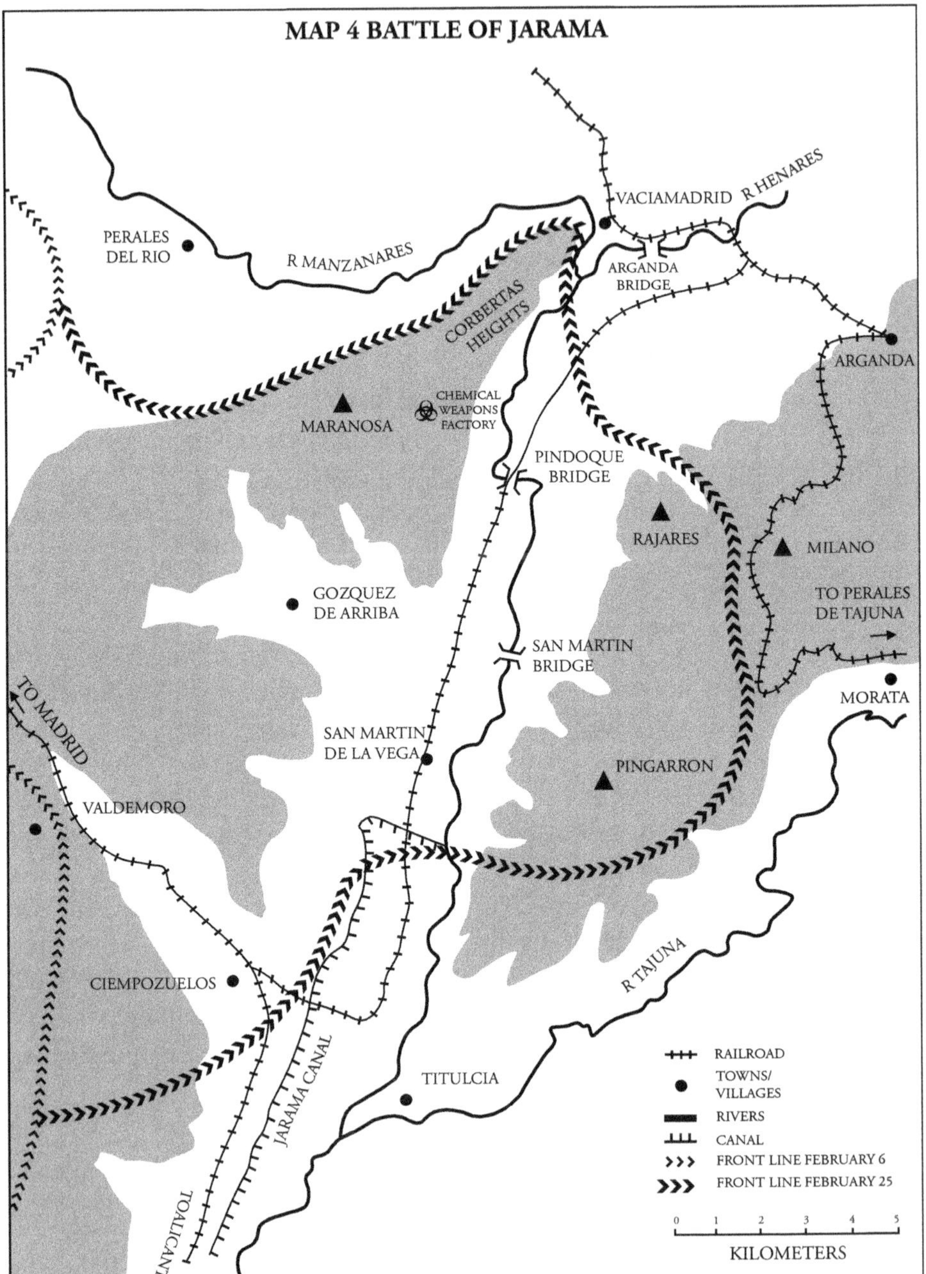
MAP 4 BATTLE OF JARAMA
PERALES DEL RIO
R MANZANARES
VACIAMADRID
R HENARES
ARGANDA BRIDGE
CORBERTAS HEIGHTS
ARGANDA
MARANOSA
CHEMICAL WEAPONS FACTORY
PINDOQUE BRIDGE
RAJARES
MILANO
GOZQUEZ DE ARRIBA
TO PERALES DE TAJUNA
SAN MARTIN BRIDGE
MORATA
TO MADRID
SAN MARTIN DE LA VEGA
PINGARRON
VALDEMORO
CIEMPOZUELOS
R TAJUNA
JARAMA CANAL
TITULCIA
TOALICANTE
RAILROAD
TOWNS/ VILLAGES
RIVERS
CANAL
FRONT LINE FEBRUARY 6
FRONT LINE FEBRUARY 25
0 1 2 3 4 5
KILOMETERS

begin on January 24 but dawn brought torrential rain which lasted for ten days, turning the ground into a quagmire. Some units tried to push forward on schedule but Orgaz ordered them back to their jump-off points, although cavalry secured the high ground southwest of Ciempozuelo.

Soviet advisors had also been suggesting an offensive in this sector, and with growing confidence in his forces Pozas proposed, on January 15, striking the enemy's Madrid salient from the Jarama Valley. The chief of the general staff, Brigadier General Toribio Martínez, and Largo Caballero agreed but Miaja wanted simultaneously to strike on the Corunna Highway battlefield toward Brunete. D-Day was set for January 27 with 35,000 men assembling south of Madrid, but the operation was delayed by political squabbling about overall command, with the Communists advocating Miaja while their opponents supported Pozas.

On February 4 the weather broke and aerial reconnaissance, together with Communications Intelligence (Comint) and espionage, meant that both sides became aware in general terms of the other's intentions.[26] The Republicans, who had nagging doubts about the effectiveness of their new brigades, immediately abandoned all plans for the offensive and went on to the defensive. Miaja and his chief of staff, Major Vicente Rojo, fearing the enemy would work their way around the southern outskirts of Madrid, assembled 4 DI (36, 41 67 BM) under Major Juan Modesto who also assumed command of 19 BM.[27] In reserve were 1bis (later 9), 5, 21 and 41 BM together with 12 BI while 11 BI was scheduled to join them.

Pozas moved 48 BM, under Colonel Evelio Jiménez, into the northern part of the valley toward what Colodny coyly called "the military factory" at the foot of Maranosa. This was actually Spain's chemical weapons factory (Fábrica Nacional de Productos Quimicos) around which the defenders had arranged 50 cylinders of chlorine gas and the Nationalist brigade leader Colonel Ricardo Rada was told not to enter the facility until it was surveyed by the chemical warfare services.[28] Half of Lieutenant Colonel Eloy Camino's 23 BM was in San Martin while Lieutenant Colonel Gerardo Sánchez-Monje's 18 BM was at Aranjuez. To the south was 9 DI (45, 46, 47 BM) under Burillo, a prewar Asalto leader and the left-wing and anti-clerical scion of a conservative, aristocratic family, who had returned from the Corunna Highway front.

Orgaz decided on February 5 to attack the following day when his men fanned out from a 15km start line and advanced 10km. Rada's brigade on the left caused confusion by striking down the Madrid Committee/Central Army boundary to take Maranosa, which became an artillery firebase, then entered the Corbertas Heights destroying most of Jiménez's brigade and overrunning the chemical factory before the defenders could use their gas.[29] On the other flank García-Escámez fought a brisk battle for Ciempozuelos with Sánchez-Monje, a prewar infantry regiment commander leading a largely Communist brigade which was short of ammunition. The defenders suffered 1,300 casualties before they were driven back to rally at the Titulcia road bridge, although Pozas did not learn this until the following day. On February 8 Sánchez-Monje would suddenly flee, be court-martialed and cashiered, leaving the brigade in the hands of one of his battalion commanders, Francisco Carro.[30] Meanwhile, Barrón's cavalry exploited weak resistance in the north to take Gózquez de Arriba, in the valley northwest of San Martin which remained in Republican hands.

The following day Rada encountered fierce resistance from 19 BM as he descended the Corbertas Heights toward Vaciamadrid, leading Varela to bring up Barrón on his right. The move occurred as black clouds heralded the return of torrential rain which turned the valleys into quagmires. The offensive caused confusion in Republican ranks. Miaja was slow to recognize the threat, believing that it was a feint before the enemy struck northwest. He dispatched southward Lister's 11 DI (1, 9 BM), two more International Brigades (14, 15 BI) and Durán's 69 BM, while Pozas created the Arganda Group under Lieutenant Colonel Arturo Mena for the southern sector down to San Martin, initially with 17 and 19 BM supported by survivors of 23 BM, a tank company, and four batteries, but units were scattered and it took time to bring order out of chaos.

February 8 saw Rada and Barrón continue to push northward aided by a short but heavy artillery preparation which routed the defenders, and the Nationalists soon overlooked Vaciamadrid and the confluence of the Jarama and Manzanares as well as reaching the banks of the Jarama and the canal. Italian and Polish battalions of 12 BI, supported by Pavlov's tanks, thwarted attempts to take the Arganda Bridge but the Valencia Highway was under automatic weapons fire. Progress was slow the following day due to the mud, while the Republicans desperately sought to push the enemy away from the Valencia Highway but succeeded only in regaining the confluence of the rivers. With Largo Caballero's support, Pozas was determined to fight a battle of attrition in the Jarama Valley while Miaja again urged an attack at Brunete. During the afternoon the clouds began to clear, the sun began to dry out the ground, and there was a brief lull as the Nationalists prepared a new drive across the Jarama.

During February 10, Varela conducted a personal reconnaissance on horseback while scouts probed the only two practical crossing points across a swollen river: the Pindoque rail bridge, a steel structure on white, stone-faced pillars, and the San Martin road bridge. Varela decided to launch an immediate surprise night attack against the former because woods would conceal his assembly while the far bank had few natural obstacles which could be covered by fire from Maranosa. Barrón and Buruaga would establish a bridgehead at the rail bridge while Asensio would take the road bridge. They would then push northeast to Alcala, with their flanks shielded by the rivers to reach the line Arganda–Morata to secure the salient.

That night Moorish infantry and engineers attacked, slit the sentinels' throats at the Pindoque bridge, overwhelmed the defending French company of whom only four escaped, then "deloused" the bridge. They missed one demolition charge which was set off but merely raised the metal structure, then deposited it virtually intact onto its foundations. Engineers laid planks across the rail lines for easier crossing and Barrón sent as many men as possible to establish a bridgehead, but by dawn the bridgehead came under heavy fire from aircraft and Pavlov's tanks.[31] The bridgehead was shielded by artillery fire from Maranosa while antitank guns were dragged across the bridge to knock out a couple of tanks. Varela capitalized on his success by bringing over cavalry which charged up the bare slopes to isolate and destroy a French battalion, while infantry with mountain guns followed to dig in among the few olive trees allowing the whole brigade to cross by 15:00. They slowly pushed back a Polish battalion who were buttressed by Pavlov's tanks and Carabineros. With nightfall Buruaga's brigade began to cross the bridge, moving onto Barrón's right to secure the Nationalist toehold but behind their lines there was much confusion.

On the right Asensio crossed the canal on the morning of February 11 to take San Martin, but machine-gun fire from across the river slowed progress toward the bridge and gave the defenders time to detonate demolition charges which again did little damage. That night Moorish troops swam the river, knifed the sentinels, then drove back 17 BM to force their way into the bush-studded hills and by noon they had taken Pingarron. Mena desperately tried to contain the advance, and to support him Pozas dispatched 11 BI to face Barrón and 15 BI with Pavlov's tanks to hold Buruaga and Asensio.

That night Varela met Orgaz and reported that crossing the river had cost him nearly 720 casualties who would be difficult to replace. Despite this they decided to press on and the next day watched as the advance slowed due to desperate resistance from the two International Brigades aided by artillery fire interdicting the Pindoque Bridge.[32] Republican pressure was growing as Maranosa's batteries helped keep the enemy at bay but on the night of February

12/13 Lister arrived opposite the bridgehead with his newly formed 11 DI which entered the line south of 15 BI.

Orgaz was determined to maintain the pressure, and during February 13 Barrón edged closer to Arganda, taking Mounts Valdeperdices and Milano to force back 11 BI and open a gap at Pajares. This allowed Barrón to turn the right of 15 BI and send cavalry up the eastern bank of the Jarama almost to Arganda. Asensio and Buruaga tried to reach Morata pushing through dripping olive groves where, as a defender later said in a poem, "Death's leaden finger beckoned again and again."[33] Progress was slow because the foreign volunteers fought tooth and nail while the attackers were now outside the range of Maranosa's guns, but the defenders were taking heavy casualties and morale was cracking. Yet the Nationalists were almost exhausted and that night Varela and Orgaz again considered their options and decided upon a last throw of the dice spearheaded by Buruaga who was given the last reserves.

The attack on February 14 would be dubbed "The Jarama's Sorrowful Day" (El Día Triste del Jarama) by Major Gregorio López Muñiz who was Varela's chief of staff. It began badly when enemy fighters thwarted a preparatory air strike while Maranosa's guns could not distinguish friend from foe in the olive groves in the center and right. There was intense Republican pressure upon the whole front but especially Buruaga's, where Pavlov's tanks broke through and routed the defenders, the situation being restored when Buruaga led his headquarters personnel in a counterattack. Unfortunately Pavlov's tanks still charged around like cavalry unsupported by infantry while his crews expended ammunition even if they were too far away to hit anything.[34] Attacks by Modesto's division upon Rada were thwarted by Maranosa's guns but Varela sent López Muñiz to Orgaz to report that he could advance no further without reinforcements and that he could barely hold his lines. Franco had already informed Orgaz that he had no spare troops and as a result the offensive was effectively closed down, although the following day Buruaga and Asensio took a couple of positions to precipitate a rout among Mena's troops who were rallied by pistol-wielding officers.

Across the lines there were major changes in command owing to a feud between the political supporters of Miaja and Pozas, which ended in victory for the former. Miaja had refused to provide reinforcements unless he was given command of the front and Largo Caballero gave in, allowing the general to extend his authority into the Jarama Valley down to Aranjuez and promptly replace Mena with Burillo.[35] Pozas had been advocating a counteroffensive and his successor agreed, although he would still have preferred to strike at Brunete.

He had reorganized his force to give Burillo command of four Communist-led divisions: Division "A" (5 BM, 12, 14 BI) under General Walter, Division "B" (17, 24 BM, 11, 15 BI) led by Colonel Gal, the Hungarian Janos Galicz, Lister's 11 DI as Division "C" (1, 18, 23, 66 BM) and Division "D" under Lieutenant-Colonel Juan Arce, a founder member of the army's prewar left-wing Unión Militar Republicana Antifascista (UMRA) with 45 BM and six Anarchist and Carabiniero battalions. To the north was Task Force Modesto built around his 4 DI, reinforced by 36, 41 BM and Brigada "E" (later 46 BM).

With 68 battalions and 59 guns Miaja faced 32 battalions with 80 guns, but his artillery was under a centralized command created with the assistance of Soviet advisor Major General Nikolai Voronov. On the afternoon of February 17 Miaja's counteroffensive began with probing attacks on each side of the salient; Modesto striking toward Maranosa and Lister toward Pingaron. During the day Nationalist casualties mounted and included Buruaga, who was replaced by García-Escámez.

The Italians were now preparing for an advance upon Guadalajara, and in the early morning of February 18 Orgaz and Varela asked Mola to urge them to begin their advance as soon as possible, but as the skies lightened the Nationalists faced a new crisis. At 07:30 Modesto's troops swept out of the fog without artillery preparation and tried to push Barrón off Maranosa but were driven back by noon with heavy casualties on both sides. Walter struck the center but he too made little progress while Lister delayed his attack upon Pingaron until 17:00, and although urged on by Miaja, he too was also held with heavy losses on both sides. He renewed his assault just before midnight and inaccurately reported that he had taken the peak.

The following day Franco and Orgaz decided to cut their losses and go onto the defensive but the Nationalists remained under heavy pressure. On February 20 Modesto renewed his attack after a three-hour bombardment, and Rada had to place cooks and engineers into the firing line to hold the enemy as the rain eased and then ceased. Pressure was maintained the following day and Lister pushed toward the San Martin bridge but was driven back by Maranosa's guns which destroyed six of his 32 tanks. On the evening of February 22 Miaja ordered Lister to renew his assault upon Pingaron which began at 08:30 the next day, leading to a bloody day of attack and counterattack watched anxiously by Orgaz and Varela who had virtually no reserves but retained the peak. Reluctantly Miaja had to concede the failure of his offensive.

The fighting began to fade, leaving the Nationalists with a salient 5km deep and 10km long on the western bank of the Jarama. It had cost them more than 7,900 casualties, while the Republicans lost some 7,370 plus 3,300

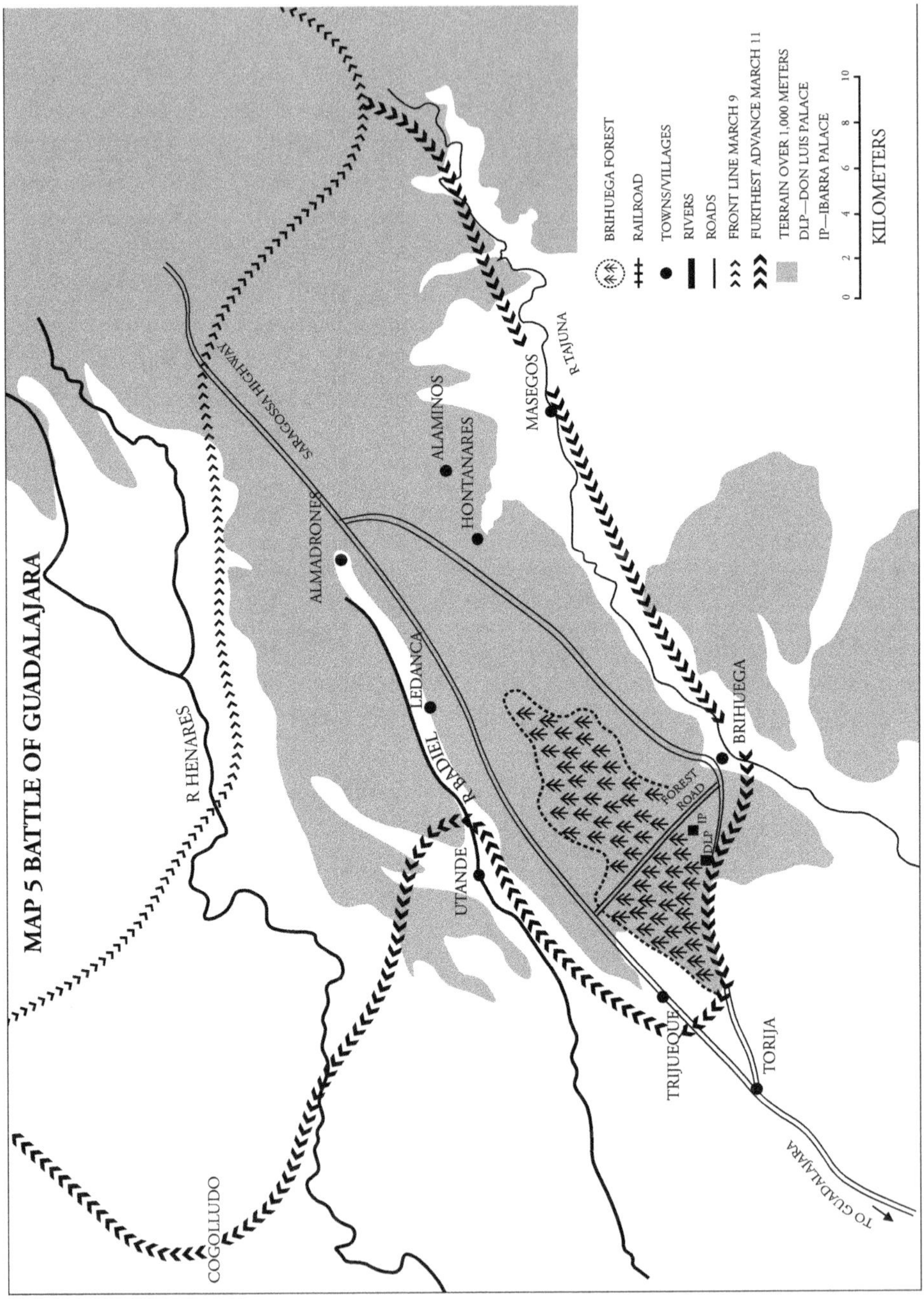
MAP 5 BATTLE OF GUADALAJARA
BRIHUEGA FOREST
RAILROAD
TOWNS/VILLAGES
RIVERS
ROADS
FRONT LINE MARCH 9
FURTHEST ADVANCE MARCH 11
TERRAIN OVER 1,000 METERS
DLP—DON LUIS PALACE
IP—IBARRA PALACE
0 2 4 6 8 10
KILOMETERS
SARAGOSSA HIGHWAY
ALAMINOS
HONTANARES
MASEGOS
R TAJUNA
ALMADRONES
LEDANCA
R BADIEL
FOREST ROAD
IP
DLP
BRIHUEGA
UTANDE
TRIJUEQUE
TORIJA
TO GUADALAJARA
R HENARES
COGOLLUDO

sick. For the Nationalists the Jarama battle had the same effect as the First Battle of Ypres upon the British Expeditionary Force, decimating the Army of Africa's limited number of professional troops who were increasingly replaced by conscript and volunteer battalions.

The heavy casualties led to strong but unfair criticism of Orgaz, whom Franco had to remove. But out of loyalty to his old supporter, on March 25, 1937, he appointed him head of MIR (Movilización, Instrucción y Recuperación—Mobilization, Instruction and Recovery), the vital recruiting and training organization that contributed so much to Franco's victory. He was replaced by the tubby Major General Andrés Saliquet with his gray walrus moustache, for whom this was a belated 60th birthday present. He had served in Cuba and Morocco and was another ardent Monarchist who had resigned his commission when the Republic was established to become involved in several plots. Despite this, at the outbreak of war he commanded a division district which became the cadre of a corps headquarters and was now further promoted.

The battle also reflected the Republican air superiority through Russian aircraft and pilots over the Madrid front from November 1936 through March 1937.[36] From their first mission on November 4 until the end of March they lost 40 aircraft but destroyed a similar number in the air and half a dozen on the ground, but their greatest impact was psychological. German fighters escorting bombers sheltered under their charges' guns while "the appearance of the Ratas had a depressing effect."[37] The Italians insisted their fighters fly defensive patrols of at least 15 aircraft over friendly lines while daytime bombing raids on Madrid ceased after November 26. By late February the Nationalists were bitterly complaining about the shortage of fighters and demanding substantial reinforcements from the Italians.[38]

Guadalajara

The failure in the Jarama finally convinced many in Franco's staff, led by his operations chief, Lieutenant Colonel Antonio Barroso, not only that Madrid was no longer of military importance but that its capture would create significant problems. Barroso, who had been the prewar military attaché in Paris, argued that even its loss would not undermine Republican determination to fight on, while the Nationalists would find that feeding the population was impossible. Yet Franco obstinately focused upon the capture, or at least isolation, of the capital, although the Jarama campaign reduced his resources for another major effort. By happy coincidence his Italian allies presented a solution by pressing him to use their expeditionary force, the Corpo Truppe Volontarie (CTV) in a decisive operation.

The CTV was activated under a former military intelligence chief Major General Mario Roatta in February 1937 from the Italian Army Mission (Mission Militare Italiana in Spagna—MMIS) and its bayonets were bloodied on a militia rabble around Malaga just as the Jarama offensive began.[39] Many of the Italian personnel were from the paramilitary Blackshirt militia (Milizia Volontaria per la Sicurezza—MSVN) which had fought the colonial war in Ethiopia in 1935–36, and Mussolini wanted to demonstrate Rome's military prowess against worthier opponents including the use of chemical weapons.[40] From January through February 1937 the Italian army accumulated in Spain 176 tonnes of liquid to create gas clouds, 50 tonnes of mustard gas, 55,500 poison gas and 2,000 tear-gas shells, while the air force assembled 100 tonnes of mustard gas and phosgene bombs.[41]

CTV strategy was considered at a conference attended by Mussolini in Rome on January 15. Malaga was considered as a military exercise with Valencia as the primary objective and Guadalajara as the secondary one. In the ecstasy of victory Mussolini wanted his warriors to drive to Valencia using a Hispano-Italian army under CTV command and he ordered preparations for the campaign to begin on February 9 with a diversion toward Guadalajara to pin down the Central Army.[42]

At this point Spanish and Italian planning began to converge. The objective of the Jarama offensive was to reach Brihuega–Guadalajara to meet the Soria Division under the reserved and pious hero of the Alcazar, Moscardó, now a brigadier general, which would push down from the north. Moscardó had been planning an advance upon Brihuega since December 20 under the direction first of Saliquet and later Mola. Franco had rejected these proposals on January 5 because they required too many troops, so Moscardó produced a less ambitious plan before the Jarama offensive was launched but this too was pigeon-holed. As the Jarama battle began to die down Franco concluded that he could use the Italians to complete the isolation of Madrid in conjunction with a renewed Jarama offensive. He agreed when his allies requested the CTV assemble around Siguenza, on the upper Henares, from where the Italians planned to drive to Valencia

But when Roatta met Franco on February 15 the Generalissimo informed him that an advance upon Valencia had no strategic benefit and proposed instead an advance through Guadalajara to isolate Madrid. As Roatta had never favored the Valencia plan he accepted the proposal which made the former diversion a major operation, but he demanded that Orgaz maintain strong pressure in the Jarama to pin down Republican reserves.[43] The end of the Jarama offensive left the CTV unsupported, but Roatta convinced himself in the coming weeks that his allies would launch the supporting attack, and on February 23 Franco gave his seal of approval to the Italian attack.[44]

The battlefield was a plateau between the deep valleys of the rivers Badiel and Tajuña running northeast to southwest and sloping from 1,500m to 700m. It was a sparsely populated, largely a bare rolling plain of clay dotted with shrubs and woods. There was a former royal parkland, the Brihuega Forest, some 12km long, bounded in the north by the Saragossa Highway and in the south by a side road from Almadrones to the walled town of Brihuega in the Tajuna Valley. The highway ran into the Castilian plain through Guadalajara to Alcala. It was joined just north of Guadalajara at Torija by a side road from Brihuega, from which another secondary road (which will be called the Forest Road in this account) bisected the forest to the Badiel Valley to Utande. At the eastern end of the forest, dominating the roads northwest to Utande and southwest to Torija, was the so-called Ibarra Palace. This was a massive, white-painted stone building which was actually a 17th-century country house, the only substantial structure in the forest apart from the Don Luis Palace some 3km away and almost half-way between Torija and Brihuega.

Roatta had 31,200 men organized into three 6,300-strong Blackshirt divisions, an army division of 7,700 men, a brigade-sized force of 3,600, an artillery train of 33 batteries (120 guns, 84 heavy), and an armored battalion with 46 CV-33/35 tankettes nicknamed "Sardine Cans" (Lattine di Sardine) by their crews. Contrary to contemporary claims the CTV was not fully motorized; indeed it had only 2,400 trucks of which 1,400 were assigned to the artillery or engineers. Roatta intended to use the Blackshirts as his spearhead but his battle plan for a 75km advance, published on March 4, was based upon a Michelin 1:400,000-scale road map!

Brigadier General Americo Coppi's 2nd Fiamme Nere (Black Flames) Division reinforced by Brigadier General Enrico Francisci's brigade (Raggruppamento Autonomo "XXIII Marzo") would break through the defenses allowing Brigadier General Luigi Nuvolini's 3rd Penne Nere (Black Feathers) Division with a tank company to go down the Saragossa Highway and occupy Guadalajara. Coppi would then take Brihuega and drive down the Torija road, link up with Nuvoloni and together would then drive to Alcala while Francisci would push into the Tajuna Valley to take Masegos.

Roatta anticipated that he would take two days to reach the Torija–Brihuega line, another two to reach Guadalajara, and a further two to reach Alcala. In reserve would be Brigadier General Edmundo Rossi's 1st Dio lo Vuole (God

Wills It) Blackshirt Division, formed only on February 17, and the army's Littorio Division under Brigadier General Annibale Bergonzoli, together with two tank companies.[45] Most of the divisional commanders were 52 years old, Rossi was a year older, and, apart from the fire-eating Francisci, had commanded brigades, although Nuvolini had also commanded a division. Francisci was highly decorated and had earned battlefield promotions but much of his career had been with the MSVN.

While Roatta anticipated cold weather with some rain, he believed the speed of his advance would expose his men only briefly to the elements. For this reason he left the field kitchens behind and his troops would receive little hot food throughout the battle. His attack was still based upon the understanding that the Nationalists would drive northeast out of the Jarama Valley to meet him around Alcala. Yet they remained ambiguous and Franco gave no firm commitment about such an attack; indeed Roatta's allies told him several times that the Nationalist troops in the valley were in no position to launch an offensive—warnings the Italian seemed to ignore.

To shield the Italian right from substantial Republican forces in the Sierra de Guadarrama, Moscardó provided 3,000 men of Colonel Ricardo Marzo's II Brigade with seven battalions, a tank company, four cavalry squadrons, and nine batteries which would advance along the Henares Valley, although the Spanish were worried that they would be unable to keep pace with their "motorized" allies. Franco had little confidence in the Italians and both he and Barroso warned Roatta that his left would be exposed from attacks across the Tajuña, but they were unable to puncture Italian complacency.[46]

They faced the 12 DI under engineer and UMRA member Lieutenant Colonel Victor Lacalle, who had helped to distribute rifles to the people in Madrid in July 1936. He had four mixed brigades (49, 50, 71, 72 BM) with only 10,700 men and 15 guns occupying poorly sited, shallow, water-filled trenches behind thin, low, barbed-wire entanglements. Yet morale was high, for on New Year's Day the division, reinforced by an International Brigade and armor, had staged an offensive which gained little ground but easily contained the resulting counterattacks. Miaja visited Lacalle to warn him of the imminent attack and sent him one of Pavlov's tank companies and two battalions which further boosted Lacalle's confidence, but the Republicans remained uncertain of enemy intentions.

The Italians assembled on the night of March 7/8 in snow, sleet, and rain, although an alarmed Franco, fearing his allies would lack air support due to the muddy state of their airfields, suggested postponing the attack. Roatta dismissed the concerns and the 40-minute bombardment by 86 guns began on time under a leaden sky with frequent rain squalls. Coppi and Francisci attacked, supported now by two tank companies, but the former quickly became embroiled in a prolonged battle with a 400-man battalion counterattacking from Almadrones with 11 tanks. This was driven off with Marzo's assistance and Italian mountain guns destroyed two tanks. With sleet and fog reducing visibility to 100m Coppi decided it was too risky to push down the Saragossa Highway and ordered his troops to dig in until the morning. There was better progress to the east where one of Coppi's regiments and Francisci advanced 17km to take Alaminos, then pushed into the Tajuna Valley taking Masegos against light resistance. Lacalle sent four battalions toward Hontanares but events the next day forced them to retreat.

Roatta belatedly realized the need for air support and was assured by his air commander, Brigadier General Vincenzo Velardi, that not only would Italian bombers be used but also German, and on March 9 the new He 111 made its combat debut against airfields at Barajas and Alcala de Henares. Velardi had six squadrons (62 aircraft) at Soria, on the other side of the Sierra Guadarrama, but Italian air support was sporadic because of cloud over the Sierra while the forward airfield at Almazan was muddy and fighters could take off only with reduced fuel and ammunition. Velardi had warned Roatta and his staff about the problems but they did not seem unduly concerned. Republican strike aircraft would also suffer from waterlogged airfields, which often grounded the SB bombers.[47]

The Italian bombers dropped 3 tonnes of bombs on enemy positions in front of Brihuega during the morning of March 9 when Nuvoloni, reinforced by a motorized machine gun company, entered the line and with heavy artillery support captured Almadrones by 11:00. He was urged on by Roatta, who had planned to be in Torija that day, but faced fierce resistance, notably from the surviving but superior enemy tanks. The battle blocked the road causing a massive traffic jam with fierce disputes between officers over priority which sometimes led to pistols being pulled, and eventually Coppi and Nuvolini had to clear the mess personally. By nightfall Nuvolini had reached the crossroads with the Forest Road, 5km from Torija, but sent an armored reconnaissance team toward Trijueque. His staff wanted the rest of the division to follow during the night but the cautious general refused, fearing ambush from the forest.

To the east Coppi's lackluster performance continued as he crawled toward Brihuega, delayed by demolitions, and by dusk was still 4km from the town. Francisci saw the problems faced by his neighbor and, on his own initiative, sent a regiment down the Tajuna Valley toward Brihuega, whose garrison had failed to establish any significant defenses. He stormed the town during the morning, capturing much-needed supplies, 135 prisoners and two guns, then established a bridgehead across the river but was too weak to take the opposite slopes of the valley. On the northern flank Marzo beat off Lacalle's counterattacks in the Badiel Valley, destroying three tanks, then took the village of Cogolludo on the northern bank of the Henares. This was the Communists' excuse to replace Martínez with Miaja's chief of staff, Major Vicente Rojo.

Upon learning of the breakthrough Miaja had alerted Pavlov and sent up reinforcements led by 11 BI, while Lister's "advisor," Soviet Colonel Aleksandr Rodimtsev, was assigned the defense of the Saragossa Highway with Lister as his second in command. Meawhile, Lacalle was pushed aside into the Badiel and Henares valleys to stop Marzo. Enemy air attacks delayed the advance of 11 BI, a tonne of bombs helping to buy Nuvolini time to reach the Forest Road crossroads, but by dusk the International troops were digging in around the highway 2km north of Trijueque as a flood of reinforcements made their way to the front. The day saw the first appearance of the Republican air force when fighters flew a reconnaissance mission. The weather would continue to be a malign influence, with snow at night and rain in the day until March 12, turning the fields into quagmires and largely confining both sides to the roads.

Roatta now ordered Coppi to remain at Brihuega while during March 10 Nuvolini cautiously pushed southward down the highway to Guadalajara but soon ran into 11 BI. The International Brigade fought hard, supported by 50 BM, and staged numerous counterattacks but was overcome with the aid of armored flame-throwers which helped to destroy a French battalion, allowing the Italians to advance a kilometer. To the east the 12 BI, led by the Italian Garibaldi Battalion and unaware of Brihuega's fall, came up the Torija–Brihuega road led by a motorcycle patrol which led to a farcical moment at Don Luis's Palace. Coppi had sent motorcycle scouts down the Torija road as he prepared to outflank the enemy facing Nuvolini. One of his scouts encountered those from Garibaldi, and, thinking they were Nuvolini's troops, asked if he was on the Torija road. When assured he was, he returned to Brihuega.

The Garibaldi Battalion marched on and occupied the Ibarra Palace, engaging Coppi's columns as they emerged from the east in a miniature Italian civil war which lasted into the evening. Roatta's offensive was rapidly running out of steam as the defenders were reinforced to 26,000 men and placed under a new IV Cuerpo de Ejercito (CE) under a gunner, Colonel Enrique Jurado, with Lacalle's 12 DI (35, 49, 50, 71 BM) on the left, Lister's 11 DI (1, 9 BM, 11 BI, 1 Shock Brigade) in the center with some women machine gunners, and the Anarchist Cipriano Mera's 14 DI (12BI, 65, 70, 72 BM) on the right.[48] The Republic also brought up four fortification battalions to strengthen the defenses of Guadalajara and Alcala. More ominously for the Italians, while their airmen were largely confined to their bases by clouds, rain, and snow showers, a Republican fighter squadron strafed the Italian columns but with little physical effect.

The offensive was rapidly falling behind schedule, so on the night of March 10 Roatta, still believing there would be an attack on the Jarama front, decided to bring Rossi's division into the line alongside Coppi. The latter was then to continue his advance south to support Nuvolini who was to press on to Torija. During the afternoon Nuvolini managed to break through, destroying another 11 BI battalion, and took Trijueque, but was left exhausted.

To push deeper he needed Coppi's support, but the Fiamme Nere's attempt to blast a way along the Torija road was a disaster. During the morning they finally took the Ibarra Palace but became totally entangled in the woods which Coppi lacked the manpower to clear and open the road. During the afternoon he attacked with a reserve battalion and a tank company but antitank guns and T-26s destroyed four "Sardine Cans" and pinned down the attackers.

That evening Roatta and his staff evaluated the situation and were forced to recognize the grim reality that they had failed to break through and that the men were exhausted by a combination of heavy fighting and debilitating weather. The only good news was that Francisci had crossed the Tajuna during the day and advanced 18km along the river to cover Rossi's flank. At 23:00 Roatta ordered his men onto the defensive while he brought up Littorio under Bergonzoli, nicknamed "Electric Whiskers," to relieve Nuvolini. Roatta continued to press Franco for an offensive on the Jarama which, the Italians claimed, he promised for the following day although this was probably wishful thinking. Ironically, given all Barroso's concerns, Marzo's brigade was beginning to outpace their allies and during the day began to threaten Lister's left, causing Miaja considerable concern.

Meanwhile, Republican aircraft exploited every break in the clouds to make irritating low-level strafing attacks upon enemy columns as the pendulum was clearly swinging toward the Republican cause, with 35,000 men now deployed on the Guadalajara front and Jurado open to ideas from Rodimtsev and Lister for a counteroffensive. Soviet military attaché Colonel Vladimir Gorev, who spoke both Spanish and English, helped produce a combined arms plan which went into effect on March 12.[49] With armored support, powerful blows struck Nuvolini's left regiment in the woods east of Trijuque, while Lister's 9 BM, supported by two more infantry battalions, 30 tanks, and six batteries, struck the right regiment at Trijuque. Nuvolini sent up eight 105mm howitzers to boost the antitank defenses but five were lost as the Italians were pushed back. Brihuega was under air and artillery fire and Coppi was slow to assemble his troops west of the town, yet despite everything Roatta remained optimistic. He informed Franco that he would continue the offensive but only if it was certain the Nationalists would strike from the Jarama. That evening he considered his options, which were to continue the advance along its current axis or make a wide swing across the Tajuna. He chose the former. As a first step during the night Bergonzoli began to relieve Nuvolini while the incapable Rossi was to relieve the inept Coppi.

The Italians also faced Republican air attacks growing in intensity and coordinated by Brigadier General Yakov Smushkevich at Alcala with 71 airplanes including 11 SB bombers and 15 ground-attack aircraft. From 08:30 they hit columns, vehicle parks, and supply dumps in 300 fighter and five fighter-reconnaissance sorties, dropping 25 tonnes of bombs and firing 200,000 rounds of ammunition, thereby destroying an ammunition depot at Brihuega. The Italians had only two batteries of eight 20mm Breda antiaircraft guns but Republican claims of catastrophic damage proved exaggerated: the CTV suffered only 230 casualties and a dozen vehicles destroyed, including a couple of armored cars, but the effects upon morale were greater. Nuvolini's antiaircraft gunners claimed a single R-5 while there were only nine fighter sorties over the CTV with four victories claimed.

The aerial onslaught continued on March 13 as the Republicans continued their attacks with 28 fighters dropping 6 tonnes of bombs and firing 50,000 rounds on Nuvolini's troops, who were again attacked by Lister's division while Mera began probing toward Brihuega in preparation for an attack across the Tajuna. Although the Nationalists had got wind of these plans and Barroso again warned his allies, they continued to ignore him. On the highway the pressure grew upon Nuvoloni, whose men abandoned Trijueque in some confusion, with some 25 percent casualties—1,480 out of 6,241 men. They rallied when they reached Bergonzoli, whose troops stabilized the line which came under steady pressure during the following day, with the 12 BI retaking the Ibarra Palace and inflicting 300 casualties to force Roatta back to the Forest Road. Velardi's strike aircraft now made a belated appearance and dropped 39 tonnes of bombs around the palace from March 15 through to March 16, when the Republican Rasante ground-attack and SB bombers struck for the first time.

That night Roatta and his subordinates again reviewed their options, including a retreat back to their start line. Roatta blamed his allies and met Franco and Mola on March 15 in what was obviously a tetchy interview.

Roatta explained that he and Mussolini considered that operations around Madrid had reached an impasse and a new offensive should be launched on a fresh front, preferably in the north, allowing the CTV to be rested. Franco vetoed not only Roatta's plea to withdraw but also his demand for an attack on the Jarama front. Faced with an impasse Roatta returned to his headquarters and that afternoon wrote two proposals: transfer the CTV to a new sector, as Mussolini desired, or continue operations on the Guadalajara front. When the letter was presented to Franco he ignored it and when the Italian ambassador Randolfo Cantalupo pressed for a decision, he claimed he was consulting his commanders.

Roatta was becoming concerned by growing signs of a counteroffensive as his troops' morale began to fail, for as well as cases of frostbite there were others of self-inflicted wounds while uninjured men tried to board ambulances. He had good cause for concern, for on the evening of March 15 Jurado outlined his ideas for a counteroffensive after his men had recovered following the recapture of Trijuequ. He decided to use air power to erode enemy strength and morale while his material resources grew to 56 guns and 60 tanks. By now Lacalle had resigned ostensibly on health grounds, but apparently because he resented being passed over in favor of Jurado, despite having seniority, and he was replaced by the Italian Communist Nanetti.[50]

The plans were discussed on March 17 at Jurado's command post by Miaja, Rojo, and numerous Soviet advisors including Pavlov, Gorev, and future marshals of the Soviet Union Pavel Batov, Rodion Malinovsky, Kyril Meretskov, Rodimtsev, and Voronov. Lister and Nanetti would strike along the plateau on a narrow front to isolate Brihuega from the west while Mera would take the town with an attack across the Tajuna. Meretskov later claimed he had signed off on the plan together with Gorev and Pavlov.[51] In a telling comment, Miaja proposed that Pavlov should be the operational commander while the Russian diplomatically proposed Lister. Gorev agreed it was politically undesirable for a Russian publicly to command Republican forces but bent to Miaja's wishes by making Pavlov *de facto* commander with Jurado signing his orders to attack the following afternoon.[52]

On the morning of March 18 Roatta flew to Salamanca with a new plea for an offensive in the Jarama to relieve pressure but Franco reiterated that his men were in no shape to launch an attack. He advised his ally to dig in and hold on but even as they spoke the situation was changing radically. The Italians were weak, especially on the center and left where Rossi's division, a green formation, was exposed in positions which mostly marked the high-water mark of Coppi's advance. Rossi had failed to secure a hill which dominated

Brihuega from the north. Bergonzoli was in a slightly stronger position, and the saving grace for Roatta was a "Second Position" being established 15km behind the front and occupied by Nuvolini and Coppi, although the latter had a regiment in the Tajuna bridgehead.

The morning of March 18 brought the usual gray skies, and the Italians could hear ominous engine noises behind the enemy lines, but otherwise the front was relatively quiet. Then at 13:10, 15 bombers, escorted by 26 fighters, struck around Brihuega, dropping 22 tonnes of bombs on one of Francisci's regimental command posts and two ammunition depots, all selected by a radio-equipped reconnaissance team that had infiltrated into the town's suburbs. The fighters then expended 12,000 rounds on ground targets and in the confusion there was an explosion as a truck carrying almost all the 20mm antiaircraft ammunition detonated. There were only 20 casualties but then Republican guns opened up, directed from observation posts on heights which the Italians had failed to secure, and as shells landed 45 assault aircraft and fighters appeared to pour another 25,000 rounds into the Italians.

As the biplanes swept over the Italian positions Pavlov's tanks began to drive eastward along the Torija road, driving a wedge between Rossi's left and Coppi's regiment in the bridgehead which Mera struck from the south. His attack had been due at dawn but heavy sleet reduced visibility and delayed the deployment of a vital pontoon bridge. Mera created a bridgehead below Brihuega but Italian light guns contained this threat until enemy heavy artillery destroyed three of them just as tanks killed the command team of Rossi's left regiment. Attempts by Coppi's men to stabilize the situation collapsed under heavy artillery fire which saw both regiments driven back from the Ibarra Palace crossroads, causing them to lose contact with Bergonzoli. The retreating troops rallied behind Rossi's reserve regiment but the division commander now became obsessed with protecting his artillery which he sent back to the Second Position and then sat subdued at the dinner table. The CTV left now fell back to a position south of Hontanares, allowing Mera to retake Brihuega during the evening.

Roatta's staff, under Lieutenant Colonel Emilio Faldella, were awaiting his return from Salamanca and did not learn of the loss of Brihuega until 19:15. This clearly exposed Bergonzoli who had personally led counterattacks in a successful defense of his positions against 11 BI, the weak and tired spearhead. Russian tanks made lone raids into his positions but his soldiers were made of sterner stuff than the Blackshirts, and their mountain guns claimed six. The situation was too critical to await Roatta's return, so Faldella telephoned Bergonzoli and both reluctantly accepted the need for a withdrawal. Grumbling, Bergonzoli's men fell back rapidly but in good order to the

Second Position anchored on Ledanca, cautiously followed by Lister, and the following day the line was extended to join Rossi around Hontanares. The new line from Almadrones to Alaminos was 15km from the original start line. Nanetti, aided by Lister, tried to push back Marzo but was easily held. The Italian consolidation of their new positions was aided by the opening on March 19 of a good airfield at Burgo de Osma which allowed their strike aircraft to hit enemy concentrations and columns.

Humiliatingly, Roatta learned of Faldella's decision from Franco during their meeting. He returned to his command post at 22:30 and 45 minutes later learned of the fall of Brihuega. To Franco's surprise, and no doubt gratitude, Jurado failed to exploit the situation and his main body did not reach the Second Position until March 20. Set-piece attacks involving 15 battalions were launched from March 21 through March 22 but were beaten off and the battle ended that evening with the Italians almost on their jump-off line. From March 23 Moscardó began to relieve his allies, with the last of Bergonzoli's troops departing on May 8.

The victory was a tremendous boost to Republican morale, with exaggerated claims made for prisoners and material taken, including 6,000 casualties, 1,200 prisoners, 65 guns, and ten tanks. It demonstrated that Madrid had succeeded in converting a militia rabble into a modern army capable of offensive operations; indeed after the spring of 1937 Soviet advisors rarely intervened on the battlefield. It was certainly humiliating for the Italians, not only because it was a defeat but also because it exposed Rome's military defiance of non-intervention agreements. Roatta suffered 2,743 casualties (415 dead, 1,832 wounded) or 16 percent including 496 prisoners, while material losses were a dozen guns and 90 vehicles, including 19 tankettes and five armored cars, 25 guns, two antiaircraft guns, 85 machine guns, 140 automatic rifles, and 822 rifles.[53] Velardi lost six airplanes while Marzo suffered 350 casualties. Jurado and Lacelle suffered 6,500 casualties, including 360 prisoners and 15 aircraft, while of Pavlov's 72 tanks 28 were hit and seven destroyed but only nine were operational at the end of the battle.[54] After the campaign 3,719 Italian wounded and sick returned to Italy.[55]

Franco briefly spoke of disbanding the CTV and dispersing its resources among the Nationalist Army but this was unacceptable to Mussolini. Instead he removed Roatta from command, although he remained in Spain, and began a substantial reorganization of the CTV under General Ettore Bastico who arrived in Spain with eight generals. Many of the Blackshirt troops were sent home in disgrace accompanied by Coppi who was given an armored brigade and would retire just before Italy quit the Axis ranks in 1943. Nuvolini was given a motorized division and would eventually become a corps commander while Rossi became an infantry division commander. Bergonzoli retained command of Littorio and was promoted to major general while Francisci's brigade was expanded into a division.[56]

Guadalajara was widely trumpeted as the defeat of a mechanized force, contributing to the traditional view that they were unable to penetrate deep into enemy lines. But the Germans recognized the CTV was really a traditional infantry force with little armored or air support, certainly not on a par with German *Mobiledivisionen*.[57] They also had a low opinion of Italian military capabilities, which Guadalajara confirmed, and there was some schadenfreude in the Nationalist rank and file with Moscardó's men observing in doggerel: "Spaniards, even the Reds, are brave. You need fewer trucks [*camiones*] and more balls [*cojones*]." Yet this was a serious setback for the Nationalist cause and especially for Franco as he consolidated power. He appears to have considered the Italian offensive a gamble and was preparing contingency plans even as Mussolini's troops advanced.

There was only one significant strategic option: to eliminate the northern enclave along the Bay of Biscay which was 200km from the Republican "heartland." It was some 300km long but only 30–40km deep and a significant prize, for it contained 1.5 million people as well as substantial mineral and industrial resources. This option was being pushed by Mola, who commanded the Army of the North, even before the Jarama offensive, and he had won Barroso's support.

The Cuban-born Mola, aged 49, was the son of an army officer and distinguished himself during the Rif War to become Director General of Security under the monarchy and he did all he could to prevent the emergence of the Republic.[58] He was dismissed after a failed right-wing coup in 1932 but given an amnesty two years later because this myopic, meticulous, and cautious officer with his vulpine features was too valuable for the Republic to dismiss and he reluctantly served it as commander of the Army of Africa, then from 1936 as military governor of Pamplona. Obsessed, like many of the Republic's opponents with Jewish–Communist–Freemason conspiracies, it was only now that this courageous, imaginative, devious, and literary-minded man became involved in plotting the overthrow of the Republic. He brought a breath of fresh air, realizing that what had previously been a purely military affair now required a political dimension.

His close contacts with the Carlists, whose heartland was in Navarre, gave him a key position in the conspiracy. Curiously both he and Franco had seemed ambivalent about the prospects of the July coup but he became a key member of the National Defense Council and Franco's most serious rival. Relations between the two were tense, for Mola was not afraid to speak his mind and at one point asked Franco: "Don't you trust my leadership any more?"[59]

During January, Mola became pessimistic about the prospects on the Madrid front and on January 26 he asked his subordinates to consider the strategic options. The 6th Division's Brigadier General Miguel Ponte proposed an offensive eastward into Aragon but concluded that there were insufficient resources to face anticipated fierce Anarchist and Catalonian resistance which would probably doom the operation. Meanwhile, Mola's former and new chiefs of staff, Colonel José Solchaga and Colonel Juan Vigón, pondered striking in the opposite direction and on February 6 met Franco to argue that this offered better prospects, partly because there were divisions within the defenders' ranks that might weaken resistance.[60]

Initially Franco refused, partly due to his obsession with the Madrid front and partly out of fear that the Nationalists would become involved in a prolonged and debilitating struggle in the northern mountains.[61] As the Italians reeled backward from Guadalajara, the foxy Mola saw his chance to switch the focus of Nationalist efforts northward. He used the air commander Kindelán as his herald to present the plan to Franco on March 20 with a request for the resources to implement it. The following day Franco was again visited by Kindelán and also Vigón, nominally in his role as the Generalissimo's personal staff advisor. Vigón, who resembled an elderly schoolmaster, was a 56-year-old engineer and ardent Monarchist who had tutored the king's sons and resigned his commission when Spain became a republic in 1931.[62] One of the most able staff officers in the Spanish Army, this Germanophile officer was in Argentina when the war broke out but returned home to work with Mola. It was he who finally persuaded Franco that no further progress could be expected around Madrid and that the Nationalists' path to victory lay through the Republican enclaves.

Mola and Solchaga came to Salamanca on March 22, were informed of the change in strategic direction, and discussed what resources Franco would receive for the first stage, the advance upon Bilbao. They departed on Holy Thursday, March 25, and within five days they and Vigón were conducting detailed planning at Vitoria. Certainly Franco was taking a gamble by investing most of his spare resources in a campaign whose success could give his rival, as well as the Monarchist cause, a significant boost in prestige.

Notes

1 His full surname was Mola Vidal, because formally both parents' family names are used but the maternal name is usually dropped. Spanish names in this book will follow this practice.
2 Arce, *Los Generales de Franco* p. 89 (hereafter Arce).
3 For the airlift see Hooton, *Phoenix Triumphant* pp. 120–123 (hereafter Hooton, *Phoenix*); Meredith, *Phoenix*, vol. 2, pp. 512–542 (hereafter Meredith); Proctor, *Hitler's Luftwaffe in the Spanish Civil War* pp. 28–29 (hereafter Proctor).
4 See Thomas, *The Spanish Civil War*, pp. 420–423 (hereafter Thomas).
5 For operations to mid-November 1936 see Martínez, *Frente de Madrid*; Aznar, *Historia Militar de la Guerra de Espana*, pp. 69–295 (hereafter Aznar); Beevor, *The Battle for Spain*, pp. 115–124, 166–169, 174–182 (hereafter Beevor); Cardona, *Historia Militar de una Guerra Civil*, pp. 65–102, 110–113 (hereafter Cardona); Colodny, *The Struggle for Madrid*, pp. 11–91 (hereafter Colodny); Hills, *The Battle for Madrid*, pp. 61–71, 83–108 (hereafter Hills); Lister, *Neustra Guerra*, pp. 79–92 (hereafter Lister); Lojendio, *Operaciones militares de la Guerra de Espana*, pp. 21–185, 239–251 (hereafter Lojendio); López-Muñiz, *La Batalla de Madrid*, pp. 1–45 (hereafter López-Muñiz); Martínez and Martínez, *De Madrid al Ebro*, pp. 57–99 (hereafter Martínez and Martínez); Perea, *Los Culpables*, pp. 74–95 (hereafter Perea); Reverte, *La Batalla de Madrid*, pp. 7–418 (hereafter Reverte, *Madrid*); Rojo, *Espana Heroica*, pp. 47–60 (hereafter Rojo, *Heroica*); Rojo, *Historia de la Guerra Civil Española*, pp. 139–398 (hereafter Rojo, *Historia*); Salas, *Ejercito popular de la Republica*, vol. 1, pp. 277–318, 467–480, 487–491, 507–515, 542–566, 569–617, 628–650 (hereafter Salas *Army*); Thomas, pp. 370–376, 385, 410–413, 432, 436–437, 468, 470–471, 473–487; Vidal, *La Guerra de Franco*, pp. 159–191 (hereafter Vidal).
6 Arce, p. 130; Martínez and Martínez, p. 100.
7 García-Escámez was "a subtle and charming Andalusian" who had been a major planner of the uprising under Mola. Thomas, pp. 201, 238.
8 For his biography and that of other Republican military leaders see Zaragoza, *Ejercito popular y militares de la Republica*, pp. 292–294 (hereafter Zaragoza).
9 The Republic renamed the Civil Guard (or Guardia Civil) the Guardia Nacional Republica.
10 Zaragoza, pp. 276–285; López-Fernández, *El General Miaja, Defensor de Madrid.*
11 Not to be confused with General Grigorii Shtern, a senior Soviet military advisor.
12 For the Corunna Highway battle see Aznar, pp. 326–333; Beevor, pp. 190–192; Cardona, pp. 113–120; Colodny, pp. 92–106; Hills, pp. 113–118; Lister, pp. 92–95; Lojendio, pp. 185–195; Martinez *La lucha en torno a Madrid*, pp. 11–59, Appendices 2 and 3 (hereafter Martinez, *Lucha*); Martínez and Martínez, pp. 99–101; Modesto, *Soy del Quinto Regimento*, pp. 73–75 (hereafter Modesto); López-Muñiz, pp. 50–64; Perea, pp. 95–100; Reverte, *Madrid*, pp. 421–527; Rojo, *Heroica*, pp. 64–68; Salas, *Army*, vol. 1, pp. 653–675, 727–748; Tagüeña, *Testimonio de Dos Guerras*, pp. 100–102 (hereafter Tagüeña); Thomas, pp. 488–490, 492–495; Rodimtsev, *Pod Nebom Ispanii*, pp. 67–103 (hereafter Rodimtsev); Saiz, *Aviacion Republicana*, vol. 1, pp. 301–336 (hereafter Saiz); Vidal, pp. 192–194; Zaloga, *Spanish Civil War Tanks*, p. 22 (hereafter Zaloga, *Tanks*); Daley, "Soviet and German Advisors Put Doctrine to the Test" (hereafter, Daley "Armor"); Zaloga, *Soviet Tank Operations in the Spanish Civil War* (hereafter Zaloga, *Soviet*).
13 The full title was Reforzada de Operaciones sobre Madrid y Cuenca del Tajo.
14 For Orgaz see Arce, pp. 180–190; Thomas, pp. 59, 89, 166, 173–174.
15 Perea, pp. 95–96. This was a back-handed compliment as Voroshilov was a military moron.
16 Colodny, n.69; Hills, p. 113; Thomas, p. 532.

17 Hills, p. 113. The perpetrator was convicted by a court-martial and immediately pardoned.
18 "Hans" was Hans Kahle, a former German officer who became a Communist. After World War II he became an East German police chief.
19 Zulueta was wounded on January 8 and replaced by Major Antolín Serrano García.
20 Daley claims the armored cars were BA-10 but they appear to have been BA-6 which had T-26 tank turrets. The Republic claimed two dozen tanks.
21 A cinema composer, Durán would later become an American citizen and United Nations' official.
22 Colodny, n.25, quoting Cardozo, pp. 233–234.
23 The 39 BM was the former Brigade "X" under Palacios, while 21 BM was under Major Francisco Gómez.
24 For the battle of Jarama see Díez, *La Batalla del Jarama* and Alcofar, *La aviación legionaria en la Guerra Española*, pp. 141–153 (hereafter Alcofar, *Air*); Aznar, pp. 355–364; Beevor, pp. 208–215; Cardona, pp. 125–131; Colodny, pp. 106–128; Engel, *Estrategia y Táctica en la Guerra de España*, pp. 33–40 (hereafter Engel, *Operations*); Hills, pp. 118–124; Kindélan, *Mis Cuadernos de Guerra*, pp. 65–68 (hereafter Kindélan); Lister, pp. 97–106; Lojendio, pp. 195–206; López-Muñiz, pp. 65–113; Manrique and Molina, *Las Armas de la Guerra Civil Española*, p. 51 (hereafter *Armas*); Martinez, Lucha, pp. 89–153; Martínez and Martínez, pp. 103–118; Modesto, pp. 80–87; Perea, pp. 100–109; Rojo, *Heroica*, pp. 68–76; Rojo, *Historia de la Guerra Civil Española*, pp. 398–417 (hereafter Rojo, *Historia*); Rodimtsev, pp. 131–157; Salas, *Army*, vol. 1, pp. 748–778; Saiz, vol. 1, pp. 380–391; Thomas, pp. 588–596; Vidal, pp. 201–207; Voronov, *Na Sluzhbe Voennoy*, pp. 102–105 (hereafter Voronov).
25 For text see Engel, *Operations*, pp. 33–38.
26 Comint is the monitoring of radio communications.
27 Modesto was his *nom de guerre*. His real name was Juan Guilloto León.
28 *Armas*, pp. 525–529; Engel, *Operations*, p. 35. See also Axis History website, Battle in Poison Gas Factory, November 23, 2017. The Maranosa factory had produced chlorine, mustard gas, and phosgene for the Rif War in the 1920s but ceased production in 1929 when Spain ratified the 1925 Geneva Protocol against chemical and biological warfare. By 1936 it was used largely for development and chemical warfare training but the production facilities were intact at the time of the uprising. The Premier, José Giral, who was both a chemist and pharmacist, ordered the transfer of the facilities near to Valencia in September/October 1936 to recommence production directed by his son. On September 28, 1936 Maranosa requested 1,000 tonnes of zinc chloride but little or no production took place (HW 21/1 AS/0029.). Apart from dropping tear-gas bombs on the Alcazar of Toledo on August 8, 1936, and claims of activity in the Sierra de Guadarrama around Oropesa, chemical weapons do not appear to have been used during the Civil War. Franco had witnessed their use in Morocco but both he and Prietro seem to have been less interested in acquiring them and more in protecting their troops against their effects, although the Nationalists did build a phosgene production facility early in 1937. See *Armas*, pp. 525–529. See also intercepted Nationalist signals in UKNA HW 21/1 AS/0053 and AS/0061.
29 *Armas*, p. 52. Jiménez was briefly a sector commander, then held administrative posts.
30 See brigade entry in Engel, *Historia de las Brigadas Mixtas* (hereafter Engel, *Brigades*). This is also available online.
31 Pavlov had 47 tanks of which 34 would be hit and 14 destroyed. Kowalsky, *Stalin and the Spanish Civil War*, ch. 14, table V-8 (hereafter Kowalsky). References are to chapters in the online version.

32 During the battle both sides suffered food and supply shortages due to disruption of the supply system.
33 Thomas, p. 592n.3.
34 Beevor, pp. 213–214.
35 Miaja became Central Army commander on February 27. Pozas was given command of the Barcelona garrison in May and later the Eastern Army, while Mena commanded a corps and would die in Mexico.
36 For air operations over the Madrid front see Alcofar, *Air*, pp. 10–179; Permuy, *Air War Over Spain*, p. 51 (hereafter Permuy); Meredith, pp. 542–568; Proctor, pp. 82–115; Ries and Ring, *The Legion Condor*, pp. 34–47, 52–54 (hereafter Ries and Ring); Jesus Salas, *La Guerra de España Desde el Aire*, pp. 126–148, 160–167, 170–177 (hereafter Salas, *Air*); Salas, *Army*, vol. 1, pp. 618–627; Håkan website. During 1936, 311 Russian pilots were sent to Spain. See Kowalsky, ch. 14, table V-6.
37 Ries and Ring, p. 35.
38 Salas, *Air*, p. 165.
39 For Malaga see Alcofar, *La Aviación Legionaria en la Guerra Española*, pp. 155–158 (hereafter Alcofar, *Air*); Alcofar, *C. T. V.*, pp. 64–73 (hereafter Alcofar, *CTV*); Beevor, pp. 200–201; Belforte, *Guerra civile in Spagna; La campagna dei Volontari italiani dale Baleari a Teruel*, pp. 89–101 (hereafter Belforte, *Teruel*); Cardona, pp. 123–124; Coverdale, *Italian Intervention in the Spanish Civil War*, pp. 206–210 (hereafter Coverdale); Engel, *Operations*, pp. 23–32; Carlos Muria, *Militares Italianos en la Guerra civil Espanola*, pp. 61–67 (hereafter Muria); Salas, *Army*, vol. 1, pp. 807–824; Thomas, pp. 582–587; Vidal, pp. 207–212. There were 372 Italian casualties including 96 dead and missing. Rodrigo, *La Guerra fascista*, p. 119 (hereafter Rodrigo).
40 For the MSVN see Crociani and Battistelli, *Italian Blackshirt*.
41 *Armas*, p. 528; Balfour, *Deadly Embrace*, pp. 309–311 (hereafter Balfour); Rodrigo, pp. 150–151. Germany provided chemical weapons in January, including 50 tonnes of 12kg mustard gas bombs, while on April 7, 1937, the SS *Aldecoa* disembarked 4 tonnes of mustard gas at Cartagena. *Armas*, pp. 528–529.
42 Coverdale, pp. 212–213.
43 For planning see Pedralli, *Guadalajara, mito e realta*, Part 1, p. 95 (hereafter Pedrialli). He does not indicate when these proposals were made but it appears to have been on February 15.
44 For Guadalajara see Garriga, *Guadalajara y sus consecuencias* and Alcofar, *Air*, pp. 158–179; Alcofar, *CTV*, pp. 75–106; Aznar, pp. 369–390; Beevor, pp. 216–220; Guadalajara Belforte, *Teruel*, pp. 103–140; Cardona, pp. 131–140; Colodny, pp. 128–147; Coverdale, pp. 225–248; Hills, pp. 113, 125–135; Kindélan, pp. 68–71; Lister, pp. 106–112; Lojendio, pp. 206–222; Martinez, *Lucha*, pp. 157–246; Martínez and Martínez, pp. 19–138; Meretskov, *Na Sluzhbe Narodoo*, pp. 155–165 (hereafter Meretskov); Modesto, pp. 87–91; Muria, pp. 71–99; Rodrigo, pp. 127–145; Rojo, *Heroica*, pp. 79–94; Rojo, *Historia*, pp. 417–437; Rodimtsev, pp. 158–210; Saiz, vol. 1, pp. 392–403; Salas, *Air*, pp. 170–177; Salas, *Army*, vol. 1, pp. 867–885; Thomas, pp. 596–603; Vidal, pp. 212–221; Voronov, pp. 105–108; Pedriali, *Guadalajara, mito e realta*.
45 "God Wills It" was the Crusaders' battlecry.
46 Martinez, *Lucha*, pp. 131–132.
47 Howson, *Aircraft of the Spanish Civil War*, pp. 265, 278 (hereafter Howson, *Air*).
48 Mera was the leading Anarchist supporter for a conventional army. See Perea, p. 102.
49 Often incorrectly called Goriev.
50 Lacalle would later command a task force in Estremadura, then a division and a corps. He died in Venezuela.

51 Meretskov, *Na Sluzhbe Narodoo*, p. 162 (hereafter Meretskov).
52 Hills, p. 133.
53 Coverdale, p. 249, n.83.
54 Kowalsky, ch. 15, table V-8.
55 Rodrigo, p. 145.
56 Bergonzoli would command an armored division, then a corps, before being captured in 1941. Francisci remained with the MSVN and was their Inspector General when he was killed during the Sicily landings.
57 This was the term used by the Wehrmacht to describe armored and motorized divisions.
58 Arce, pp. 101–131; Thomas, p. 173.
59 One reason Mola lost to Franco in the race for supreme command was that the largely Monarchist military leadership believed that he was a Republican while he loathed the Falange. Thomas, p. 422.
60 For planning see Salas, *Air*, pp. 185–186; José Manuel Martínez Bande, *Vizcaya*, pp. 16–25 (hereafter Martinez, *Vizcaya*). José Solchaga Zala should not be confused with José Iruretagoyena Solchaga who served on the Madrid front.
61 Martínez and Martínez, p. 135.
62 For Vigón see Arce, pp. 297–299; Thomas, p. 614.

CHAPTER 2

The New Armies

Spain now faced a protracted civil war. By the winter of 1936–37 there were more than half a million men under arms, increasingly conscripts of the 1933, 1934, and 1935 classes (*quintas* or *reemplazos*) aged 19–21. Many were the rural and urban poor who endured grinding poverty, undoubtedly reflected in their physical condition, although no figures are available for the numbers rejected on medical grounds.[1]

They were generally brave and would display stoicism in appalling conditions. Many were illiterate, making them cannon fodder, while the literate were required for more technically demanding or administrative tasks. For many, the war was marked by long stretches of boredom on quiet fronts, apart from the occasional short bombardment or raid.[2]

For all the contemporary romantic references to "Spanish trenches," the terrain, together with the paucity of men and material, meant Great War-style trench systems were rare, especially as the Spanish were reluctant to dig trenches which tended to be narrow, shallow, and lacking latrines, which made them malodorous in the summer.[3] Each side relied upon a thin crust of battalion and company strongpoints sited for all-round protection on hills, farms, villages, or towns (sometimes with pillboxes or bunkers) covering a couple of lines of barbed-wire entanglements. They might have mortars, antitank, or infantry support/mountain guns, and, more rarely, field artillery batteries.

Organization

By the spring of 1937 the Republic had 235,500 men and women under arms in its central and eastern heartland and 99,500 in the Biscay enclave in the north, rising by May Day 1938 to 689,130 men in the heartland alone.[4] They were a people-in-arms for whom victory meant the prospect of a better life; indeed many became literate during the war, making them readier to make a sacrifice for victory. They went to war as volunteer militias (*milicia*) in columns organized by all the Popular Front's social and political elements, although this created near anarchy at the front and real anarchy in Aragon and Andalusia where Syndicalist columns were dominant. Their common backgrounds provided a cohesion akin to a regimental spirit within columns, but even minor threats could lead to panic-stricken flight, while many returned home when the front was quiet.[5] Political or trade union leaders became military leaders but this was no guarantee that they could command bodies of men, their tactical capabilities usually being restricted to leading frontal assaults while they were too impatient to organize coordination with neighboring columns, other arms, or services.

During the late summer of 1936 the militias' weaknesses became apparent not only to the exasperated cadre of professional officers remaining in the War Ministry, but also to the politicians. The perennial problem with volunteer forces is that the flood of recruits in the first flush of enthusiasm soon becomes a trickle. There was widespread opposition within the Popular Front to the professionals' demands for the return to a conventional army because of the raw wounds generated by the uprising. Ultimately, the need both to generate a steady flow of troops and to establish a disciplined body were reluctantly recognized by the influential Communists. Premier and War Minister Largo Caballero together with his cabinet also saw the political advantages as the first step to restoring the authority of central government which dissolved after July 1936.

On October 15, 1936 the Popular Army (Ejercito Popular) was officially activated and on October 29 conscription was introduced with the classes of 1932–35 being the first of 27 to be mobilized.[6] Recruits were given two or three weeks basic training before being sent to units where they might receive further training.[7] By the spring of 1937 there were armies nominally under central government command, those under the Catalonian government (Generalidad), or l'Exèrcit de Catalunya, holding the line from the Pyrenees to Teruel, and the troops under the three authorities in the northern enclave. The Popular Army always remained under firm political control with a War Council chaired initially by Largo Caballero until his resignation on May 17, 1937, when his Navy and Air Minister, Indalecio Prieto, became Defense Minister until dismissed by Premier Dr Juan Negrín who assumed the portfolio for himself.

The creation of the new Republican Army owed much to Under-Secretary for War General José Asensio and Colonel Segismundo Casado who had to shoehorn the anarchic militias into a conventional army based upon an easily implemented but radical organization. During the Great War the combatants discovered their traditional "square" organization—an infantry division of two brigades each of two three-battalion regiments—restricted tactical control and they adopted a "triangular" pattern with three regiments. Each regiment was the core of a flexible combined-arms task group or battle group including artillery, engineers, signalers, and supply troops which could provide flexibility for semi-autonomous operations. While the conservative prewar Spanish Army retained the traditional organization, radicals proposed a more flexible organization, the composite or mixed brigade (Brigada Mixta-BM) which incorporated tactical organization experience gained from suppressing the Asturian uprising of 1934. It resembled the British Army brigade of 1914 with four infantry battalions and was adopted from the fall of 1936.[8]

The BM, nominally with 3,850 men, was easily created by combining militia columns of similar political hue. Yet Largo Caballero had to act cautiously, and the decision to create the BM was not published until October 4, with implementation from October 31, Lister's 1 BM being a Communist formation.[9] As a sop to the revolutionaries, from October 16 each unit, formation, and headquarters was given a commissar who ensured the political reliability of the military commander and the welfare of the men.[10] The Commissar General was Foreign Minister Julio Álvarez del Vayo who ensured that by the spring of 1937 125 of 168 battalion commissars were Communists or secret Communist sympathizers like himself.

Although the BM were supposed to have five artillery batteries, a motorized reconnaissance squadron, and an engineer company, lack of resources saw this reduced in November to a three-gun battery plus an antitank company and a support group with mortars and/or infantry guns and a cavalry platoon which raised nominal strength to 4,095. By the end of 1936 43 BM had been created, mostly on the Madrid front, then the reorganization gradually spread north and south with 106 created by the end of March and 166 in the Republican heartland by the end of 1937. Shortages of equipment meant many BM were purely infantry formations, sometimes of 1,500–2,500 men, some with only three battalions.[11]

From December 1936 two or three BMs were grouped with an artillery battalion (*grupo*) of three batteries, an engineer battalion, signal, medical and transport units into infantry divisions (DI). From March they formed army corps (CE) and ultimately the Republican heartland had 74 DI in 22 CE.[12] The corps and armies would be assigned support forces including cavalry brigades, usually used for protecting lines of communications and internal security, engineers and artillery batteries often assigned to a grouping (*agrupación*). In May 1937 it was claimed that the Republic had 451 batteries with 1,680 guns.[13]

Armor remained a contentious subject, benefiting, like aviation, from improved fuel and advances in mechanical engineering to enhance performance and reliability. The tank was developed as an infantry-support weapon to help suppress centers of resistance and this was their role in Spanish doctrine, which was heavily influenced by the French.[14] One of the most influential postwar designs was the British Vickers 6-ton tank, the basis of the Russian T-26, which was used extensively by both sides.

During the 1920s the concept of tanks replacing cavalry rapidly to exploit battlefield success led to two very different solutions. America's J. Walter Christie created a vehicle with a unique chassis of large road wheels for greater cross-country range and speed and the Russians adopted this as the Bystrokhodny Tank (Fast Tank-BT) and sent some to Spain. The other solution deployed in Spain was a small, automobile-sized vehicle whose prototype was built in a domestic garage to become the turretless two-man Carden-Loyd tankette. Developed by Vickers as a cheap armored fighting vehicle for reconnaissance and as a mobile machine gun, it was the basis of Italy's L3/35 or Carro Veloce 33/35 (CV-33/35) and Germany's Panzerkampfwagen I (PzKpfw I) tank with twin turret-mounted rifle-caliber machine guns both of which appeared in Spain.

To support the Republic, Krivoshein led the first Russian tank detachment with T-26s, which arrived in October 1936, but lacked logistical support in the form of repair facilities and spares—the perennial problem with all Red Army mechanized forces. The detachment suffered 59 percent vehicle casualties in its first month, with 16 of the 87 tanks destroyed. Krivoshein would return to Russia in January 1937, escaping the purges despite his Jewish background, and would distinguish himself during World War II to become head of armored training from October 1941 through February 1943.[15] Operations were initially under Arman, a Latvian-born tank battalion commander who had studied engineering in Paris as a teenager. He too returned to Russia in January 1937, was given a mechanized brigade, and was then jailed for two years but reinstated to lead armored formations until he was killed in August 1943.

In December 1936 Pavlov brought replacements, many drawn from his 4th Mechanized Brigade, who merged with Krivoshein's survivors to create 1 Brigada Blindada (1 BB) initially with two tank and one transport battalion, later expanded to four battalions: three tank and one armored car. In the late spring of 1937 a second tank brigade was created together with an armored car battalion and they were combined into the Armored Vehicles Division

(Division de Ingenios Blindas—DIB) activated in April 1937.[16] This was purely an administrative organization which was augmented by a motorized infantry battalion and a regiment of BT tanks and became 1 DIB after Republican Spain was split in April 1938, with 2 DIB activated to control armor in the south. Similar tank-heavy organizations were also used by tank/armored divisions of the British, French, and Soviet armies but these lumbering formations proved no match for the agile and better-balanced *Panzerdivisionen*. A shortage of Russian manpower meant that 40 percent of tank crews were Spanish and this steadily grew until, by October 1937, chief military advisor Lieutenant General Grigorii Shtern informed Voroshilov that there was no need to send any more tank crews. There appear to have been fewer than 150 Russian tanks in Spain at any one time during the Civil War and, although superior to enemy vehicles, they were hamstrung by a combination of poor mechanical reliability and inadequate support.

Surprisingly, although Spain gave its name to irregular or guerrilla (small war in Spanish) warfare, now called asymmetric operations, this would not feature prominently in the new conflict. The Spanish Army encountered it in Morocco but in prewar Spanish Army doctrine, "guerrilla" was used to denote a skirmisher. With Russian technical assistance the Republic would create a guerrilla organization but despite occasional successes it remained an irritant rather than a threat to the Nationalist rear.[17] Command and control was almost impossible due to a shortage of reliable, mobile radio transceivers, and it was difficult to find sanctuaries where retreating bands could shelter when harried by Nationalist counterinsurgency forces who used ferocious repression to cow potential resistance.[18] However, the guerrillas did prove a useful source of intelligence, and the Republicans also landed agents behind enemy lines in Caudron C 600 Aiglon trainers.[19] These agents were organized by the general staff's Information Section (Servicio de Información, SIM) under Major (later Colonel) Manuel Estrada, an energetic officer who provided high-quality information aided by a commando unit, Batallón Especial and the Russian-organized Comint.[20]

Across the lines the Nationalist Army was, as Winston Churchill famously observed of Russia in October 1939, "A riddle wrapped in a mystery inside an enigma.2"[21] In contrast to the in-depth studies of Alpert and Salas on the Republican Army at the time of writing (2018) there appears to be, even in Spanish, no equivalent work on the Nationalist Army.

Many historians have accepted Republican propaganda claims that it consisted only of Fascists (Falangists), the Spanish Foreign Legion, Moors, Germans, and Italians. Like all good propaganda it has a core of fact and the foreign presence in the Nationalist forces was numerically stronger than in the Republican Army, yet the Nationalist Army remained a largely Spanish force. By the end of the war only 32,000 (3 percent) of 1,024,500 men were in the Italian corps, and even here the majority were Spanish, while 35,000 (3.4 percent) were African troops.[22]

Five prewar divisional districts provided the framework for the Nationalist Army: 2nd at Seville, 5th at Saragossa, 6th at Burgos, 7th at Valladolid, and 8th at Corunna, creating columns which were then expanded into brigades. From the end of March 1937 static, territorial divisions were created around Madrid while the former divisional districts were expanded into regional corps headquarters, e.g. 6th Division became Sixth Corps on April 26 and 8th Division became Eighth Corps on May 15. In April three mobile reserve divisions (11th, 12th, and 13th) were activated to reinforce the Madrid front and others were converted or activated to total 28 divisions by July 1937 and 54 (including two cavalry divisions) by the end of 1938, organized into army corps augmented from April 1938 by divisional groups (*agrupación de divisións*).

The divisions were largely infantry formations with an artillery battalion of three batteries each of three or four guns, an engineer battalion, a cavalry squadron, and auxiliary troops, but each was unique in organization and, like German panzer divisions, appeared to reflect the commander's preferences.[23] Most used the prewar "square" model sub-divided into two regiments (*agrupacións* or demi-brigades). Four "Navarrese" divisions formed in November 1937 were divided into three *agrupacións* and during 1938 divisions were increasingly reorganized on triangular lines (with either *agrupacións* or regiments) with the process accelerated from October 1938 to be adopted by 38 divisions by the end of the war.[24] Usually there were 10–12 infantry battalions or battalion equivalents, although static formations might have twice this number, while 21st Division uniquely had two cavalry brigades and two infantry brigades until March 1938.

Divisions largely consisted of conscript battalions (*batallónes*) augmented by battalions of the Foreign Legion and Falange (*banderas*), Carlist Requetés (*tercio*), and Moorish demi-battalions (*tabor*). Franco ensured the militias posed no political threat to the regime by formerly incorporating them into the army on December 20, 1936 without consulting their political masters.[25] The Falange and Requeté units continued to be raised by their supporters but equipped and led by officers appointed by GHQ, while the Foreign Legion, whose name reflected the fact that it could accept foreigners, remained largely Spanish, unlike its French namesake. The Legion expanded from six to 19 battalions, attracting volunteers because they were, like the Moors, elite units frequently used as the spearhead of the Nationalist Army, often in high-priority offensive and defensive missions.[26] This was reflected in their casualties: the Legion, which reached a peak strength of 14,000, suffered 37,400 casualties including 8,400 dead, while of 78,504 Moors deployed in Spain nearly 67,000 (85 percent) became casualties, including 11,500 killed.[27]

Southern Army commander General Gonzalo Queipo de Llano introduced conscription on the day he raised the banner of revolt but Franco did not issue a conscription decree until August 8, 1936. Eventually the Nationalists would raise 15 reserve classes of men aged 18–33 who were woven into a framework of the prewar regiments on Nationalist territory. Conscription was extended into captured territory and augmented by prisoners of war, many of whom were considered trustworthy enough for the front line.[28] The less trustworthy served in labor battalions and all were closely watched, with any attempt at mutiny or desertion brutally suppressed.[29]

The numbers of battalions, and the ratio of "private" units to conscript varied throughout the war but snapshots are possible. At the beginning of April 1937 the field army had some 300,000 men in 464 battalions, of which 40 (8.6 percent) were Italian or Spanish troops under Italian command and the equivalent of seven (1.5 percent) were African troops. There were 66 (14 percent) Falange, 48 (10 percent) Requeté, and 20 (4.3 percent) volunteer battalions, but 261 (56.25 percent), were conscripts, and if the ten Foreign Legion battalions were included then the figure rose to 58 percent.[30] By the end of the war there were some 665 battalions with front-line divisions of which 34 (5 percent) were Italian or Italian-led, 74 (11 percent) were African, 18 (3 percent) Foreign Legion, 82 (12 percent) were Falange, 24 (3.5 percent) were Requeté, but 429 (64.5 percent) were conscript units.[31]

The Nationalists inherited a handful of obsolete Renault FT 17 tanks but from September 1936 received German PzKpfw I tanks for infantry support with a training and support detachment Gruppe Imker (Beekeeper). This was commanded until the end of the war by Thoma who acted as inspector general of the Nationalist armored corps even when training was transferred to MIR in the spring of 1938.

The PzKpfw I tanks which the Germans called Drohne (Drones) and the Nationalists called Black Men (Negrillos), were first issued to the 1st Tank Battalion (1 Batallón de Carros) activated on October 1, 1936 from the Regimento de Infanteria 27 "Argel" at Cáceres.[32] In the spring the battalion became part of the 2nd Battalion/Tank Regiment (Regimento de Carros de Combate) with two companies of German tanks and a reserve company.[33] The battalion was steadily expanded and from June 25 it created units with captured

T-26s or Russians (Russos), and by August had four Negrillo companies and one Russo. In October 1937 it divided into two battalion-sized groups with an antitank battalion.[34]

On March 1 the Foreign Legion formed its own tank battalion (Bandera de Carros de Combate) to give the Nationalist armored corps 1,538 men by June 6, 1938 and 163 tanks: 67 Negrillos, 39 Russos augmented with Renault FT 17 and Trubia 1936. On October 1, 1938 the battalions were merged into the Tank Task Force (Agrupación de Carros de Combate) with armored car and motorized antitank companies. This was renamed Northern Tank Task Force on November 1938 with 66 Negrillos and 41 Russos, while a newly activated Southern Task Force had nine T-26s. An integral part of the armored corps were antitank batteries, with ten activated in 1936, expanding to 17 by September 1937, with 170 x 37mm guns and 20 captured 45mm guns, and 28 batteries by mid-1938 with 290 German guns and some captured weapons.[35]

Both sides created a strategic reserve during the summer of 1937. On June 3 Franco ordered each of his six corps to create a division numbered from 100 upward, with the last number indicating the corps.[36] It was only in September that Prieto and Rojo created the Reserve Army (Ejercito de Maniobra) headquarters in Aragon, initially from the V and XVIII CE but later reinforced by the new XX, XXI, and XXII CE.[37] It was initially administered by its chief of staff, Colonel Frederico de la Iglesia, but later XX CE commander Colonel Leopoldo Menéndez was assigned to command it.

Leadership

Expanding armies require leaders and the Nationalists inherited 8,000 of the 13,500 regular officers and 2,000 of the 6,200 reservist officers but only 1,200 reservists augmented the Republic's 5,500 regular officers, while 3,000 served neither side.[38] The Republic's shallow pool of professionals for both senior command (corps and army) and key staff positions meant that one corps in 1938 was commanded by a Medical Corps officer!

The Nationalists had the initial advantage of Africanistas who generally proved competent and dynamic leaders, as well as a pool of professional non-commissioned officers (NCOs).[39] When Franco absorbed the militias in December 1936 he also created a network of up to 28 professionally run officer-training schools with training unified under Orgaz as head of the MIR from March 1937. Young, usually middle-class men with a *bachillerato* and two months' front-line experience entered the schools after an entrance exam followed by a 21–24-day course to graduate as provisional officers (*alféreces provisionales*). A specialist course of up to three months then followed in their preferred arm of service. The schools produced 4,000 young officers by the spring and a total of 22,936, although their high casualty rate meant the troops often referred to "provisional officer, certain corpse."[40]

While platoons were led by dynamic young leaders, it was a sad fact that as casualties and promotions removed their predecessors the quality of Nationalist company and battalion commanders declined.[41] In part this was due to the albatross of prewar military education which emphasized learning by rote rather than providing intellectual stimulation. It created a pathological fear of responsibility and yearning for precise, detailed orders and was exacerbated by the stultifying effects of prewar garrison life, with the emphasis upon routine, bureaucracy, and seniority.[42] As one writer observes: "What the academies seemed to produce was no more than another class of bureaucrats, without any regard for their real proficiency for military command."[43] This did not encourage dynamic leadership, a major reason for the uprising's failure, while the traditional parochialism of each branch of the army hindered cooperation.[44] The problems were reflected in Spanish doctrine, with its emphasis upon set-piece battles, and a 1932 corps-size war-game required a day's paperwork to generate orders. Promotion in the Nationalist Army was often based upon seniority rather than merit, while the desire to maintain army prestige meant that there was a reluctance to remove dead wood. Yet from brigade to corps level most Nationalist commanders were promoted within their capabilities.

The Republican Army suffered the same problems and bureaucratic tendencies, especially amongst senior officers, many of whom were promoted beyond their capabilities due to loyalty rather than merit. They also "took refuge in over-bureaucratisation and established a paper army" with "wordy" orders, which Russian commentator Serebryakov criticized in an after-action report on the battle of Brunete.[45] There was also a severe shortage of trained staff officers. In April 1938, for example, Lieutenant Colonel Eduardo Sáenz was the only qualified officer in the Estremadura Army, the others being a temporary lieutenant and a militia officer. Central Army commander Pozas would complain bitterly of being milked of staff officers, yet staff officer training did not begin until October 1938.[46] Those professionals who served in the Republican Army were often regarded, sometimes correctly, as being rebel sympathizers, with suspicion leading some to be, in the contemporary Communist expression, "repressed." The remainder fought for the Republic out of loyalty, ambition or even like Miaja from opportunism, but some such as Miaja's last chief of staff, Colonel Manuel Matallana, while loyal, maintained contacts with friends across the lines.

Largo Caballero and Asensio centralized Republican officer training and reopened branch (infantry, artillery, engineers) schools around Valencia on September 9, 1936 to provide three- or four-month courses while the Generalidad and the northern enclaves had their own establishments, yet until the appointment of General Mariano Gámir on October 12, 1938 there was no training supremo. The shortage of instructors, many demoralized because they were not officially regarded as "loyal," aggravated the poor standard of training. Many cadets, even university students and teachers, lacked the required educational standards and Catalonian officers received a frosty reception from Anarchists who felt they were a new generation of bourgeoise young gentlemen. All commands organized training courses to meet their own requirements.[47] The Russians also opened the Red Army's training facilities to the Spanish and qualified 300 infantry, 60 artillery, 80 engineers and signalers, together with some 60 tank crew during 1937 alone.[48]

War schools (*Escuelas Populares de Guerra*) produced 11,200 officers while corps and divisional educational establishments produced 15,000 and a further 10,000 came directly from militias, but few reached the standard of the Nationalists' *alféreces provisionales.* Junior leaders came from artisans, artists, activists, and intellectuals within the militias and were augmented by non-commissioned officers from the prewar army and paramilitary forces. There were battlefield promotions (*oficiales en campaña*) but by July 1938 these totaled only 7,237 with another 2,225 commissioned later, but their quality was generally poor while many well-educated members within the ranks did not apply for fear of being on the losing side. Many militia leaders struggled to meet the complex administrative and tactical challenges, so that from brigade to army level there were many unfitted for their role and subject to constant pressure over political and ideological issues, but their "ignorance was hidden behind a bluff confidence sustained by a ferocious discipline." Only a few, such as the Communist Modesto, would rise to the challenges and prove very effective corps commanders.[49]

Because of political control over the armed forces Republican decision-making reflected internecine political rivalries. These were aggravated by the knowledge that there were only limited resources, and while a southern thrust might split Nationalist territory, retake the Andalusian breadbasket, and disrupt the enemy's prime supply route through Seville and Cadiz, it required a substantial redistribution of resources and would not achieve strategic surprise. A westward thrust through Aragon to relieve the northern enclave using the ill-equipped and poorly organized Catalonian forces would enter the Nationalist heartland.

Republican strategy had to be pared down to a series of operations designed to weaken the enemy army and would display Tactical Level success but Operational Level failure.[50] Franco always took up the gauntlet and turned these attacks into battles of attrition, which the Republic could not win, although they also strained Nationalist resources. Like Ulysses S. Grant in the American Civil War, Franco aimed to weaken his enemies to enable his forces to strike rapid, spectacular, and decisive offensives which ultimately would win the war.

The most influential Republican military leader was Rojo, an army officer's son who was 41 when the war broke out. He was in the top four of his class and after service in Morocco his career from 1922 focused upon military education; indeed he had the air of a school master, editing texts on tactics, weapons, and firepower. This extremely capable and well-educated officer joined the general staff as a major in February 1936.[51] A conservative and devout Catholic, and possibly, like Miaja, a member of the anti-Republic UME, he remained true to his oath and stayed with the Republic.

Promoted lieutenant colonel in October 1936 he became Miaja's chief of staff but his modesty and lack of charisma meant he posed no political threat and his widely admired professionalism overcame any suspicions of disloyalty.[52] He planned all the Republic's offensives and with the formation of the Negrín government in May 1937 as a colonel he became chief of the general staff earning a promotion to brigadier general. In 1939 he emigrated to Latin America, although most of his family remained in Spain, and was an instructor to the Bolivian Army, but after 15 years military and religious contacts helped negotiate his return home. There he was formally charged with "military rebellion," given a suspended 30-year sentence followed by a pardon and he died in June 1966, uniquely still respected by his former enemies.

Rather like Stalin in pre-1957 Russian histories, Nationalist sources regarded Franco as the fountainhead of all military success, and he certainly became the sole arbiter of Nationalist strategy following Mola's death in June 1937. He was an Africanista and former chief of the General Staff who seems to have been little influenced by contemporary military thought.[53] Perhaps it was a Moorish-style superstition that led him to keep the mummified hand of St Teresa of Avila on his office desk. His bravery, dynamism, and professionalism made him the army's youngest brigadier general in 1926, while his Moroccan experiences led him to encourage his generals in the Civil War to adopt an "indirect approach" and tactics based upon rapid maneuver rather than frontal assaults.[54]

He was a man of contrasts, personally ultra cautious and militarily wary, yet sometimes given to wild flights of fancy.[55] Although he instructed his generals to abandon territory to avoid exposure, he engaged in bloody battles of attrition, often for strategically irrelevant points which exasperated his foreign allies. His obsession with symbolism, such as relieving the Alcazar of Toledo and regaining lost ground such as Teruel, might have been instinctive or a determination to erode enemy military strength at every opportunity. He was certainly indifferent to human suffering, snubbing the wife of Colonel Domingo Rey d'Harcourt, who vainly defended Teruel, and would shun old friends who had failed to show enthusiasm for The Cause.[56]

Army command requires a polygamous marriage between the commander, his general staff, and his senior subordinates, although these relationships within the Nationalist Army remain uncertain. What is certain is that the Italians and Germans had little influence upon Nationalist decision-making; indeed, advice offered too forcefully would arouse Franco's considerable ire. His sharp changes of strategy in 1937 and 1938 owed more to his subordinates and the professional flexibility of his staff, who in Salamanca worked on the floor above him.[57] He would often host informal meetings at night in his apartment when ideas might be aired for later examination, but as the Levante campaign demonstrated, he could obstinately ignore advice.[58]

His first chief of staff was 58-year-old Africanista Brigadier General Fidel Dávila, an infantry officer who had fought the Americans in Cuba and regarded himself as a liberal.[59] As a staff officer he fought in Morocco but when Spain became a Republic he went into the reserves to become a full-time Monarchist conspirator. He resembled a successful businessman and was always courteous and loyal, being described by a colleague as "pure and austere." During the uprising he seized Burgos then became chairman of the National Defense Council, chief of staff and head of the Technical Board (*junta técnica*) or provisional government. He would become commander of the Army of the North after Mola's death and from February 1938 simultaneously Defense Minister, as lieutenant general. Although bureaucratic he was indefatigable and honest as well as being an extremely able administrator who became one of the architects of victory.

He would be succeeded by the capable Germanophile Colonel Juan Vigón, the Northern Army chief of staff, who had earlier been Franco's personal staff advisor and was also a Monarchist, like the Air Force and Navy commanders General Alfredo Kindélan and Admiral Juan Cervera. In between these appointments, or when either was otherwise engaged, the deputy chief of staff, General Francisco Martin, would take their place. Other key members were the other architect of victory, the Operations Chief Barroso (who became a colonel), the Organization Department's Colonel Luis Villanueva, the Service

Department's Lieutenant Colonel Manuel Villegas, and the Information Chief Colonel Luis Gonzalo Vitoria.[60] The last was responsible for intelligence and benefited from aerial photography and Comint, as well as organizing the famed Fifth Column through Colonel José Ungria's Servicio de Información y Policía Militar (SIPM), one network of which provided detailed information on enemy rail movements.[61]

Foreign troops

Foreign volunteers formed seven International Brigades (BI) in the Popular Army but the Brigadistas were regarded as a mixed blessing by many xenophobic and anti-Communist Republican officers.[62] They were the result of foreign Communists spontaneously joining the militias after the uprising, then writing to their national parties advocating a Foreign Legion of trained soldiers.

Eventually Stalin authorized the Comintern, the worldwide coordinating body for Communist parties, to instruct national parties on September 18 about "the recruitment of volunteers with military experience" who were to be sent to Spain.[63] The French Communist Party created an organization to move recruits southward while national parties were allocated quotas, which meant that up to 60 percent of the men dispatched were Communists or Communist sympathizers but were joined by thousands of non-Communist volunteers.[64] Some went from a spirit of adventure, while most were idealists willing to risk their lives both to stop the spread of fascism and to support the revolution. Hundreds of German and Italian émigrés believed that victory in Spain would be the first step toward liberating their homelands.[65] About 80 percent of the men were literate members of the working class and generally they were physically superior to their Spanish comrades.

Once across the frontier the men assembled at Albacete, as brigades were organized under French Communist leader André Marty, with his distinctive beret and moustache. Men from similar national backgrounds were grouped into platoons, companies, and battalions to provide some form of cohesion, but despite the Comintern's admonishment to seek men with military experience few recruits knew even how to load a rifle.[66] When 11 BI was created in October 1936 only 42 percent of 515 volunteers had done military service, although their first battalion commanders had faced each other on the Western Front. Most Brigadistas were aged 18–36 who had little or no wartime or military experience, the exception being the French, most of whom had been conscripted during their lives.[67] The first four International Brigades were activated from October through December 1936 as mixed brigades, and from September 27, 1937 they would officially replace the Spanish Foreign Legion.[68]

The Brigadistas were portrayed as the Republic's shock troops but, despite their *esprit de corps*, inadequate training and poor leadership meant their operations became massacres of the innocents, like the German Army at the First Ypres or the British Army at the First Somme. Their diversity meant that they lacked a uniform tactical doctrine, or even common square-bashing drills, and the Communists' political investment meant a demand for a rapid return at the price of limited training.[69] While a World War II British and American soldier might receive at least three months of initial training before joining units to learn battlefield skills, the Brigadistas were lucky to receive two months' initial training, although this was better than their Spanish comrades. Worse still, much of this time was wasted in endless political meetings, with protestors marked for arrest as Trotskyist-Fascists.[70]

Inadequate training was exacerbated by leaders selected for political rather than military capabilities in an early form of "ticket-punching."[71] Strutting around with their highly prized pistols in leather holsters, these leaders, mostly Communists, had a toxic combination of dynamism and military ignorance. The Party, like the Nazis, tended to think of The People in the abstract rather than the personal, and at the front these two traits were expressed in unsupported bayonet charges or demands to hold ground to the last man, a trait shared with the Nationalist military leadership. Human frailty was ignored and when units failed because men were pushed beyond endurance, Party leaders immediately sought scapegoats with drum-head courts martial and executions, often on the flimsiest of pretexts.[72]

Witch hunts for spies, saboteurs, and Trotskyists at Albacete, enthusiastically supported by Marty, undermined unit morale and cohesion as men became aware of their incompetent leaders, and declining morale was reflected in a constant stream of deserters, while many of those who returned home abandoned the Party.[73] The witch hunts directed by NKVD secret police, with imprisonment in secret jails, created an atmosphere of hysterical paranoia as the Soviet Union exported not only weapons to Spain but also the Purges.[74] It led many Brigadistas, especially non-Party members, to believe they were fighting for repressive rather than progressive humanity.[75]

Some 35,000 men from 53 countries served in the International Brigades although there were never more than 18,000 foreign troops in the Republican Army at any one time.[76] Soviet sources suggest the Brigadistas suffered 20,000 casualties (60 percent) but another source says 55,161 including 17,620 dead and missing, but this figure includes Spanish troops.[77] Heavy casualties left few survivors to pass on vital lessons as the British Battalion demonstrated. In July 1937 it entered the Brunete battlefield in a scattered formation as a precaution against air attacks and artillery fire, but eight months later marched to the front in a column of fours without scouts, and a complete company was captured.[78]

Heavy casualties and dwindling numbers of volunteers meant that from 1937 Spanish troops increasingly fleshed out the BIs, which became only nominally "international." Indeed by December 1937, of 48,814 men, only 21,089 (43 percent) were foreigners.[79] This decline paved the way for the Republic to accept diplomatic moves to withdraw foreign volunteers and the Brigadistas held their final parade on October 28, 1938. But only 4,600 had departed by mid-January, leaving 6,000 to fight as individuals in the Catalonian campaign.[80]

For all their heroism and dedication, the International Brigades represented one of the most cynical publicity stunts since the Children's Crusade, providing cannon fodder to publicize the Republican cause. As one commentator observed: "They cannot be said to have given an example of discipline or military ability to the Spanish troops, nor was their achievement greater than that of the Republican Army or at least its best fighting units."[81]

The foreign volunteers most familiar with the terrifying witch hunts were the 1,653 members of the Red Army who served in Spain.[82] Some were undoubtedly volunteers anxious to fulfill their internationalist duty and fight fascism but many, like the Germans and Italians on the other side, were happily volunteered or drafted.

The dispatch of general-level officers required Central Committee authorization and to conceal their presence they, like their German and Italian equivalents, received code names. Many volunteers were high fliers, both literally and figuratively, who served tours averaging six months, but ranging from three months to a year, so the numbers of advisors (including Navy and civilian technicians) fluctuated. In early November 1936 there were 835 (including 245 tank crew and 379 aircrew), in October 1937 the figure had dropped to 557 (including 349 Red Army of whom 107 tank crew and 141 aircrew), to 250 by October 1938 and 218 by January 1939.[83] The last group of 25 arrived in Spain on February 7, 1939 and all departed in mid-March 1939. From November 1936 they had a direct radio link to Moscow and also their own internal radio links, but the latter were not always reliable and there were often serious breakdowns in communications.

The total number of advisors, including Navy, NKVD, and technicians, was reportedly 1,878, of whom some 600 were non-combatants. Of these 168 were killed or missing, including six military advisors/instructors, the heaviest losses being from the 770 airmen and 351 tank personnel with 99 (12.85 percent) of the former and 53 (15.1 percent) of the latter killed or missing.[84] Moscow, like Berlin and Rome, intended to send instructors rather than combatants but the "instructors" soon found themselves fighting alongside their allies in what the Americans later called "mission creep." Officers most affected were in formations up to army-corps level, including machine- gun and artillery instructors such as Lister's advisor, former rifle regiment commander Rodimtsev, whose duties took them near the front lines despite Stalin's admonishment to stay away from artillery fire. The combat role of tank and air crew made it impossible to obey Stalin's directive.

Yet relatively few advisors served with army corps and most worked at army headquarters or ministries. Front-line army advisors included another former infantry regiment commander, Batov, who arrived in December 1936 and departed injured in August 1937. He would later be a distinguished tank commander and would crush the Hungarian Rising in 1956. Future Marshal Malinovsky was in Spain between January 1937 and May 1938, Mikhail Shumilov would command troops at Stalingrad in 1942, while gunnery specialist Mitrofan Nedelin would be the first commander of the Strategic Missile Force before dying in a missile explosion in October 1960.

The most senior advisor was Stalin's crony Colonel General Grigorii Kulik, who was with the Central Army to May 1937, but from 1935 had been head of the Red Army's Main Artillery Directorate responsible for weapon development. An ignorant, bullying buffoon, his appointment to direct weapons development was like expecting an 18th-century coachman to master a 20th-century automobile and contributed to the Soviet Union's defeats in 1941.[85] Brigadier General Voronov worked under him before and after service in Spain as a gunnery specialist. He would succeed Kulik in the Artillery Directorate and become an architect of victory. By contrast his successor in Spain, Brigadier General Nikolai Klich, was arrested in June 1941 as a front artillery commander and executed in September 1941 for command failures.

General staff advisors included Major General Meretskov, former chief of staff to the Far Eastern Army. He departed in May 1937, and at the end of 1940 was briefly chief of the general staff but was replaced in January 1941 by future Marshal Georgii Zhukov. He served in minor roles against Germany and Japan despite falling into the clutches of the NKVD for a short but painful period in 1941.[86]

The advisors could make only recommendations or suggestions to their Spanish hosts, and even this was hamstrung by the perennial shortage of interpreters. Worse, they were often relatively junior officers who, as Malinovsky observed, were asked to advise on matters beyond their professional knowledge, rather like hundreds of Red Army officers promoted after the "repression" of their predecessors.[87] Whether or not the advice was accepted depended upon their host, although Russian control of armor and aviation made such advice offers that their hosts could not refuse. While the advisors often found enthusiastic support for their presence the lack of urgency, the so-called *mañana* culture which also exasperated the Germans, caused frustration especially because Moscow held the advisors responsible for the success or failure of operations.[88]

Liaison with the Spanish forces was initially through military attaché Gorev, who arrived in late September 1936 and departed in October 1937. He had served as an advisor in China a decade earlier, then became the GRU chief spy (*rezident*) in the United States from 1930 to 1934, returning to command a mechanized brigade. Four months after returning to Russia he was arrested and in June 1938 shot.[89]

The Chief Military Advisor held the rank of lieutenant general and directed Soviet military activity in Spain through advisory branches. Because the Russians were short-handed, these advisory branches supervised other missions; the aviation advisor, for example, being responsible for communications, weapons, and maintenance. All three chief military advisors had GRU connections; indeed the first, the Latvian Janis Berzin, was its former head but was arrested in November 1937 and executed in July 1938 for involvement in a counter-revolutionary organization. His replacement Grigorii Shtern served in the Far East, then became head of National Air Defense, only to be arrested in June 1941 and executed four months later together with most of the former Soviet air leadership, many of whom had served in Spain. The last, Kuzma Kachanov, would have a similar role in China until February 1941, then became an army commander but his failures led to a drum-head court-martial and death.

Table 2.1: Soviet Chief Military Advisors

Name	Period
Janis Berzin	October 1936–August 1937
Grigorii Shtern	August 1937–April 1938
Kuzma Kachanov	April 1938–February 1939

Nationalist attitudes toward their allies were also ambivalent with the substantial Italian military presence proving especially irritating, in that they would sometimes ignore Spanish senior officers.[90] At the urging of senior Italian officers in Spain, notably Roatta, Mussolini agreed on December 12,

1936 to dispatch troops and on December 23, the MMIS landed at Cadiz with 3,000 men. With reinforcements they became on February 17, 1937 the Volunteer Corps (CTV) under Roatta.[91] The majority, 51.5 percent, were the poorly trained MVSN organized into three "triangular" divisions while the regulars, largely conscripts, formed the fourth binary (two-regiment) division.[92] The 35,222-strong corps also had the brigade-sized MVSN XXIII de Marzo, armored and artillery groups and engineers, to absorb 17.5 percent of the Italian Army and nearly 26 percent of the active MSVN.[93] The CTV's defeat at Guadalajara in March 1937 saw Roatta replaced by Bastico, the disbandment of two MVSN divisions, and the distribution of their men into the expanded "XXIII Marzo" Division and the newly activated Fiamme Nere (Black Flames) Division. The last was disbanded in October 1937 and its men formed a third regiment in "XXIII Marzo."

From February 1937 Rome also equipped two Spanish brigades, the Flechas Azules (Blue Arrows) and Flechas Negras (Black Arrows), each of 2,500 men of whom 5 percent were Italians, mostly commanders and specialists. These were organized into two regiments (six battalions), an assault demi-battalion, and a mountain artillery group. In August/September 1937 the CTV reformed its Armored Group with 5,999 men in two tankette battalions (four companies), a support and an infantry battalion, while at the end of the year the CTV received another three heavy batteries. It now had 38,250 men and a new commander, General Mario Berti, while in March 1938 the Flechas Negras Brigade was expanded into the Flechas Division and all were supported by an artillery command of 25 batteries (116 guns). The last reinforcements, 5,679 men, arrived in the summer of 1938, bringing CTV strength to 37,387 in August 1938, but diplomatic pressure to reduce the foreign military presence in Spain saw the withdrawal of 9,752 troops and airmen the following month, including 5,076 MVSN of XXIII Marzo, whose remaining troops were absorbed by the nine-battalion Littorio Division.[94]

A new commander, Major General Gastone Gambara, was appointed on October 24, 1938 and the CTV again reorganized, with the Hispano-Italian Flechas Division reverting to its original name of Flechas Negras while the Flechas Azules Brigade was expanded into two divisions, Flechas Azules (Blue Arrows) and Flechas Verdes (Green Arrows) with a total of 18 battalions. The Armored Group was reorganized into two Italian tank and one Spanish motor-mechanized battalions, each of two tank companies, and a mixed battalion with another Italian tank company to give the CTV 28,012 men.[95] Italy sent 78,846 men to Spain and they suffered 15,463 casualties (19.5 percent) including 3,700 dead.[96]

By contrast only 19,000 Germans, mostly from the Luftwaffe, served with the Condor Legion in Spain where they lost 298 dead (173 to enemy action, the rest to accidents and illness), including 28 tank crew of whom five were lost in action.[97] The prime land force was Gruppe Imker, also known as Panzerabteilung 88, activated from a cadre of II/4 Panzer Regiment on September 23, 1936 and commanded until the end of the war by Thoma. He had been associated with motorized troops since 1922 and was a member of the first panzer demonstration formation in 1933.[98] While Imker was not a combat unit, some German personnel did receive combat experience and participated in 192 actions.[99]

Some 8,000 Portuguese served in Nationalist battalions and also as pilots, while Irish fascist General Eoin O'Duffy created the 15th Foreign Legion Bandera from 700 of his followers and adventurers but failed to maintain Hibernia's military reputation before they were withdrawn in June 1937.[100] The Foreign Legion also had a 500-man French unit, while perhaps 1,000 individual volunteers from Europe and Latin America joined the Nationalist Army's ranks.[101]

Doctrine

Battles would be dominated by the Great War mantra, "artillery conquers the ground, infantry occupies it."[102] The ease with which artillery concentrations could be assembled had tipped the traditional balance between offensive and defensive operations firmly in favor of the latter at all levels, with the French calculating that defensive casualties would be about a third of combatants while offensive casualties would be twice that figure.[103]

In defense, infantry deployed in depth, shielding the gun line with dispersed automatic weapons to cover barbed-wire entanglements, which together restricted battlefield movement. Overcoming these defenses required overwhelming artillery force secretly concentrated on a narrow sector, with guns neutralizing rather than destroying the defenses, engaging enemy artillery (counter-battery fire), destroying enemy command and control, as well as stunning the defending infantry. The attacking infantry operated in regimental/brigade combined-arms battle groups within divisional task forces to break through the defenses and threaten the gun line which would be forced to retreat.

Victory is achieved only by large-scale offensive operations, and while the Tactical Level challenges had been solved by mid-1918, exploiting this success at the Operational or Strategic Levels remained a significant problem.

Maneuver was severely restricted at the Tactical Level by artillery damage to both ground and communications, while the scale of the artillery train acted as a millstone around the attackers' necks. By contrast the defenders' communications, especially railroads, would be intact allowing them to bring in reinforcements, including artillery, to create rapidly a new defensive position, making the supreme Power of the Defense an article of postwar military faith.[104]

At the Operational Level, progress deep into the enemy lines on a narrow front would create a salient exposed to enemy fire and counterattacks. The solution was a broad advance of a few dozen kilometers to an easily defended line from which enemy counterattacks could be repelled, a step-by-step approach which the British General Sir Henry Rawlinson described as "bite and hold," and this became the basis of a military catechism.[105] Most armies, including the Spanish, followed, to a greater or lesser degree, French doctrine, which envisaged a succession of limited offensives to chew chunks from the enemy and ultimately expose him in an indefensible salient which would have to be evacuated. It was a concept similar to maneuvering a large piece of furniture by shifting its weight from side to side. In such operations the degree of junior leader initiative varied from zero with the French to almost 100 percent with the Germans, but whichever approach was used the enemy would be slowly pushed back.

At the very end of the war on the Western Front the British were experimenting with mobile forces based upon equine and mechanized cavalry, with motorized infantry and even cyclists to assist Operational Level exploitation. They exploited fissures in a disorganized defensive system to penetrate the enemy rear and take key communications points such as railroad stations and crossroads. This concept was absorbed into postwar doctrine for exploitation and to screen the main force as it consolidated on its objective or helping to seal defensive breaches.[106] The supremacy of the defense and limited offensives became the One True Faith and was reflected in Spanish Army doctrine defined by *Doctrina para el empleo táctico de las Armas y los Servicios* of 1924 and by the *Reglamento para el empleo táctico de las Grandes Unidades* of 1925 as well as the *Reglamento Táctico de Infantería* of 1929. However, these placed a greater value upon maneuver than the French, questioned their obsession with centralization, and were more ambivalent about the power of the defense as their joint campaign during the Rif War in the 1920s demonstrated.[107]

For heretics like Mikhail Tukachevsky in the Soviet Union, Heinz Guderian in Germany, as well as Great Britain's Basil Liddell Hart and John Fuller, these mobile forces pointed the way to the future. They believed that tank-tipped motorized battle groups operating within divisional-sized mechanized task forces not only could rapidly penetrate the Tactical Zone but also provide Operational Level exploitation, striking hundreds of kilometers into the enemy rear. By cutting communications to prevent the defenders rallying they could achieve massive encirclements. Interestingly the great German offensives of 1918 were spearheaded not by Storm Troop (*Stosstruppe*) divisions but *Mobildivisionen*—infantry divisions with improved transport—while until 1942 the Wehrmacht's armored and motorized formations were also referred to as *Mobildivisionen.* Indeed the panzer division was essentially a motorized Great War *Mobildivision* with a tank regiment replacing one of the three rifle regiments.[108]

Despite a huge investment in resources, the Russian mechanized formations encountered severe logistics and communications problems, as Voroshilov and Kulik were quick to point out.[109] This influenced the Red Army purge from 1937, with "deep strike" advocates suffering the harshest treatment. By contrast the Germans spent much time solving these problems although the summer campaign of 1940 would demonstrate that the Wehrmacht retained senior-level skeptics.

The faithful dismissed the heretics' ideas as science fiction. They recognized the value of infantry-supporting tanks at the Tactical Level and supporting mobile groups at the Operational Level. Yet they were certain that the field gun would remain the tanks' prime enemy, as in the Great War where the 54 Infanteriedivision's guns broke up two major tank attacks during 1917: in April during the Nivelle offensive and in November at Cambrai. Many agreed with Kulik that, just as machine guns restricted infantry movement, so antitank guns would have the same effect upon tanks.[110]

Cavalry were retained for advances over rough country or for screening the flanks but, like their European contemporaries, both armies also relied upon equine power for transport at the Operational and Tactical Level to pull wagons and guns. It appears that Nationalist troops, especially at battalion level, may also have relied upon packhorses, which could easily carry around 115kg or more, or mules which could carry at least 150kg.[111]

Air Forces

The Spanish conflict exploited the post Great War revolution in aviation technology. By 1918 most air forces consisted of single-seat fighters and what the British called "corps aeroplanes," two-seat, single-engined biplanes used for reconnaissance, artillery fire direction, and ground attacks. Daytime bombers were usually high-speed versions of these airplanes, while lumbering heavy bombers flew night attacks.

Technical developments from the late 1920s fueled the revolution with reinforced aluminum alloy shells replacing the tradition wire-braced timber/metal tube structure to create a more aerodynamically efficient airframe aided by retractable undercarriages, greater internal volume and superior power–mass ratios. The new generation of combat aircraft included bombers faster than most contemporary fighters, even when fully loaded, making them difficult to intercept and leading British Prime Minister Stanley Baldwin to claim in 1935: "The bombers will always get through."

The Americans pioneered this technology but leading European air forces emulated them from 1935, with the Russian Tupolev SB Katiuska, German Heinkel He 111, and Dornier Do 17.[112] In response, fighter design changed from dogfighters with light armament (two or four rifle-caliber machine guns) to high-speed bomber interceptors whose heavier armament could inflict greater damage. The Russians hedged their bets with the I-15 dogfighter biplane and I-16 interceptor monoplane, the Germans developed the Messerschmitt Bf 109 interceptor monoplane, but the Italians would retain the traditional Fiat CR.32 biplane, all of which would appear in Spanish skies.

The Russians provided the backbone of Republican air power, and until May 1937 were led by Smushkevich, a capable officer who had been both air brigade commander and commissar before arriving in Spain. He got on well with Army Air Force commander Colonel (later Brigadier General) Ignacio Hidalgo de Cisneros, a left-leaning aristocrat who would become a secret Communist during the winter of 1936/37.[113] Smushkevich appears to have been replaced by future Soviet Air Force commander Major General Vsevolod Lopatin until September 1937, Brigadier General Evgenii Ptukhin until February 1938, and Colonel Aleksandr Andreiev until February 1939.

Hidalgo de Cisneros became the commander when the Army and Navy Air Forces were merged into the Fuerzas Aereas Republicanas Españolas (FARE) on May 19, 1937, with a maximum strength in 1937 of some 330 (excluding aircraft in the Biscay enclave and seaplanes), including a core of 250 Russian aircraft, and 300 combat aircraft in the summer of 1938, supported by the army's antiaircraft artillery force, the DCA (Defensa Contra Aeronaves).[114]

The FARE focused upon supporting ground operations at the Tactical-Operational Level. Fighters were to achieve air superiority over the battlefield and to intercept enemy bombers but occasionally were used for ground-attack missions and reconnaissance. Bombing was more the prerogative of the strike arm whose Katiuskas and Rasantes, according to a 1937 Russian report, flew 45 percent of sorties against troop concentrations, 24 percent against airfields, and 22 percent against rail or industrial targets. Urban areas were rarely attacked, partly because they did not feature in Russian aviation doctrine and partly because the Spanish government did not approve of it. The Communists would keep details of this force close to their chests, even from the FARE commander.[115] Defense Minister Prieto would later allege that neither Hidalgo de Cisneros nor Smushkevich would tell him how many aircraft were available or even the number of airfields being used in the air regions![116]

The government could not confront the Russians because Moscow was the Republic's sole source of modern combat aircraft and delivered 644.[117] By contrast France delivered only 100 modern, but obsolescent, combat aircraft, with 190 trainers and transports, while "commercial sources" supplied about 125 combat aircraft (many suitable only for training) and 100 trainers or transports.[118] Only 34 Grumman GE-23 Delfin (Dolphin) two-seat fighters proved suitable for first-line service, equipping a two-squadron group. The remainder, together with the survivors of the 140 prewar combat aircraft, operated in various formations until reorganized in the autumn of 1937 into eight squadrons (*escuadrillas*) in three groups (*grupos*) in a second-line operational wing (*escuadra*) for coastal patrol and home defense. The last was important because of raids, especially upon coastal cities, by Majorca-based Italian bombers.

Russian Polikarpov fighters formed a fighter wing with I-16 Mosca (Fly) equipping a *grupo* of up to seven squadrons, while I-15 Chato (Snub Nose) equipped another with four squadrons.[119] The bomber wing had up to two *grupos* each of up to four squadrons equipped with the Katiuska (Katy) twin-engined bomber and R-5 Natasha or R-5SSS Rasante (Skimmer) single-engined biplanes, one of these squadrons later becoming a night-bomber unit.[120] But the FARE inherited the Soviet Air Force's greatest weakness, demonstrated during the Winter War with Finland, of inadequate long-range photo-reconnaissance, for only six Katiuskas modified for this role were delivered in April 1937 with cameras.[121]

By July 1, 1937 only 267 remained of the 360 aircraft sent to Spain, and 45 of these needed major repairs.[122] Two months later Shtern reported the bomber force was down to 70 aircraft, including 28 SB, and he vainly sought 200–250 fighters and 110–120 SB.[123] Smaller Russian reinforcements brought FARE strength to 300 (151 fighters and 115 strike) by the summer of 1938 but by December the figures were 140 and 70 respectively and by January 12, 1939 there were only 30 serviceable fighters.[124]

Nationalist air power rose from a nominal 450 land planes in 1937 to 575 during the second half of 1938, attrition eroding this figure to 453 by February 4, 1939 because German and Italian factories had difficulties replacing aircraft, although the latter's deliveries to Spain amounted to 10 percent of total aircraft production in the second half of the 1930s.[125] A Spanish return of December 23, 1938 showed that the Nationalists were supported by 469 aircraft, excluding seaplanes, of which 42 were in the Balearics.[126] Nationalist air power provided strong but not overwhelming numerical superiority and good air support on several fronts simultaneously.[127]

In 1936 Kindélan, one of Spain's first military pilots, had only 75 combat aircraft and 2,150 personnel from the prewar air arms, but the Arma de Aviación (Air Arm) or Aviación Nacional rose to 90 by the summer of 1937 and by December 1938 had a nominal of 225 landplanes in 23 squadron-sized *grupos* of two *escuadrilla*.[128] Within the *escuadrilla* prewar active officers commanded 21 of 27 fighter units but only 15 of the remainder.[129] In November 1937 Kindélan created a Brigada Aérea Hispaña (Spanish Air Brigade—BAH) with six bomber, two fighter, and a reconnaissance *grupos* and a nominal 60 aircraft which became 1 BAH when 2 BAH was created in August 1938, with the two fighter *grupos* (joined by a third in January 1939) and six bomber *grupos* (60 aircraft), giving a total strength excluding seaplanes of 165 aircraft. These two brigades each had some 60 aircraft, twice the size of the three-bomber *grupo* 3 BAH activated in March 1939.

Republican air power faced not only problems with aircraft but also aircrew; indeed a pilot shortage grounded many I-16s between July and September 1937.[130] The problem was exacerbated because in February 1937 the Republic formally dismissed 333 Air Force officers, many of whom were already with the Nationalists, leaving as few as 65 serving with the Republic, together with 2,150 NCOs and other ranks.[131] The loyalists were augmented by foreign volunteers and mercenaries, some of whom remained until the fall of 1938

Poor aircrew training was a major problem for both sides. Financial stringency restricted fuel for prewar training, so Spanish airmen had only a few hours basic flying and little combat training, a problem they shared with the Russians who were lucky to fly 15 hours a month; indeed many Russians joined units with only 30 hours in their log books.[132] A Russian report noted that from October 25, 1936 through July 1, 1938, 147 aircraft (nearly 38 percent) of 388 Soviet-built were lost in accidents, while another report covering the period to mid-March 1938 noted that 88.5 percent of accidents were due to pilot error.[133]

Italian pilots joined units after 80–85 hours but the more comprehensive German system saw their pilots join with 200–300 hours, including instrument training for bad weather and night flights.[134] Yet in Spain even they suffered a high accident rate in severe weather conditions, especially crossing mountain ranges, and 160 German aircraft with 46 crew were lost in accidents which cost the Italians 100 aircraft.[135] Training courses were arranged in Russia, Germany, and Italy as well as within Spain, the Nationalists, under Major Gerardo Fernández Pérez, emulating their Italian allies.[136]

The first new Spanish pilots joined the FARE from May 1937, although the Spanish were already providing 40 percent of SB crews, mostly gunners and radio operators. The Republicans also used French private air clubs.[137] Russian aircrew numbers began to drop from mid-1937, with 311 pilots in 1936 of whom 21 were killed or missing, a figure which dropped to 276 (47 killed and missing) in 1937 and 183 (31 killed and missing) in 1938.[138] In September 1937 Shtern recommended withdrawing Soviet aircrew but they would remain until November 1938.

Italian and German air power provided significant benefits to the Nationalist cause from the earliest days of the war. Italy's Aviazione Legionaria (AL) was the largest foreign air force under Velardi until May 1937, General Mario Bernasconi to January 1939, and finally Major General Adriano Monti, and included a small strategic force in the Balearic Islands. Italy sent 5,699 men to support it, with a peak strength in August 1938 of 2,169 on the Iberian peninsula and another 519 on Majorca. The figure includes 1,435 aircrew, who suffered 365 casualties, including 175 killed, while 215 aircraft were lost, 115 to enemy action, as the AL flew 86,000 sorties and dropped 11,584 tonnes of bombs. Only 29 bombers were lost, seven to enemy action including one on the ground, none in strategic air attacks.[139]

AL squadrons (*squadriglie*) were organized into groups (*gruppi*) each of three fighter or two bomber/observation squadrons of nine fighters, or six bomber/observation aircraft. By December 1938 there were nine *gruppi* on the mainland with a nominal 240 landplanes and four in the Balearics with a nominal 55. Industrial weakness kept Italian squadrons under strength and in April 1937 there were only 96 aircraft on the mainland and 160 two months later, with spares shortages reducing serviceability.[140] In September 1938 seven squadrons were deactivated with their aircraft handed to the Nationalists, while the personnel returned home, and by February 1939 the AL had 149 aircraft on the mainland and 43 in the Balearics.[141]

The Condor Legion, which trained 500 Spanish aircrew, was commanded by a major general, first the corpulent Hugo Sperrle to October 30, 1937, then

Helmuth Volkmann, and from December 1, 1938 the Red Baron's cousin, former Condor Legion chief of staff Wolfram von Richthofen.[142] Despite an establishment of 5,500 it had only 5,000 Germans organized into squadrons (*staffeln*) of 12 aircraft with three to four each in the fighter and bomber groups (*gruppen*), augmented by a reconnaissance and a seaplane squadron.

There were usually a maximum 125 landplanes at the front, but by the end of 1938 this dropped to 55 before rising to 142 in February 1939. One advantage it provided the Nationalist cause was in long-range photo-reconnaissance, first with the Heinkel He 70F and later with the Dornier Do 17E which were augmented by the Italian Savoia S.79.[143] In addition the Luftwaffe provided an antiaircraft battalion with three batteries of 8.8cm heavy and two batteries of 3.7 and 2.0cm medium and light guns and lost 21 men killed in action.[144]

While the first generation of German aircraft proved wanting, the second generation, partly developed by Richthofen and arriving from the spring of 1937, outclassed everything else in the Iberian sky and could be dispatched without significantly restricting the expansion of the Luftwaffe. By contrast Italy's fighters were almost all obsolescent, although Captain Joaquin García Morato, the leading ace of the Civil War, scored most of his 40 victories in a Fiat CR.32. Aero-engine development was so poor that most bombers needed three engines to achieve performances that the Germans and Russians could produce with two.

The Sinews of War

The Russians, Germans, and Italians fighting their proxy war in Spain had jointly developed military equipment until 1934; indeed the Condor Legion's first aircraft, tanks and antitank guns were covertly developed within the Soviet Union from 1926 through 1933.[145] Although each side believed the other had access to a cornucopia of modern armaments, this was in short supply and both sides fought a war on a shoestring. It is worth noting, for example, that of 21 battalions in the Nationalists' Tank Regiment (Regimento de Carros), 17 were infantry units.

In the aftermath of the coup, the Nationalists gained the lion's share of the Spanish Army's weapons inventory (see Table 2.2) because the professionals of the Army of Africa had higher priority for equipment.[146] Both sides immediately turned to their friends and sympathizers for more weapons and ammunition but would never acquire enough to meet their wishes.

The Great War saw weapons produced in numbers which dwarfed prewar imagination and by the armistice, Europe had thousands of guns, hundreds

Table 2.2: Weapons inventories, summer 1936

Weapons	Republicans	Nationalists
Rifles	275,000	325,000
Automatic rifles	879	1,896
Machine guns	750	1,100
Schneider Mod 1908 70/16 light guns	About 120	73
Schneider Mod 1906 75/28 field guns	About 250	390
Heavy artillery	About 232	477
Skoda Mod 1919 76.5/40 AA guns	10	6

Heavy artillery consists of Schneider Mod 1919 105/11, Vickers Mod 1922 105/22 and Schneider Mod 1917 155/13 howitzers and Krupp Mod 1913 150/27 guns.

of thousands of automatic weapons and millions of rifles. With the war's conclusion the defeated armies saw most of their weapons scrapped, while the victors sought more cost-effective means of reducing their inventories. The best weapons were retained to meet peacetime requirements and to allow for modest expansion. Some of the surplus was provided to allies and friends at favorable rates, while the remainder were sold commercially either for onward sale or scrap.[147]

For Europe's armament manufacturers the 1919 Versailles Treaty ended a golden age. The second half of the 19th century saw metallurgical, chemical, and mechanical advances create continuous revolutions in armament development, so weapons purchased in one decade were obsolete in the next. By the 20th century armies had rifle-barreled, breech-loaded, steel weapons using "smokeless" high-energy nitro-cellulose propellants and explosives. Cannon benefited from recuperators to absorb recoil force and provide high, accurate rates of fire, leading to their prewar name of Quick-Firers. Since the beginning of the 20th century, development of conventional armaments—artillery, automatic weapons, and rifles—has become and largely remains evolutionary rather than revolutionary.

With the conclusion of the Great War, Europe's armaments works faced bleak prospects for wartime surplus; a general horror of war, and demands for financial stringency, meant little political support for large armaments orders. Apart from some development and upgrading work, domestic orders for basic armaments dried up, while limited demand from Eastern Europe, the Middle East, China, and Latin America saw fierce competition which cut profit margins to, or even through, the bone. The armament works did not fall totally silent but the faint sounds of activity echoed through empty workshops.

The Communist propaganda machine, which campaigned for 15 years in favor of pacifism and against armaments, made a dramatic U-turn and organized demonstrations and petitions demanding arms for Spain.[148] It was easier to demand arms for Spain than to produce them because the western democracies had few to spare and had difficulties equipping their own armies. France, Czechoslovakia, Mexico, and Poland would contribute arms to the Republic for a variety of motives: to deflect the potential threat from Germany, ideological conviction, and financial gain.[149]

Diversification and niche markets helped many companies to survive: Great Britain's Vickers, for example, produced mountain howitzers for the Spanish Army and helped to defend the Iberian peninsula from maritime threat by arming almost every Spanish warship and most of the coastal defense batteries.[150] Czechoslovakia's Skoda provided the Republic with all its antiaircraft guns, a growth market, together with antitank guns. Demand for Stokes-principle mortars as well as what were at the time called "automatic rifles" also helped companies remain in business, while augmenting rifle company firepower were the new fully automatic pistols, or sub-machine guns as John T. Thompson called them, regarded by most armies as "police" weapons.[151]

There were exceptions: Italy's militaristic fantasies ensured its factories profited from export successes which concealed Rome's industrial problems until World War II, while the newly industrialized Soviet Union produced 7,000 guns between 1928 and 1935 and 11,000 armored vehicles between 1930 and 1934.[152] But when the western democracies began to rearm from 1935, they did so from a narrow industrial base and production was barely in its stride when World War II broke out. This may be illustrated by comparing British and French artillery inventories in November 1918 and September 1939 (Table 2.3). The urgent need to rearm meant that there was little spare capacity, while few of the smaller powers, including Spain, possessed the industrial resources for substantial expansion; indeed Madrid had only three plants capable of producing artillery: at Trubia, near Oviedo (augmented by facilities at Corunna), Seville, and Palencia.

The Russians delivered arms both to the Republican heartland and the northern enclave against an increasingly effective Nationalist air–sea blockade. By contrast the Nationalists' mastery of the seas, enforced by their Italian

Table 2.3: Comparison of British and French artillery inventories, November 1918 and September 1939.

Type	France		Great Britain	
	Nov 1918	Sept 1939	Nov 1918	Sept 1939
Field (75–90mm)	10,119	8,298	3,206	1,315
Medium (100–159mm)	3,819	428	2,634	835
Heavy (160mm and above)	510	106	561	128

French data from Musée de l'Armée, courtesy of M. Christophe Pommier, curator of Département d'Artillerie.

Table 2.4: Arms supplies to the Republic

Type	1936	1937	1938–39
Tanks	123 (0)	200 (49)	25
Artillery	215 (120)	425 (255)	760
Automatic weapons	10,910 (1,535)	13,725 (1,835)	9,050
Rifles	84,265 (84,450)	279,180 (140,200)	175,000
Combat aircraft	220 (22)	372 (36)	248

Note: Numbers in parentheses denote additional deliveries to the northern enclave.

Table 2.5: Arms supplies to the Nationalists

Type	1936	1937	1938–39
Tanks	97	116	85
Artillery	40	795	230
Automatic weapons	575	4,515	6,600
Rifles	57,500	273,665	102, 800
Combat aircraft	292	607	349

Note: Tanks excludes command and training vehicles.

friends, ensured supplies could reach them unhindered. The estimated supply of arms to both sides is given in Tables 2.4 and 2.5 and show the Nationalists received fewer weapons than their enemies, apart from aircraft, in 1936 and 1937 but little apart from ammunition in 1938 until after the Munich crisis.[153]

Hundreds of arms dealers sold weapons, with the first "private" sale to the Nationalists in August 1936 of 11,000 Mauser rifles by former German air ace Josef Veltjens, acting as a front man for Luftwaffe commander Field Marshal Hermann Goering.[154] Most private sales were to the Republic, whose purchasing commissions were devoid of technical knowledge and business acumen. Sometimes they purchased obsolete weapons: small arms that used gunpowder and were suitable at best only for second-line duties, or cannon without recuperators. This restricted firing rates and accuracy compared with the Quick-Firers which equipped almost all Nationalist batteries. Approximately 85 percent of the artillery in the Republican heartland consisted of Quick-Firers but in the northern enclave it was only about 80 percent.

The majority were functional weapons but they were often delivered in small quantities and limited munitions.[155] This left the Republic with the logistical nightmare, the northern enclave alone having artillery of 19 different calibers. Ammunition was an especial problem and even with domestic production, Rojo noted 105mm howitzers would consume a day's supply with one barrage. Modesto complained of having only 80 shells a day, while the Nationalist battlefield salvage organization noted that the Republicans had 235 types of shell and 388 types of rifle cartridge.[156]

While Italy was a more consistent supplier of arms and ammunition, exploiting large stocks of captured Austrian weapons, its limited industry restricted both quantity and quality, but by the end of the war 136 of 148 Spanish batteries had Italian ordnance.[157] The German armament works were still suffering from the restrictions of the Versailles Treaty, as Hitler tried vainly to expand the German Army which would never be completely equipped with modern, domestically produced weapons. In 1939 many divisions had Great War weaponry while others, including several panzer divisions, benefited from weapons seized from Czechoslovakia in 1939. Consequently, Germany could send only a small amount of modern equipment such as tanks, antitank and antiaircraft guns but most weapons were of Great War vintage. The most significant exception was the MG 13 general-purpose (heavy/light) machine gun which proved too delicate for army use but was widely used in German aircraft. With the introduction of the more robust MG 34 the German Army used the opportunity to clear its shelves of weapons which were largely gathering dust.

Similar motives drove Russian arms supply, known as Operation *X*, directed by ballroom dancing Defense Minister Voroshilov and personally authorized by Stalin.[158] The Soviet Union delivered modern arms such as tanks, while the diversion of the SB bombers slowed modernization of the bomber regiments. Yet the Russians also cleared their armories of British, American, and Japanese weapons supplied to Imperial Russia during the Great War, older weapons supplied by Russian factories before the Great War, or those captured during the Russian Civil War. This included British 60pdr (127mm) howitzers and Lewis automatic rifles, the Maksim-Tokarev (PMT) and American Colt Model 1895 machine guns together with Springfield and Japanese Arisaka rifles.[159]

Both sides also exploited domestic facilities but only Trubia remained in Republican hands after the uprising. It produced 16 guns and 16 Model 1936 tanks, together with small-arms ammunition before falling to the Nationalists, who built another nine tanks. The other plants were harnessed to the Nationalist war machine and during the war they produced some 310 pieces of artillery, 8,616 automatic weapons, 136,000 rifles, together with tonnes of ammunition.[160] The Nationalists also established a battlefield salvage and recovery organization which discovered 1,877 guns, 25,300 automatic weapons and 576,300 rifles, together with substantial amounts of ammunition, all of which was turned against its former owners.[161]

The Republicans could use the naval arsenal at Cartagena to produce 105mm shells but usually used converted plants, especially in Barcelona, where Russian technical advisors helped an automobile factory produce rifles, small-arms ammunition, and spares for T-26s while a toy factory produced shells.[162] Production largely focused upon ammunition with some 3,600 tonnes of artillery and 900 tonnes of small-arms ammunition in the year to September 1937, and by the summer of 1938 35 tonnes of artillery ammunition a month but only 2,000 rifles appear to have been produced.[163]

With parts supplied from the Soviet Union, or copied from existing aircraft, the Republic built 237 I-15 airframes in Reus from August 1937 through January 1939 but shortages of engines, instruments and machine guns meant that only 141 entered service together with 14 of 100 I-16 by February 1939.[164] The Russians were exasperated by what they perceived as a lack of dynamic industrial leadership and Stalin rebuked the Spanish ambassador, Marcelino Pascua, in February 1938 when the latter sought further Russian arms shipments.[165] Yet in the summer of 1937 the NKVD arrested German aircraft builder Antonius Raab, who played a leading part in creating factories, because he employed Anarchists and Trotskyists.[166]

Fuel for the armor, artillery, and transport was obtained with imported oil to refineries in Barcelona, Seville, and Tenerife in the Canaries. The Nationalists had a steady flow from the United States which supplied some 2 million tonnes, mostly by the Texas Oil Company (Texaco) and Standard Oil, while private deals and its friends supplied a further 1.5 million tonnes, the same as the amount that the Republic received from Russia and commercial sources, although it was estimated that 15,000 tonnes of gasoline were imported by July 1938.[167]

The oil was important because increasingly both sides relied upon the internal combustion engine. At the outbreak of war there were 109,176km of road in Spain, of which 70,522 were paved state highways, and 334,800 vehicles, of which some 250,000 were trucks and buses, while the prewar army had small numbers of Hispano-Suiza, Ford, Mercedes Benz, and Dodge trucks and was modernizing its fleet.[168] Automotive factories around Barcelona allowed the Republic to build more than 1,000 vehicles during the war, including some 385 trucks.[169]

Both sides' patrons provided vehicles, Germany sending some 3,100, including some 1,600 trucks, while Italy provided more than 6,700, including 4,250 trucks.[170] The Soviet Union sent 8,760 trucks as well as various specialized vehicles but both sides also used commercial sources, with the Republic acquiring nearly 100 from Belgium, about 180 from France, some 90 from Germany, and 560 from Great Britain, while the Nationalists received 1,400 from Germany. But the prime supplier of trucks was the neutral United States. A figure of 12,000 to the Nationalists is often quoted but is actually to the whole of Spain from 1936 through 1938. The Republic received about 5,800 from various sources while the Nationalists received about 6,100, augmented during the first quarter of 1939 by another 3,900.

The railroad remained the prime means of Strategic and Operational transport. After the uprising the Republic retained control of most of the track, locomotives, and rolling stock (wagons and coaches) as well as Madrid, which was the hub of the national network.[171] The latter advantage was lost when the tide of battle swept into the capital but the Republic retained superior interior communications to the end of the war. While the Nationalists increased their grip on the network in terms of track and trains, they gained little advantage because the battle lines cut most of the major railroads, effectively leaving them branch lines. This made Strategic Level movement more time-consuming because trains had to take indirect routes to a threatened front often over single-track lines.

Most of the west Andalusia network came under Nationalist control, coordinated by engineer captain José Rivero de Aguilar, leaving the Northern and MZA (Madrid, Zaragoza, Alicante) networks split, with the Republic controlling 55 percent (823) of the former's and 69 (780) percent of the latter's locomotives (181).[172] The Republicans also had 39,700 items of rolling stock and controlled 5,043km of track, or 68 percent. Both administrations quickly established control over the rail companies and in October 1937 the Republic merged them into the state-controlled Red Nacional de Ferrocarriles (National Rail Network). Constant use left railroads little time for maintenance but the Republic suffered more, for many rail workshops were converted to military production. Another problem was the loss of more than a quarter of all rail workers who opted for the glamor of fighting at the front rather than the mundane operation of the vital rail network.[173]

Despite this the railroads continued to operate but with increasing priority given to military traffic, which rose to 49 percent during the Nationalist spring/summer offensive of 1938 which captured 4,000km of line. The campaign split the Republic in two, with the majority of the 35,100 wagons and coaches leaving less than 19 percent (6,500) in the central zone, of which 4,000 were unserviceable.[174] The Nationalists also had problems with Saragossa becoming the heart of their rail system, but it appears to have been a bottleneck with 500–800 wagons stuck there at any one time.[175] However, they made more efficient use of their rail system, aided by advice from Italian experts.[176]

Notes

1 For the conscripts and their lives see Matthews, *Reluctant Warriors*, pp. 181–182, 184 (hereafter Matthews); Alpert, *The Republican Army*, pp. 109–110 (hereafter Alpert). Matthews notes that in 1938 on the Madrid-based Central Army front there were 2,175 deserters and defectors to the Nationalists and some 1,800 from the Nationalists. For desertion see also Alpert, pp. 168–172, 307, who notes that better-educated conscripts in the Republic's technical services were especially likely to cross the lines.

2 For the daily lives, conditions, and concerns of both sides' troops see Alpert, pp. 160–162, 164–165, 167; Matthews, pp. 102–136, 155–159.

3 In March 1937 Franco issued instructions for defense in depth and banned defense based upon continuous trench lines.

4 *Armas*, pp. 50–51; Payne, *The Spanish Revolution*, p. 350, quoting *Katalonskaya Operatsiya*; Thomas, p. 542.

5 Matthews, pp. 19–23.

6 For the Popular Army see Salas, *Army*, vol. 1, pp. 178–180; Salas, *Air*, pp. 177–181; Matthews, pp. 24, 26, 34–62. See also Engel, *Brigades*.

7 Alpert, pp. 157–158.

8 Salas, *Army*, vol. 1, pp. 504–507; Herrero Perez, *The Spanish Military and the Evolution of Warfare 1899–1939*, pp. 251–260, 313–314 (hereafter Herrero Perez). For the Mixed Brigade histories and background see Engel, *Brigades*. See also the website militar.org.ua/militar/hm/historia-militar-espana-guerra-civil-brigada-ejercito-republicano.html.

9 Based upon Engel, *Brigades*, pp. 5–6.

10 *Ibid.*

11 Herrero Perez, pp. 315–316.

12 Engel, *Brigades*, Appendices 3, 4; Herrero Perez, pp. 317–318, 321.

13 Thomas, p. 677. This figure may well include antitank and antiaircraft batteries. By 1938 the Nationalists reportedly had 290 artillery batteries and the Republicans 200.

14 Herrero Perez, pp. 281–285, 341–342. Foreign thinkers had little influence, although some of General John Fuller's works on the future of mechanized warfare were translated into Spanish and read by Rojo. Herrero Perez, pp. 271–277.

15 After the 1939 Polish campaign he participated in a joint victory parade with General Heinz Guderian, the brains behind the Wehrmacht's Panzerwaffe.
16 *Armas*, p. 32; Kowalsky, ch. 15; Salas, *Air*, Appendix 41; Zaloga, *Soviet*; Zaloga, *T-26 Light Tank* (hereafter Zaloga, *Tanks*); Daley, *Armor*; and Candil, *Carros de Combate*, pp. 91–94 (hereafter Candil).
17 Alpert, pp. 70–72; Kowalsky, ch. 13.
18 The Republic's 50, 75, and 76 DI would command the guerrillas with a nominal 20 brigades. 50 DI became a conventional formation in May 1938. Engel, *Brigades*, p. 5, Appendices 3 and 4.
19 Howson, *Air*, pp. 22.
20 Alpert, p. 308.
21 For the Nationalist Army see Beevor, pp. 197–198; Engel, *Historia de las Divisiones del Ejército Nacional* (hereafter Engel, *Divisions*). See also Larrazabal, *Air*, pp. 147, 177–181, Anexo 40; Matthews, pp. 34–62, 102–136, 155–159; Thomas, pp. 504–508.
22 *Armas*, p. 54.
23 Herrero Perez, pp. 318–322.
24 The honorific "Navarrese" was assigned to the 1st, 3rd, 4th, and 5th Divisions.
25 Matthews, pp. 30–32.
26 For the Legion and the Moors see Balfour, pp. 272–279, 304, 307–308, 313–315. An Irish battalion was later disbanded.
27 Balfour, p. 313.
28 See Matthews, *Our Red Soldiers*.
29 For Nationalist conscription see Matthews, pp. 29–30, 37, 147–150.
30 Salas, *Air*, p. 178.
31 Based upon an analysis of the order of battle information in Engel, *Divisions*.
32 "Negrillo" has a racist meaning.
33 For Nationalist armor see Candil, pp. 88–90; Cappellano and Battistelli, *Italian Light Tanks*; Daley, *Armor*; Herrero Perez, pp. 330–340; Salas, *Intervencion*, Anexo 8; Zaloga, *Tanks*, pp. 20–23, 32.
34 Salas says that the Nationalists had 13 T-26s in late June 1937, while Candil says that the Nationalists used 98 T-26s and cannibalized another 30.
35 Salas, *Intervencion*, pp. 555.
36 The 150th and 151st Divisions were created from the Moroccan Corps and Canaries garrison. Martínez, *La ofensiva sobre Segovia y la batalla de Brunete*, p. 143n.165 (hereafter Martinez, *Brunete*).
37 The name means Operations or Maneuver Army, but the best translation is Reserve Army.
38 Herrero Perez, p. 301.
39 Alpert, p. 307.
40 Alpert, pp. 147, 150, 153; *Armas*, p. 51; Herrero Perez, pp. 301–304; Thomas, pp. 507–508.
41 Herrero Perez, pp. 306–307.
42 Herrero Perez, pp. 66–68, 250–251; 306–308, 311. See orders in Engel, *Operations*.
43 Herrero Perez, p. 70.
44 For parochialism see Herrero Perez, pp. 70–82.
45 Alpert, p. 306; Herrero Perez, pp. 305–308, 310–313; Serebryakov, *Brunetskaya Operatsiya Respublikanskoi Armii Ispanii* (hereafter Serebryakov).
46 Alpert, pp. 148–149.
47 Alpert, pp. 144–153.

48 Kowalsky, ch. 14.
49 Alpert, pp. 151–152, 304, 307; Beevor, p. 279; Herrero Perez, pp. 302–308.
50 Howson, *Arms for Spain*, p. 109 (hereafter Howson, *Arms*).
51 Thomas, p. 476, 663n2, 950; Zaragoza, pp. 295–300. Rojo's autobiography is *General Vicente Rojo: Mi Verdad.* See also Blanco, *Franco y Rojo* (hereafter Blanco); Martinez Paricio, *Los papeles del general Rojo.*
52 On February 12, 1939 he was promoted to lieutenant general but at his own request this was cancelled a month later. See "Iron Machine's" comments of February 25, 2015 in the Spanish Civil War section of the Axis History Forum.
53 For Africanistas and Franco see Balfour.
54 Balfour, pp. 290, 295, 309; Herrero Perez, p. 321; Jensen, *Franco*, pp. 87, 91–97 (hereafter, Jensen).
55 Significantly he committed to the July 1936 coup only on its eve. Balfour, pp. 258, 263, 267; Hills, pp. 147–166.
56 For Franco see Blanco.
57 GHQ, codenamed Terminus, moved to Burgos in November 1937.
58 Thomas, p. 504, based upon Cervera's memoirs.
59 For Davila see Arce, pp. 272–275; Thomas, p. 690.
60 For Franco's staff see Martinez, *Los cien ultimos dias*, p. 39 (hereafter Martinez, *Ultimos*).
61 For Ungaria see Herrero Perez, p. 245n.49.
62 There are numerous books on the International Brigades, mostly chronicles. Alcofar, *Spansky*, focuses upon their creation and early operations while other useful works are Alvarez, *Historia Política y Militar de la Brigadas Internacionales*; Castells, *Las Brigadas Internacionales de la Guerra de España*; Delperrié de Bayac, *Les Brigades Internationales*; Johnston, *Legions of Babel*; Landis, *Death in the Olive Groves*; Sanchez and Blanco, *Las Brigadas Internacionales.*
63 Beevor, p. 157.
64 Beevor, pp. 157–158; Thomas, pp. 454–455.
65 Thomas, p. 453.
66 Beevor, p. 162.
67 Alpert, pp. 220–221; Thomas, p. 479n.3.
68 Alpert, pp. 219–224.
69 Romilly, *Boadilla*, pp. 48, 77.
70 Beevor, pp. 127, 157–162. I would like to thank my good friend Will Fowler for details of wartime training.
71 "Ticket-punching" is a U.S. Army term which means taking an assignment to ensure promotion.
72 Beevor, p. 197; Thomas, p. 491.
73 Alpert, pp. 222–223; Kowalsky, ch. 13, quotes adverse Comintern reports on BI political work during 1937.
74 Beevor, p. 221, quoting Kulik on the subject; Thomas, pp. 457–459. NKVD stands for Narodnyy Komissariat Vnutrennihh Del, or People's Commissariat for Internal Affairs.
75 Thomas, pp. 457–459, 781.
76 Lefebvre and Skoutelsky, *Las Brigadas Internacionales*, p. 16, and Academy of Sciences of the USSR, *International Solidarity with the Spanish Republic 1936–1939*, p. 370 (hereafter *Solidarity*), give figures of 32,256 and 32,109, the latter based upon figures published by the League of Nations Military Control Commission in October 1938 which later discovered another 400 in jail. Kowalsky, ch. 13, n.22, says that archive evidence suggests up to 50,000 served in the BIs. Alpert, p. 309.

77 Beevor, p. 366, quoting Andreu Castells, *Las Brigadas Internacionales en la Guerra de España*, pp. 383–384. *Solidarity*, p. 370.
78 Rust, *Britons in Spain*, pp. 75, 153 (hereafter Rust).
79 Alpert, p. 222.
80 Thomas, pp. 851–853.
81 Alpert, pp. 223–224.
82 For Soviet military advisory assistance to Spain see Kowalsky, chs. 12–15; *Solidarity*, pp. 298–331; Alcofar, *Los Asesores Sovieticos*, pp. 35–74 (hereafter Alcofar, *Asesores*).
83 Kowalsky, ch. 12, tables V-1 and V-2. The October 1937 figure is based upon Thomas, p. 984n.3, and qualified by *Solidarity*, p. 329n.2.
84 Kowalsky, ch. 12, table V-3.
85 Stalin authorized his execution in 1950.
86 Despite claims in Alcofar, pp. 61–62, future Marshal Zhukov never served in Spain. His namesake was a naval advisor.
87 Beevor, pp. 163–164.
88 Beevor, p. 164; Kowalsky, ch. 16.
89 Thomas, pp. 617, 731. For Soviet officer biographies see Parrish, *Sacrifice of the Generals* (hereafter Parrish), and websites: warheroes.ru; Dmity Churakov's Red Army Soldiers Repressed in Aleksandr Kiyan The Workers' and Peasants' Red Army site (rkka.ru) and also Generals in World War II (generals.dk).
90 Thomas, p. 568.
91 For the CTV see Alcofar, *CTV*, Coverdale, pp. 166–171; Rodrigo, pp. 117–118. The Spanish sometimes said CTV stood for "Cuando Te Vas?" or "When are you going?"
92 The Italian Army was being reorganized into binary divisions.
93 Murias, p. 48; Rodrigo, p. 145.
94 Alcofar, *CTV*, pp. 165–166; Nasseas, pp. 153–161; Thomas, pp. 855–856.
95 Jesus Salas *La Intervencion Extranjera*, Anexo 8 (hereafter Salas, *Intervencion*).
96 Rodrigo, p. 32; Thomas, pp. 978–979.
97 Ries and Ring, p. 282.
98 See Herrero Perez, pp. 333–336, 338.
99 Thomas, p. 977.
100 Thomas, pp. 592, 592n.1, 979–980.
101 For foreign volunteers in the Nationalist Army see Baxell, *Unlikely Warriors*, pp. 386–391 (hereafter Baxell); Keene, *Fighting for Franco*, pp. 6–8, 115–127, 152–172, 197–210, 222–239, 250 (hereafter Keene).
102 See Doughty, *The Seeds of Disaster*, pp. 6, 9–12, 77–78 (hereafter Doughty).
103 Doughty, p. 77–78.
104 Doughty, pp. 77, 84–89, 97–98, 103–111, 115–116. For British ideas see Bond, *British Military Policy between the Two World Wars*.
105 See Lloyd, *Passchendaele*, pp. 52, 78, 157, 292, 295–296, 372n.22.
106 Doughty, pp. 176–179.
107 See Doughty, pp. 90–92; Herrero Perez, pp. 245–246, 248–250.
108 For the development of German and Russian armored doctrine, and the problems encountered see Habeck, *Storm of Steel*, pp. 20–24, 52–70, 75–76, 99–103, 126–127, 132–135, 139–143, 156, 167–170, 176–179, 188–194, 196–199, 201–205, 208–231, 233–244, 250–254, 270–273. For British developments in mechanization and armored forces see Harris, *Men, Ideas and Tanks*.

109 Hooton, *Stalin's Claws*, pp. 11–13 (hereafter Hooton, *Claws*).
110 Zaloga, *Tanks*, p. 26.
111 The 115kg limit is from the British War Office manual, *Animal Management* (London: HMSO, 1933).
112 The Skorostnoi Bombardirovschik (SB) or Fast Bomber was often called the SB-2, a misunderstanding of its full designation, which translates as Fast Bomber, with two M-100 engines or SB 2-M-100.
113 Beevor, p. 153.
114 For the Republican Air Force the most detailed account is Saiz. See also Alcofar, *Asesores*, pp. 75–86; Howson, *Air*, notably pp. 20–25; Salas, *Air*, pp. 142–145, 207–210, 213–214; Thomas, pp. 548, 678; Permuy, *Air War Over Spain*; Permuy, *Spanish Republican Aces*; Shore, *Spanish Civil War Air Forces*. Håkan's Aviation Page, Air War in the Spanish Civil War 1936–39, http;// surfcity.kund.dalnet.se/scw.htm (hereafter Håkan site). The chief of staff in 1938 was Lieutenant Colonel Antonio Martín-Luna who commanded air operations in the Biscay enclave during 1937.
115 Alpert notes that it was difficult to determine who was actually responsible for air force policy and that Hidalgo de Cisneros's memoirs are "singularly uninformative" on this issue, Alpert, pp. 236–237.
116 Beevor, p. 153, 200; Thomas, p. 521. The FARE built some 400 airfields and airstrips for maximum flexibility. Howson, *Air*, pp. 20–25.
117 Howson, *Air*.
118 *Ibid.*
119 The Nationalists called the I-16 Rata or Rat.
120 The R-5SSS is often called R-SSS or R-Z and some sources suggest that only this aircraft was delivered to Spain.
121 Hooton, *Claws*, p. 135; Howson, *Arms*, p. 288.
122 Kowalsky, ch. 14.
123 Kowalsky, ch. 10.
124 Saiz, vol. 3, pp. 891–906.
125 Neulen, *In the Skies of Europe*, p. 25 (hereafter Neulen); Salas, *Army*, vol. 4, pp. 3364–3365.
126 Salas, *Air*, Anexo 8.
127 Of 418 Italian aircraft delivered to Spain by September 22, 1937 only 42 were for Spanish squadrons. Coverdale, p. 277.
128 Arce, p. 89. For Nationalist air power see Howson, *Air*, notably pp. 25–28; Salas, *Air*, pp. 198–202, 208–213, Anexo 10; Shore, *Spanish Civil War Air Forces*; Håkan site. See also UK National Archives HW21/2–4 which are British Comint reports on the Italian Air Force covering most of the Civil War. Fighter and observation grupos had 12 aircraft while bomber units had six.
129 Alpert, p. 235.
130 Kowalsky, ch. 14.
131 Arce, p. 89; Alpert, p. 235.
132 Hooton, *Claws*, pp. 199–200 and *War Over the Steppes*, pp. 46–47, 54–55.
133 Kowalsky, ch. 14, tables V-4 and V-5. Polish and Russian sources suggest that 248 Russian fighters were lost to enemy action, including 38 on the ground, while 130 were lost to accidents. The figures for SB are 40 to enemy action and 33 to accidents.
134 For Luftwaffe training see Hooton, *Phoenix*, p. 159.
135 Neulen, p. 25; Proctor, p. 253; Ries and Ring, p. 227, Appendices L and M.

136 Howson, *Air*, pp. 20–25; Neulen, p. 26. Only 40 airmen were trained in Germany. Some Spanish airmen trained at Lipetsk, the temporary home during the late 1920s for many of the Condor Legion leaders, including Richthofen.
137 Howson, *Air*, pp. 23–24; Kowalsky, ch. 14.
138 Kowalsky, ch. 14, table V-6.
139 For the AL see Alcofar, *Air*; Alcofar, *CTV*, p. 165; Neulen, p. 25. See also Logoluso, *Fiat CR.32 Aces of the Spanish Civil War*; Pedriale, *Guerra di Spagna e aviazione italiana* and *Ali di Guerra sulla Spagna*; Permuy, pp. 54–56; Rodrigo, p. 324. Axis History Forum, Spanish Civil War section on subject Aviazione Legionare y Aviacón Nacional from May 2014.
140 Salas, *Army*, vol. 4, pp. 3364–3365; UK National Archives (UKNA) HW 21/2 AS/0144 and 0181; HW 21/4 AS/0320 and AS 0389.
141 Ries and Ring, p. 189; Thomas, pp. 855–856.
142 For the Condor Legion see Arias, *La Legion Condor en la Guerra Civil* (hereafter *Arias*); Forsyth, *Aces of the Legion Condor*; Gonzalez Alvarez, *Aspectos Militares de la Guerra Civil* (hereafter Gonzalez Alvarez); Hooton, *Phoenix*, pp. 120–145; Proctor; Ries and Ring.
143 Howson, *Air*, pp. 117–120, 179–181, 270–273.
144 In Spain the 8.8 was also used to provide direct fire support for infantry. The gun was used in the antitank role during the fall of 1918 but not apparently in Spain.
145 Russo-German cooperation has many accounts. For Russo-Italian cooperation see Calvett Clarke, "Italo-Soviet Military Co-operation in the 1930s," in Stoker and Grant (eds.), *Girding for Battle*, pp. 177–199. Rheinmetall developed the 37mm antitank gun as the Pak L/45, then the Pak 31, and finally the Pak 35/36 which was copied by the Russian as PP O 1930g or 1 K, with some apparently delivered to Spain as Gorischka. But they preferred a version with a 45mm barrel such as the PP O 1932g or 19-K, many of which were sent to Spain, and the PP O 1937g or 53-K, while the 19-K gun was used in T-26 and BT tanks as well as in BA-6 armored cars as the 20K.
146 *Armas*, pp. 97–129, 176.
147 Prewar Spain benefited from this largesse of tanks and heavy artillery from France. During the Civil War some 90 percent of the imported artillery came directly or indirectly from wartime inventories.
148 For the British left-wing author George Orwell's comments see Beevor, p. 159.
149 Howson, *Arms* is the best source for Republican arms supply but has been qualified by Spanish research. *Armas* together with Molina and Permuy, *Importación de Armas en la Guerra Civil Española* (hereafter *Importación*), and Salas, *Intervencion*, are the most detailed accounts of deliveries to both sides. See also Beevor, pp. 329–331 and correspondence in *Revista de Historia Militar*, # 9, 11, 17, 18 (2001), with Artemio Mortera's criticisms and information. This can be seen in sbhac.net/Republica/Fuerzas/Armas/Polemica/Salas.htm. For the background see Maiolo, *Cry Havoc*.
150 Howson, *Arms*, p. 81.
151 Both Germans and Russians called them Automatic Pistols-Maschinenpistole/Pistolet-Pulemyot.
152 Hooton, *Claws*, p. 7.
153 Data based upon Coverdale, pp. 87, 103, 106–108, 113, 177; Howson, *Arms* and *Aircraft*; *Armas*, *Importación*; Salas, *Army*, vol. 3, pp. 2590–2592, vol. 4, pp. 3418–3422 and Mortera's articles; also correspondence in the Axis History Forum website. Aircraft exclude seaplanes. Tank and aircraft figures are accurate while the rest are rounded to the nearest five. Nationalist figures include equipment for Allied forces. Artillery included infantry support, mountain, field, and heavy ordnance but not Minenwerfer, light, antitank and antiaircraft guns.

154 Veltjens also sold arms to the Republic on Goering's behalf. Beevor, pp. 329–330. He would serve in the Luftwaffe and be killed in an air crash in 1943.
155 Howson, *Arms*, pp. 28–29.
156 Based on *Armas*; Alpert, p. 50; Modesto, p. 213. The shortage of shells meant that all Republican offensives were based upon infiltrating the enemy defenses and none began with extensive artillery preparation.
157 Salas, *Intervencion*, p. 560.
158 For Operation "X" see Kowalsky, chs. 9, 10, 16. See also Alpert, p. 242.
159 Alpert, pp. 242–243; Howson, *Arms*, p. 127; Kowalsky, ch. 10; *Solidarity*, pp. 329–330.
160 Salas, *Army*, vol. 3, pp. 97, 128. The Nationalists produced the M1938, an improved Hotchkiss M1922 automatic rifle.
161 Motera notes that from the outbreak of the war to July 13, 1938 the organization recovered 413 guns and 131,739 rifles. The larger figure may include material seized after the Republican surrender.
162 For Catalonian war industry see Voltas, *La Guerra Civil a Catalunya*, pp. 84–93 (hereafter Voltas).
163 Based on *Armas*, *Importación*, and Kowalsky, ch. 13.
164 Howson, *Air*, pp. 195, 200; Kowalsky, ch. 10.
165 Kowalsky, ch. 13.
166 Howson, *Air*, pp. 20–25.
167 Howson, *Arms*, pp. 72–74; *Importacion*, p. 545; Thomas, p. 417n.2, 943.
168 Cayon Garcia/Munoz Rubio, *Los Transportes y Las Comunicaciones Durante la Guerra Civil*, p. 4 (hereafter Cayon Garcia/Munoz Rubio, *Transport*).
169 For vehicles see discussion on the Gran Capitan forum under Vehiculos a motor en la Guerra Civil from September 9, 2007 through December 26, 2017. See also Thomas, pp. 943, 981–982.
170 Both figures include vehicles sent to support their expeditionary forces.
171 For the rail system see Cayón Garcia and Muñoz Rubio papers *El Ferrocarril como Sector Estratégico Durante la Guerra Civil Española* (hereafter Cayón Garcia/Muñoz Rubio, *Railway*), and Cayon Garcia/Munoz Rubio, *Transport*, pp. 7–12. Wais, *Historia de los Ferrocarriles Espanoles*, pp. 641–644; Garcia Lomas, *La Explotación de Ferrocarriles* (hereafter Garcia Lomas).
172 Garcia Lomas, p. 150.
173 Cayón Garcia/Muñoz Rubio, *Railway*, pp. 10–11.
174 Garcia Lomas, p. 158.
175 Garcia Lomas, p. 157.
176 Thomas, p. 573.

CHAPTER 3

Decision on the Northern Front

The Bilbao Campaign

The campaigns against the enclave benefited from Mola's success in September 1936 when he took Irun on the French border to isolate the region, part of the town being burned by Anarchists before they withdrew. Later he relieved the siege of Oviedo, but during the fall and the winter of 1936/37 his attention was focused upon Madrid, which allowed the Basque Army (Euzko Gudarostea) to try to relieve pressure on the city.

On November 30, 29 battalions and six ox-drawn batteries struck at Villarreal de Alava (Villareal) to seize the key heights north of the town and anchor the Basques' eastern defenses. The attackers' overwhelming numerical strength drove back the 638 defenders under Lieutenant Colonel Ricardo Iglesias to reach most of their objectives, and by December 3 they had cut the railroad from the coast to Vitoria but were stopped by two battalions of Nationalist reinforcements.[1] Villareal cost the Nationalists 255 casualties, with only 31 dead, but for the Basques it was a pyrrhic victory with 4,300 casualties including 1,000 dead, many due to inadequate medical facilities. Appalled, the Basque government now decided to remain on the defensive and to accelerate work on the defenses of Bilbao, the Iron Belt (Centurion de Herero), which it had authorized on October 9.

Mola's immediate response to the crisis on December 6 was to split the forces of the Saragossa-based 6th Division. Its commander, the Monarchist Brigadier General Miguel Ponte, retained responsibility for the Aragon front while Mola's chief of staff, Colonel José Solchaga, received an autonomous command designated 1 Task Force (1 Agrupación) facing westward as the Navarrese militia columns were reorganized into four Navarrese brigades. Solchaga was replaced by Vigón.[2]

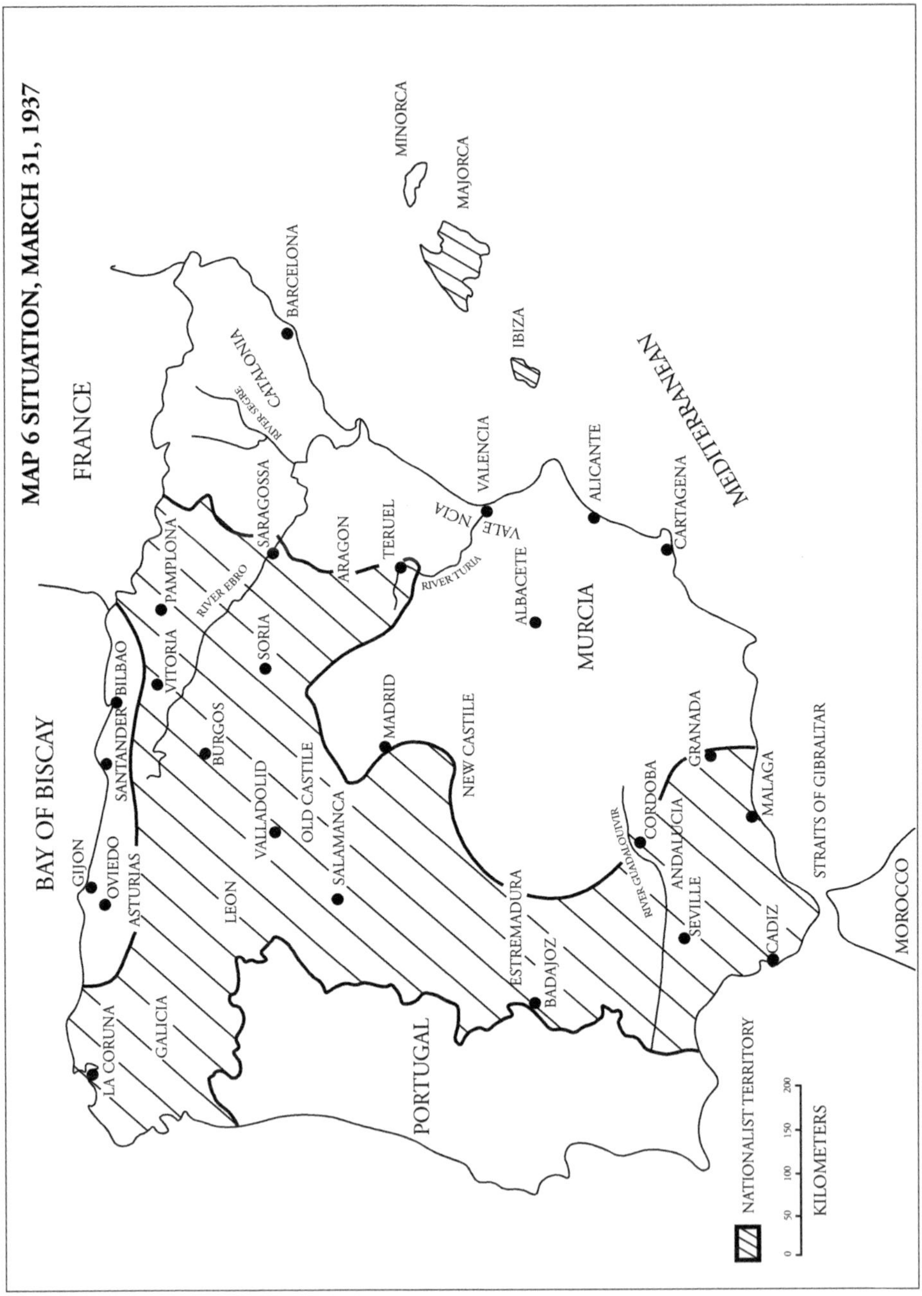

MAP 6 SITUATION, MARCH 31, 1937

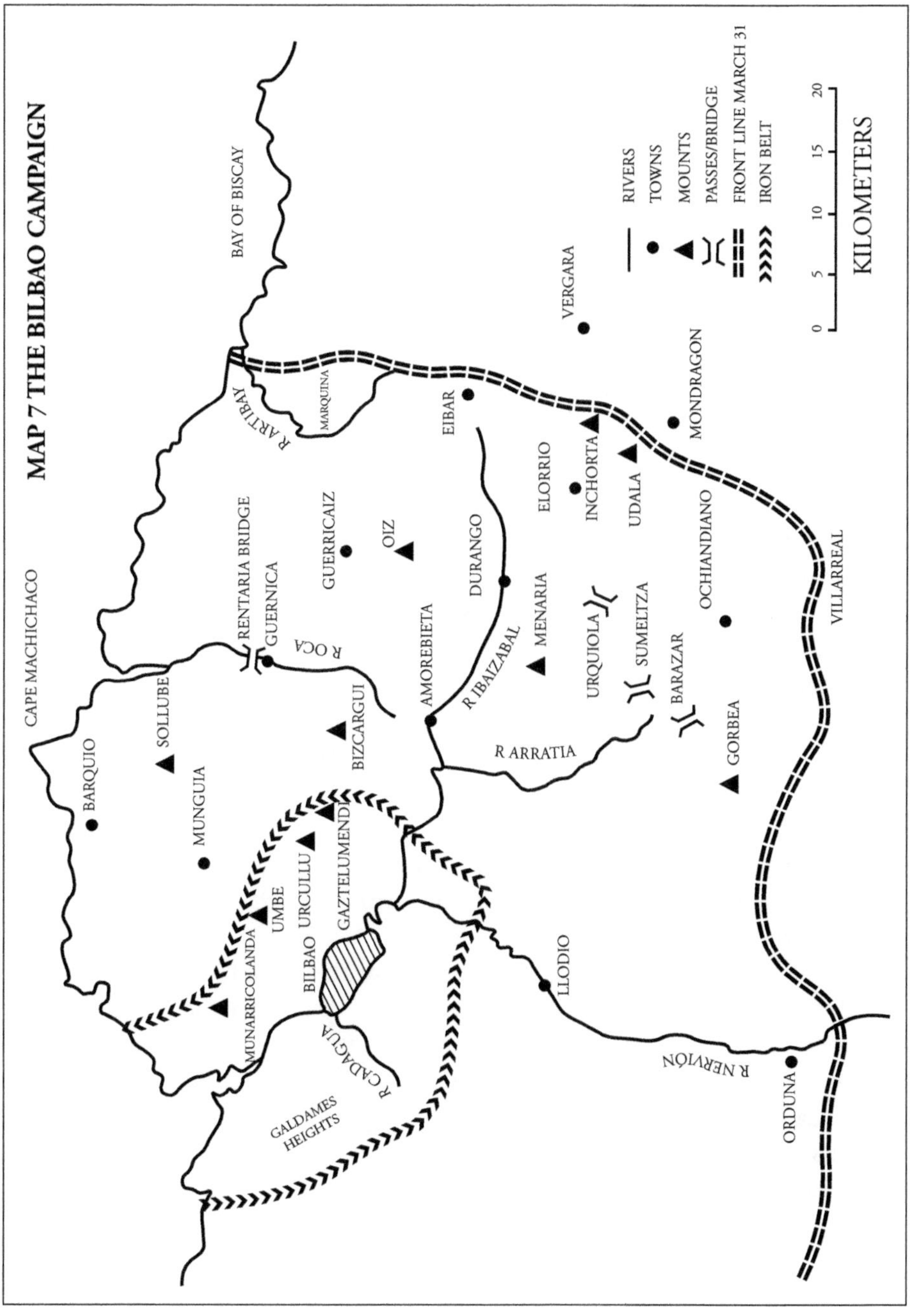
MAP 7 THE BILBAO CAMPAIGN
BAY OF BISCAY
CAPE MACHICHACO
BARQUIO
SOLLUBE
MUNGUIA
RENTARIA BRIDGE
GUERNICA
R OCA
GUERRICAIZ
OIZ
BIZCARGUI
AMOREBIETA
DURANGO
R IBAIZABAL
R ARTIBAY
MARQUINA
EIBAR
VERGARA
ELORRIO
INCHORTA
UDALA
MONDRAGON
MENARIA
URQUIOLA
SUMELTZA
BARAZAR
OCHIANDIANO
VILLARREAL
GORBEA
R ARRATIA
UMBE
URCULLU
GAZTELUMENDI
MUNARRICOLANDA
BILBAO
R CADAGUA
GALDAMES HEIGHTS
LLODIO
R NERVIÓN
ORDUNA
RIVERS
TOWNS
MOUNTS
PASSES/BRIDGE
FRONT LINE MARCH 31
IRON BELT
0 5 10 15 20
KILOMETERS

The campaign to take Bilbao and the remainder of the enclave was shaped by geography, with mountain barriers running east–west restricting direct access to the coast. The Basques held almost all the heights along the front and, while the valley of the River Artibay offered an easier advance to the rail and road hub of Durango, Mount Oiz (1,026m) hindered progress to the River Oca, with the town of Guernica (now Gernika) near its mouth. The river was a potential barrier but beyond it the going was easier, leading to the lower valley of the River Nervion, at the heart of which was the great industrial city of Bilbao shielded in the west by the Galdames Heights which were 822–998m high.

The original plan envisaged an advance on three axes down river valleys converging upon Bilbao. They were westward from Vergara along the Ibaizábal through Durango, from Villarreal in the southeast along the Arratia and through Orduna in the southwest along the Nervion. However, the hilly terrain in the south was favorable to defense in depth, and an attack from the east would be exposed to envelopment, but the strongly held heights north of Villareal were in a salient which could be attacked from two sides. Once they fell, Mola, like a carpenter, could plane along the grain of the terrain to roll up the enclave.

The offensive would be directed by Solchaga's Group using the four Navarrese brigades (Brigada Navarra) created during the winter as a 27,900-strong reserve strike force: the 1st under Lieutenant Colonel Rafael García-Valiño, 2nd under Colonel Pablo Cayuela, 3rd under Colonel Rafael Latorre, and 4th under Colonel Camilo Alonso Vega with a total of 32 battalions (13 Requete, 7 Falange and 12 conscript). Franco wanted to deploy the full force of the CTV in the north but Bastico regarded this as a secondary operation and would permit only the Italian-led Flechas Negras under Brigadier General Alessandro Piazzoni to be transferred north from March 28 to raise Solchaga's strength to 39,500.[3]

The plan, published on March 29, called for the main blow from Villarreal by Alonso Vega's double-strength (9,927 men) brigade which would retake the heights lost in December. On his right the weakest of the Navarrese brigades (4,343) under Latorre would launch a diversion from the east while García-Valiño, with the second-strongest Navarrese brigade (5,410), would strike westward through the mountains on Latorre's right to cut the Villarreal–Durango road. Afterward Alonso Vega and Latorre would occupy Ochiandiano, then the former would advance northwestward to take the Barazar and Sumeltza passes leading to the Ibaizabal Valley west of Durango. Latorre and García-Valiño would advance to the Urquiola Pass to the east ready to descend upon Durango. Meanwhile, Cayuela's brigade would hold the

30km line from Mondragon north to the sea until early April when Piazzoni's Flechas Negras took over the coastal sector.

They would receive fire support from 33 batteries (100 guns) under Colonel Carlos Martínez de Campos, while 153 aircraft—85 German, 40 Spanish and 28 Italian—would ensure air domination.[4] Although Vigón delegated the conduct of air operations to air commanders, the Condor Legion leaders, Sperrle and Richthofen, intended to implement the Luftwaffe doctrine of Tactical-Operational Level air support published as Luftwaffe Regulation 16: *Conduct of the Air War* (Luftwaffe Dienstvorschrift 16, Luftkriegführung or LDv 16) only two years earlier.[5]

While there would be close air support in the Forward Edge of Battle Area (FEBA), the emphasis was upon the interdiction of communications and communications centers at the Operational Level to disrupt resistance, although many air forces regarded these as "Strategic" missions. Both Luftwaffe officers would also have been familiar with Paragraph 186 which stated: "Attacks against cities made for the purpose of inducing terror in the civilian populace are to be avoided on principle."[6] In view of the later controversy over Guernica it is worth noting that the Condor Legion's single-engined aircraft, notably fighter group J/88, were at Vitoria while the multi-engined aircraft were 100km away, with bomber group K/88 at Villafria, 6km north of Burgos, in an air terminal built in 1932 exclusively for foreign airlines flying into Spain.[7]

Since November 15 the defending Northern Army (Ejército del Norte) was nominally under the 60-year-old Moroccan-born Brigadier General Francisco Llano de la Encomienda, one of the few active generals loyal to the Republic. He appears to have been a somewhat passive personality who would be sidelined by the Basques as he had been by the Catalans and Anarchists the previous year. He had little authority and at one point plaintively telegraphed Largo Caballero to ask whether or not he commanded the Basque forces. In January the Basque president, José Antonio Aguirre, who regarded Llano de la Encomienda as the "personification of incompetence" made his army autonomous and in the face of this snub the general moved his headquarters to Santander in February and left the Basques to conduct their own defense.

The military reforms in the Republican heartland were applied late by the Northern Army with brigades formed by the Asturians from February and by their allies from March 26, to give a nominal force of 16 Basque, 12 Santanderino, and 19 Asturian brigades, with 192 battalions, and on March 31 these were organized into four corps.[8] The Northern Army had 101,000 men and were supported by 83 tanks, most of them Great War Renaults, 30

BA-6 armored cars and 300 guns of 14 different types, a high proportion of which were obsolete. There were 60 aircraft supported by 40 antiaircraft guns, most of them of light and medium caliber.[9]

The Basque Army (Ejército de Euzkadi) element was grouped into divisions barely a week before the offensive and had the 1 DIE (Division de Infanteria Euzkadi) facing east, 2 DIE in the southeast with on its right 3 DIE holding Mount Gorbea, while the mountains south of Bilbao were held by 4 DIE.[10] They had 37,000 men supported by 16 Trubia M-1936 tanks, ten BA 6, 100 guns (about 20 heavy), and 51 aircraft, including 16 I-15 and Letov S.231 fighters, under future FARE chief of staff Lieutenant Colonel Antonio Martin Luna-Lersundi, but the multiplicity of types made maintenance a nightmare and severely reduced serviceability.[11]

In an age fascinated by defensive fortifications it was no surprise that the Basques decided to create their own Maginot Line, the Iron Belt, as their ultimate guarantor of independence. The U-shaped defenses in the lower valley of the Nervion had a northern face 25km long, an eastern face of 12km, and a southern face of 40km. It consisted of field and concrete fortifications behind barbed-wire entanglements, sometimes only 6km from Bilbao. At the government's insistence it was designed to protect not only the port and industries of Bilbao but also the airport and even the reservoirs, ignoring Frederick the Great's comment that, "He who defends everything, defends nothing." There were planned to be 1,400 concrete pillboxes, observation posts, and shelters, supporting trenches which were supposed to be a meter deep.[12]

The Belt was divided into five sectors: the 5th ran along the northern bank of the Nervion with the key heights of Mounts Munarricolanda and Umbe, the line extending eastward from the Munguia–Bilbao road to become the 4th then turned south at the 311-meter Mount Gaztelumendi to the River Ibaizabal. The 3rd Sector was between the Ibaizabal and the Nervion, while the 2nd and 1st sectors covered the southern side to the sea, split by the River Cadagua. The most extensive defenses, up to three lines of trenches, were in the 4th and 5th sectors between Mount Gaztelmundi (which had a single line of trenches) and the south bank of the Ibaizabal, while most sectors had only one or two lines of trenches. Llano de Encomienda's chief of staff, Lieutenant Colonel Gustavo Montaud, had overall responsibility for the defenses but the designer was an engineer, Captain Pablo Murga, assisted by a Basque Monarchist rail engineer, Captain Alejandro Goicoechea. Together they supervised detailed design and construction work by a team of 13 architects together with 14 industrial and mining engineers.

Then, on October 28, the Austrian consul was stopped as he tried to board a British ship and found to have detailed plans of the Iron Belt which had come from Murga. He was shot on November 19 while Goicoechea came under suspicion but was cleared after an interview with his friend President Aguirre and assumed control of the project. At the last minute, Montaud tried to change the plans but it was too late for anything except the most minor alterations, as 8,500 workers began digging the trenches and pouring concrete, some 70 centimeters thick, for 180 positions. Only 28 percent of the structures would be completed. Construction slowed during the winter, when the work force dropped to 2,500, but by late February some 13,300 men were working on the positions, the work costing some 50 million pesetas.[13]

Much of this effort, such as trench systems to cover the coastal road from Santander, was wasted while many pillboxes and bunkers were not camouflaged, either deliberately or through ignorance. Worse still, the designers placed the Main Line of Resistance (MLR) on forward instead of reverse slopes which exposed them to enemy fire. The need to hold a long perimeter meant that the system, at a kilometer deep, was eggshell thin and all of this was known to the Nationalists. On February 27 Goicoechea rolled up the plans, put them in his automobile, then drove south until he crossed the lines where he presented them to Mola. When Franco was shown the plans he quickly spotted the weak point at Mount Gaztelumendi and reportedly exclaimed, "What a mistake. What a huge mistake!"[14]

Even if Mola had not been aware of the defensive weaknesses they would have remained a liability to the Basque defense. A few years later Hitler would observe that he avoided building defensive systems on the Eastern Front because his generals were always looking longingly over their shoulders and seeking an excuse to retreat into them.[15] Extensive propaganda meant the Basque defenders sought the sanctuary of the Iron Belt and were reluctant to meet the enemy in the field.

On March 31 Alonso Vega attacked at 09:40 after 60 guns, with German bombers, pounded the heights north of Villarreal for 90 minutes, then German fighters strafed positions indicated by the Spanish troops with cloth signal panels.[16] The 2 DIE defenses were shallow, trenches barely waist deep, and easily crushed by the heavy artillery fire which allowed the Navarrese to take the heights north of Villarreal within 30 minutes, but García-Valiño, with only half the artillery support, made slower progress. The Condor Legion also sought to impose its influence upon the battle by striking the communications hub of Durango and, through heavy bombing, made it a "choke point" by filling the down-town roads with wreckage and rubble to prevent the movement of men and supplies.[17]

Yet reinforcements did flow southward as the 2 DIE recovered from its shock to resist fiercely and, by holding Mount Gorbea for eight weeks, prevented Solchaga from rolling up the Basques' southern defenses. Rain was now falling, further slowing the Navarrese advance and finally halting it on April 2. It resumed briefly on April 4 when the Navarrese, supported by armor and some 50 aircraft, began to envelop Ochiando, which caused the terrified Basques to flee after they had suffered 1,000 casualties. The heavens opened but did not yet drown the fighting: a Basque counterattack from Mount Gorbea was held on April 5 and two days later the Barazar, Sumeltza, and Urquiola passes were taken. But Mola could ask no more from his troops and ended the offensive which had become a damp squib after opening with such high hopes. The Nationalists had driven a 15km-long and 20km-wide salient into the enemy lines but had created a cul-de-sac, and there was a fortnight's lull while Mola and Solchaga pondered their next moves.

Llano de la Encomienda could only rage on the sidelines, but he was not totally impotent and on April 6 he ordered four Asturian and Santanderino brigades together with artillery eastward under the command of Colonel Arturo Llarch Castresana while the Santander fighter squadron reinforced the Basque fighters.[18] The defenders used the time to strengthen their positions, the Basques mobilizing more men and receiving new arms shipments, which gave them 140 guns. The Russians were so alarmed that Gorev was dispatched with a 26-man staff to put more fire in Republican bellies, as he had at Madrid, but he would have little influence upon events, as the front burst into flames once again on April 20, for the Basques regarded him as "inexperienced in war."[19]

Solchaga recognized that he could not expand the Ochiando salient but his advance had exposed enemy positions southeast of Elorrio, whose elimination would open the way to Durango. Latorre's brigade remained in the salient while Alonso Vega's was transferred north to Vergara where it replaced part of Cayuela's brigade. Cayuela would strike the Elorrio salient from the east with a demi-brigade while García-Valiño, using one of Lattore's demi-brigades, would squeeze it from the west and take the strongpoint at Mount Udala. Meanwhile, Alonso Vega would strike westward to take Mount Inchorta to open the passes on either side of Mount Udala, with roads from Mondragon and Vergara respectively through Elorrio to Durango.

The offensive reopened on April 20 with the usual massive artillery preparation involving 180 tonnes of shells which had a devastating effect upon the defenders' shallow trenches.[20] Once again rain began to fall but

García-Valiño broke through and turned north to storm Mount Udala on April 24, and by the end of the day he had taken Elorrio aided by the sudden flight of two Anarchist battalions. The Basque front was now collapsing and García-Valiño advanced upon Durango, which fell on April 28. Frequent air attacks on the roads added to the defenders' difficulties and on April 22 bombing cut communications between the Basque headquarters at Elorrio and the front line.

Meanwhile in the east Alonso Vega had faced fierce resistance at Mount Inchorta where a failed frontal assault cost him 325 casualties. An outflanking maneuver from the south, aided by the fall of Mount Udala, allowed him to take Mount Inchorta on April 25. He then advanced north toward Eibar and Marquina (also Markina) and into the flank of Carabiniero Major Ricardo Gómez García's 1 DIE which fell back. Alonso Vega rapidly took Eibar on April 26 and Marquina on April 27, while Piazzoni's Flechas Negras moved along the coast and briefly reached Marquina before Mola firmly slapped Piazzoni on the wrist to prevent him stealing Alonso Vega's thunder.

The disasters in the east fueled secret peace discussions between the Church and the Basque government. The Archbishop of Toledo, Cardinal Isidro Gomá, tried to persuade the Basques to surrender and sought Italian and Vatican support. On April 25 Franco's brother and secretary, Nicolás, informed the Italians that the Nationalists would be willing to accept the Basque surrender and allow Basque leaders to go into exile, although some would have to face justice for politically motivated crimes. Similar terms were transmitted to Aguirre by the Vatican's Secretary of State Cardinal Eugenio Pacelli (later Pope Pius XII), a message intercepted by Valencia and kept secret. In May Aguirre rejected the Vatican's proposals possibly because he hoped that the Iron Belt would hold back the Nationalist tide, but the discussions would bear fruit during the Santander campaign.[21]

The Nationalists now prepared to sweep westward with the River Oca the last remaining barrier before the Iron Belt, and it was against this background that the little market town of Guernica, which had 4,000 people, was bombed on April 26. To a world living in the shadow of the bomber and hearing a stream of horror stories in which aerial bombardment destroyed civilization, Guernica was a nightmare come true. It was an indiscriminate aerial attack that reduced the defenseless town to scorched rubble, with hundreds of inhabitants slaughtered in order to terrorize the Basques into surrender.[22]

Descriptions and discussions of this terrible event have focused upon "Who" and "What," neglecting "Why" because of the paucity of documentary evidence.[23] There are, however, four uncontestable facts: the town was bombed

Nationalist troops form up on a misty morning to continue their advance on the northern front. Battle flags were carried to help commanders follow the progress of the infantry who were supported by a mixture of vehicles and pack trains of mules and horses. (Photo by José Demaría "Campúa")

Franco and General Fidel Dávila (right) discuss the concluding stages of the Teruel campaign. Dávila would be the mastermind behind the Nationalist victories not only against the northern enclave but also in the Aragon, Levante and Catalonia. (Photo by José Demaría "Campúa")

Franco and Mola emerge from church in Burgos with their demeanor clearly reflecting their changed status. Franco had just been proclaimed head of the Nationalist state, down-grading Mola who had been the "Director" behind the military uprising. He was blamed for its limited success and was reportedly suicidal for a few weeks until Nationalist fortunes changed.

Richthofen (second from right in background) with Spanish allies and forward command team during the Vizcaya campaign which he regarded as an excellent opportunity to demonstrate the value of air power in supporting armies. He was often exasperated by the failure of his allies to exploit his successes and the accidental destruction of Guernica occurred as he tried to prove his point.

by the Condor Legion, the Spanish Nationalists were complicit in the events, it was not a terror attack, and Guernica was not supposed to be the target!

For the Germans, and especially the Luftwaffe, the Spanish conflict was both a laboratory and a showcase. Sperrle and his chief of staff Lieutenant Colonel Richthofen followed the official doctrine set out in LDv 16, *Luftkriegführung*, drafted and published in 1935 by Lieutenant General Helmuth Wilberg, who would head Special Staff W (Sonderstab W) which dispatched German men and materials to Spain.[24] The Luftwaffe's role was to support the traditional services at the Tactical and Operational levels, especially the latter, focusing upon enemy communications to prevent the movement of troops and supplies. Consequently the Germans sought to paralyze enemy communications by striking choke points such as Durango. It was the value of air power at the Operational Level which Sperrle and Richthofen were anxious to demonstrate, although they did launch a few strategic raids upon economic targets in Bilbao. They also provided support at the Tactical Level, with bombers and fighter bombers supporting assaults and breaking up enemy attacks, but the Spanish frequently failed to exploit the opportunities, which frustrated the Germans.

When the Nationalist advance was resumed and Durango taken, Sperrle and Richthofen spotted a new opportunity as the Basques retreated toward the Oca where the lowest crossing points were the road bridge at Guernica and the Rentaria rail bridge some 2km to the north. There was another road bridge 8km south of Guernica with a road running east to the village of Guerricaiz (now Gerrikaitz), 10km from both Guernica and Durango.[25] The Basque left would have to retreat along the coastal road to Guernica or take the inland route through Guerricaiz.

As Solchaga's new offensive got into its stride, Richthofen was excited by the prospect of letting loose the Condor Legion to compound the misery of the retreating enemy. He noted in his diary on April 25: "The possibility exists to harass the enemy further to the north and in the region Marquina–Guernica, to entrap portions of them," although the enemy were actually in the area of Marquina and Guerricaiz. That day, he ordered his fighter-bombers and reconnaissance aircraft to attack the roads between Marquina and Eibar while his bombers and the Italians struck Ermua, 3km west of Eibar, where the road forked north to Guerricaiz and south to Durango. He noted attacks upon the Eibar–Durango and Elorrio–Guernica roads, but the Elorio road actually circles north of Mount Oiz to Guerricaiz. The Ju 52 bombers used 250kg bombs to block Ermua, and in his diary, after noting his formations had been ordered to be ready for the morning, he concluded: "Our hopes are raised considerably."

At 06:00 on April 26 Vigón telephoned Richthofen and as a result the Condor Legion bomber formation, K/88, "was tasked to go to Guernicaiz [i.e. Guerricaiz], two villages at the crossroads west of Marquina, in order to harass and halt the retreat of the Reds, who have to pass through there." An hour later Vigón gave Richthofen a situation report indicating that García-Valiño's brigade was on the eastern slope of Mount Oiz, i.e. southwest of Marquina, and was "pressing further to Guernica (to the north) and is expected to take Durango from the northeast." But if they were pressing north then their objective had to be the nearest communications hub, Guerricaiz.

Vigón now expected an advance into and west of Marquina. In response Richthofen repeated the previous day's tactics with the fighters and reconnaissance aircraft striking the roads in the area Marquina–Guernica–Guernicaiz (i.e. Guerricaiz), while K/88, after returning from Guerricaiz, was "to attack the roads and bridges … just eastwards of Guernica [which] must be closed off and ought to at last blossom out as a success against the personnel and materiel of the enemy." Vigón reportedly said that the Navarrese would press on "in such a way that all the roads south of Guernica become blocked off." Yet a glance at the map makes it clear he was referring not to Guernica but to Guerricaiz, and this is confirmed when he added, "If that can be achieved, we shall then have the enemy around Marquina fully trapped."

Richthofen's operations staff at Durango claimed they knew nothing about Guernica although it was a rail head for the coastal railroad which ran through the town to the Rentaria bridge. There was also the nearby Unceta small-arms factory, while two battalions of 4 Basque BM garrisoned the town.[26] Richthofen was determined to isolate the battlefield east of the Oca by destroying the Guernica bridges while the Spanish were concerned that the enemy might assemble reserves around Guernica for a counteroffensive. That morning a Condor Legion He 45 reconnaissance aircraft reported large movements of people and vehicles into Guernica, not realizing that it was market day.[27]

Richthofen wished to destroy not only the enemy reserves east of Guernica but also the Rentaria rail bridge, both to trap the retreating Republicans and to prevent reinforcements crossing the Oca yet he also wanted to turn Guerricaiz into a choke point. His operations staff telephoned the Vitoria-based J/88 to strafe roads east of Guernica, and Major Robert Fuchs's K/88 at Villafria was apprised of Richthofen's intentions for the bombers. It is likely that there was confusion between Guernica and Guerricaiz which probably led Fuchs to believe he was to turn Guernica into a choke point using his Ju 52s, while the new He 111, under Captain Rudolf Freiherr von Moreau, would drop the Rentaria bridge exploiting its superior bomb sights.[28]

That afternoon Moreau's He 111 aimed nearly 8 tonnes of bombs at the Rentaria bridge, which was undamaged, and along an east–west axis across the town while 26 Ju 52s and some Do 17s dropped 45 tonnes of bombs, including 2,500 incendiaries, on a north–south axis down the eastern side of the town. Three Italian S.79 bombers dropped 5.4 tonnes on Guerricaiz.[29] The bombs missed Guernica's two hospitals but ignited vats of olive oil and the spreading flames destroyed, or seriously damaged, some 80 percent of the buildings. As the luckless inhabitants fled into the surrounding fields 16 German fighters strafed them, believing they were enemy troops, The Basque government claimed there were 2,500 casualties including 1,654 dead, but later research suggests that the death toll was about 300.

In his evening report to his allies Sperrle noted his aircraft had struck the enemy rear, roads north of Mount Oiz and into Guernica, as well as the Rentaria bridge, but not Guernica itself.[30] Richthofen was unaware Guernica had been bombed but on April 27 noted with some puzzlement reports that the town was burning. Three days later he visited the town and was shocked at the damage, which he blamed upon Anarchists, but when a furious Mola learned the truth he banned any repeat missions. The bombing of Guernica certainly demoralized the defenders as the front collapsed, and increasingly they looked over their shoulders to the illusory protection of the Iron Belt.

García-Valiño pushed on from Durango to reach the Oca by April 29 and quickly established a bridgehead across the river at Guernica, but on April 30 there was a brief pause to resupply the vanguard and reorganize the Nationalist forces. The Saragossa-based 6th Division was elevated to Sixth Corps, now under General José López Pinto, the former military governor of Cadiz, while Solchaga's task force became the 1st Division, although it would be renumbered 61st on May 23. Solchaga relieved Alonso Vega's exhausted brigade on May 3 with the 5th Navarrese Brigade formed by Colonel Juan Bautista on April 30. In addition the Flechas Negras were brought across the Oca to cover the coastal flank, and from May 3 were reinforced by Francisci's XXIII de Marzo Group while in the south Latorre's brigade was transferred to the south of Mount Gorbea.

The Basque Corps still held Mount Gorbea and this would remain the southern anchor almost until the fall of Bilbao. President Aguirre, exasperated at the failure of his army, and apparently upon Gorev's recommendation, assumed command of the I CEE on May 5, with Major Ernesto de la Fuente as his chief of staff. He activated another two brigades and 5 DIE under Major Pablo Beldarrain with two Basque and a Santanderino brigades to cover the coastal route. The reinforcements from the Asturias and Santander were now distributed among the

Basque forces: an Asturian brigade to Gómez García's 1 DIE and two to Colonel Joaquín Vidal's 2 DIE. Civil Guard Lieutenant Colonel Juan Ibarrola's 3 DIE still held Mount Gorbea but had swung back to cover the Arratia Valley, while Civil Guard Colonel Daniel Irezábal's 4 DIE continued to hold the mountains south of Bilbao. This gave 92 battalions to cover completion of the Iron Belt where work continued frantically after the unions called up everyone from 18 to 50 to work on the defenses, providing a work force of 15,000, many from factories, which disrupted war production which was already weak.

In a desperate effort to ease the enemy air superiority the Republic tried to send aircraft to the enclave through French air space. The long distances, bad weather, and the zealousness of Non-Intervention organization officials plagued these efforts and only 20 aircraft reached the Basques before the fall of Bilbao.[31] With the Nationalist naval blockade tightening, the only reliable means of reaching the outside world from the enclave was with the French airline Air Pyrénées, which had to run the gauntlet of fighters which shot down two Airspeed Envoys.[32]

The defenders' morale was briefly boosted after Piazzoni, on his own initiative, led a Flechas Negras battalion northward from Guernica along the coastal road to take the small fishing port of Bermeo on April 30 and then continue up the road toward Cape Machichaco. Mola learned of this rash move only the following day and was especially concerned because Beldarrain's 5 DIE held the high ground to the west around Mount Sollube (684m) and might cut the coastal road, which it promptly did south of Bermeo. The isolated Piazzoni pulled his forces around Bermeo and awaited relief from Alonso Vega and Francisci, who broke through on May 4 after Piazzoni suffered 290 casualties.[33]

The Bermeo fiasco demonstrated the importance of taking mounts Sollube and Bizcargui (563m) north and south respectively of the Guernica bridgehead. García-Valiño struck the latter from May 1 but fierce resistance and the need to relieve the Flechas forced Mola and Solchaga to rethink. Bautista's brigade was brought into the bridgehead to win its spurs by taking Mount Sollube, striking on May 5 with strong air support from the south to outflank the enemy. By May 8 the Navarrese had reached the Baquio–Munguia road, then, despite two days of counterattacks by Beldarrain, they fought their way up the slopes to take the heights on May 13, only to lose them to a counterattack. By striking into the enemy flank Bautista removed this threat and his men once retook the heights on May 14. He was aided by the revitalized Flechas, with XXIII Marzo on their left, who resumed their coastal advance with strong Condor Legion support.

They reached Cape Machichaco, took Belderrain's two remaining mountain strongpoints on May 14 and 19, and then opened the coastal route to push 5 DIE ever closer to the Iron Belt. His neighbor, Gómez García of 1 DIE, was also pushed back as García-Valiño took Mount Bizcargui on May 11 but García-Valiño was briefly delayed by counterattacks on May 15. The advance was soon resumed but the XXIII Marzo was withdrawn from the line on May 20, to be expanded into a division and replaced three days later by the newly raised 6th Navarrese Brigade under Colonel Maximino Bartoméu.

Valencia desperately and vainly launched diversionary offensives at Huesca and La Granja but by now Solchaga's vanguard was barely 5km from the Iron Belt's northern face which his field guns bombarded. He still needed to remove the last barriers to the Iron Belt, the twin anchors of Mount Manaria, southwest of Durango, and Mount Gorbea. Cayuela struck from Durango with a demi-brigade along the Ibaizabal Valley to take Amorebieta on May 17 while the other demi-brigade enveloped the northern part of Mount Manaria. Simultaneously the rested Alonso Vega fought his way through the Barazar Pass on May 22 to link up with Cayuela on May 24 and take the last height before the Iron Belt, leaving Latorre to pin down 3 DIE around Mount Gorbea.

As the Nationalists approached the Iron Belt the weather again broke, leaving them at least 5km from the fortifications, and while Vigón issued orders on May 28 to assault the fortifications it was a fortnight before Solchaga could begin. The defenders' collapse destroyed Valencia's confidence in the military abilities of both Aguirre, ironically dubbed by the Basques "Little Napoleon" (Napoleontxu), and Fuente. On May 27, Defense Minister Prieto appointed Brigadier General Mariano Gámir, an apolitical Basque officer with prominent eyebrows, to command I CEE, and he flew into Santander two days later to assume command, leaving Llano de Encomienda, who was the same age as him, directing the Asturian and Santandarino forces. Gámir was an able staff officer, described as a military theorist, who had once been director of the Toledo Infantry School and had previously commanded Republican forces around Teruel.[34]

His chief of staff was Major Angél Lamas, an incompetent Nationalist sympathizer, yet the two seemed to improve the Basque Army, which was further boosted by the arrival of Czech arms but had only 12 aircraft until it received 16 Chato fighters from the heartland in late May. Central government interest in the Basques was reflected in the fact that a number of senior Communist figures were flown in by Air Pyrénées, while on June 4 the Italian Nino Nanetti, who had distinguished himself at Guadalajara, assumed command of 6 Basque Brigade/1 DIE on June 4 as the bearded former chief of the general staff General Martínez also arrived as representative of the Central government's staff.

Gámir inspected his command and on June 6 informed Prietro that with his troops' low morale and equipment shortages Valencia should prepare for the loss of Bilbao. He reported that he needed 70 battalions to hold the Belt but only half his 92 battalions were about to enter the defenses and many were under strength due to losses in the long retreat. The defense would have to rely upon (north–south) 5, 1, and 2 DIE with about a dozen brigades, although he had just created the Division de Enlace de Euzkadi (Euzkadi Liaison Division) with two brigades to cover the western approaches to Bilbao and the coastal road to Santander.

A defensive system is like a diamond—where there is a flaw it may be split by a hard blow. The Iron Belt had two flaws: the sharp angle around Mount Gaztelumendi exposed the whole system and was further weakened by inadequate fortifications at this spot. Vigón's plan for splitting the Belt recognized these weaknesses and he ordered an assault upon Gaztelumendi from north to south by Bartoméu, Bautista, and García-Valiño, while the remaining brigades pinned down the enemy through diversions, probes, and bombardments. They would be supported by more than 35 batteries, including 13 Italian, with 144 guns including 305mm howitzers, as well as 100 aircraft, and on the first day they would overcome the last barriers to the Belt. On the second day García-Valiño would strike the western slope of Mount Gaztelumendi and outflank the defenses, while Cayuela on his left would strike the eastern part of the Belt. Bartoméu and Bautista would break through the Belt on the remaining heights, then the former would begin rolling up the northern defenses while the latter supported 1st Brigade's advance upon eastern Bilbao.

The rain and low cloud of early June gave the Nationalists time to bring up supplies, replace losses, and make their final preparations, but the weather also dealt a heavy blow to the Nationalist cause. Mola wanted to discuss the future campaign with Franco at Burgos, and on June 3 he flew out of Vitoria in his Airspeed Envoy with his staff aide Major Francisco Senac and his adjutant Colonel Gabriel Pozas. But in the cloud his aircraft crashed into the Brujula mountains near Castil de Peones and all on board were killed. Mola was six days short of his 50th birthday and his death, following that of Sanjurjo also in an air crash, left Franco with a morbid fear of air travel which he avoided for the rest of his life.[35] Surprisingly he was replaced not by Vigón but by Dávila, who would direct most of the successful Nationalist campaigns until almost the end of the war. Vigón, who would become Army chief of staff in

September 1937, appears to have held no grudge and would act as a roving chief of staff with the two men working hand-in-hand for most of the war, like a duet on the same piano.

A week later, on June 11, the front erupted into life following a seven-hour artillery bombardment augmented by bombers, the Italians alone flying 30 sorties, and from June 1 through June 18 they would fly 22 missions to drop 140 tonnes of bombs on the Belt.[36] The shallow trenches around the fortifications could not withstand the weight of enemy fire and Solchaga's brigades punched a 2km hole in the line while also sweeping through the last barrier to the Belt. They were spearheaded by García-Valiño who advanced 3km, assisted by two tank companies, a Condor Legion signal team, four artillery bombardments, and 35 tonnes of bombs, although a Condor Legion Hs 123 ground-attack aircraft (light dive bomber) was shot down.[37] Meanwhile, the Condor Legion's 88mm antiaircraft guns were used to subdue resistance from pillboxes.

At dawn the next day García-Valiño repulsed a major counterattack by 1 DIE and at 07:00 a five-hour artillery preparation began, reinforced by 70 bombers which dropped 100 tonnes of bombs. As his troops advanced about midday, one of Bautista's battalions exploited a weak point at Mount Urcullu to punch a hole through the Iron Belt and in the confusion some 20 enemy battalions abandoned their positions in panic allowing him to advance 3km. His neighbors helped to exploit the success and by the end of the day there was a 5km gap in the Iron Belt. Aguirre telegraphed Valencia begging for assistance after reporting the enemy had broken through the Iron Belt after two days of horrific artillery and air bombardment which was impossible to resist. During the night all the troops outside the Iron Belt were withdrawn into it but during the following day (June 13) Bartoméu took another 5km of the northern Belt despite a desperate counterattack. Simultaneously Bautista and García-Valiño advanced toward the Nervion to take the last heights before Bilbao while the Flechas and Cayuela also joined in the assault.

The Iron Belt was lost and that evening Auirre summoned a conference of his military advisors at the Carlton Hotel and asked if Bilbao could be held. Gámir said nothing while Gorev advocated a battle for the Basque capital as well as the demolition of bridges over the Nervion, and Prieto sent a message demanding the destruction of industrial sites of potential use to the enemy. To put steel into the defenders' hearts, on June 14 the 1 and 2 DIE received foreign commanders, Colonel Joseph Walter Putz and the Italian Communist Nanetti respectively. Putz was a former French Army officer and previously commander of 14 BI, while Nanetti had shown military ability at Guadalajara.[38]

Their presence briefly rallied the Basques who briefly slowed the enemy advance, but the following day García-Valiño crossed the Nervion and pushed toward the suburbs, causing panic among Putz's and Nanetti's troops who began to flee across the river. As the Nationalists pushed down the Nervion Valley, Bartoméu and the Flechas entered the northern suburbs, the former taking the airfield on April 16, but during the day Bartoméu was wounded and temporarily replaced by Lieutenant Colonel Venancio Tutor. With the city on the verge of falling the Basque government ordered its troops to cover a general withdrawal westward, but there were two opposing ideas about Bilbao's future. Left-wing battalions were willing to destroy everything of value in the city but Basque Justice Minister, Jesús Maria Leizaola, brought in four Basque Nationalist battalions to thwart them and for good measure he also released political prisoners.

The Nationalist advance continued remorselessly during June 16 to inflict heavy casualties on Putz's men and by the next day the command posts of both Putz and Nanetti were in the city center as the Basque government moved to Villaverde de Trocíos in Santander while food and water began to run out and electrical power ceased. Some Basque leaders escaped by air to France, including Aguirre who was flown out by Air Pyrénées, but the Health Minister, Dr Alfredo Espinosa, and the Basque Army artillery chief were both captured when their aircraft landed on a beach near San Sebastian.[39] The Flechas reached the northern bank of the Nervion to push 5 DIE across the river as refugees fled across the rail bridge, while Nationalist sympathizers became more active and sniped at the retreating troops. At dawn on June 18 the remaining Basque units were ordered to withdraw from Bilbao, the last departing early the following morning, but the retreating columns were under frequent air attacks, one of which killed Nanetti.

The prospect of leaving their province was too much for the Basque troops, many of whom deserted or surrendered, reflecting an astonishing provincialism for the 20th century. The morning of June 19 saw an uneasy calm in Bilbao where white flags and the Nationalist banner were being put out of windows and the Fifth Column began to occupy buildings. As the sun rose García-Valiño's two tank companies roared into the city center to be greeted by Nationalist sympathizers, but tensions remained until the 1st Navarrese Brigade's infantry marched in during the late afternoon following the surrender of six or eight Gudari battalions and occupied Bilbao, Gámir formally informing Valencia at 21:00.

The Nationalist advance continued westward. Alonso Vega crossed the upper Nervion around Llodio, some 12km southwest of Bilbao, while Latorre marked

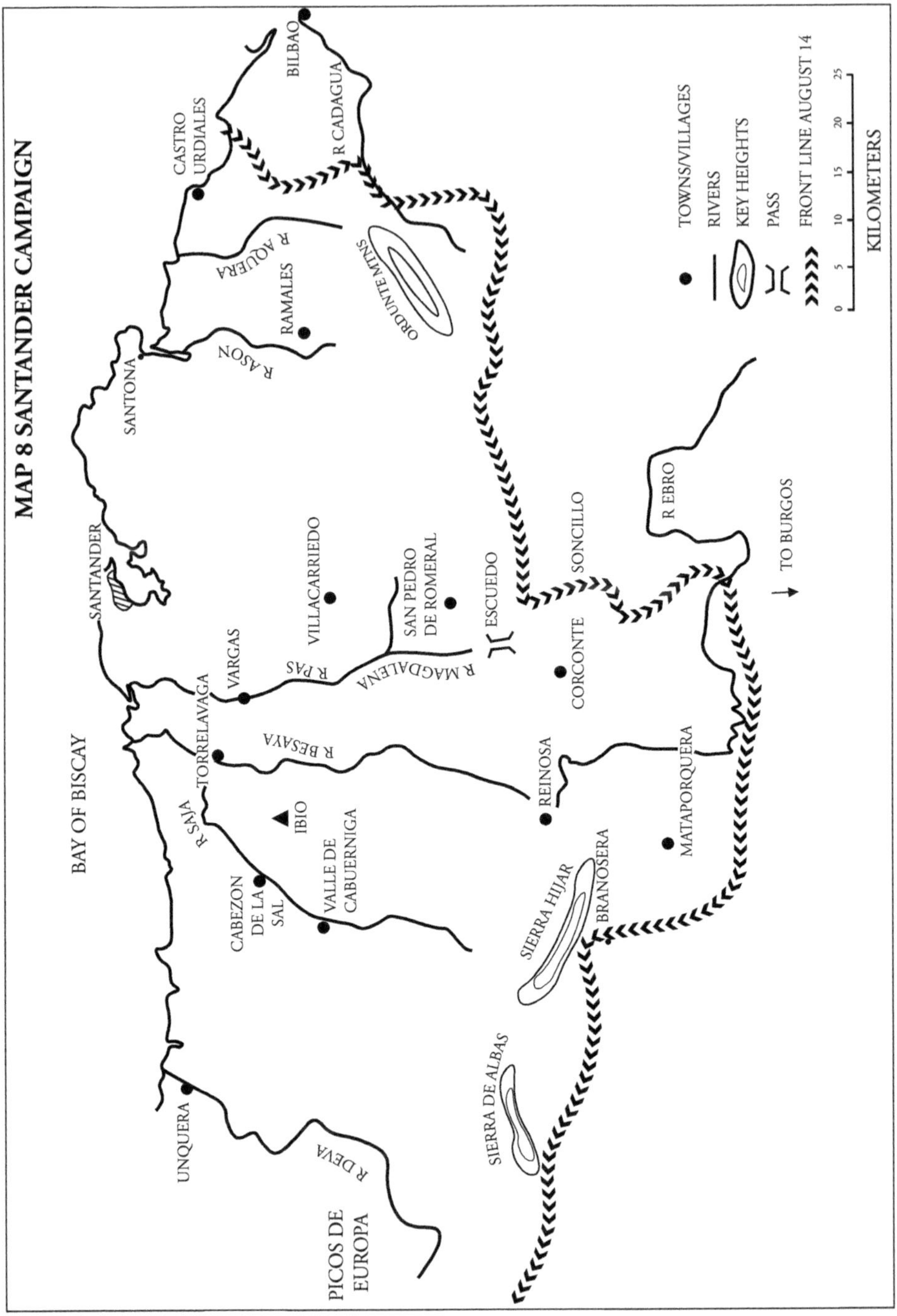

MAP 8 SANTANDER CAMPAIGN

time with him in the extreme south. Tutor advanced along the western bank of the Nervion to its mouth, while García-Valiño and Cayuela pushed into the heights west of Bilbao to take the remainder of the Iron Belt from the rear. As the last Basques abandoned the Iron Belt, Franco issued a directive on June 22 for the occupation of Santander and a second, two days later, for the occupation of the Asturias. During the last days of June and the early days of July the Nationalists succeeded in occupying the whole Basque province of Vizcaya, but increasing resistance from the heights on Santander's borders and the need to replace losses and bring up supplies meant that the offensive was ended on July 5.

The Nationalists had secured Spain's Ruhr with tremendous industrial and economic benefits for their cause at the cost of 30,000 casualties, including 4,500 dead, of whom 516 and 106 respectively were Italian, while the Republicans suffered 35,000 casualties, including 10,000 dead. Interestingly 13 of the 15 tanks lost by the Nationalist armored corps in the North from March through October 1937 were in the Bilbao campaign.[40] The Basque defeat owed much to the Nationalists' naval blockade, which restricted the import of war material and food, as well as their unchallenged air dominance over the battlefield, which allowed them to interdict communications. Yet the Basques were also the agents of their own downfall: they failed to create an organization to replace battlefield losses, leaving many battalions under strength, and they delayed creating brigades and divisions until the very eve of the enemy offensive, leaving green staffs and leaders with the twin burdens of organizing resistance and simultaneously learning their duties. By contrast the professionalism of the Nationalist leadership, as much as the superior firepower so carefully accrued, was the key to their victory both now and later.

The Santander Campaign

The Nationalists intended only a brief pause but the enforced lull following the fall of Bilbao gave them time to rest and prepare. The Italian squadrons, for example, were ordered on June 15 to make every effort to prepare for the Santander campaign and restock supply depots. Trains with a total of 160 tonnes of bombs and small-arms ammunition were sent north from Seville with the last being dispatched on June 24.[41]

The Italians were straining at the leash even before the Iron Belt fell and on June 11 had proposed pushing down the Ason Valley to complete the isolation of the Basque state. Franco carefully considered the offer for three days before rejecting it because his forces were making good progress and the move would not aid a new attack upon Santander, and his decision was confirmed by the Basque collapse. Having considered the options, he selected the envelopment of the salient in the Escuedo Pass and Reinosa areas as the center of operations to crack the mountain defenses, but he intended the Italians to have a major role in the campaign.[42] On June 22 and 24 he ordered the capture of the Reinosa salient, the occupation of Santander province, and the destruction of enemy forces to hamper their retreat into the Asturias, with D-Day set for July 10.[43]

But on July 6 the Republicans struck at Brunete (see Chapter 4) and caused a month's delay. This gave Gámir, who had assumed command of the Northern Army on June 25, time to reorganize his command and to send Llano de Encomienda and Martínez ignominiously back to Valencia.[44] Valencia's growing influence of the enclave was reflected on August 6 by the loss of territorial designations, as formations were redesignated in sequence with the rest of the Popular Army. Commanders of the Basque Corps (now XIV CE) were rapidly rotated until the appointment of Lieutenant Colonel Adolfo Prada, but he had only 12 brigades and 68 guns while Ibarrola retained divisional command, although Gómez García replaced Putz who returned to the heartland. The Santandarino Corps became XV CE under Colonel José García Vayas, with 73 guns, while the Asturian corps was split into XVI and XVII CE. Gámir had a total of 160,000 men, with some 260 guns of 25 types and 13 calibers ranging from 37mm to 210mm, 40 tanks, and 20 BA 6 armored cars, but air support continued to be weak with 64 aircraft, including 15 Chatos, of which 44 were serviceable.[45] In late June Valencia dispatched eight Russian-manned I-16 fighters to Santander and during August another eight, together with four I-15, while a few more aircraft were shipped into Gijon.[46] Relations between the defenders were strained and mutual distrust was not assuaged by accurate rumors that the Basques were negotiating a surrender with the Italians on conditions similar to those proposed by Cardinal Pacelli.[47]

As the last embers of the Brunete offensive were extinguished, Franco ordered Dávila on July 26 to resume the destruction of the northern enclave as soon as possible and returned the two Navarrese brigades, aircraft, and artillery he had borrowed to meet the crisis. This gave Solchaga's swollen 61 Division six brigades, which were augmented by two Castilian of Brigadier General Antonio Ferrer's 62 (Castilian) Division to give a total of 73 battalions and 62,000 troops. The 2nd and 6th Navarrese Brigades had new commanders: Colonel Agustin Muñoz Grandes, an old friend of Franco who had escaped from Republican Spain earlier in the year, replaced Cayula in the former while Colonel Miguel Abriat replaced Tutor in the latter.

Dávila also received much of the CTV, now under Bastico, which had been substantially reorganized after Guadalajara, and sought to recover its battered reputation. It had the army's Littorio and MVSN's recently expanded XXIII Marzo Divisions under Bergonzoli and Francisci respectively, together with Brigadier General Luigi Frusci's Fiamme Nere Division, Piazzoni's Flechas Negras, the IX de Mayo Regiment, and a mechanized Mobile Group (Grupo Celere), a total of 32 battalions including six Spanish with 28,000 men. Dávila could call on 86 field and medium batteries (48 Italian) with some 300 guns, while air dominance was assured by 220 aircraft: 80 Italian and 140 evenly divided between the Condor Legion and Spanish squadrons.[48] Perhaps less welcome was the arrival of Franco himself who brought with him part of his own headquarters from Salamanca ready to look over Dávila's shoulder.[49]

Dávila had used the enforced rest to revise his plans constantly in the light of experience during the advance upon Bilbao. The Republican lines ran south from the coast, where they held key heights blocking the coastal route to the Ordunte Mountains (Montes de Ordunte), then curved westward. East of the steep-sided, 1,011m Escudo (Shield) Pass (Puerto del Escudo), the lines in the eastern Cantabrican Mountains (Cordillera Cantábrica) bulged to create a 25km-deep salient with Mataporquera in the west. The salient was between the Nationalist-held towns of Soncillo and Branosera and ran across the upper Ebro Valley, which in turn led to Reinosa that lies between the Ebro and Besaya valleys. From Mataporquera the Republican line ran westward along the Sierras de Hijar and de Albas into the Asturias. The prime routes to Santander from the south were through the Escudo Pass and down the River Magdalena (which rises in the pass), a tributary of the Pas, and from there down the Pas or from Reinosa down the River Besaya, both of which reached the Bay of Biscay west of Santander, both of which meant fighting at heights between 800m and 1,700m.

Santander's defense consisted of Prada's XIV and García Vayas's XV CE, whose divisions were augmented by Asturian brigades to give 86 battalions. Prada blocked the eastern approaches, with 49 and 51 DI defending the coast to the Ordunte Mountains, 52 DI held the heights to the west near the Escudo Pass, while 48 DI was in reserve. Prada had more than 36,100 men, 68 guns (including light artillery), 16 Trubia tanks, and ten BA 6. García Vayas shielded the southern approaches with the Escudo Pass and the salient held (east to west) by 55, 53 and 54 DI with Ibarrola's 50 (Basque) DI on the shoulder shielding Reinosa, together with the Independent 177 BM on its left while the corps' reserve, near the coast, was the Asturian 57 DI. Each division was in echelon with a brigade in the front line, one holding a second or third line and one in reserve, although many of the 100 battalions were under strength and together had only 80,000 men supported by 73 guns, 19 former Polish Renault FT 17 tanks, and three BA 6.

The Republican decision to hold the Mataporquera salient was a major error of judgment, for it exposed most of García Vaya's formations to attack from three sides and left them only one escape route—the railroad and the road north from Mataporquera. A shorter line would have been stronger, required fewer troops, yet still defend the Magdalena/Pas and Besaya routes northward. They and the coastal road were the most obvious axes for the offensive and Dávila's outline plan issued on August 8 called for the main blow to be launched on either side of the Mataporquera salient to reach Reinosa and the Escudo passes, with the main blow coming from the west.

Vigón's detailed plan, issued on the evening of August 11, created a task force (*Agrupación*) for each axis: A under Ferrer, B under Bastico, and C under Solchaga.[50] Solchaga, or the 61st Division, would be the spearhead from the western side of the salient with García-Valiño's, Alonso Vega's, and Bautista's brigades together with Colonel Luis Faurie's 2 Castilian Brigade—a total of 48 battalions (32,800 men), 55 batteries (165 guns), and a tank company supported by 120 aircraft. They were to take Mataporquera, then advance down the road and railroad to Reinosa, linking up with the Italians to envelop the salient.

From Reinosa, Solchaga would drive down the Besaya to the crossroads of Torrelavega, where part of his task force would advance north to Santander while the remainder drove along the coast into the Asturias. Bastico had Littorio, XXIII Marzo, and Fiamme, and Colonel José Gistau's 1st Castilian Brigade, a total of 43 battalions (31,400 men) and 54 batteries (110 guns), together with the mechanized group that included four tankette companies. He would strike the Mataporquera salient from the east, take the Escudo Pass, then drive down the Magdalena and Pas valleys to Vargas on the coastal road and from there north to Santander. Ferrer had the Navarrese brigades of Muñoz Grandes, Latorre, and Abriat, together with the Flechas—a total of 31 battalions (21,500 men) and 15 batteries (50 guns). The Navarrese would strike across the Ordunte Mountains into the valley of the River Ason to take the crossroads at Ramales, while the Flechas would drive along the coastal road, the two then securing eastern Santander.

The offensive began on August 14 after an hour's bombardment, and on Solchaga's front García-Valiño, on the left, struck at the Sierra de Hijar supported, like Bautista on the other flank, by a mobile group of three mountain batteries. He pushed back Ibarrola's 50 DI to the headwaters of the River Saja to secure the Nationalist left, then his brigade was relieved by Faurie. Supported by tanks and the Condor Legion, Alonso Vega in the center smashed through Major Eloy Fernández Navamorales's 54 Division, aided by a bombardment that continued for an hour after his infantry moved out, the advance supported by an artillery group of eight batteries. Navamorales's men briefly rallied at Suano, 5km southwest of Reinosa, which acted as a breakwater, but its fall allowed Alonso Vega to reach the outskirts of Reinosa by dusk on August 15 and take the town on August 16.[51] Bautista on the extreme right supported him by pushing up the road to Mataporquera.

In the east Bastico, flanked by demi-brigades of Gistau's Castilian Brigade, broke through Lieutenant Colonel Francisco Bravo's 53 DI and 55 DI, and as XXIII Marzo cut the Santander–Burgos road the remainder advanced upon the pass where Bravo was reinforced by 179 BM/55 DI, a Carabinero battalion, the corps artillery battalion with 14 guns (two heavy), and the Northern Army Tank Regiment (Regimiento de Carros del Ejercito del Norte). Consequently, progress was slow on the second day as XXIII Marzo pushed toward the Escudo Pass, but IX de Mayo took the heights to the northeast which dominated the Magdalena Valley. Despite fierce resistance during the afternoon of August 15 Littorio on the left pushed westward along the road from Corconte, at the southern end of the Escudo Pass, toward Reinosa.

García Vayas staged counterattacks using the reserve brigades of 50 and 55 DI and committed his reserve, 57 DI, in a vain effort to restore the situation but in the face of enemy air attacks XV CE was beginning to collapse, which placed Gámir and his Russian advisors in a dilemma.[52] They had lost all confidence in García Vayas and wished to replace him with the Communist former Guardia Civil officer Lieutenant Colonel Francisco Galán, who had distinguished himself on the Madrid front and arrived on the northern front in early July to assume command of 51 DI. But García Vayas remained very popular in Santander, which he had held since the 1936 coup, and after dithering Gámir decided to leave him in place but appointed Galan commander of XIV CE.[53]

During August 16 the situation deteriorated alarmingly, for not only did Alonso Vega take Reinosa but Bautista took the heights northeast of Mataparquera to cut the escape routes north. Simultaneously he linked up with Littorio, which committed the Mobile Group's armor in an inconclusive clash with Gamír's tank regiment. Together they isolated 22 battalions, or more than 10,000 men of 53 and 54 DI, a substantial part of García Vayas's forces, which Bautista Sánchez and part of Gistau's brigade mopped up. The following day XXIII Marzo took the Escudo Pass and on August 18, despite fierce storms which would last two days, Bastico began pushing down the slopes: Littorio advanced along the Santander–Burgos road to reach the Pas while on its right the Fiamme took San Pedro del Romeral to advance upon Villacarriedo in the face of fierce resistance which caused heavy casualties. That day saw Gamír face a new threat in the east, where the Flechas broke through Major Victor de Frutos's 49 DI and began to drive along the coast as Ferrer's brigades pushed into the heights. Simultaneously, the Condor Legion's bombers struck airfields to neutralize the remaining Republican air power, although sufficient fighters remained to generate fierce air battles on August 21 and August 22. At dusk the German fighter pilots attacked vehicles in missions they called "Hunting for the Pot" (*Kochenjagd*).

Solchaga's advance northward down the Saja and Besaya began on August 19 as Bastico pushed down the Pas Valley, with the Fiamme reaching Villacarriedo, only 25km from Santander, where it was held by stubborn resistance. On August 20, as Solchaga approached the coastal road at Cabezon de la Sal and Torrelavega, XV CE's front collapsed except in the Pas Valley, where resistance remained strong, especially against the Fiamme, which faced numerous counterattacks before it took Villacarriedo on August 22.

On that day, as Bautista entered the Besaya Valley between García-Valiño and Alonso Vega and reached a point 20km west of Villacarriedo, the Republican leadership, with Aguirre in the chair, met to consider the situation. The military leaders were pessimistic and Valencia ordered a retreat into the Asturias, but this became difficult on August 23 when Mount Ibio, which dominated the coastal road, fell to García-Valiño who was then relieved by Abriat.

Catastrophe also loomed in the east where the Flechas had taken the port of Castro Urdiales, while Muñoz Grandes and Latorre, with Gistau's Castilians, pushed northwest to outflank the next potential defensive position along the River Aquera. Prada was ordered to withdraw on August 21 to the next potential defensive line along the River Ason, but that night four battalions of 49 and 51 DI abandoned their positions and another dozen soon followed their example opening Gamír's left.

On August 23 the Basques ignored Gamír's orders to withdraw westward and instead marched north to the small port of Santona. There 22,000 men assembled and their commanders reopened negotiations with Piazzoni for an honorable surrender, which occurred the following day under the Santona Agreement (Pacto de Santona), with the only condition being that their lives would be spared and they would be able to take a ship to safety. But three days later Spanish pressure caused the Italians to renege on the agreement. Upon learning of the Santona Agreement, Franco and Dávila were furious with the allies and Dávila immediately countermanded it on the grounds that Piazzoni had made it on his own initiative and without the approval of Burgos. The unhappy Italians forced most of those in the ships to disembark, although more than 500 wounded were allowed to sail, and the following morning began marching the Basques into prison camps.[54]

On August 24 Gámir again ordered a general withdrawal westward into the Asturias but his plan was compromised when Bautista took Torrelavega to cut the coastal road to Gijon, then, with Alonso Vega, beat off an attack by 52 DI. By now morale in Santander had collapsed and there were riots as the Fifth Column rose, despite 26 battalions remaining in and around the city. The following day the Republican leadership abandoned Santander, some including Gámir fleeing by submarine to Gijon, while thousands of desperate people also sought escape by sea only to be drowned in the attempt.

As part of Alonso Vega's brigade, together with Littorio, entered the city at dawn on August 26, the garrison surrendered and 17,000 men became prisoner. But the Nationalists did not rest upon their laurels and Alonso Vega sent part of his brigade to join García-Valiño who advanced westward along the coastal road toward the Asturias. He took Cabezon de la Sal on August 27 and sent troops south along the Saja to meet Abriat, who was pushing northward, meeting him two days later at Valle de Cabuerniga. The advance westward was joined on August 30 by Alonso Vega. The following day they reached the River Deva in Asturias, while on September 1 Abriat took the coastal town of Unquera and established a bridgehead across the river, most of which remained in Republican hands as Dávila closed the campaign. Only two Santanderino and four Basque brigades succeeded in reaching the Asturian sanctuary.

The campaign was the most spectacular success of the Civil War, with 86 battalions destroyed and 60,000 prisoners taken, including 20,000 Santanderinos. Of a dozen Basque and a dozen Santanderino brigades, only eight and six battalions respectively were left while only 14 of 27 Asturian battalions evaded the envelopment. The victory owed as much to Nationalist numerical superiority in artillery and aircraft as the attackers' leadership, and together they exploited poor enemy dispositions with limited material strength compounded by a general demoralization.[55] Incomplete figures intercepted by the British for Italian air operations show that they flew 1,215 sorties, including 262 bomber, 39 ground-attack and 24 reconnaissance, during which they dropped 231 tonnes of bombs, and on September 19 they urgently requested from Rome 1,200 tonnes of bombs.[56] The Nationalists also took much booty, including 14 tanks, 80 guns, and 15,000 rifles, sufficient for 22

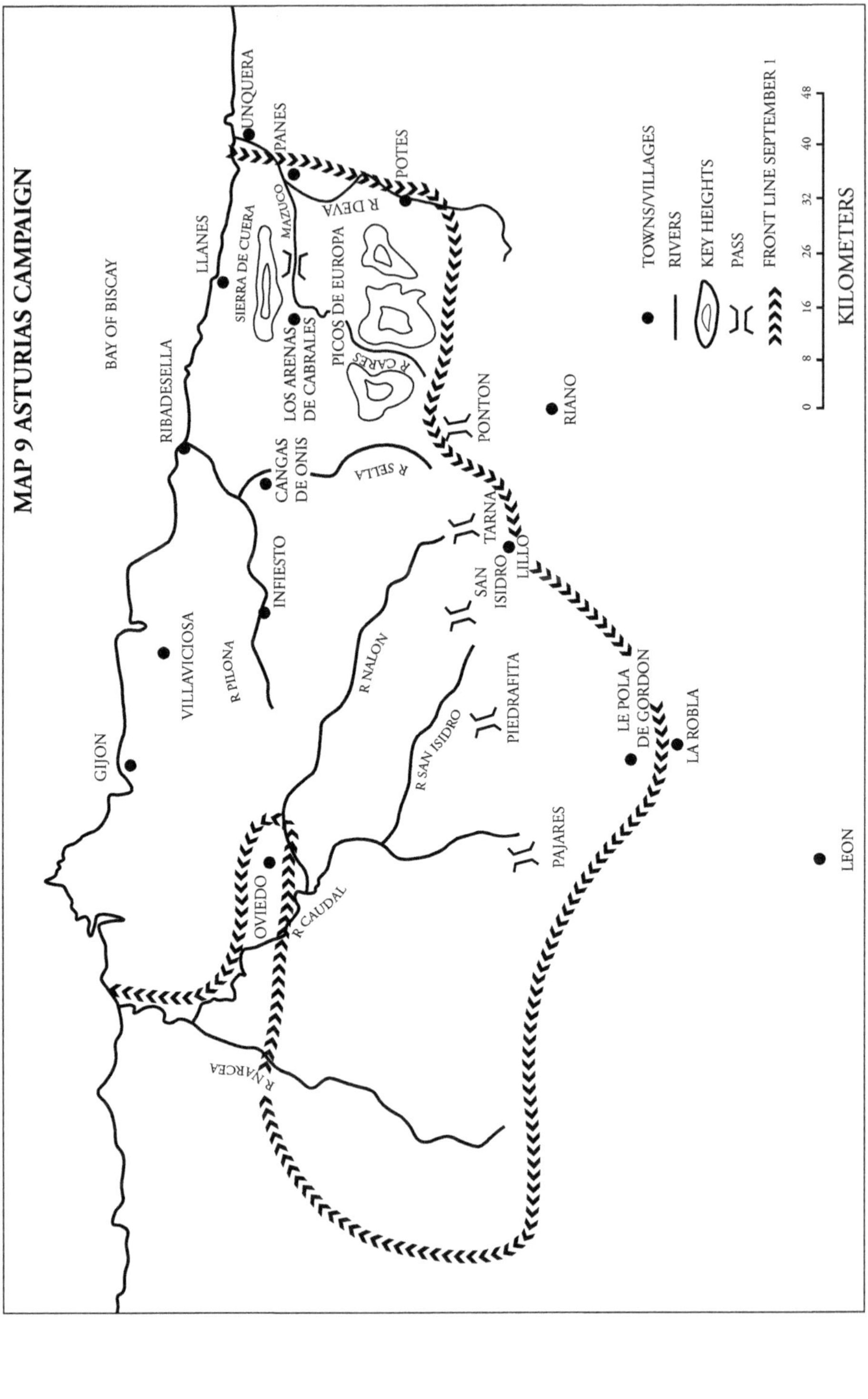
MAP 9 ASTURIAS CAMPAIGN
BAY OF BISCAY
UNQUERA
PANES
POTES
LLANES
SIERRA DE CUERA
MAZUCO
R DEVA
PICOS DE EUROPA
LOS ARENAS DE CABRALES
R CARES
RIBADESELLA
CANGAS DE ONIS
R SELLA
PONTON
RIANO
TARNA
LILLO
SAN ISIDRO
INFIESTO
VILLAVICIOSA
R PILONA
R NALON
PIEDRAFITA
R SAN ISIDRO
LE POLA DE GORDON
LA ROBLA
GIJON
PAJARES
OVIEDO
R CAUDAL
LEON
R NARCEA
TOWNS/VILLAGES
RIVERS
KEY HEIGHTS
PASS
FRONT LINE SEPTEMBER 1
0 8 16 26 32 40 48
KILOMETERS

infantry battalions.[57] Their casualties were relatively light, some 2,900 men, of which 2,000 were suffered by the Italians who had fought in the more easily defended valleys.

The Asturias Campaign

The Republic's northern enclave was now only 125km across and 75km deep, making its fall inevitable sooner or later. Dávila was determined to make it sooner, for with the fall rapidly approaching he recognized the weather would break and winter might give the defenders a six-month respite. Franco's staff ensured he had adequate supplies, which allowed the advance to be renewed on September 1.[58] Unusually for the Spanish Army, instead of issuing a detailed instruction, Dávila simply issued an outline one, leaving detailed planning to his corps commander.[59]

The Asturias was the bailiwick of the Nationalist Brigadier General Antonio Aranda, an infantry officer who had distinguished himself in the heroic siege of Oviedo, which he had held against overwhelming odds.[60] His 8th Division was upgraded to VIII Corps on May 15 and he now had (west to east) the 83rd, 81st, and 82nd Divisions under Colonel Pablo Martín Alonso, Brigadier General Salvador Múgica, and Lieutenant Colonel José Ceano-Viva respectively, while in the Oviedo salient were Aranda's mobile reserve, Colonel Vicente Lafuente's 108th Division and the static Oviedo Brigade under Colonel Garcia Navarro, a total of 41 battalions and 33,000 men.

Aranda would act as the anvil for the twin hammers of Solchaga and Ferrer, with the 61st and 62nd Divisions which were unchanged since taking Santander. Their combined strength was 54,960 men (84 battalions), supported by Múgica's 81st Division with 19,700 men. During September the Republicans launched a desperate diversionary offensive from Barcelona toward Saragossa and this led to the withdrawal of Bastico's troops, but the Nationalists could still count upon 250 guns together with 200 German and Spanish aircraft.

The Republican defenses in the east of the enclave followed the north–south line of the River Deva, stiffened by the Sierra del Cuera some 10km to the west, before leading into the Picos de Europa (Europe's Peaks) some 20km inland. One road ran through rolling coastal countryside north of the Sierra and another from Panes westward along the valley of the River Cares to Los Arenes de Cabrales (Cabrales) and then to Cangas de Onís on the River Sella. The Picos, which are split into three massifs with the western one split by the Cares, which has created a 1.5km-deep gorge, feature several peaks over

2,600m. These were the Asturians' bastion with only tracks into the northern massifs from the Panes–Cangas de Onís road.

The Cares flows north then east, with the River Sella flowing from near the Ponton Pass north to the coast at Ribadesella, with a tributary of the Pilona flowing eastward past Infiesto. The Republican line west of the Picos wound through the Cantabrian Mountains, bulging southward at La Pola de Gordon, where it defended the entrance to three rivers flowing northwest of Oviedo to the sea. These rivers were, east to west, the 153km-long Nalon, the San Isidro, a tributary of the Caudal, and the Caudal itself, and to deny enemy access to them the Republicans would have to hold the passes (east to west) of Tarna (Nalon), San Isidro, and Piedrafita (San Isidro) and Pajares (Caudal). With Oviedo still almost surrounded and linked by a narrow corridor to Nationalist territory, the only practical solution was to repeat the successful strategy at Santander and strike from the east and south.

Solchaga was on the Deva and planned to outflank the Picos from the north. Alonso Vega would advance along the coast followed by García-Valiño, who would then swing south to take the Sierra del Cuera. South of these heights Bautista and Abriat would advance westward to Cabrales and Cangas. Muñoz Grandes and Latorre would pin down the enemy in the Picos while Ferrer's 62nd Division would strike west of the mountains at the Tarna and San Isidro passes as Múgica struck at the Piedrafita and Pajares passes. With the enemy line taken off its foundations Ferrer and Múgica would advance northwest to complete the relief of Oviedo while Lafuente and Garcia Navarro would strike north from Oviedo to Gijon and meet Solchaga's troops, driving along the coast, and south to meet Múgica.

The Council of Asturias under the vain Socialist Belarmino Tomás had established a regime whose repressive policies matched those of the Soviet Union at that time. It was shocked by Gámir's failure to hold Santander and even as the Nationalists approached the Deva the council declared Asturian territory independent, sacked Gámir on August 29, and replaced him with Prada, a Communist in all but name.[61]

Prada, aged 54, was a regular officer who had retired when the Republic was established and acted as a tutor for potential students to military academies. He rallied to the government and served on the Madrid front where he became a corps commander. He had arrived in the enclave only a few weeks earlier and it is unclear why he was so rapidly promoted. Continuity of command was maintained by retaining Major Francisco Ciutat, himself a Communist, as chief of staff and they reorganized the army as best they could, aided by Gorev. However, the rural population was largely conservative and there was an active Fifth Column which on one occasion ambushed a brigade near the coast at Aviles and inflicted many casualties.[62]

Prada had 14 divisions with only 25 brigades (113 battalions), including four Basque and two Santanderino, but all were understrength leaving him with a total of 80,500 men and 196 guns as well as miniscule air support including a dozen fighters.[63] Lieutenant Colonel Javier Linares held the west of the enclave with 35,000 men of XVII CE (59, 60, 61, 62, and 63 DI), leaving the key defense of the east to Gálan's XIV CE with 49, 50, and 51 DI on the Deva, XV CE (still under García Vayas) with 53, 52, 54, and 55 DI in and around the Picos, and XVI CE (Lieutenant Colonel José Gállego) west of the Picos with 57 and 58 DI.

The offensive opened on September 1 with the usual massive air and artillery bombardment, the Condor Legion ground-attack aircraft using carpet bombing for the first time. But this was to be no walk-over and after the initial shock the Republicans fought stubbornly.[64] The campaign would be a prolonged conflict fought in conditions of frequent fog, drizzle increasing to downpours, and decreasing temperatures, conditions that at least one Navarrese commander, the military historian Colonel Ramon Salas, regarded as the most exhausting of the war.

Alonso Vega had the easiest task, for he was able to break out of the Deva bridgehead at Unquera with armored support and by September 4 had advanced some 20km, pushing back 50 DI to take Llanes and forcing the defenders to create an *ad hoc* force, Division A, from its two coastal brigades. The remaining brigade was in the Sierra de Cuera where García-Valiño and later Alonso Vega became involved in what would prove to be a prolonged and debilitating battle. The threat to Alonso Vega's brigade, and the fierceness of Republican resistance, slowed his advance westward and it reached the River Sella to take Ribadesella only on September 27. Alonso Vega was not with them, for he was wounded on September 6 and replaced by Colonel Heli Ronaldo Tella.

The Sierras, which are 30km long and only 6km from the sea, consist of a series of east–west ridges with steep slopes. They are more than 800m high, with the tallest heights, mostly in the south, being Pico Turbina (1,315m) and Pena Blanca, actually three peaks of which the highest is 1,176m. The road south from Llanes to Cangas runs through the El Mazuco Pass in the western part of the Sierras, 16km south of Llanes, the pass being dominated on the northeastern side by the Sierra Llabres and to the south by the Penas Blancas and Pico Turbina.

It was Solchaga's intention for Alonso Vega (later Tella) to drive along the coast while García-Valiño pushed down the Mazuco Pass to link up with

Bautista and Abriat as they advanced toward Cangas. Their operation began well, with Abriat taking Potes on September 2, but as they pushed westward the defense in the Sierra was strengthened with 54 DI and reinforcements from XV and XVI CE, some of which created the *ad hoc* Division B.[65]

The first attacks, on September 6, were beaten off as Bautista tried to strike from the south, but despite overwhelming air and artillery support (15 batteries) progress was grindingly slow, the defenders sometimes rolling barrels of explosives down the slopes. By September 8, 54 DI had been reduced from 6,000 to 1,644 men but the defenders were aided by the rapidly changing weather and on that day clear, sunny skies gave way to clouds, rain, and even fog. On September 11 Tella was brought in on García-Valiño's left and the two were now being supported by the heavy cruiser *Almirante Cervera* as the Condor Legion used incendiary bombs. But the defenders were sometimes able to reduce the effects of the bombardment by hugging the enemy positions.

Dávila was now so concerned about the lack of progress that he considered recalling the CTV which had been deployed to meet the Republican relief offensive toward Saragossa.

Renewed attacks saw Tella penetrate the Sierra Llabres on September 13 as Bautista, supported by Abriat, struck from the south toward the Pico Turbina. The writing was now on the wall, and that day Prada ordered the preparation of a new defense line west of the Mazuco Pass. The following day García-Valiño drove a wedge into the pass, which he secured on September 15, while Bautista took Pico Turbina and pushed along the southern road to take Cabrales supported by Abriat. The Republicans fell back to the Bedon but retained a foothold in the heights. Tella and Abriat, with 16 battalions, vainly tried to storm the heights on September 16 but the following day Abriat encircled them from the south and linked up with Tella, although rain and fog grounded air support. Division B continued to resist stubbornly but when the Navarrese took the peaks on September 22 the surviving defenders retreated to the new defenses west of the pass. A force which reportedly never exceeded 5,000 had held back more than 30,000 for a fortnight in a truly epic struggle but, ultimately, it undermined the defense of the Asturias.

The Nationalists hastily reorganized and after a brief pause consolidated their hold east of the Picos despite heavy rain. On October 10 Cangas de Onís was taken, bringing the Navarrese to the burst banks of the Sella which prevented any further exploitation of their success, but they had now outflanked the Picos de Europa bastion which was rapidly abandoned.

While the battle for the Sierra de Cuera had slowed the Nationalist advance from the east it had also sucked in substantial forces from XV and XVI CE, especially the latter, to weaken the defense of the southern passes. Aranda was able to exploit this when he joined the battle on September 9 using Múgica and Gistau to strike the southwestern face of the La Pola de Gordon salient to take the Pajares Pass. The Nationalist advance began in a rain storm and against bitter resistance, which meant that it took three days to take La Pola de Gordon, but Múgica's men fought their way over the heights shielding the pass which fell on September 19.

All too aware of the weakness of the southern defenses Prada, on September 13, placed the remnants of XVI CE under Linares of XVII CE, who used the remnants to create two *ad hoc* task forces, Divisions C and D, and to coordinate their operations more effectively he created the León Passes Defense Group (Agrupación de Defensa de los Puertos de León) to hold the passes. Their frequent and ferocious counterattacks now halted Múgica's advance and delayed the fall of the Piedrafita Pass. Fearful that his forces would be stuck in the mountains during the winter, Dávila changed tack and decided upon a new advance from the south.

He gave Aranda tactical command of Solchaga's left, the brigades of Muñoz Grandes with Latorre, now freed by the enemy's abandonment of the Picos de Europa, and with Ceano's 82nd Division they struck east of the Pajares Pass on September 25. Ceano struck from Lillo while the Navarrese advanced from Riano on September 25 toward the San Isidro and Tarna passes respectively. The Navarrese fought their way along the Sierra de Tarna, north of the pass, which fell on September 30, easing Ceano's advance to the San Isidro Pass which was in his hands by October 1. After regrouping the Nationalists began to push down the Nalon and San Isidro valleys from October 5.

Republican morale was now collapsing both at the front and in the rear. The politicians demanded draconian action to restore discipline by shooting those who withdrew, but reports that Prada executed a score of officers, including three brigade and six battalion commanders, may be exaggerated.[66] Certainly two 54 DI officers caught trying to flee in a speed boat loaded with silver were shot, but mass shootings would probably have encouraged surrender and desertion. The Mayor of Gijon fled and there were arrests of even the pro-Republican Asaltos on the charge of disloyalty.

On October 14 the Nationalists renewed their advance against declining resistance and the following day Aranda and Solchaga met at Infiesto, some 30km southeast of Gijon. Republican Premier Negrín in far away Valencia demanded the Asturias fight on but, after hearing a pessimistic report from their military leaders on October 17, the Council of the Asturias decided upon flight by sea led by its leaders, Tomás, Prada, Ciutat, and Galán, while most of the Russians were flown out.[67] Prada reached the heartland and in March 1938 replaced Casado as commander, first of the Andalusian Army and then the Estremadura Army. He became the last commander of the Central Army on March 12, 1939 and surrendered weeks later. The Nationalists jailed him and after his release he lived in Madrid, where he died in 1962. Galán reached the heartland in November and would later distinguish himself.

The capture on October 19 of Villaviciosa, some 15km away from Gijon, heralded the final act, with a Fifth Column rising on October 20 to seize control of the port and capture 22 battalions.[68] The commander of the Trubia arms factory, Colonel José Franco, possibly the only senior officer in the area, surrendered Gijon and ensured the safety of some 200 political prisoners, although he would later be shot by the victors. The following day the Nationalists entered Gijon, and the northern enclave ceased to exist, with most of the defending forces either returning home or surrendering. Several thousand took to the mountains to fight a guerrilla war of declining effect, leading to a ferocious counterinsurgency campaign which largely contained the threat by March 1938, although the embers remained and would occasionally flare into life over the next decade.

The success of the Nationalists' northern campaigns was aided by their artillery and air superiority but these were catalysts. The Nationalists focused their efforts on key parts of the front and succeeded because of the tactical skill of their leaders at all levels, possibly reaping the first benefits of the centralization of Nationalist Army training. The absence of unity among the defenders was as severe a handicap as their limited armaments, and ultimately the Nationalist determination to crush the enclave outweighed the nationalism and political will of the defenders. They suffered some 133,000 casualties and 100,000 prisoners, many of whom entered the Nationalist Army's ranks after being "purified," together with a substantial amount of war material which included, according to a Republican report, 58 batteries with 188 guns including 26 heavy.[69] The Nationalists themselves suffered some 110,000 casualties but gained control of 1½ million people and control of a third of the country's industrial production, including almost all the steel and 60 percent of coal.[70] The 65,000 men freed allowed Franco to create a strategic reserve which he now proposed to use to end the war.

With the elimination of the Republican enclave the Army of the North was reorganized for a campaign eastward, still under Dávila, while Vigón after the war became Air Minister and held senior technical posts.

Notes

1 For Villarreal see Aznar, pp. 298–304; Beevor, pp. 203–204, 226; Engel, *Operations*, pp. 75–83.

2 For a contemporary view of these brigades see Aragon Gomez, *Con Intendencia Militar de las Gloriosas Brigadas Navarras.*

3 For the Bilbao campaign see Alcofar, *Air*, pp. 191–195, 198; Arias, pp. 15 9–181; Aznar, pp. 393–426; Beevor, pp. 223–236; Cardona, pp. 147–155, 168–170; Coverdale, p. 279; Engel, *Operations*, pp. 91–104; Hildago, *La Ayuda Alemana a España*, pp. 135–142 (hereafter Hildago); Kindélan, pp. 75–86; Lojendio, pp. 269–290; Martinez, *Vizcaya*, pp. 75–197; Martínez and Martínez, pp. 156–172; Meredith, *Phoenix*, pp. 576–595; Muria, pp. 99–110, 185–186; Proctor, pp. 117–144; Saiz, vol. 2, pp. 431–453, 489–500; Salas, *Air*, pp. 185–192, 230–235; Salas, *Army*, vol. 3, pp. 1851–1945; Salas, *Guernica*, pp. 75–11 (which has much useful information about the campaign to the end of April); Alcofar, *Air*, pp. 180–195, 198–201; Alcofar, *CTV*, pp. 113–123; Permuy, pp. 56–57; Proctor, pp. 117–144; Ries and Ring, pp. 56–68; Sole and Villarroya, *Espana en llama*, pp. 77–92 (hereafter Sole and Villarroya); George Steer, *The Tree of Gernika* (with some useful maps) (hereafter, Steer); Thomas, pp. 612–617, 623–631, 680, 687–688, 690–693; Vidal, pp. 229–247; Håkan site. The Spanish Civil War & Legion section of the Axis History Forum website often has much valuable detail.

4 Strength on March 31 from Salas, *Guernica*, Annex 7. The Condor Legion had 32 bombers while the Italian aircraft were all fighters but were later joined by bombers.

5 See James S. Corum, *The Luftwaffe*, pp. 140–144 (hereafter Corum); Engel, *Operations*, p. 94.

6 Quoted in Corum, pp. 143–144.

7 Howson, *Arms*, p. 2n.

8 Engel, *Brigadas*; Vizcaya, p. 27. They were I CE de Euzkadi (CEE); II CE de Santanderino (CES), and II, III CE de Asturio (CEA.).

9 Thomas, p. 542. The BA 6 used the same turret as the T-26 tank.

10 The Nationalists were unaware of these changes when they attacked. Martinez, *Vizcaya*, pp. 36–37.

11 Howson, *Air*, pp. 164, 192–196, 213–218; Salas, *Guernica*, pp. 112–113, Appendix 14.

12 For the Iron Belt see Martinez, *Vizcaya*, pp. 46–47; see also Cinturon de Hierro website.

13 This was equivalent, at prewar exchange rates to $3,482,000 or $61,000,000 in early 21st-century terms.

14 Martinez, *Vizcaya*, p. 46. Sketch 4 is based upon Goicoechea's plans. He would gain postwar fame designing the trains used in the Irun–Madrid express, the TALGO or Tren Articulado Ligero Goicoechea Oriol.

15 The same problem was encountered by Hindenburg and Ludendorff on the Western Front during the fall of 1918 and by Hitler on the Eastern Front in 1943.

16 During the day Nationalist batteries fired 150 tonnes of shells while 7.75 tonnes of bombs were dropped. Salas, *Air*, p. 187.

17 Salas, *Guernica*, Annex 14, shows that there were two missions involving eight bomber sorties which dropped more than 7.75 tonnes of bombs.

18 Salas, *Guernica*, pp. 91, 118, Annex 14.

19 Steer, p. 99.

20 During the day the Italians flew 96 sorties, UK NA HW 21/2 AS/0158.

21 See Axis History forum website and "Buscaglia's" comments of May 31, 2006 on the background to what became the Santona Pact.

22 For the bombing of Guernica see Gonzalez Alvarez, pp. 204–219; Hildago, pp. 142–145; Meredith, pp. 585–587; Saiz, vol. 2, pp. 443–446; Salas, *Army*, vol. 3, pp. 1884–1895;

Salas, *Guernica*, pp. 121–167, Appendix 33, based upon BA-MA RL7/57 and RL2/V, and Appendix 35: Testimony of Lieutenent Colonel Karl von Knauer on February 6, 1974; Sole and Villarroya, pp. 82–92; Thomas, Gordon and Max Morgan-Witts, *The Day Guernica Died* (hereafter TMW); Steer, pp. 236–245. See also Arias, pp. 166–177; Corum, pp. 124–154; Beevor, pp. 231–233; Hooton, *Phoenix*, pp. 131–132; Nasseas, *Air*, p. 194; Proctor, pp. 127–129; Sole and Villarroya, pp. 82–92; Vizcaya, p. 106ff; Thomas, pp. 624–629. BA MA N671/1. UKNA HW 21/2 AS/0158.

23 The Spanish seem content to blame these events on the Germans and few Spanish documents have emerged about Guernica.

24 The doctrine, its evolution, and development to 1940 are discussed in Corum, pp. 134–144.

25 In German they are written Gernika and Gerika, and Steer also used this name for Guernica, while transcripts from Richthofen's diary sometimes refer to Guernicaiz for Guerricaiz. The confusion between the two names has led several German accounts to claim that Italian bombers struck Guernica, but Italian signals and Richthofen's diary state that they bombed Guerricaiz. For the geography see Martinez, *Vizcaya*, Map 7, and Steer.

26 TMW, p. 106. Unceta produced the Astra 400/Model 1921 pistol which was the standard weapon of the Spanish armed forces and law enforcement. It also produced sporting weapons and a submachine gun. Steer, p. 230. During the Monarchy aerial gas bombs were filled in a Guernica factory. Armas p. 425. A Nationalist press officer would later tell an American journalist, "We bombed it and why not?"

27 For evidence on decision-making on April 25–26 see Richthofen's diaries together with TMW, pp. 52–53, 103–107, 117–123, 170, 174, 186–187, 205–213. Much of this is based upon the memories of Lieutenant Hans Asmus, the Assistant Operations Officer.

28 Richthofen's entry of April 27 noted that he was worried about communications and there were only two unreliable radio/telephone stations. Richthofen's forward headquarters had only a field telephone link and communications were improved only from late April with the provision of two frequencies to direct air operations from Burgos, followed by a radio truck in May. Meredith, pp. 578, 585–587n.48. In Salas, Annex 35, Knaur notes that he first bombed Guerricaiz, then the Rentaria bridge. Fuchs would distinguish himself during the 1940 Norway campaign and on the Eastern Front.

29 HW 21/2 AS/0158.

30 Sole and Villarroya, pp. 82–83.

31 The enclave received 8 I-15 fighters and some 14 Koolhoven FK 51 light bombers. Howson, *Air*, pp. 192–201, 213–215; Salas, *Air*, pp. 214–218; Thomas, p. 680.

32 For this airline see Howson, *Air*, pp. 291–292. Radio and wire communications between Bilbao and the outside world remained uninterrupted.

33 Alcofar, *CTV*, pp. 116–119.

34 For Gamir see Zaragoza, pp. 256–258.

35 Arce, pp. 130–131; Jensen, p. 84. The aircraft was originally smuggled to the Republicans and crossed the lines in the hands of a defecting pilot. Howson, *Arms*, p. 93.

36 Coverdale, p. 280; HW 21/2 AS/0187.

37 Half the six Hs 123s would be lost in the Northern Campaign. Howson, *Air*, pp. 186–187.

38 Putz was a Great War veteran and a French Army reserve officer who resigned his commission to join the Republicans but regained it at the outbreak of World War II. He would serve with the Free French forces and his regiment, spearheaded by a company of former Spanish Republican troops, would be the first Allied troops into Paris in August 1944. He was killed in Alsace in January 1945. See Beevor, *D-Day*, pp. 500–504.

39 Howson, *Air*, pp. 49, 86–87.
40 Salas, *Intervencion*, Anexo 8.
41 UKNA HW 21/2 AS/0187 and 0191.
42 Coverdale, p. 280.
43 Martinez, *El final de frente norte*, pp. 41–42 (hereafter Martinez, *Final*).
44 Llano de la Ecomienda returned to find himself virtually retired. Martínez was arrested upon his return and court-martialed for treason but cleared and became military governor of Madrid. Following Casado's March 1939 coup he became a minister in the National Defense Council, refused to flee, was captured and executed in June 1939.
45 Martinez, *Final*, p. 29.
46 Howson, *Air*, pp. 192–201, 213–215; Salas, *Air*, pp. 244–245.
47 Murias, pp. 119–128; Thomas, pp. 681–682, 720–721. Also see Axis History forum website and "Buscaglia's" comments of May 31, 2006. He reports that there was correspondence in July between the Italian leaders of the Flechas Negras and the Basque leadership.
48 On August 11 the Italian air liaison officer in Salamanca informed Bernasconi that the Nationalist government authorized new bombing of Santander "if the Italian command considered it necessary." UKNA HW 21/3 AS/0230. The Germans had only 27 fighters.
49 For the Santander campaign see Alpert, p. 239; Arias, pp. 181–184; Aznar, pp. 465–484; Beevor, pp. 237–238; Belforte, *Teruel*, pp. 179–214; Cardona, pp. 182–187; Coverdale, pp. 281–284; Engel, *Operations*, pp. 163–174; Hildago, pp. 155–159; Kindélan, pp. 101–103; Larrazabal, *Air*, pp. 244–249; Lojendio, pp. 290–303; Manca di Mores, *L'Impiego dell'Artilleria Italiana nella Guerra di Spagna*, pp. 109–169 (hereafter Manca); Martínez, *Final*, pp. 21–105; Martínez and Martínez, pp. 172–181; Murias, pp. 111–119; Alcofar, *Air*, pp. 210–214; Alcofar, *CTV*, pp. 123–141; Permuy, p. 63; Proctor, pp. 157–161; Ries and Ring, pp. 88–94; Saiz, vol. 2, pp. 544–557; Salas, *Army*, vol. 3, pp. 1947–1982; Sole and Villarroya, pp. 96–97; Thomas, pp. 717–720; Vidal, pp. 275–282; Håkan site. Details of Italian air operations can be found in UK NA HW 21/3.
50 For planning see Engel, *Operations*, pp. 163–169; Martinez, *Norte*, pp. 43–59.
51 The town's industrial facilities were captured intact because the workers refused to allow sabotage. On August 18 Navamorales fled to France by air.
52 Martinez, *Final*, p. 72n.74.
53 Galán's brother José was a divisional commander at the battle of Brunete.
54 Coverdale, pp. 284–294; Murias, pp. 119–128; Nasseas, *CTV*, pp. 134–141; Rodrigo, pp. 167–170. Aguirre's part in these events is uncertain. By November half the Basque prisoners had been released, 5,600 remained in jail, while 5,400 were drafted into labor battalions. Although 510 death sentences were handed down only 57 were apparently carried out. See "Buscaglia's" comments of May 31, 2006 in the Axis History Forum website.
55 On August 29 Bastico reported that his forces had expended 45,000 shells. Martinez, *Final*, Anexo 6.
56 UK NA HW 21/3. Figures are missing for August 19–20, possibly because the Italians were grounded. An unusual feature of these operations was the use of the Breda Ba 65 ground-attack airplane as either a fighter or reconnaissance aircraft.
57 The Renaults became the Nationalists' 6th Tank Company and nine captured Trubias were joined by nine new vehicles.
58 For the Asturias campaign see Arias, pp. 184–188; Aznar, pp. 517–530; Beevor, pp. 301–302; Belforte, *Teruel*, pp. 224–228; Cardona, pp. 194–196; Engel, *Operations*, pp. 183–188; Hildago, pp. 159–164; Kindélan, pp. 103–104; Lojendio, pp. 303–326; Martinez, *Final*, pp.

109–188; Martínez and Martínez, pp. 181–191; Permuy, p. 63; Proctor, pp. 162–169; Ries and Ring, pp. 94–102; Saiz, vol. 2, pp. 558–572; Salas, *Air*, pp. 259–270; Salas, *Army*, vol. 3, pp. 1982–2019; Thomas, pp. 728–733; Vidal, pp. 292–296; Håkan site.

59 Engel, *Operations*, pp. 183–185, quotes the operations orders which are dated September 1 but must have been published earlier.

60 Thomas, pp. 236, 309–310, 384–385.

61 Gámir would be flown to France, then the "heartland," but his conduct in the north was much criticized. He was given only an infantry brigade until October 12, 1938 when he became Inspector General de Instruccion Militar.

62 Thomas, p. 729n.3.

63 Another figure is 79,500 men with 176 guns, 3,870 automatic weapons, and 45,340 rifles. Salas, *Army*, vol. 4, Cuadro 40.

64 During the campaign the Condor Legion dropped 2,500 tonnes of bombs while their 88mm guns fired 22,500 shells. Ries and Ring, p. 102.

65 A detailed account of the defense of the pass may be found on the El Mazuco impossible defense website based upon Blas, *La guerra civil en Asturias, Tomo 2*, pp. 369–383 (hereafter Blas).

66 Alpert, p. 168.

67 Tomas became the FARE's Commissar General. Gorev was not flown out until later.

68 Four fighters escaped to France and eight were captured. Ries and Ring, p. 101.

69 Armas, p. 267.

70 The Italians suffered 1,941 casualties including 401 dead and missing. Rodrigo, p. 157.

CHAPTER 4

High Tide for the Republic: Brunete and the Aragon Offensive

Battle of Brunete

Observing the northern enclave as it crumbled, the Republican heartland could indulge only in futile hand-wringing. Attempts to pull enemy forces away were made on May 31 by the Central Army around La Granja and by the Eastern Army in Huesca on June 12, but these were half-hearted affairs lacking resources and quickly faded away.[1] This was because, once victory at Guadalajara had secured Madrid's safety, Valencia wished to keep its powder dry for a major offensive to gain the strategic initiative, and much effort was spent during the spring of 1937 considering how to achieve this goal.

The prospects of success rose when Franco transferred most of his reserves to the enclave, but where best to strike? Realizing that the substantial Nationalist First (Madrid) Corps, which held the capital's western suburbs, was exposed, the Central Army's commander and chief of staff, Generals Miaja and Rojo, had been advocating an attack upon Brunete since the dark days of December. They recognized the 54,000 Nationalists, like the wartime French 2nd Army at Verdun, depended upon a single supply line, the Estremadura Highway, running westward through Navalcarnero to Talavera. This lay a mere 6km south of Brunete through which, on March 22, Rojo and Miaja once again advocated attacking to isolate the tip of the enemy salient and five days later produced an outline plan.

Bizarrely, Largo Caballero was cool toward the plan precisely because of the enthusiastic support of chief Soviet advisor Kulik, for the premier was fighting a rearguard action against growing Communist influence and recognized success at Brunete would increase the Communist-dominated Central Army's prestige. Also opposing it were chief of staff Colonel Aureliano Alvarez-Coque de Blas (Coque), supported by his operations chief, Colonel Segismundo

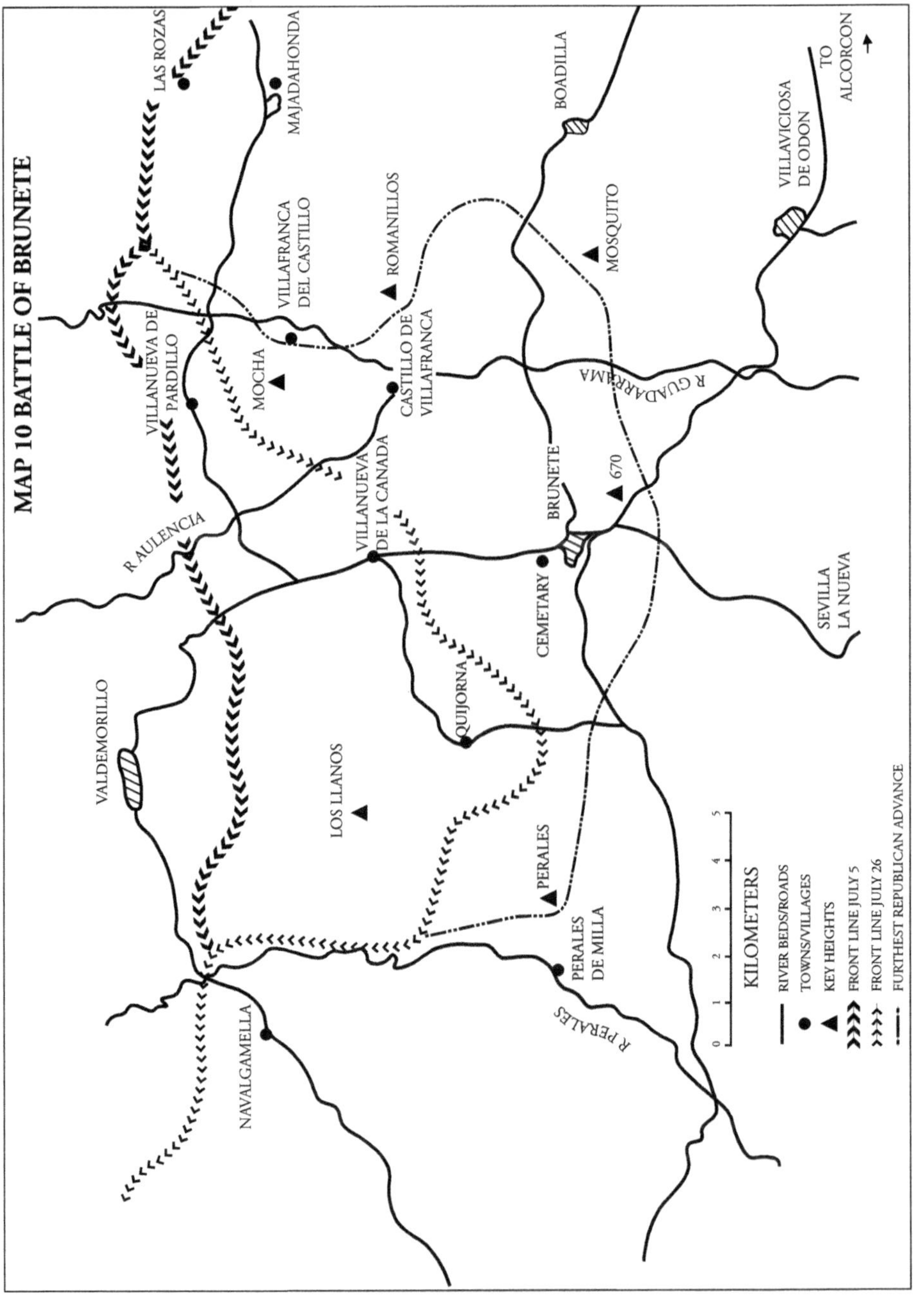
MAP 10 BATTLE OF BRUNETE
LAS ROZAS
MAJADAHONDA
BOADILLA
TO ALCORCON
VILLAVICIOSA DE ODON
VILLAFRANCA DEL CASTILLO
ROMANILLOS
MOSQUITO
VILLANUEVA DE PARDILLO
MOCHA
CASTILLO DE VILLAFRANCA
R GUADARRAMA
R AULENCIA
VILLANUEVA DE LA CANADA
BRUNETE
670
CEMETARY
SEVILLA LA NUEVA
VALDEMORILLO
QUIJORNA
LOS LLANOS
PERALES
PERALES DE MILLA
R PERALES
NAVALGAMELLA
KILOMETERS
0 1 2 3 4 5
RIVER BEDS/ROADS
TOWNS/VILLAGES
KEY HEIGHTS
FRONT LINE JULY 5
FRONT LINE JULY 26
FURTHEST REPUBLICAN ADVANCE

Casado, and a month later, on April 22, they produced an alternative for a three-pronged offensive further west. The Brunete attack was incorporated as a secondary operation together with one at Oropesa, which lay northwest of Talavera on the Madrid–Merida road. The Brunete and Oropesa attacks would isolate the enemy First Corps while the main thrust would be toward Merida in Estremadura, to split Nationalist Spain in two, with D-Day set for May 7.[2] The offensive would be commanded by former IV CE commander Jurado, aged 44, a gunner and Rif War veteran who had shown considerable competence in the battles around Madrid and had been IV CE commander at Guadalajara.[3]

Coque's ambitious plan required Central Army resources but the vain Miaja was loath to transfer them, especially when Largo Caballero rubbed salt in the wound by eliminating the Brunete attack. The Russian advisors, recognizing that success at Merida would enhance "the Spanish Lenin's" prestige, now encouraged Miaja to delay transferring forces, and D-Day passed quietly. A new D-Day was set for May 21 but on May 14 the Communist-dominated FARE refused to provide air support for the Estremadura offensive and the next day the Communists, exploiting a political crisis in Barcelona, ambushed Largo Caballero at a cabinet meeting and forced his resignation as both premier and war minister, to be replaced in the former role by Negrín while Rojo replaced Coque, then sidelined Casado to remove opposition to the Brunete operation. Strangely, although he cancelled the Estremadura offensive, it was a concept with which he became obsessed—Plan "P."

Rojo's objectives were to destroy the First Corps and draw enemy reserves from the northern front. He substantially increased the assault force from the nine brigades proposed in March to 20, possibly influenced by his Soviet advisor, Malinovsky. However, Rojo was a traditionalist who believed in the direct destruction of the enemy forces rather than cutting their supply lines—the prime purpose of the Merida plan—and he now focused upon expanding his original plan into an ambitious double envelopment of First Corps.

The double envelopment concept reflected the pre-Great War obsession with battles of encirclement, such as Hannibal's victory at Cannae, although it proved impossible to implement. In Madrid the secondary southern probe would be launched from the southern suburbs by II CE, which was under Lieutenant Colonel Carlos Romero, appointed only on July 1. The son of an army officer, Romero retired when the Republic was established and focused on Freemason, diplomatic, and engineering work but rallied to the government in July 1936. The main blow would be launched by V

(Modesto) and the new XVIII CE around Brunete which controlled the road system north of the Estremadura Highway. Both assault forces would be concentrated upon narrow fronts, as wartime experience suggested that this was more effective.[4]

Modesto was a 29-year-old Andalusian who worked in a saw mill before joining the army and serving in Morocco where he rose to the rank of corporal. This cachet earned him the leadership of the Communist militia after he joined the Party in 1930, and in the summer of 1936 he would expand it into their elite Fifth Regiment. He lacked political skill or ambition but was a very competent leader, although autocratic, sarcastic, and brutal. During World War II he served with the Red Army and died in Prague in 1969.[5]

The Brunete battlefield resembled a Roman arena framed in the north and the east by high ground sharply rising from 620m to more than 700m with peaks such as the Romanillos Ridge in the north and the Mosquito Ridge in the southeast. Two rivers run north-to-south in wide valleys: the Perales in the west and the Guadarrama in the east, fed by its tributary the Aulencia, the two rivers separated by a low, shrub-covered 640-meter ridge along which ran what would become the offensive's prime supply route, the Valdemorillo–Navalcarnero–Brunete road. It was overlooked by the eastern heights from which observers could direct artillery fire.

The gently undulating valleys featured large, open fields used mostly for cereals, with numerous small olive groves, mostly along the banks of the Guadarrama, and short oaks and olives in a wood straddling the road 3km north of Brunete. The numerous streams feeding the rivers form deep gullies which scar the plain and are often dry during the summer. The area is sparsely populated—the largest town of Valdemorillo had only 2,000 people while Brunete had half that number and the other villages even less, with Villanueva del Castillo having only 50.

The Valdemorillo–Brunete road was of beaten dirt, as were the lanes criss-crossing the plain. Where these lanes met were small abandoned villages: from west to east in the Perales Valley Quijorna and to the south Perales de Milla, in the upper Guadarrama Valley Villanueva de la Cañada which lay on the road south to Brunete and northeast to Las Rozas passing through Villanueva del Pardillo. South of the last, on the western bank of the Guadarrama, lay Villafranca del Castillo (hereafter Villafranca). All of these had been turned into strongpoints by the Nationalists.

Rojo's plan, published on June 24, called for a preemptive strike against a reported enemy offensive on the southern front as well as loosening the enemy grip on Madrid and would be launched between July 1–5.[6] The northern force, under Miaja's personal control, would advance in four phases beginning with a nighttime advance of 6km without preparatory artillery preparation to the edge of the strongpoints. Villanueva de la Cañada and Quijorna would then be stormed to open the way initially to Brunete but ultimately to the Estremadura Highway. In the key second phase Brunete would be occupied and Modesto would then send a brigade-sized, tank-tipped motorized column south to take Navalcarnero and cut the highway. Meanwhile, Jurado would extend the Republican bridgehead eastward across the Guadarrama into the heights and toward both Boadilla and Villaviciosa to secure the salient's communications as well as shielding the bridgehead's eastern flank.

Reserves would assemble north of Villanueva de la Cañada to aid Jurado's advance southeast to the Estremadura Highway and then to Alcorcon, whose fall would tighten the Republican grip on the road. He would also expand the bridgehead by taking Las Rozas. Once the highway was cut the Republican forces would squeeze the life out of First Corps like a boa constrictor, a task which would be aided by splitting the pocket in two.[7] Romero would strike northwestward from the Villaverde-Usera sector in the general direction of Alcorcon to link up with the northern advance, although Russian observers would later criticize the lack of armor and artillery assigned to Romero who had little ammunition.[8] Once the salient was eliminated the troops were to prepare for an assault a week later upon the Jarama salient.

Rojo was worried about the corps' ability to conduct a flexible battle using their initiative to exploit local successes especially in a command structure of officers, commissars and Soviet advisors, where most divisional commanders and commissars were Communists with their own agenda. In an accompanying document, *Conditions for the Execution and Characteristics for the Madrid Front Maneuver* (*Condiciones de Ejecucion y caracteristicas de la Maniobra en el Frente de Madrid*), he emphasized the fact that the enemy was weak and over-extended and urged his commanders to ignore threats to their flanks because success depended upon surprise and audacity.[9]

For the main blow in the north, Miaja had 85,000 men, with 20 brigades, 100 tanks, and 33 batteries with 96 guns, including two 240mm howitzers, while for direct support there would be a dozen antitank batteries with 45mm guns.[10] Miaja would be supported by 500 trucks, with Modesto and Jurado each having 200 to exploit tactical opportunities, but the vehicle fleet included only 74 ambulances despite an anticipated daily casualty rate of 1,600. Romero's two divisions would be supported by 30 tanks, seven field and five antitank batteries with 34 guns.[11] The supply dumps were adequate for a relatively short battle, including 375 tonnes of gasoline and oil.[12]

Most of the FARE would support the offensive which would be shielded by half the DECA's antiaircraft batteries, nine of them covering railroads. Air strength is usually given as 200 aircraft in 13 squadrons but hopes that the first 200 Russian-trained pilots would reach the front for the offensive were dashed. Before they arrived the Russians withdrew pilots from several fighter squadrons and it appears that only nine, with 133 aircraft, were actually available, including 50 serviceable fighters.[13] The air campaign against airfield and communications centers would begin from D-4 and be extended to enemy factories and troop columns from D-2. The northern attack would be supported by 15 fighters in the ground-attack role.

To conceal Miaja's concentration, the divisions moved to the front in small units to carefully camouflaged assembly points. From June 25 through July 4 the gunners arrived and began to familiarize themselves with the battlefield and their targets, while Modesto, with his divisional and brigade commanders, conducted personal reconnaissance of the sector from July 3.[14] Radio communications, all encrypted, were kept to a minimum, while rumors were spread that the concentration was for an offensive into the Sierra de Guadarrama with a diversion at Brunete.

The deception initially succeeded when the Nationalists, inevitably, got wind of the offensive and air reconnaissance confirmed in late June reports from observation posts of preparatory work. Yet Army of the Center commander Saliquet remained uncertain about enemy intentions until the day before the attack. The First Corps' front was over-extended, running east from the River Perales to the southern outskirts of Madrid. Its commander, Brigadier General Luis Valdés, had in the line, from west to east, Colonel Irutetagoyena's 11th Division, Colonel Asensio's 12th Division, and Colonel Juan Yagüe's 14th Division, while General Barrón's 13th Division, the "Black Hand" (*La Mano Negra*) as it was called, was regrouping and reorganizing around Navalcarnero with 13,000 men. West of the Perales was the Seventh Corps, under Varela, whose front extended into the Sierra Guadarrama. On June 28 he had activated Colonel Ricardo Serrador's 71st Division to hold Navalagamella on the boundary with First Corps, and this would act as the shoulder to the enemy breakthrough. From June 3 through June 16 there had been major changes on the Madrid front, with 71st Division becoming 11th Division and 75th Division becoming 71st Division, while the need for Operational Level reserves saw Eighth Corps create, on June 3, 108th Division, and the Moroccan Corps the 150th Division. On July 4 Franco ordered Dávila to pull 5th Navarrese Brigade out of the line and be prepared to send it to the Army of the Center.[15]

The Brunete front was part of Irutetagoyena's sector, with his III Brigade under Lieutenant Colonel Abelardo Mancebo having its command post in Brunete, but Republican intelligence had little detailed information about the defenses.[16] The front line consisted of battalion strongpoints at Quijorna, Villanueva de la Cañada, and Villanueva del Pardillo, while there were company strongpoints at Villafranca and the nearby Castillo de Villafranca, at the confluence of the Aulencia and the Guadarrama. They were organized for all-round defense, with a double trench line and one or two rows of barbed wire 300m away, all covered by machine-gun positions in stone buildings. Most strongpoints had a couple of antitank guns, but even if tanks penetrated the outer defenses they could not drive down the villages' narrow streets. Mancebo had a conscript battalion at Villanueva del Pardillo and two Andalusian Fascist battalions, one split between Villanueva de la Cañada and Villafranca while the other held Quijorna and Castillo del Villafranca. At Brunete were 60 officers, signalers, and clerical staff with crews for two antitank guns, which were its only defense, and there was also a casualty clearing station with 20 doctors, nurses, and stretcher-bearers. There was little artillery support: two 105mm howitzers at Villanueva de la Cañada, where Republican intelligence claimed there were four, a 75mm battery at Quijorna and around Navalgamela a battery, each of 75mm and 105mm guns together with two 155mm howitzers. The defenders had sparse air support, consisting of only an understrength Italian fighter group and a Spanish reconnaissance squadron, a total of 35 aircraft.

Only from June 30 did the Nationalists become aware that there was a serious threat to First Corps with a steady stream of deserters warning of major blows at Quijorna and Brunete. Despite Valdés's illness his well-run corps responded and on July 4 he ordered Barrón to send two Moorish tabors and a 155mm battery to reinforce the line, one company occupying the Los Llanos Ridge north of Quijorna to act as a breakwater and to maintain contact with Serrador. On July 5 deserters not only confirmed the strength of Miaja's threat but also warned of Romero's planned attack, yet the defenders remained confident to the point of complacency. That afternoon Miaja's troops assembled at Valdemorillo to hear speeches by Negrín and Prieto exhorting them to new efforts then formed up at dusk.

They marched south from 22:00, led by Campesino's 46 DI followed by Lister's 11 DI which later crossed the Valdemorillo–Brunete road, while Walter's 35 DI remained in reserve. Modesto had ordered Campesino's two brigades to take the Los Llanos Ridge and Quijorna, while Lister's three brigades would isolate and storm Brunete before seizing jump-off points for Walter's advance southeast upon Villaviciosa. Jurado's spearhead was Carabiniero

Lieutenant Colonel José Maria Galán's 34 DI which was to isolate, then storm Villanueva de la Cañada with one brigade while using the other two to hold the western Aulencia. Once the village fell, Galán was to push eastward along the Brunete–Boadilla road supported by 15 DI under Gal. Their left would be covered by Major José Maria Enciso's 10 DI which would take Villanueva del Pardillo and Villafranca. Miaja retained operational control of Walter's division, Kléber's 45 DI, Duràn's 47 DI, and the tank reserve, a total of 20,000 men and 23 guns.[17]

The troops marched down the valleys and assembled near their objectives awaiting the bombardment which came down at 05:30 on July 6. Limited ammunition restricted it to 30 minutes, with the corps batteries striking Quijorna and Villanueva de la Cañada while the army artillery group struck the enemy rear. Owing to the absence of suitable observation posts, as well as clouds of dust, it was difficult to correct fire, especially upon small targets such as antitank guns, thus wasting most shells. Lister decentralized fire control, which made his batteries more responsive to the situation, in contrast to Jurado who insisted on authorizing all changes in the fire plan, which was not coordinated with the air force.

Consequently Galán's assault went awry and only after strengthening his assault force did he penetrate the defenses, although a dozen of his tanks, unsupported by infantry, were picked off by antitank guns.[18] In the early afternoon a frustrated Jurado ordered first the corps cavalry then Gal's two International Brigades to join the assault while Miaja demanded he take the village, "and if the infantry would not go forward, to place a troop or battery of guns so as to fire behind our own troops to make them do so."[19] The International Brigades were scheduled to advance upon Boadilla but could not bypass Villanueva de la Cañada due to the defenders' fire and were forced to turn westward during the late afternoon. For two hours they battled their way into the northern and eastern trenches but were unable to enter the village. They and Galán renewed their assault at 19:00 after further artillery preparation and the support of 25 aircraft, but the village did not fall until 07:30.[20] The defenders had lost a third of their men, including an alleged 500 prisoners, but had bought Varela 24 hours while the two assault divisions became hopelessly intermingled thanks to what was described as Jurado's and Galán's "marginal disorganization and helplessness."[21]

As the battle raged Modesto faced his own problems, for when Campesino tried to isolate Quijorna he discovered the village defenses extended through a wired trench line to the walled cemetery some 700m to the southeast. He hastily regrouped his assault brigade, delaying the attack until after dawn and thus alerting the defenders, who stopped them. A new artillery bombardment was arranged but Campesino's men remained in their foxholes owing to intense fire while an evening attack upon the cemetery was repulsed. The assault upon Los Llanos also failed, leaving both strongpoints in enemy hands, with Campesino's other brigade content to dig in along the east bank of the Perales. The failure to isolate Quijorna allowed it to be reinforced by two battalions and a battery of 155mm howitzers!

By mid-morning reports trickling into Miaja's headquarters painted an alarming picture of assault forces boxed-in by the strongpoints, leaving Lister isolated 5km ahead of the main force, without artillery and dependent upon a trickle of supplies brought in by mule or packhorse, and frustrated by growing resistance. Miaja ordered him to hold his ground until Villanueva had been taken, then during the afternoon he suddenly halted all attacks following false aerial reports of large troop movements in the west and retained Walter to meet this imaginary threat.

Lister, screened by the Battalion Especial, was injured when he fell off his horse, but before dawn he and his men had assembled in woods north of Brunete. At 05:00 his men came out of the mist to envelop Brunete and took it within 90 minutes, inflicting 32 casualties and taking 60 prisoners. However, with his artillery unable to move in the dark and fearing exposure to a counterattack, Lister remained in the village until 09:00 as the sounds of battle grew behind him. He reluctantly pushed forward until token enemy resistance led him to dig in around Brunete and along the Guadarrama.

The Nationalist response was far more dynamic. Despite discovering at dawn the telephone line to his divisional headquarters had been cut by the Battalion Especial, Mancebo managed to alert corps headquarters together with Varela at Seventh Corps and Saliquet at army headquarters. Valdés's staff promptly contacted the Villaviciosa garrison and ordered it to hold the bridge over the Guadarrama at all costs and reinforced them with a Moroccan tabor. Meanwhile, Saliquet ordered Barrón to dispatch anything he had to support Mancebo.

Barrón sent Lieutenant Colonel Jose Alvarez to Villaviciosa, where he organized a scratch force including 320 rear area soldiers as well as Civil Guards. But instead of confining himself to holding the Guadarrama bridge, he advanced upon Brunete and pushed back Lister. By 11:00 Alvarez had established his little command on heights which dominated the town around Hill 670, some 3km southwest of Brunete, then beat off a tank-tipped attack and by the end of the day was reinforced by the First Corps' tabor. Meanwhile other troops marched up from Sevilla la Nueva to establish another two

General Juan Vigón would be one of the architects of the Nationalist victory both as an army chief of staff and as an éminence grise influencing strategic decisions. He was a Germanophile but it was his efficiency that made him one of the few Spanish officers whom the Germans respected. He was certainly not one for whom petulant Condor Legion leaders would refuse to provide air support.

The Heinkel He 51 fighter was developed based upon experience gained at Lipetsk in the Soviet Union. As a fighter it proved inferior to the new generation of Soviet fighters but it proved a valuable fighter-bomber providing tactical air support to Nationalist troops. In the background is a Fokker F/VII/3 tri-motor transport which also helped to fly in Moorish troops. Similar aircraft were used as bombers by both sides.

Lieutenant Colonel Wolfram von Richthofen, a cousin of the Red Baron, pictured at the front with newsreel cameraman. Like most of the Luftwaffe's senior leaders he had received refresher training during the late 1920s in the Soviet Union where many of the Condor Legion's first generation of aircraft were developed. The second generation which replaced them were developed under his direction.

The Republican Army was originally based upon militias whose own leaders were augmented by military and para-military officers. This is symbolised by this picture of one of the most distinguished militia commanders, Major Enrique Lister (left) and General José Miaja, whose reputations were made on the Madrid front. (Courtesy of Marx Memorial Library, London)

reinforced-battalion battle groups a kilometer west of Brunete as a Foreign Legion bandera dug in east of the village, effectively hemming in Lister. All through the day and the night he battered the enemy with air and artillery support but to no avail.

Valdés was temporarily replaced on July 8 by Yagüe, who also retained his division, and with Saliquet responsible for the army the battlefront needed a new leader. This was the cool but flamboyant 46-year-old Varela who established his headquarters at Sevilla la Nueva. Always impeccably dressed with white gloves and his medals, which he was even reputed to wear on his dressing gown, this Carlist son of a regimental bandmaster joined the army as an enlisted man.[22] He so distinguished himself that he ended the Rif War as a colonel after twice winning Spain's highest military award, the Cruz Laureada de San Fernando. He later broadened his experience in military missions, including visits to Germany and France, but was jailed in 1932 for supporting a right-wing uprising.[23] He organized the Requetés but was again jailed in Cadiz, only to be released by Queipo de Llano, and would rise ultimately to corps command.[24] He assumed operational control not only of Barrón's division but also Asensio's 12th Division, although the new front had received only six battalions and two batteries on the first day.

With prospects for starting the Santander offensive clearly evaporating, Franco informed Davila that it would be postponed for several days and he began to milk the northern front of artillery together with German and Italian aircraft. On July 7 he decided to transfer both Bautista's 5th and Alonso Vega's 4th Navarrese Brigades to the Madrid front and formally suspended the Santander offensive. The previous day he ordered the two newly formed Operational Level reserve divisions: Buruaga's 150th Division at Caceres, and Lieutenant Colonel Carlos Gómez-Avellaneda's 108th Division in Galicia, transferred to Saliquet, the latter to dig a new defensive line covering the northern approaches to the Estremadura Highway.[25] Meanwhile Barrón dispatched six battalions and three batteries to prop up the front.

In Madrid Romero's assault in the southern outskirts of Madrid proved disastrous. Following a 40-minute artillery preparation, it struck Yagüe's division occupying a 4km-deep Western Front-style trench system.[26] Some tanks, unsupported by infantry, penetrated forward defenses but were exposed to heavy fire which destroyed two. Romero's men had received little training in offensive operations and advanced in dense formations vulnerable to defensive fire and eventually went to ground.[27] Romero tried to crank up the offensive with an early afternoon bombardment but the supporting tanks arrived late, stopped 300m from the front line, expended their ammunition, then withdrew leaving three wrecked vehicles and the infantry on their start line. A third attack in the early evening was no more successful and a counterattack drove back Romero's men who had nothing to show for their heavy casualties. Further attempts in the next days saw no significant improvement, ending Romero's contribution to the campaign at a cost of nearly 2,450 men.[28]

Miaja, now fighting alone in the north, spent July 7 trying to exploit the fall of Villanueva de la Cañada but was contained by the arrival of more enemy reserves, while artillery fire directed from the eastern heights increasingly harassed traffic making for Brunete. The problems of trying to supply a two-corps offensive down a single road were now becoming apparent and Miaja had to use half his engineers to keep it open. Meanwhile, Varela ordered Barrón to establish two defensive lines, across the roads to the south and in the east to protect the back door to the Madrid front.

Campesino continued knocking at Quijorna's door and also tried to take Los Llanos with generous support from Smushkevich's airmen and half of Modesto's tanks. A daylight assault upon Los Llanos was beaten off when the tanks came under accurate antitank fire but a night attack by fresh troops took the ridge, Modesto claiming some Moors shot themselves in the belly.[29] Two attacks were launched upon Quijorna, which was becoming Miaja's ulcer, but both were smashed and an attempt to reinforce Campesino was thwarted by road congestion.

With the fall of Villanueva de la Cañada, Lister's artillery arrived and he tried to make amends for the previous day's mistakes. He made poorly coordinated attacks around Hill 670 to get a jump-off line for an advance upon Villaviciosa but the Nationalist battle groups drove them off aided by 20 guns. But at 18:00 Hill 670 finally fell to a bayonet attack, although Jurado's continued failure to push southeast forced Lister to extend his flank 5km northeast of Brunete. Miaja still refused to release Walter's division but one of its brigades was allowed to advance along Campesino's and Lister's boundary in an attempt to take the crossroads 4km south of Quijorna, but when they encountered enemy troops the brigade went to ground. The first two days had cost the Republic some 4,060 casualties, including Romero's troops.[30]

The offensive's success had depended upon the Republic breaking out quickly, but divisional and corps leadership was clearly inadequate. With Modesto pinned down, everything depended upon the slender reed of Jurado, who was ordered to push on to Boadilla. But his divisions stubbornly refused to advance, causing traffic jams on the road to Brunete and he was unable to bring order out of the chaos. He was slow to make decisions, and hours elapsed between verbose orders being drafted and sent forward by motorcycle courier because telephone lines were frequently cut by shell fragments and the officers were unfamiliar with radios.[31] Orders to take Villafranca, for example, were dispatched at 07:30 but took so long to reach Enciso that he did not begin until 13:00.

Consequently Galán made little progress upon Romanillos and Boadilla while Gal was still licking his wounds after taking Villanueva. Eventually one brigade crept toward the Guadarrama, plagued by air attacks, only to scatter with the appearance of Jurado's cavalry sent up in support. It regrouped and by nightfall established a bridgehead on the eastern bank of the Guadarrama on the slopes of the Mosquito Ridge 4km west of Boadilla. This threat to the Madrid Corps' back door was serious and Varela acted with characteristic decisiveness.

He ordered Asensio to move his division headquarters to Boadilla to head the *ad hoc* Guadarrama Temporary Division (División Provisional del Guadarrama) while Irutetagoyena and Yagüe took over his Madrid front sector. At first Asensio had only three battalions, too few to reinforce the Villanueva del Pardillo garrison who were still able to beat off Enciso's attack, but soon he had eight battalions and seven batteries. Despite the stiffening defense, Enciso drove the enemy off the Mocha Ridge to reach the outer defenses of Villafranca, further increasing Varela's concern about the salient's eastern front.

Meanwhile the flow of Nationalist reinforcements increased and by the end of the day Varela had received a total of 31 battalions and nine batteries. Meanwhile, six battalions of Buruaga's 150th Division arrived around Perales de Milla to strengthen the defense in the southwest of the salient, as Serrador's division dug in along the Perales up to Navalagamella. Barron's "Black Hand" was sealing off the southern front of the salient with orders to hold the line as near Brunete as possible and not to surrender a centimeter of land.[32]

For the Republicans July 8 was another day of frustration, with Quijorna's defenders still resisting Campesino and being reinforced by another infantry battalion, yet Miaja still refused to release Walter. Campesino, his vanity fed by claims that he had the best troops in the army, staged another poorly coordinated and vain assault upon Quijorna at dawn. But his sixth and last attempt was heralded by a 30-minute mid-morning bombardment by six batteries each assigned a specific target, then six battalions executed a pincer movement to fight their way through the village. The battle for the village ended at dawn on July 9 after 80 hours of combat but Campesino reported only 200 prisoners because part of the garrison escaped. The village had cost Modesto 14 tanks and much of his artillery ammunition expended almost randomly. Campesino's failure was due to poor intelligence and his inability to organize combined-arms assaults, which allowed the defenders to take cover during bombardments, then man their fire steps before the Republican infantry arrived.[33]

Lister was facing growing artillery fire and his attempts to push southwest toward Sevilla la Nueva during July 9 made slow progress under numerous counterattacks. Barrón had now split his division into two brigades but he gradually lost the high ground near Hill 670, allowing 11 DI to extend its line to the Guadarrama bridgehead which was still only 2km deep. This meant Gal was unsupported as he tried to take both the Romanillos Ridge, held by a Moorish tabor, and the Mosquito Ridge which forced him into a divergent attack as Miaja kept demanding Jurado advance eastward. Asensio's line was like a great S running in an arc covering Villafranca and Romanillos Ridge, then sweeping westward to the Mosquito Ridge, but during the day it was strengthened by ten battalions and seven batteries, giving Barrón 15 battalions, a third in reserve, and Asensio nine supported by 11 and eight batteries respectively.

Despite receiving reinforcements from Buruaga, Gómez-Avellaneda, and Yagüe, Asensio remained severely overstretched, but the two ridges acted as breakwaters while numerous company counterattacks helped to slow the enemy, who were still 800m from the Romanillos peak by dusk.[34] Meanwhile Galán's men sat passively at Castillo de Villafranca officially "mopping up" as Jurado also remained an interested spectator. To the north Enciso was slowly drawing the noose on Villanueva del Pardillo, whose defenders met every probe with withering fire. In an effort to break the deadlock here, Miaja brought Kléber's division out of reserve and sent it through the night to reinforce Enciso.

During the day Franco, accompanied by operations chief Barroso, drove to Barrón's command post to determine the dangers posed by the attack from Brunete, then visited Varela. Ever the optimist, Varela was straining at the leash to launch a counteroffensive once the whole of Buruaga's 150th Division arrived, but the cautious Franco ordered him to await the arrival of the two Navarrese brigades to restore the front line to its pre-battle position. Nevertheless Varela was determined to clear the right bank of the Guadarrama and squeeze out the enemy salient. His optimism was boosted by the continued arrival of reinforcements and by the following day he had 26 battalions in the front line with 12 in immediate reserve. The most serious problem was a shortage of artillery, with only 40 guns available, but growing Nationalist air power was beginning to act as a counterbalance.

Miaja, his right now secure along the Perales, made a belated effort to breathe life into the offensive on July 9 by ordering Jurado to break out from the

Guadarrama bridgehead toward Boadilla and, if possible to attack and occupy Villaviciosa. Modesto was to secure the right flank and then push down the Perales, a task assigned to one of Campesino's brigades, which over the next couple of days slowly pushed Buruaga back 2km toward Perales, taking the Perales Ridge to the north. Miaja finally released his grip on Walter who was sent to hold the line west of Brunete where Lister again made little progress, partly because of a shortage of armor until the following day.

Much depended upon Jurado, whose bureaucratic inertia continued to disappoint, but there was one brief ray of hope when Kléber, using half his men, isolated and then stormed Villanueva del Pardillo, but attacks upon Villafranca by Enciso and Galán merely piled bodies on the wire. Kléber would have been better deployed further south where Gal's attempts to push forward were pinned down by artillery fire and numerous counterattacks.

The offensive was now running out of steam and the emphasis during the next three days was increasingly upon securing rather than gaining ground as General Logistics took control. The task of providing half-a-dozen divisions with food, water, fuel, and ammunition over a single, narrow road would have been formidable for experienced officers, but for the Republican Army's half-trained staff it was almost impossible.[35] These difficulties, compounded by air attacks and artillery bombardment, meant forward units received only a fraction of their requirements and left only 15 tanks serviceable on July 11. Meanwhile Nationalist reinforcements continued to arrive to strengthen the line, which received 26 battalions and five batteries on July 9. By contrast, the Nationalist supply situation was improving daily, with a torrent of men and material. Varela now had 50 battalions including the two Navarrese brigades, while the 108th Division, having given two battalions to Asensio, was building a second defensive line to doom any faint Republican hopes of isolating the Madrid garrison.

During July 10 Kléber slowly isolated Villafranca, but despite receiving 46 tanks his hopes were dashed by the arrival of the vanguard of Bautista's 5th Navarrese Brigade which relieved the town by dusk of the following day to provide the Nationalists with a useful bridgehead on the Perales. In a fit of optimism, Jurado planned a new assault upon Villafranca, but during the day Asensio received another six battalions and two batteries to secure his position. Their arrival doomed Gal's attempts to take the Romanillos and Mosquito Ridges on July 11, leaving him severely understrength with the Franco-East European 13 BI having only 2,800 men. Despite receiving five fresh battalions, Modesto decided not to push his head deeper into the furnace, and his men were now digging in and setting up wire entanglements while fighting off enemy probes. On the night of July 11/12 he formally informed his divisional commanders that they would temporarily go on the defensive.

On the opposite flank an exasperated Miaja purged XVIII CE, relieving both Jurado and Galán "for health reasons" when the real reason was that like many Spanish officers they lacked initiative.[36] Galán was replaced by Major Joaquin Zulueta and Jurado by Casado, whom Miaja asked whether or not he could further expand the shoulders of the salient by striking north of Villafranca. Casado, a cavalryman from a military family was head of President Manuel Azana's military household at the outbreak of war and became operations chief in October 1936 but was dismissed when the Communists refused to support the Estremadura offensive.[37] The 44-year-old was an irascible man owing to peptic ulcers which sometimes left him bed-ridden and his pessimism increased when he reached his headquarters. There he learned that the men were exhausted with two brigades reported completely demoralized; indeed the 13 BI had to be relieved. Only 14 guns were serviceable and there were loud complaints about Communist influence upon decision-making. When Casado sought to postpone the attack Miaja overruled him, and it was so poorly coordinated that Enciso, Zulueta, and Kléber not only were unable to take Villafranca but also the Mocha Ridge.

Even for atheists Brunete was a vision of hell, with the blazing sun pushing the temperature at times up to 50°C (122°F), baking hard the ground and drying up almost every waterway, condemning the infantry to a raging thirst, sending some men mad, and causing heat-stroke to tank crews. Both sides sought to relieve their thirst, with Asensio organizing motorized water tankers to raise the ration from 5.5 to 8 liters a day, but it was never enough.[38] There was the constant rumble of artillery which caused acrid blazes in the dry vegetation, adding to battlefield smoke and dust clouds as well as the constant sickly stench of the decomposing corpses that littered the battlefield like black balloons attracting swarms of flies. The shouts of leaders and the screams and moans of the wounded added to the cacophony, which included American machine gunners in Gal's division wasting ammunition in seven-round "shave-and-a-haircut-two-bits" bursts. The strain on the troops saw many suffering battle fatigue to a greater or lesser degree, while the desperate desire for water forced men to drink from any source, leading many to suffer diarrhea or dysentery.

Worse still was the appearance of the Nationalist Air Force now making an all-out effort to snatch back the air superiority established by Chato and Rata fighters during the offensive's first days, which allowed Katiuskas, Natashas, and Rasantes to strike the defenders.[39] The Nationalists rapidly transferred squadrons from the north, with the Italians flying about 100 sorties per day from July 6, as another three Italian fighter squadrons joined the fray, reinforced from July 17 by five bomber squadrons. On July 8 all eight squadrons of the Condor Legion flew their first mission, joining six Spanish squadrons to give the Nationalists a total of 265 aircraft. The Republic added two more squadrons (20 aircraft) on July 10 but they remained numerically inferior to their enemies, although the Nationalists had only a single squadron of modern Bf 109 fighters capable of matching the Ratas.

The Nationalist bombers, such as the Italian BR 20 and S.79 together with the German Do 17 and He 111, had qualitative superiority, although the triple-motored Savoias and Junkers remained the main "bomb trucks" both day and night, the Italians and Italians each dropping 106 tonnes of bombs during the battle.[40] Republican antiaircraft batteries could do little to stop them, as most had the short-range 20mm Oerlikon—its high firing rate made it deadly to low-flying aircraft but also caused ammunition shortages. The Republicans used their aircraft less intensively, and in 25 days flew exactly 3,000 sorties with a maximum of 180 on July 23. Fighters flew six or seven sorties throughout the long hours of daylight for a total of 1,670 sorties, but their strike forces often remained in their nests as enemy bombers flew two or three sorties a day to compensate for the shortage of artillery.

By July 13 the Nationalists established air superiority, and formations of up to 50 aircraft roamed not only the battlefield but also struck airbases from July 10, destroying only three aircraft on the ground. This forced the Republicans to use airfields further from the battlefield; the ground-attack aircraft were 80km away, which reduced their time over the hard-pressed troops. Operating both day and night the Nationalist bombers blasted communications and troop concentrations, the latter by carpeting the area with small bombs, Italian S.79s flying 33 sorties and dropping 7.5 tonnes of bombs from July 10 through July 19. When the Nationalist infantry attacked they were often supported by He 51 fighter-bombers which hovered over the defenses, then repeatedly bombed and strafed the defenders who were demoralized by what seemed very personal attacks. Air power would contribute greatly to the Nationalist victory, and "the enemy had a numerical superiority over the Republicans' aviation and overwhelming superiority in heavy bomber aircraft."[41] The air campaign cost the Nationalists 23 aircraft, 8 percent of their strength, and the Republicans 43, or 29 percent of their strength, leaving only 30 serviceable Ratas on the Madrid front. They were forced to disband the SB bomber group but would later activate a night-bomber squadron with 12 Rasante.[42]

Despite numerous local crises Varela and Saliquet continued planning the counteroffensive and on July 13 published their proposals. They involved a double envelopment of the Brunete salient from east and west, a concept that so enthralled Franco that he hoped that afterward Varela would drive north through the Sierra de Guadarrama to the Alto del Leon Pass.[43] Varela set D-Day for July 18, the first anniversary of the army uprising.

As the plan was published Casado was reluctantly launching a new assault upon the eastern face of the salient. Gal's latest attempt to expand his bridgehead suffered the predictable setback as both sides were fought to a standstill, with Asensio forced to relieve four battalions while seven of his batteries were down to a single gun.

On July 15 Miaja reluctantly accepted that his army could do no more, having suffered 11,000 casualties, including 1,750 sick, and he ordered it "to rest, to build up reserves to withstand any enemy offensive action in the first place, and in the second to enable offensive action on our part in the near future." The prospects for holding the salient were poor because the exposed defenses marked the offensive's high-water mark. Worse, the infantry lacked entrenching tools, so the work of digging the trenches and stringing the wire had to be done by 4,500 engineers, although their efforts did ensure that there was a double trench line along the Perales and up to Brunete.[44]

A Nationalist counteroffensive was anticipated around July 16–17, with the greatest threat perceived in the west where 25 battalions had been identified while 8,000 infantry were reported on the eastern side. Although Modesto and Casado were exposed Miaja insisted there would be no withdrawal, but he may have had concerns about repercussions from the failure. He is alleged to have taken time off to remove evidence from archives that he had once belonged to the UME. Casado also feared reprisals for his "failure" especially as he had always opposed this offensive, but his efforts to seek relief were thwarted until July 30 when he was finally allowed to report sick and be replaced by another regular officer, Lieutenant Colonel Enrique Fernández-Heredia.[45]

Meanwhile, the final details of Varela's plan were completed as the Navarrese brigades of Bautista and Alonso Vega arrived in the central front from July 11 through July 12 in a move which involved some 50 trains in a triumph of staff work.[46] The two brigades were trucked into the battlefield and assembled by the night of July 16 to spearhead the envelopment of the salient. Bautista would strike in the east and Alonso Vega in the west, while Barrón pushed from the south, together with task forces created from 108th Division and independent units, which would advance from the Brunete area toward Quijorna and Villanueva de la Cañada. One of Asensio's brigades, north of

Bautista, would retake Villanueva del Pardillo, leaving the other in reserve. On D+1 Buruaga's 150th Division would advance from Navalagamella to envelop Valdemorillo, supported by the remaining divisions.[47] If successful the offensive would deprive the Republic of some 60,000 of their best troops with all their equipment and gain some 4,000 square kilometers of territory, but the plan was wildly optimistic and based upon the unlikely assumption that the enveloped Republican elite troops would have gone like lambs to slaughter. Varela had 45 batteries and urged his subordinates to be liberal with shells and frugal with lives.[48] He had 55 tanks which he wished to disperse in penny packets but Thoma insisted on striking *en masse* and they were attached to Barrón.

For four days the Nationalists prepared and probed around Villafranca and between Los Llanos and Quijorna. Their airmen roamed the battlefield at will, bombing and strafing to reduce the flow of supplies and erode vehicle strength as well as real and suspected troop concentrations, which disturbed sleep if nothing else. When the Nationalist attack began there were few buildings standing in the Republican-held villages. The Republicans frantically strengthened their defenses and tried to provide some depth while assembling reserves from already battered formations. There continued to be heavy fighting around Villafranca where Kléber launched a new attack on July 16 after a 105-minute bombardment by 35 guns, but antitank guns stopped his armor while machine guns scythed down the infantry.

The Nationalists struck at dawn on July 18 with a heavy bombardment and strong air support, estimated at 160 sorties, but the tired defenders quickly dashed the high hopes. Varela had made a serious error in timing the offensive for the anniversary of the army uprising, a timing correctly anticipated by the defenders who were alert before the first shells fell.

In the west Alonso Vega penetrated Campesino's defenses to establish a bridgehead across the Perales opposite Los Llanos but was eventually stopped 2km from the ridge, then driven back across the river having suffered 1,100 casualties. Campesino and Walter stopped Buruaga's support attack up the eastern bank of the Perales. In the south Barrón fought a bloody battle for Hill 670, and while Lister repelled the first two attacks, the tanks' machine guns failing to suppress the defenders, a surprise third assault not only drove him off that peak but also exposed the surrounding heights which fell easily. Barrón tried to press home his advantage, with his troops reaching Brunete four times but always driven out.

On Casado's front, Lister's retreat from Hill 670 led to the collapse of Zulueta's right-hand brigade, and its northward flight exposed Lister's left which swung back in the first stage of the collapse of the Republic's Guadarrama salient. Here Zulueta and Gal were also pushed back, with heavy casualties reducing the bridgehead to a third of its previous size but they never broke and made the Nationalists pay a high price for every step forward. Bautista stormed northward from Villafranca to expand the Nationalist bridgehead until Enciso and Kléber eventually contained his attack and inflicted heavy losses.

Undaunted, the Nationalists renewed their attacks on July 19 with Alonso Vega switching his attack further south to support Buruaga's new advance north toward the Perales Ridge. Campesino beat off Buruaga's first two attacks but during the afternoon a third, following a four-hour bombardment, saw the attackers fight their way into the defenses to take the ridge after an all-night struggle. The remaining Nationalist formations inched their way forward despite numerous counterattacks.

Bautista now struck southwest from the Mocha Ridge to take Castillo de Villafranca and threaten what was left of the Republican's Guadarrama salient. Within this salient intense artillery fire pushed Zulueta off the Romanillos Ridge, while the pressure to the south caused Miaja to withdraw Gal's exhausted division. The following day Casado launched a counterattack along his whole front but he failed to gain ground and further weakened the surviving troops.

The Republicans were on the verge of collapse. The shortage of reserves meant that many units had to remain in the line under heavy fire while receiving little hot food or cool water and on July 23 the spirit of the 13 BI broke. It was down to 500 men and refused to return to the front to aid Enciso. Its commander, Vicenzo Bianco, attempted to restore discipline by shooting a mutineer and was almost lynched by his comrades. Some 300 men then began to march northward, aiming to reach Madrid, and Gal telephoned a warning to Casado who in turn consulted Rojo. They agreed to let the mutineers leave the battlefield "lest there should be shooting and that were further to demoralize the troops at the front." Once out of the danger zone the mutineers were intercepted by Asaltos and an infantry battalion backed by armored cars and were disarmed. The ringleaders were executed on the spot and the survivors were "reeducated," then distributed among other units.[49]

Even Lister's men were demoralized, although they had lain within the eye of the hurricane under artillery fire. During the night of July 20/21 Lister, who detested Modesto, went over his head to Miaja and requested relief, only to be asked to hold out for two or three days more. By contrast Campesino had virtually destroyed his division through incompetence leaving it unable to any longer shield the Republican right, so he was relieved by Durán's division and the exhausted troops sent to rest camps.

The relief was achieved during a relative lull on the battlefield which lasted until July 24 as the Nationalists regrouped troops, restocked supply and ammunition depots, then assembled 130 guns, while on July 22 Buruaga relieved an exhausted Iruretagoyena. Franco and Saliquet had abandoned their overambitious plans to envelop the Brunete salient and now opted to ensure that it was no longer a threat to the Estremadura Highway. Alonso Vega and Bautista were transferred to flank Barrón's division and the three would bulldoze the enemy back from Brunete, starting on July 24. The enemy recognized the growing threat which they estimated at 40–45 battalions along the Perales in the west, 12 battalions in the south, and 14–15 battalions in the east, supported by 100 guns, 80 tanks, and 150 aircraft.[50]

After an hour-long bombardment the Nationalist infantry at 07:00 rose from their trenches. Walter and Durán contained Buruaga and Alonso Vega on the Nationalist left but on the right Bautista crashed through the lines and drove Casado's right north of the Brunete–Boadilla road. This was cut by Álvarez's brigade, as Asensio cleared the east bank of the Guadarrama to expose Brunete further. Barrón exploited the earlier success on the heights south of Brunete to approach the town from the southwest through a gap in Lister's defenses and retook it at 11:45.

Lister withdrew north to the walled cemetery, which dominated the road to Villanueva de la Cañada, supported first by his neighbor Walter and then by Anarchist Major Mera's 14 DI, which entered the salient that day to relieve Lister. Mera fortified the woods north of the cemetery, beat off every attack, and frequently counterattacked, while Walter put two battalions and a tank company into the cemetery. Throughout the day Republican gunners were under constant fire directed from the Mosquito and Romanillos Ridges which also interdicted the road, although by the end of the day some 1,500 seriously injured patients had reached Republican medical centers.

Mera attempted to relieve the cemetery with a night counterattack but this was smothered by artillery fire the moment it left the tree line. The battle for the cemetery continued to rage until the afternoon of July 25 when a Moorish tabor broke up a counterattack and a sergeant successfully urged his platoon to attack. Their charge was joined first by a company, then the whole tabor, a neighboring Spanish battalion, and finally the whole brigade. The defenders abandoned the cemetery and joined Mera's men in the woods which, by unhappy accident, was being bombed.

The defenders now stampeded northward to Villanueva de la Cañada, a German fighter-bomber pilot reporting: "Mixed in with the fleeing troops were escaped horses and pack animals, then cars, and ... tanks crawling slowly along

… everything in wild flight."[51] Their flight caused one of Walter's brigades to join the panic which opened a gap in the Republican lines, and nothing, not even the deployment of tanks and cavalry, was able to stop the rout. Walter executed several of this brigade's officers and eventually established a new line covering the Quijorna–Vallanueva de la Cañada road supported by Durán who held Quijorna in the west. Rojo ordered that "disorderly retreat" be "punished with the utmost severity" while Modesto ordered machine guns to be set up in the rear to gun down anyone who quit the front line.[52] Meanwhile, Miaja used the shortening of the line to create a reserve of six brigades, withdrew Lister and Mera's divisions, and reorganized his artillery.

In the last three days the Republic suffered some 5,500 casualties, including 1,245 sick, but there was no serious threat to the new defenses, for the Nationalist counteroffensive had spent itself, with Barrón content to follow the retreating enemy whom Asensio squeezed from the east. The Republicans were left with Quijorna, Villanueva de la Cañada, and Villanueva del Pardillo because the Nationalists were in no condition for another set-piece offensive, and July 26 was spent in bloody bickering for advantageous terrain. Franco and Saliquet drove over to see Varela, who had received so many deserters that he was convinced the enemy was broken and that another push would take him to the Sierra Guadarrama. It was clearly tempting for Franco, but after some deliberation he decided that this was too great a gamble, and as he wanted the Navarrese brigades to continue the conquest of the north he closed down the battle.

Although the butcher's bill is usually reported as 15,000 Nationalist and 23,000 Republican casualties, it appears to have been smaller, with the Nationalists suffering about 14,300 plus 2,075 sick, including 3,100 dead and missing, of whom up to 630 were taken prisoner. The highest casualties were suffered by Asensio (3,772) and Buruaga (3,317) while Barrón had 2,271 and the Navarrese 1,800 each. Republican casualties were officially reported as between 9,500 and 11,300 wounded and some 900 sick and 219 dead, but these relate only to seriously wounded men who reached the rear hospitals. The figure, excluding missing, was 18,600, of whom 1,000 were killed, with 9,450 sick, and in contrast to the Great War only a third of casualties were due to artillery rather than two-thirds.[53] The loss of so many battle-hardened troops was bad enough but it was the material losses that proved so damaging. The Nationalists captured 67 machine guns and 2,500 rifles, while Soviet records show that nearly half the tanks were put out of action with more than a fifth (21) totally destroyed.[54] The Republic would never again be in a favorable military situation and the captured material would soon be turned against its former owners.

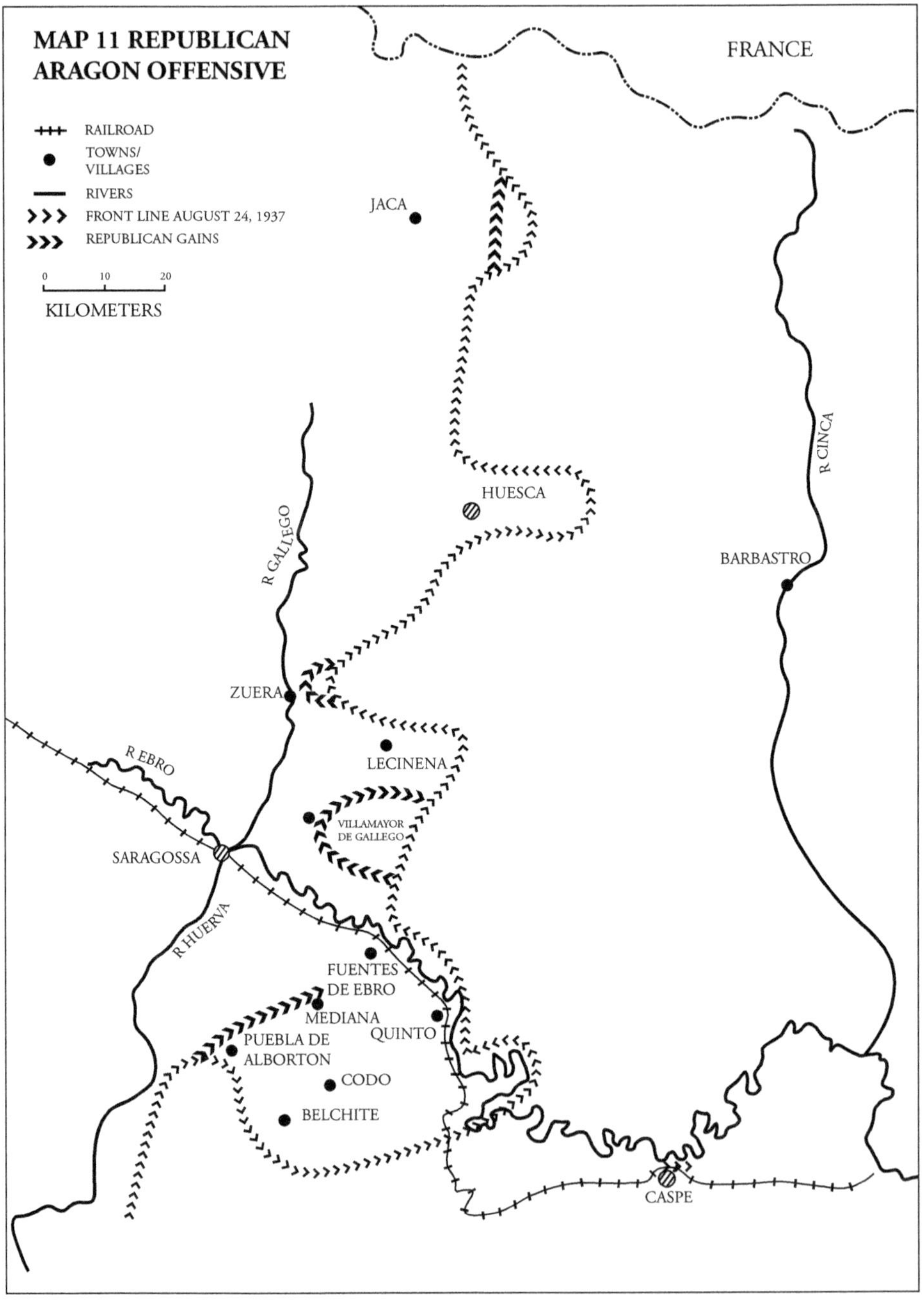
MAP 11 REPUBLICAN ARAGON OFFENSIVE
RAILROAD
TOWNS/ VILLAGES
RIVERS
FRONT LINE AUGUST 24, 1937
REPUBLICAN GAINS
0 10 20
KILOMETERS
FRANCE
JACA
HUESCA
R CINCA
R GALLEGO
BARBASTRO
ZUERA
R EBRO
LECINENA
VILLAMAYOR DE GALLEGO
SARAGOSSA
R HUERVA
FUENTES DE EBRO
MEDIANA
QUINTO
PUEBLA DE ALBORTON
CODO
BELCHITE
CASPE

Both sides claimed victory in what proved to be the decisive battle of the Civil War and one with echoes of Cambrai. In each case a breakthrough failed to overcome the defenders' hurdles and lost much of the ground gained in a riposte. There were numerous causes for the defeat, notably the Republic's failure to exploit the breakthrough due to lack of initiative and the absence of a motor-mechanized force to exploit success. There was also a fear of isolation reflected in the obsessive effort to reduce strongpoints in their rear.[55] The Russians were critical of Spanish combined-arms operations, their failure both to carry out reconnaissance, and provide forward artillery observers which meant the gunners often fired wildly, wasting precious ammunition.[56] While the Nationalists undoubtedly shared many of their enemy's weaknesses their commanders displayed initiative bordering on recklessness. But their superior combined-arms skills boded well for the future as they commenced the advance upon Santander.

The Aragon Campaign

The forces battered at Brunete had little time to recuperate, for they were sent north into Aragon as the Spanish political carousel turned again. In May 1937 tensions within semi-autonomous Catalonia between the government and the left erupted into violence, which provided the pretexts for Valencia to intervene and the Communists to crush their Anarchist rivals.[57]

They had Valencia's blessing, especially to eliminate Anarchist control of rural Aragon, which they began on August 11 after the harvest.[58] Modesto's corps received Prieto's secret orders to destroy Anarchist collective farms and occupy the offices of the Council of Aragon in Caspe without reference to the Eastern Army under Major General Sebastián Pozas at Lérida.[59] Lister occupied Caspe on August 10, but this inevitably led to protests from Anarchist troops, who provided a substantial portion of the Eastern Army, and now spoke of turning their guns on the Communists. This worried Prieto who berated Lister over exaggerated reports of a massacre when they met the following day. While the Anarchists were restrained it was vital for Valencia to keep them on the leash while justifying the arrival of elite Communist troops in Aragon.

The imminent fall of Santander provided the excuse for an offensive, ostensibly to draw away enemy resources from the enclave. Pozas had three corps with nine divisions: north of the Ebro X CE under Colonel José Gonazález, and south of the river the XII and XI CE under Colonel Pedro Sánchez and Major Antonio Gil respectively, but Valencia now inserted its own forces into the front line rather like the ribs of a corset. For the operation

Pozas organized his forces into four mixed task forces (*Agrupación*) and on August 20 ordered the envelopment of Saragossa from each bank of the Ebro in a four-day offensive. On Gonazález's front this would involve Groups A, B, and C formed around the 27, 45, and elements of 26 DI, while on Sánchez's front Modesto's V CE arrived as Group D.

The battlefield would be the broad, undulating Ebro Valley with its numerous villages, fields, and olive groves cut by irrigation channels, but it also extended into the uplands and foothills of the Pyrenees. Some fighting would take place in the Pyrenees, whose peaks and largely east–west ridges, some with peaks up to 1,000m, extended 30–40km into northern Spain. The Nationalist line consisted of two salients, with a small salient north of the Ebro at Lecinena and a larger one, 55km broad and 20km deep, south of the river between Quinto on the river and the key communications hub of Belchite, the line then following the River Huerva southward toward Teruel.

North of the river, following a diversion toward Jaca by Gonzalez's X CE, Group A under Major Manuel Trueba with four brigades of 27 DI, three batteries, and two tank companies would advance upon Zuera, which lay on the River Gállego just north of Saragossa. It would cross the river, then form a mechanized column to drive down the Saragossa road and enter the city during the late evening. On its left Group B, with two brigades under Kléber, would strike toward Villamayor del Gállego with 41 DI and three batteries and having taken the town send a motorized group into Saragossa arriving simultaneously with Group A.

Major José Hernández de la Mano's Group C, with two brigades, would strike across the Ebro into the Belchite salient to isolate Quinto, be absorbed by Modesto's Group D, and both would then capture Quinto on D+1. Modesto, with seven brigades, 15 batteries, and 35 tanks, would strike around Belchite and advance up the Ebro between Mediana and Quinto, secure the area, then send a motorized brigade into Saragossa simultaneously with Groups A and B. In a subsidiary operation XII CE's 24 (Major Antonio Ortiz) and 25 (Major Alejandro Gallo) DI with nine brigades, would advance into the Belchite salient from the west to take Puebla de Alborton, isolate and then storm Belchite. The Republic was committing 31 brigades, nine in reserve, with 125,000 men, 110 guns, 100 tanks, and 90 aircraft into what was essentially an ambitious diversion. Rojo again urged his commanders to press on and not be diverted by enemy forces in the rear while he ordered the FARE to provide maximum support for the infantry.

Republican confidence was high, for they knew that the 300km front from the French frontier through the provinces of Huesca, Saragossa, and Teruel was lightly defended. There were strongpoints in towns, villages, and peaks, augmented by shallow trench systems on each bank of the Ebro. They were under the Nationalist Fifth Corps with headquarters at Saragossa with 67,140 men in 78 battalions and 50 batteries under Ponte. He was a very safe pair of hands, having already beaten off several Anarchist attacks and had split his command at the Ebro. North of the river was Brigadier General Gustavo Urrutia's 51st Division with 22,270 men and six batteries together with Colonel Antonio Civera's Garrison Brigade (Brigata de Posición y Etapas) at Huesca (also Osca) with 7,750 men. South of the river was Brigadier General Mariano Muñoz Castellanos's 52nd Division with 17,400 men and 11 batteries supported by Colonel Alfredo Galera's Mobile Brigade with 6,480 men and five batteries.[60] The corps also had Brigadier General Mariano Santiago Guerrero's 105th Division in Operational Level reserve with 9,370 men and six batteries.

Pozas, accompanied by Rojo, established his command post at Bujaraloz, 40km east of Fuentes de Ebro, and at dawn they waited for news. North of the river Groups A and B struck before dawn on August 24 against Urrutia's I Brigade in the north and II Brigade in the south. The Republicans infiltrated enemy lines, Trueba striking two hours before Kléber to reach the Gállego, wade across and envelop Zuera defended by 640 men. But they were unable to take much of the town, and Urrutia sent reinforcements which helped drive most of the enemy back across the river, although they retained a toehold in the town. Kléber's performance was lackluster and he was held in the hills outside Villamayor and was content to blame his failure upon "strong resistance."[61]

The southern bank was defended by Muñoz Castellanos's I Brigade (Colonel Francisco Barba) with six battalions, of which half were in the Belchite-based First Demi-Brigade (Lieutenant Colonel Eduardo San Martin) with 2,270 men and ten light guns, while two battalions with 1,200 men and nine guns defended Quinto. Here Republican progress was marginally better, as Hernández de la Mano successfully crossed the Ebro to isolate Quinto. Modesto split his task force into four columns. The first under Major Luis Rivas, one of Lister's brigade commanders, was to advance with a cavalry brigade to the Ebro between Mediana and Fuentes de Ebro and there establish a jump-off line for the fourth motorized column, the rest of Lister's 11 DI, which was to drive into Saragossa spearheaded by 25 tanks. The second column was Walter's 35 DI and was to take Quinto, while Major Nilamón Toral would lead the remainder of the division and part of Gallo's 25 DI in the third column to besiege Belchite and nearby Codo, with the remainder of Gallo's troops to open the Mediana–Belchite road.

Rivas's column infiltrated the enemy lines from the evening of August 23 to reach his objectives, but attacks from 09:00 upon Mediana and Fuentes de Ebro were beaten off, the latter by two Civil Guard companies. When Lister arrived at noon in a convoy of tanks, trucks, and buses he could do nothing except set up camp. Meanwhile, Toral's column isolated Belchite and Codo, being joined by Sánchez's troops, while Walter, reinforced by two of Lister's battalions, stormed the village of Quinto. Some of the defenders held out in the village cemetery and Walter's request for air support to mount a third attack was denied by Modesto's Russian air advisor on the grounds that there were too few defenders!

Despite this, and the fact that only 800 prisoners were taken, there was cautious optimism among the Republicans, although there was disappointing news during August 25 where, north of the river, Trueba's bridgehead was being slowly contracted while Kléber continued futile frontal attacks upon Villamayor's defenses. South of the river it took all day to storm Codo, whose Requeté battalion garrison was wiped out, while Walter finally succeeded in crushing the enemy at Quinto, but mopping up continued into the early evening. Lister, reinforced by two Anarchist brigades, took Mediana, then vainly tried to ram his way through the Mediana–Fuentes de Ebro defenses. Behind him Sánchez tightened the siege of Belchite, whose 1,000-man garrison was joined on the town walls by many civilians including the mayor, Ramón Alfonso Trallero.[62] The defense was boosted by numerous cellars in the houses, often linked by tunnels to provide the defenders shelter and freedom of movement. The siege was undermined because up to 15 percent of the shells hitting the town failed to explode, creating a significant postwar hazard.

Modesto's attention was focused upon Lister's front, which he reinforced on August 26 with Walter's division and a brigade, then demanded immediate progress upon Saragossa, but the attacks were all beaten off. North of the Ebro, Treuba held his positions while Kléber had clearly learned nothing and was bleeding dry the Italian 12 BI whose commander Carlo Penchienati was replaced by Nino Raimondi. The situation was little changed on August 27, although Kléber was reinforced by the whole of 44 DI.

South of the river, Sánchez took Albortón but Belchite defied four besieging brigades, which were content to hold the line, leading Pozas to send the corps commander a "very unpleasant" message about his failure to storm the town. Sánchez took the hint and launched his first assault on August 28, but it was repelled, as were Lister and Walter's attacks toward Saragossa. To buttress the front south of the Ebro Barrón's 13th Division was ordered up from Madrid and arrived from August 26, on which day Buruaga's 150th Division was ordered to join it, the two with artillery reinforcements being brought in by 365 trains as Santiago's 105th Division also entered the line.[63] They were facing their old adversaries at Brunete in much the same weather conditions of blazing sun, clouds of dust, and the accompanying thirst.

Pozas halted further attacks, except upon Belchite, and spent the following day reorganizing and planning. Lister's task force was reinforced by Ortiz's division but Lister's division was withdrawn from the line and replaced by a divisional-sized Group F under Captain Nicanor Felipe, commander of 143 BM. With these changes the Republic renewed its assault upon the gateway to Saragossa on August 30 but was again repulsed, Walter having to come to Oritz's aid when his division was pinned down. At Belchite the siege lines were tightened but ten Ju 52s were able to drop supplies into the town as the Nationalists desperately tried to relieve the siege from August 30, but their attacks made little progress against stubborn resistance.

The following day Sánchez renewed his assault upon the town and fought his way into the outskirts but this was not enough for Pozas. He now gave Walter the honor of taking the town, a decision bitterly criticized both within the corps and in many Eastern Army formations. It took Walter a day to replace most of the Anarchist brigades around Belchite, but his attack on September 2 penetrated the town and by 19:30 he was claiming victory, although he admitted some mopping up was needed. In fact numerous pockets of resistance remained with 200 managing to break out at night, and it was not until the evening of September 5 that the town fell, Mayor Trallero dying during the last desperate hours.

North of the river Trueba continued to hold on at Zuera while Kléber trumpeted the capture of Villamayor when actually two Polish battalions that had reached the town were isolated and destroyed with only 130 men returning. An attack from September 22 through October 6 destroyed the Nationalist salient southeast of Jaca held by Colonel Alberto Caso Agüero's I Brigade, but this was the last Republican success, for, ironically, in partially succeeding in relieving pressure on the northern enclave the Republic contributed to its own failure. With adequate Spanish forces to conclude the campaign against the enclave, Franco withdrew the CTV's Hispano-Italian Flechas Negras and Flechas Azules Brigades on August 31 and September 2 respectively and sent them with two Italian artillery groups to the Aragon front on August 29. The brigades formed the new Flechas Division under Roatta with 14,571 men and nine batteries and this entered the line north of the Ebro on September 8 to support Urrutia and Civera. It helped Urrutia iron out Treuba's and Kléber's salients from September 24 through September

28, supported by 80 guns and a dozen tankettes.[64] Fighting continued in the Pyrenees and around Jaca until early November but otherwise operations north of the Ebro had ended.[65]

After the usual bloody bickering for terrain advantage, the front flared up again a month later. As Lister occupied Caspe, a consignment of 50 BT-5 tanks, designed to exploit tactical breakthroughs, was unloaded at Barcelona and issued to the International Tank Regiment under Colonel Stepan Kondratev. Russian, Bulgarian, and Canadian commanders were in many vehicles with a Russian driver/mechanic and a Spanish loader, the language barriers frequently causing confusion and accidents.[66] Yet Walter decided they would provide the perfect means to support a desperate operation to relieve pressure in the Asturias. He planned to take Fuentes de Ebro, then drive into Saragossa using his division supported by a T-26 battalion, but on October 12 he decided to use the International Tank Regiment instead.

Kondratev received his orders at 23:00 on October 12 and his tanks then drove 50km to the front arriving the following morning to be informed that they would carry the Spanish Battalion of 15 BI on their rear decks, ten men per tank. This would be the first time infantry had gone into battle in this way and there were no fittings to hold on to, leading to considerable opposition to the idea, but Kondratev was forced to obey orders.[67] He received no information on the battlefield or the defenses and was essentially told to get on with it, and the tanks set off 90 minutes late in the early afternoon supported by half a dozen guns with little ammunition.

The 43 BTs set off at 30mph over uneven ground with their passengers bouncing off the decks, with some being crushed by following vehicles. The tanks crossed the Republican trenches and drove into an irrigated sugar cane field where they got bogged down and became perfect targets for artillery and antitank guns. The regiment lost 19 tanks, while a third of its crews became casualties in what has been described as the swansong of Russian tank operations in Spain. Lister commented: "This was one of the stupidest operations of the entire war."[68] Yet Modesto blamed him for the failure, which caused a permanent rift between them and as a result 11 DI did not serve in V CE until March 1938.[69] Interestingly, Pozas blamed Walter for failing to focus upon primary objectives.

The failure of the Republican offensive to provide any relief to the enclave was demonstrated by the fact that the Nationalist reserves, including 65 aircraft, all came from the Madrid front. The offensive may have cost the Republic some 15,000 casualties and the defenders about half that. Walter's division remained at the front as Lister's was withdrawn on September 10 and sent to

Alcaniz under XXI CE to rest and reorganize as part of the recently formed Reserve Army under Colonel Leopoldo Menéndez.

Meanwhile, Negrín completed the suppression of Catalonian autonomy at the end of October by moving the government from Valencia to Barcelona. In part this represented the traditional centrist ambitions of the Spanish government but it also reflected a desire to stimulate the Catalonian industry's contribution to the war effort. Once established Negrín steadily undermined the Catalan government of President Luis Companys and avoided all personal contact with him while the Catalans increasingly regarded the Eastern Army as an army of occupation.[70]

The Hectic Fall

Unknowingly, Negrín had placed himself in harm's way, for the Nationalists were considering an offensive in Aragon. The idea was floated by Barroso as early as July, but eliminating the northern enclave took priority. On September 15 Barroso again looked at Aragon and proposed an offensive south of the Ebro to retake Belchite and then drive eastward to split the Republic in two.[71] Once Catalonia had fallen, Valencia then Madrid would be taken, but for that, he wrote, "we should have all the trumps in our hand."[72] A fortnight after the fall of Gijon, on November 5, Franco accepted this proposal but his restless ambition led him to extend the scope of the offensive to both sides of the river, with the fall of Madrid still regarded as the final act, although some in his headquarters, together with his allies, urged him to give it priority.

After the northern enclave's destruction Franco frantically expanded and regrouped his forces using captured material to help activate a dozen divisions during the first week of November, half by expanding brigades.[73] To improve command and control he had already created from October 23 the Castile, Galicia, and Navarre Corps under Varela (promoted to major general) and Brigadier Generals Aranda and Iruretagoyena.

Earlier Franco had begun to reorganize and expand his forces in Aragon, starting on October 20 when Moscardó took over Fifth Corps.[74] This was renamed the Aragon Corps four days later and was joined by a reserve corps (Cuerpo de Ejercito de Reserva) with four divisions, the new Flechas Division, and a cavalry brigade. The devout Moscardo, aged 59, was in semi-retirement when the uprising began, having fought in Cuba, the Philippines, and Morocco. Under the Republic he focused upon military education, heading and famously holding the Toledo Military Academy. His promotion to brigadier general was some consolation for the execution of his son, in whose memory he would wear a black cloak of mourning for the rest of his life. He was passionate about football, was closely involved with the Olympic movement, and was described by an English observer as "a tall, reserved, gentle-mannered man, a little awkward, rather punctilious: happy enough with a few people he knew well, but shy in company."

Moscardo's forces were concentrated north of the Ebro, but he participated in detailed planning for the Aragon offensive with his corps and Berti's reorganized CTV north of the river, while to the south were Aranda and Iruretagoyena. Varela's Castile Corps was in GHQ reserve while Barrón and Buruaga's divisions were assigned on November 5 to the new Morocco Corps under Yagüe, who was succeeded in First Corps by Ponte. The reorganization of the Nationalist Army reflected an impending change in the scale of operations from multiple brigades to multiple army corps.

Varela and Yagüe were soon transferred to the right of the planned new front, as Franco on November 11 redesignated Saliquet's command the Army of the Center and South of the Ebro (Ejercito del Centro al Sur de Ebro), while five days later he ordered Davila's Army of the North renamed the Army North of the Ebro with Aranda's, Iruretagoyena's, and Moscardó's corps, and this was activated on December 7. Many in the Nationalist leadership doubted the wisdom of attacking Aragon and Catalonia, which were perceived as the Anarchist heart of Republican resistance with an estimated 300,000 troops, but it was not this fear that forced Franco to abandon his grand design and delay the Aragon offensive for four months.

It was simply impossible to activate, man, equip, and train so many new divisions within the two-month deadline, yet the most serious problem was providing adequate artillery support. Franco used this excuse on November 28 when a change in strategy, designed to maintain the offensive momentum, led to a new plan to take Madrid and neutralize enemy forces within the salient and shorten his front. The prime axis of the attack would be the Saragossa–Madrid Highway through Guadalajara, offering Berti's CTV the opportunity for revenge, with the River Tajo securing the left while Saliquet split the assault force into three task forces (*Agrupacións*). Yagüe's Group A would be on the right with five divisions, 21 batteries and two tank companies, Berti would lead Group B in the center with three divisions and a Spanish tank battalion, while Varela's Group C on the left would have six infantry and one cavalry divisions, 25 batteries, and two tank companies. The assault would be supported by 350 guns and the full force of German and Italian air power as well as 1 BAH, but the difficulties of assembling adequate supplies, with only 400 trains from December 6 through December 15, meant that D-Day was delayed until December 18.[75]

Rojo, recently promoted to brigadier general, had anticipated that the enemy would strike in the Aragon, where it was easier to assemble the victorious forces of the northern campaign.[76] On October 27 he informed the government that while the enemy might attack Madrid, the bloody nose they had received at the beginning of the year would probably dissuade them. Therefore, "I consider the Aragonese theater the most likely venue in the immediate future."[77] He made timely dispositions, assembling in the region most of the strategic reserve army with 13 divisions in five corps under Iglesia as acting commander.[78] The Popular Army had been steadily expanded by calling up the 1930 and 1938 classes in August 1937, and the 1939 class in October 1937 to give a total strength of 221,700.[79] But the Republic's material resources were strained to the limit and a report to Moscow noted that by September 1 the Republic had only 209 serviceable tanks: 123 on the Madrid front and 63 in Aragon, 80 having been destroyed or captured.[80]

Aerial reconnaissance and Comint, together with observations by guerrillas and what would later be called Special Forces, accumulated incontestable evidence by late November of an enemy offensive against Madrid. All were pessimistic about Madrid's prospects but when Prieto asked how the Republic would respond, there was the usual absence of unity. Rojo dusted off Plan "P," the Estremadura offensive, but with most of the strategic reserve in Aragon this would take too long to prepare and time was clearly at a premium. The alternative was Plan "H" to preempt the enemy offensive by striking a target which did not require a significant regrouping and would force Franco to divert forces.

In December 8 President Azana met Prieto and Rojo, who presented him with the options but made clear that Plan "H," an assault upon the provincial capital of Teruel (also Terol), was the only feasible one. Prieto was enthusiastic about the plan, which would enhance the prestige of his ministry because the Nationalist front was exposed and lightly held, so there was a high probability of success which would boost both his personal and government prestige throughout Europe. Success would also have Strategic and Operational Level benefits, freeing communications, especially north to south. Rojo described the operation as an "offensive-defensive battle" which aimed to achieve "limited destruction of the enemy" and obtain "a definite advantage for further exploitation."[81] However, given Franco's paranoid determination not to lose any important location, it also brought the prospect of another battle of attrition which the Republic could not win.

This desperate gamble was assigned to the Levante Army (Ejército del Levante), activated on August 24 from XIII and XIX CE, under Colonel Juan

Hernández Saravia, a gaunt 57-year-old gunner with a broad smile that reflected his affability.[82] A left-wing supporter of the Republic, he had briefly resigned his commission when a right-wing government was elected. He became a secretary in Azana's military household and was briefly war minister in August 1936 but was dismissed after the fall of Talavera. He would be promoted to brigadier general on Christmas Eve. For that operation he was given three corps from the strategic reserve: Lieutenant Colonel Juan Ibarrola's XXII (Northern Column), Colonel Leopoldo Menéndez's XX (Central Column), and Lieutenant Colonel Enrique Fernández de Heredia's XVIII (Southern Column) CE. The operation would involve a dozen divisions, half from the strategic reserve including Lister's, Duran's, and Walter's, a total of 77,000 men supported by 120 guns, 104 tanks, 3,230 vehicles, 2,350 horses and 150 aircraft.[83] With limited artillery ammunition the Republic again intended to rely upon nighttime infiltration, and for propaganda purposes the Republic planned to leave the International Brigades in reserve.

D-Day was set for November 13 but heavy snowfall disrupted preparations. Rojo briefed commanders from December 7 through December 11, and to aid the concentration all civil rail traffic ceased from December 6 through December 14.[84] With the weather beginning to ease, divisional commanders dispatched scout teams behind the lines on the night of December 11/12 to help update battle plans on the morning of December 13. There was a last-minute dispute between Lister and Ibarrola over artillery preparation, with Rojo supporting the former to confine it to specific strongpoints just before the infantry attacked. By December 14 orders went out to begin the offensive and, as more snow fell, the Republican infantry began to infiltrate the enemy lines.

Notes

1 For these offensives see Alcofar, *Air*, pp. 196–198; Beevor, pp. 234, 275, 277; Cardona, pp. 162–168; Engel, *Operations*, pp. 129–143; López-Muñiz, pp. 115–147; Martinez, *Brunete*, pp. 61–100; Martínez, *La gran ofensiva sobre Zaragoza*, pp. 37–56 (hereafter Martinez, *Zaragoza*); Martínez and Martínez, pp. 200–206; Thomas, pp. 688–689.

2 For the background to Brunete see Beevor, pp. 274–275; Cardona, p. 144; Hills, pp. 137–138, 142–146.

3 At the time of the uprising he was scheduled to command the African Army artillery.

4 XVIII CE was formed only on June 28 and was Jurado's consolation prize for the abandonment of Plan "P."

5 Thomas, pp. 492, 836; Zaragoza, pp. 168–190.

6 For the plan see Engel, *Operations*, pp. 145–154; Martinez, *Brunete*, pp. 120–130, Appendices 4 and 5. Rojo described it as "almost perfect," Rojo, *Heroica*, p. 87.

7 The Republican plan resembled the Soviet Operation *Saturn* which ended in 1943 with the recapture of Stalingrad.
8 Serebryakov, pp. 95–96, noted that Romero had only 1,300 75mm and 1,800 105mm shells respectively. This made any attempt to break through the Madrid defenses a challenge, to say the least.
9 See Engel, *Operations*, pp. 152–154.
10 Serebryakov, p. 10, claims that the Republic committed 105,000 men to the offensive including reserves. He noted an acute shortage of heavy artillery. He said there were 133 tanks including 21 in reserve.
11 Serebryakov, pp. 10, 15, says that Romero was supported by ten tanks and then says 12 Renault FTs.
12 Serebryakov, pp. 95–96.
13 Kowalsky, ch. 14, section VI; Saez, vol. 2, p. 506; Salas, *Air*, p. 237; Serebryakov, pp. 10, 79–80. Serebryakov claims that there were 45 I-16, 17 I-15, 15 SB, and 56 ground-attack aircraft, while Saez, on the basis of Soviet documents, gives the figures on July 5 as 38, 13, 23, and 63, but two Chato squadrons may be excluded. Modesto, p. 101, gives 140 aircraft. One of the first pilots to return home was promptly shot down and captured at Brunete.
14 Serebryakov, p. 27.
15 Martinez, *Brunete*, pp. 119, 143n.165, 154n.177.
16 See Engels, *Divisions*, pp. 30, 126.
17 For Brunete see Alcofar, *Air*, pp. 201–210; Arias, pp. 217–224; Aznar, pp. 427–464; Baxell, pp. 227–228, 234; Beevor, pp. 277–286; Cardona, pp. 173–180; Engel, *Operations*, pp. 145–162; Hildago, pp. 150–155; Hills, pp. 147–166; Kindélan, pp. 91–100; Lister, pp. 132–149; Lojendio, pp. 331–345; López-Muñiz, pp. 151–192; Martinez, *Brunete*, pp. 101–233; Martínez and Martínez, pp. 206–222; Modesto, pp. 101–120; Proctor, pp. 145–155; Rojo, *Heroica*, pp. 97–112; Rotmistov, pp. 231–270; Saiz, vol. 2, pp. 505–529; Salas *Air*, pp. 235–244; Salas, *Army*, vol. 3, pp. 1695–1764, Cuadro 30, 31, 33; Serebryakov, pp. 28–98; Thomas, pp. 710–717; Vidal, pp. 257–270. Casas, *Brunete*, has many contemporary reports and interviews with combatants. *Solidarity* has much information about International Brigade participation.
18 On July 6 alone, 23 of 57 Republican tanks were hit, four were set ablaze, and ten left immobile. See Salas, *Army*, vol. 3, Cuadro 33.
19 Hills, p. 152.
20 The British Battalion shot several prisoners whom they believed had tried to escape behind a human shield. Baxell, pp. 227–228.
21 Serebryakov, p. 32.
22 Thomas, p. 432.
23 Some officers felt that Spain should emulate the Reichswehr. Herrero Perez, p. 242.
24 During World War II he was a leading opponent of Spain entering the war on Germany's side.
25 Each Navarrese brigade had 11 battalions and three or four batteries and each division had a dozen battalions and five or six batteries. Martinez, *Brunete*, pp. 178–179.
26 For Romero's attack see the over-critical comments of Serebryakov, pp. 16–17, 20–28, 33–35, 40–42.
27 The dense infantry formations during the German riposte at Cambrai in November 1917 contributed to their failure to recover all the lost ground.
28 Salas, *Army*, vol. 3, Cuadro 30.
29 Modesto, p. 100.
30 Salas, *Army*, vol. 3, Cuadro 31.

31 The Red Army's leaders had the same problem and rapidly lost control in 1941. Yet Shtern had a radio link to the Spanish general staff and maintained a constant stream of reports about enemy air activity. Kowalsky, Section VII: Communications Engineers and Advisors. The Republic had 300km of telephone wire in reserve. Serebryakov, p. 93.
32 The division eventually had 16 battalions in three brigades, and six batteries with a company of Russos.
33 A critique of Campesino's assault appears in Serebryakov, pp. 47–48. The Red Army displayed similar shortcomings during the Winter War with Finland in 1939–1940. See Hooton, *Claws*, pp. 143–144, 146.
34 Asensio would eventually have 15½ battalions.
35 Unlike the French staff at Verdun.
36 Jurado would become Chief of the DECA, becoming a brigadier general in August 1938, and would command the Catalonia Army Group in January 1939. He ended his days in 1965 as head of Uruguay's cartography service. Galán was given a division on the Teruel front and was then commander of the XXIII CE in Andalusia for a year from November 1937. After the war he served in Red Army academies and ended his life in 1978 as an instructor to the Cuban Army.
37 Zaragoza, pp. 237–245.
38 Matthews, p. 111.
39 For air operations see Permuy, pp. 61–62; Ries and Ring, pp. 68–84; Salas, *Air*, pp. 235–244; Serebryakov, pp. 79–90; Vidal, p. 269; UKNA HW 21/2 & 21/3.
40 Coverdale, p. 281.
41 Serebryakov, p. 65.
42 Howson, *Air*, pp. 264, 278; Saiz, vol. 2, p. 530n.1, gives 88 which must include accidental losses.
43 Martinez, *Brunete*, pp. 178–181, Appendix 7.
44 By July 30 these men had dug 10km of trenches and laid 50km of wire.
45 Casado was promoted to colonel and in 1938 was rapidly promoted to command a corps, the Andalusian Army, then the Central Army.
46 Martinez, *Brunete*, p. 154n.177.
47 Engel, *Operations*, pp. 157–159.
48 Republican intelligence estimated enemy artillery support at 60 batteries.
49 The brigade was disbanded, then reformed on August 4 with three new battalions. Morale was poor in other International Brigades due to losses. Even the British Battalion mutinied on July 28 and a Soviet document noted that from August 1 through November 1 4,000 members were sent for "reeducation." Baxell, p. 234; Beevor, pp. 285–286. Several unit commanders left Spain in despair, including the 12 "Garibaldi" BI's Randolfo Pacciardi.
50 Serebryakov, p. 65.
51 Ries and Ring, p. 77.
52 This became a favorite expedient of the Soviet Red Army during 1941 and 1942.
53 For casualties see Casas, Anexo 3; Martinez, *Brunete*, pp. 231–232; Salas, *Army*, vol. 3, Cuadro 30, 31; Serebryakov, pp. 75, 93–94; Thomas, p. 715. The Brigadistas suffered 31 percent casualties or 4,239. Beevor, pp. 285–286, based upon Soviet documents; Cardona, p. 180.
54 Kowalsky, ch. 15, table V-8, although Salas, *Army*, vol. 3, Cuadro 33, using Spanish archives, says that 33 tanks were destroyed.
55 Serebryakov, pp. 18–19. The Red Army demonstrated the same weaknesses against Finland in 1939–1940 and during the 1942 Kharkov offensive. See Martinez, *Brunete*, Appendices 11 and 12.

56 Serebryakov, pp. 57–60, 75, 93–94.
57 For the crisis see Beevor, pp. 294–296; Hills, pp. 169–170; Thomas, pp. 651–661. It also caused Largo Caballero to lose the premiership.
58 See Lister, pp. 151–162; Thomas, pp. 723–725.
59 Lister noted the considerable efforts made to conceal the true reason for the transfer of V CE to Aragon. But Soviet advisors certainly knew, and Lister, who had worked in the Soviet Union, discussed the matter with one in Russian. Lister, p. 154.
60 Martinez, *Zaragoza*, p. 88.
61 For the Aragon campaign see Alcofar, *Air*, pp. 214–222; Alcofar, *CTV*, pp. 147–163; Arias, pp. 237–241; Aznar, pp. 485–516; Beevor, pp. 296–300; Belforte, *Teruel*, pp. 215–224; Cardona, pp. 189–193; Coverdale, pp. 347–351; Engel, *Operations*, pp. 175–182; Herrero Perez, p. 327; Hills, p. 167; Lister, pp. 162–169; Lojendio, pp. 345–359; Manca, pp. 173–183; Martinez, *Zaragoza*, pp. 75–172; Martínez and Martínez, pp. 224–236; Modesto, pp. 123–136; Murias, pp. 187–190; Permuy, p. 63; Rojo, *Heroica*, pp. 115–128; Saiz, vol. 2, pp. 579–598; Salas, *Army*, vol. 3, pp. 1773–1849; Thomas, pp. 722–723, 725–728; Vidal, pp. 282–292; Voltas, vol. 2, pp. 237–249.
62 Half the 4,000 inhabitants had been evacuated long before the Republican attack.
63 Garcia Lomas, p. 153. Fifth Corps created a new reserve, 151st Division, under General Anatolio de Fuentes Garcia with nearly 11,000 men.
64 Manca, pp. 176–183.
65 Martinez, *Zaragoza*, pp. 172–183.
66 Beevor, p. 297.
67 For this disastrous attack see Beevor, p. 297; Kowalsky, ch. 15, section VI; Modesto, p. 135; Zaloga, "Soviet 'Final Reinforcements' and Tanks," pp. 34–35; *Solidarity*, pp. 96–98. Kondratev would commit suicide after his tank brigade was isolated during the Finnish War in 1940. Hooton, *Claws*, pp. 118–120. During World War II Soviet infantry routinely went into battle on the decks of tanks.
68 Lister, p. 168.
69 Tagüeña, p. 128.
70 Thomas, pp. 772–774.
71 For Nationalist planning see Hills, p. 169; Kindélan, pp. 104–116; Martinez, *La Battalla de Teruel*, pp. 18–28 (hereafter Martinez, *Teruel*).
72 Martinez, *Zaragossa*, p. 14.
73 For details see Engel, *Divisions*.
74 From October 21 through December 31, 5,716 trains, including 1,780 for troops, were run. For rail see Garcia Lomas, pp. 153–154.
75 Garcia Lomas, p. 153–154.
76 Martinez, *Teruel*, pp. 239–43; Salas, *Army*, vol. 3, pp. 2043–2082. Barroso had great respect for Rojo who had been one of his pupils at staff college; the feeling was reciprocated. Hills, pp. 169–172.
77 Martínez and Martínez, pp. 239–240.
78 The original XXI and XXII CEs were joined in September by V CE, and in October by the reformed XVIII CE which had been temporarily disbanded on September 22, and the new XX CE.
79 For Republican planning see Hills, p. 169; Martinez, *Teruel*, pp. 28–34.
80 Kowalsky, ch. 15.
81 Beevor, p. 315. Compare also with French doctrine in Doughty, pp. 97, 106, 115–116, 187.
82 Zaragoza, pp. 262–264.

83 The directive is in Engel, *Operations*, pp. 189–192. Casa-Vega, p. 19; Kowalsky, ch. 15. The Reserve Army was now deactivated.

84 Cayón Garcia/Muñoz Rubio, *Railway*, pp. 18–19.

CHAPTER 5

The Pendulum Swings: Teruel and the Aragon Offensive

The Battle of Teruel

Teruel was seized by the rebels at the outbreak of the Civil War and quickly became the tip of a narrow salient some 20km wide and 25km long, which pointed like an accusing finger at Valencia. The salient was frequently attacked, the last upon Albarracin during the battle of Brunete.[1] Built around a 700-year-old walled city on a 915-meter rocky knoll, Teruel had 13,000 inhabitants and was a vital communications center at the confluence of the Rivers Turia and Alfambra. It overlooked the crossroads of the Saragossa to Sagunto Highway, the road north to Alcaniz on the Ebro, and south to the Valencia Highway, these following the river valleys.

The city is surrounded by mountains reaching more than 1,000m with gorges, fang-shaped peaks, and vertically sided ridges with rounded tops, notably the northwest–southeast Sierra Palomera, west of the Alfambra Valley, bounded in the north by the Sierra de Lidon and in the south by the 1,165m Celadas Heights (Altas de Celadas), their eastern slopes covered with shrub or woods, while the western ones tend to be bare of vegetation. Southwest of the city are the Sierra de Albarracin and Montes Universates, and together these heights contribute to the area's notoriously harsh climate, especially during the winter when the temperature usually drops to -10°C.

The two key heights looming over the city in the forthcoming battle were La Muela (The Tooth) and El Muleton (The Fleece). The 1,086-meter El Muleton to the north is on the southern edge of the Celadas Heights, but more important to the northwest was "the grim, dark giant"—1,053m La Muela, a 3km-diameter plateau with steep eastern and southern edges but a more gentle approach from the north.

The Saragossa Highway runs up the Jiloca Valley through the small towns of Concud and Caude, entering a plain around Concud. Across the Turia a

Table 5.1: Republican order of battle

Corps	Commander
V	Modesto
XIII	Balibrea
XVIII	Fernández-Heredia
XIX	Vidal
XX	Menéndez later Galán
XXI	Perea
XXII	Ibarrola

Table 5.2: Nationalist order of battle

Corps	Commander
Galicia	Aranda
Castile	Varela
Morocco	Yagüe

highway runs southeast through the Escandón Pass to the port of Sagunto, while along the Alfambra lies the Alcaniz road running north through Perales del Alfambra, Alfambra, and Peralejos, while the road runs south down the Turia Valley through Villastar to the Valencia Highway. Teruel itself had suburbs on either side of the Turia but the walled area had a religious complex in the northwestern district including the seminary and the convents of Santa Clara and Santa Teresa. The largely administrative southeastern district included the civil governor's palace, the Bank of Spain and the Hotel Aragon.

The salient's 60km-long perimeter was held by Muñoz Castellanos's 52nd Division from his headquarters at Santa Eulalia, with 20,560 men nominally in four brigades under colonels. Barba's I Brigade, the former Belchite salient garrison, now held the southern face of the salient with 4,500 men in five conscript battalions on the eastern bank of the Turia and one in reserve north of Teruel. The western and northern faces were held by Juan Cremades's II Brigade and Natalio Lopez Bravo's III Brigade respectively. Domingo Rey d'Harcourt's IV Brigade was an urban garrison of 1,950 men, mostly rear-echelon personnel but including a single Falangist infantry battalion, as well as some 120 paramilitary police. Fire support consisted of four batteries, half on La Muela, and a single antitank gun.

Dávila was certainly aware of the salient's vulnerability, for in early October Colonel Anselmo Loscertales warned about the poor state of the defenses, while a month later Rey d'Harcourt requested reinforcements. But the Nationalist

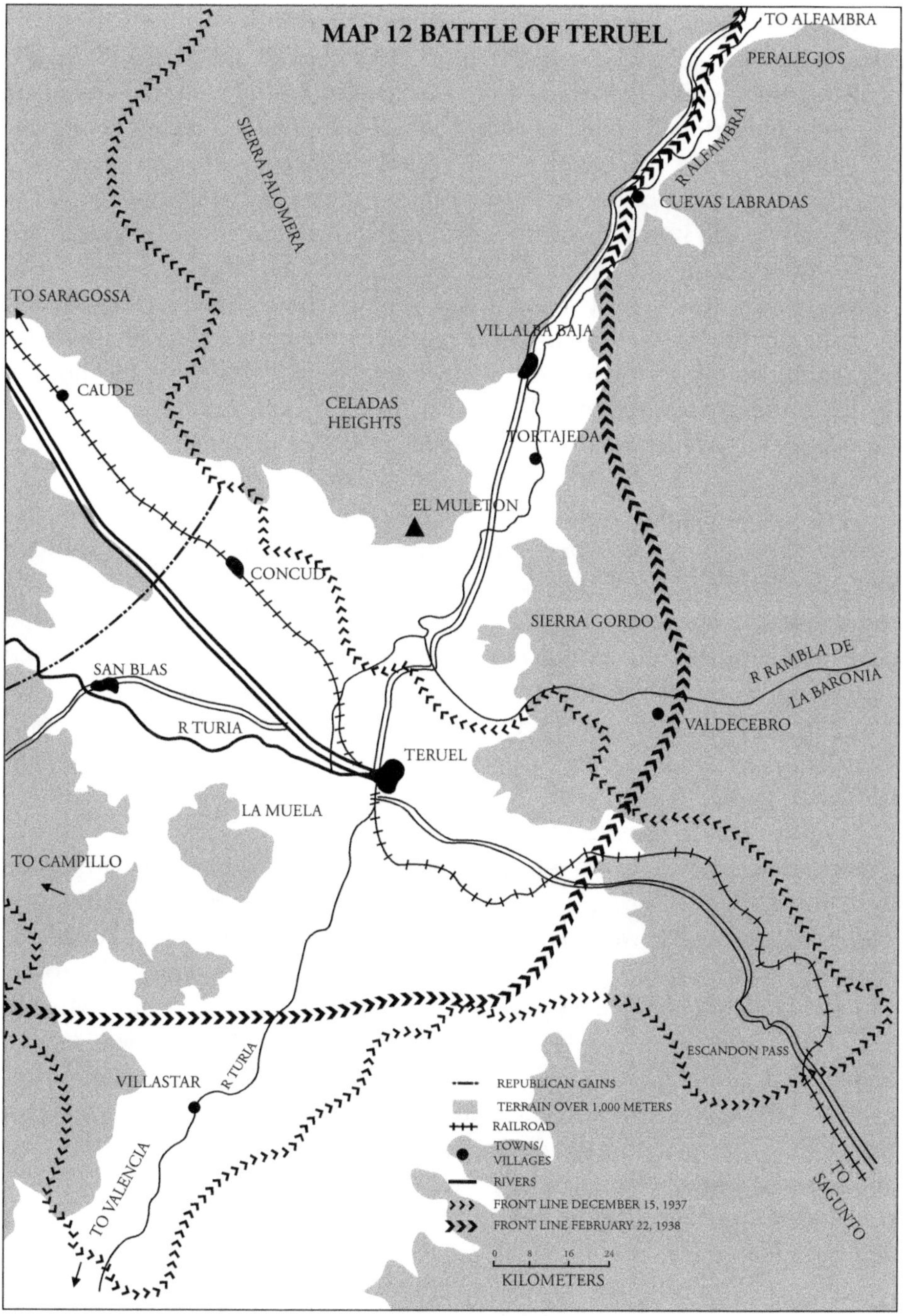
MAP 12 BATTLE OF TERUEL
TO ALFAMBRA
PERALEGJOS
R ALFAMBRA
CUEVAS LABRADAS
SIERRA PALOMERA
TO SARAGOSSA
VILLALBA BAJA
CAUDE
CELADAS HEIGHTS
TORTAJEDA
EL MULETON
CONCUD
SIERRA GORDO
R RAMBLA DE LA BARONIA
SAN BLAS
VALDECEBRO
R TURIA
TERUEL
LA MUELA
TO CAMPILLO
ESCANDON PASS
VILLASTAR
R TURIA
TO VALENCIA
TO SAGUNTO
REPUBLICAN GAINS
TERRAIN OVER 1,000 METERS
RAILROAD
TOWNS/ VILLAGES
RIVERS
FRONT LINE DECEMBER 15, 1937
FRONT LINE FEBRUARY 22, 1938
0 8 16 24
KILOMETERS

GHQ focused upon its own offensive plans and ignored Teruel, just as the Allied high command would ignore warnings about the Ardennes seven years later. Signs of an attack were detected on December 11 and Rey d'Harcourt, a 52-year-old gunner, assembled a two-battalion reserve on the Saragossa Highway and stripped his own infantry battalion to strengthen Barba's brigade.

During the night of December 14/15 the Republicans infiltrated Cremades's and Lopez Bravo's positions. They often assembled undetected outside the wire by dawn and stormed positions using their own heavy weapons, although with artillery being used from 07:15 only against the larger positions.[2] But Lister, on Ibarrola's front, contributed to the first day's setbacks. The Concud garrison detected and pinned down the assembling 11 DI as it awaited a bombardment. Tanks then had to be brought up and the town did not fall until the afternoon at the cost of 105 casualties. On Fernández-Heredia's front 64 and 34 DI pushed into a gap in the defenses west of Teruel but Cremades withdrew slowly and, like Lopez Bravo, restricted the enemy advance.

Muñoz Castellanos learned of the breakthrough before midnight and created two battle groups with a total of 1,100 men: one going to Concud and the other acting as his reserve. He and Rey d'Harcourt kept Dávila informed although the army commander telephoned Franco only at 10:30 the following day but had ordered Múgica's 81st Division to make a forced march to Teruel, grabbing five battalions from other divisions as he did so, while artillery was also sent south. Dávila also had four meetings at Muñoz Castellanos's command post to assess the situation before discussing it with Moscardó and Kindélan.

Múgica arrived on December 16 using his two brigades to reinforce Cremades and Lopez Bravo while his "borrowed" battalions shielded Caude from the east. But during a day of blizzards Lister pushed up the highway north of Concud and westward to take San Blas to await the arrival of Major Pedro Martínez Cartón's 64 DI which took the heights west of the town. Meanwhile Fernández-Heredia's 34 DI approached La Muela, while Ibarrola's 25 DI advanced upon Teruel from the north. Ibarrola and Fernández-Heredia linked up during the afternoon to achieve the Republican Army's greatest feat of arms—the isolation of a brigade that was pinned down by Menéndez's corps. Rey d'Harcourt feared he would not last longer than 24 hours and asked for and received Muñoz Castellanos's permission to pull back Barba's brigade—a timely decision, for an hour before the request Hernández Saravia ordered an assault upon Teruel.

The noose around Teruel slowly tightened on December 17 with Menéndez pushing Barba up the Sagunto Highway while the others strengthened the outer siege line and pushed toward Teruel. The end of the day saw two Nationalist task forces created north and south of the Turia under Munoz Castellanos and Múgica but Aranda's Galicia Corps was now ordered to the front. The tubby Aranda, who had just turned 49, was an engineer, a cartographer, and a staff officer who helped plan the Rif War's decisive Alhucemas Bay amphibious operation.[3] He was a freemason, a liberal, and a staunch Monarchist who helped to crush the Asturias uprising of 1934, but when the uprising began this cool, jovial, and cunning man convinced Republicans that he was loyal to them. He then seized Oviedo for the rebels and held it in an epic siege. He was described as "studious, intelligent, of clear ideas and with a tremendous capacity for work." He loathed the Falange and after Franco's victory was involved in several Monarchist plots leading to his arrest in 1943. He would be the last of Franco's Civil War generals to die, in 1979.

During the day Dávila activated the Teruel Operations Army (Ejercito de Operaciones de Teruel) while Franco dispatched seven heavy batteries augmented by 13 (later 24) Italian batteries. The following day the Republic pushed back Teruel's defenders to seize the Muela firebase during the late afternoon. Meanwhile, Barba's troops withdrew toward the town while groups of civilians carrying white flags fled in the opposite direction. Prieto demanded his troops do nothing to endanger civilians unnecessarily and evacuate them if possible.

As the crisis deepened on the morning of December 19 Rey d'Harcourt informed Muñoz Castellanos that he would defend the city. The following day, Rey d'Harcourt's 53rd birthday, the Republicans probed the suburbs, although the last bastions east of the Turia did not fall until the morning of December 23. With their backs literally to the wall the 3,700 defenders were joined by some 4,000 civilians, including children, with Rey d'Harcourt and half the troops in the administrative district and the remainder in the religious district under Barba. On December 22 the attackers entered the city walls but would have to make frontal assaults upon strongly held buildings. As they pushed into the city center civilians cowered within cellars while bullets and icy blasts swirled along the streets.

Aranda, who now had all of the 81st and 84th Divisions with part of 82nd, had begun his relief operation. Supported by 55 guns, some of which arrived without ammunition, the 82nd Division pushed from the north and the 81st from the south against fierce resistance and on December 19 Aranda's command post was bombed.[4] Reluctantly Franco recognized more substantial reinforcements were needed to prevent the loss of a provincial capital before the end of a "triumphal year." He decided to milk the Madrid assault force and on December 20 ordered Varela's Castile Corps headquarters to join Aranda together with four divisions (54th, 61st, 62nd, and the remainder of 82nd), 21 divisional and eight army batteries as well as a tank group.[5]

On December 22 Varela, Vigón, Saliquet, Yagüe, and artillery commander Colonel Martinez de Campos met Franco at Burgos where he took the momentous decision to toss the Madrid project into the trash can and relieve Teruel. A directive issued just after midday on December 22 called for the liberation of Teruel and split the front into two corps sectors: north and south of the Turia (Cuerpo de Ejército del Norte/Sur del Turia) under Aranda and Varela respectively while Yagüe's Morocco Corps was ordered to join them as Dávila moved the Teruel Operations Army command post to Ojos Negras, some 70km from Teruel.[6] Everything depended upon Teruel holding out, and as the Republicans prepared to storm the city Franco sent Rey d'Harcourt a stream of messages begging him to hold out: "Hold on and have confidence in Spain as Spain has confidence in you."

By December 24 Aranda and Varela had 78,000 men supported by 390 guns, with Dávila determined to relieve the city from the west using the direct route along the Turia Valley. Air superiority was assured, for on December 16 Volkmann and eight Condor Legion squadrons arrived followed by 14 Italian and eight Spanish, including the BAH to give the Nationalists 35 squadrons by mid-January.[7] Republican air strength over the battlefield would slowly increase to 300 aircraft.[8]

But snow showers and poor visibility delayed the attack until December 29, giving Aranda time to withdraw the exhausted 52nd Division while 82nd Division commander, Colonel José Ceano-Viva, suffered a serious head wound and was replaced by Colonel Francisco Delgado Serrano.[9] The attack began with a two-hour artillery bombardment then bombers dropped 100 tonnes of bombs. Volkmann supported Aranda while Bernasconi's Italians supported Varela. As biplane fighters strafed trenches, the Nationalists' assault began but the infantry were silhouetted against the snow, making them easy targets.

Aranda used Colonel Antonio Sagardía's 62nd Division to retake Concud, but Sagardía's attack was disrupted by artillery fire directed from observation posts to the east, despite attacks by the 150th Division. A Falange battalion entered the town but was driven out and three attempts on December 30 also failed, although by nightfall Sagardía held positions dominating the town. Lister's defenders were exhausted and were relieved that night by 68 DI (Major Justo López) who was driven out on New Year's Eve, but Sagardía, having suffered 1,177 casualties including 189 dead and 805 sick, was relieved by Barrón.

Ibarrola appealed to Lister to return to the line, leading to a rare clash between two very different men. The Basque Ibarrola, a Civil Guard captain at the outbreak of war, was deeply religious, while Lister was an atheist Communist. However, the Basque's amiable personality and loyalty to subordinates meant that Lister would later observe that knowing him was one of the best memories of the war.[10] Yet he refused to sanction the return of his exhausted men to the front, pointing out that 58 had lost feet through frostbite. The crisis passed and shortly afterward Lister was promoted to lieutenant colonel.

The end of the month saw Yagüe's Corps, reinforced by 42 batteries, enter the line in the north, taking over the 5th, 54th, and 108th Divisions, then extending its line southward. Yagüe, who had just turned 46, was a doctor's son who had been a cadet with Franco and together, after serving in Morocco, they crushed the 1934 Asturian uprising.[11] The white-haired Africanista was an early supporter of the Falange and a close friend of its founder, Jose Antonio Primo de Rivera, but did not join the military plotters until 1936. He spearheaded the advance across Andalusia and Estremadura and earned the nickname "The Butcher of Badajoz" after executing hundreds in the city. His calmness during crises and battlefield flexibility meant that he was a reliable pair of hands. With the capture of Concud and heavy snowfalls, fighting on Aranda's front died down, but the need to clear the heights north of the valley led Buruaga's 150th Division on January 2 to push down from positions opposite Caude, where he was shortly joined by Barrón's division to advance 5km by January 4.

On December 30 Varela began the main relief operation south of the Turia using the 61st, 1st, and 82nd Divisions, while his 81st Division, north of the river, sought to retake the high ground west of Teruel beyond the San Blas–Campillo road as a secure base to retake La Muela. He struck in the afternoon but only García-Valiño's 1st Division had any success, seizing the heights dominating the San Blas–Campillo road. Varela maintained the pressure and on December 30 Muñoz Grandes's 61st Division pushed back Fernández-Heredia while Varela's perennial optimism rose when aerial reconnaissance reported La Muela deserted as Muñoz Grandes reached its foot, despite fierce, tank-tipped counterattacks.

On New Year's Eve Varela, now supported by 44 batteries, pushed on through fog and snow showers.[12] Múgica closed on San Blas from the north and took the town on New Year's Day but could advance no further. Just before midday Muñoz Grandes took La Muela while García-Valiño pushed up the western bank of the Turia and reported Teruel's outskirts were within reach, and Dávila received a garbled version of the message, briefly leading

The great blizzard which interrupted the battle of Teruel front brought great hardship to front-line troops. This group of Nationalist officers in the rear were clearly affected by the freezing conditions. (Photo by José Demaría "Campúa")

An abandoned T-26 on the Teruel front. With their high velocity 45mm guns (also used as antitank weapons) these vehicles were superior to anything supplied by the Germans and Italians and several dozen were acquired to equip Nationalist tank units and even the CTV's armored group. (Photo by José Demaría "Campúa")

him to believe that the city was on the verge of relief. Varela's advance upon Teruel sparked panic among the defenders, the Socialist Lieutenant Colonel Andrés Nieto's 40 DI, who abandoned the city. They returned shamefaced four hours later without the Nationalists inside or outside the city learning of the debacle.[13]

The New Year's Eve snow showers grew into a huge blizzard which lasted four days and blanketed the battlefield with more than a meter of snow, thus ending large-scale operations for a fortnight. The snow muffled the sounds of fighting to provide the illusion of peace but the cold grounded airmen and trapped 600 vehicles on the Sagunto Highway, where many suffered cracked engine blocks and frozen radiators. Only the most powerful trucks could move along the icy roads while smaller vehicles skidded. Republican rail traffic also suffered and was reduced to 53 trains, half medical, from December 30 through January 4.[14]

As the temperature dropped to -18ºC the cold sapped the troops' energy, searing their lungs, numbing limbs and ears, and creating a longing for sleep. Many succumbed to the sleep eternal while others tried desperately to remain awake, often turning to coffee or brandy, although the alcohol was more likely to accelerate their deaths. Thousands on both sides suffered frostbite and had limbs amputated to save their lives.[15] To prevent their weapons freezing, men wrapped the mechanisms and carried them within threadbare uniforms, many of the Nationalists having been unable to exchange their summer uniforms for winter ones. Women donated pullovers and balaclava helmets but it was not enough, and the only warm clothing was made by the men themselves slitting a blanket to wear as a poncho. The absence of trees meant that there was little firewood—Moors chopped down Condor Legion telephone poles—but fires could attract shells or mortar bombs.[16]

Only those behind Teruel's walls were sheltered and had access to firewood from wrecked buildings. Nationalist propaganda described Teruel as the new Alcázar de Toledo, but now the attackers were not a militia rabble but battle-hardened troops who began to reduce the strongpoints. If loudspeaker appeals to surrender failed, engineers, covered by automatic weapons or armored vehicles, dashed out to place demolition charges to blast holes in the walls. Where even this was too dangerous, artillery fired at point-blank range, and once the infantry were within buildings there would be a vicious battle with bomb and bayonet, the lower storeys falling easily while the upper ones were bitterly defended.

All hope of relief ended after Modesto's V Corps entered the line south of Teruel on New Year's Day. Ignoring the blizzard, Modesto reacted with his usual dynamism the following day, supported by seven batteries and two tank companies, to push Varela back to La Muela which Menéndez was unable to retake. Meanwhile, Nieto, determined to take the city and wash away the stain on his division's reputation, began by taking the Santa Teresa convent in the northwest and the civil governor's palace in the southwest on January 3. Building by building he reduced the two enclaves whose defenders had suffered more than 1,000 casualties and were short of food, water, and medicine. With no sign of relief Rey d'Harcourt bowed to the inevitable and, through the auspices of the Red Cross, he and the Bishop of Teruel, Anselmo Polanco, agreed to surrender on January 7 and did so the following day. During the afternoon the civilians were allowed to leave and in the evening the defenders came out with their hands up to be trucked out as the Republicans prepared to defend their gains.[17]

Even before the big freeze, Franco on January 3 had ordered a change in direction, abandoning an approach along the valleys and trying instead to take the heights north of the city while Varela pinned down the enemy.[18] Aranda's earlier success provided a secure left flank and as visibility began to improve on January 14 Dávila ordered an attack to secure the northern heights down to the lower Alfambra and especially the Celadas Heights and El Muleton. This would bring the Nationalists 6km north of Teruel and help secure communications to Saragossa.[19] But nothing could be done until mid-January when the thaw left snow-topped peaks and hard or firm ground. The lull gave Hernández Saravia time to reorganize the Levante Army which had, from north to south, XIII CE (39, 42 DI, and equivalent of a third division), V CE (47, 35 DI), XVIII CE (34, 70 DI) and XIX CE (41, 64 DI), with XX CE (68 DI), 40 DI, some 44 batteries and four tank companies in reserve.

Dávila now adopted a bite-and-hold approach supported by 470 guns under Martinez de Campos, now promoted to brigadier general, although Spanish artillery doctrine made them very dependent upon good visibility for correcting fire in range-finding. Until 1917 corrective fire lasted up to a week before the main artillery preparation (fire-for-effect), and this denied the attacker surprise. Afterward predicted fire techniques were developed. These involved surveying gun and target positions, then allowing for gun status, elevation, location, wind speed and direction, temperature, and propellant efficiency to provide instant fire-for-effect. By 1918 this was standard practice among west European armies but not in the Spanish Army, and throughout the latter stages of the Civil War an hour of corrective fire preceded Nationalist artillery preparation.[20]

Aranda's attack was by 5th and 84th Divisions under Colonels Bautista and Galera respectively and they faced Menéndez, with Colonel Julio Michelena's 39

DI and 42 DI of Lieutenant Colonel José Balibrea's XIII CE to the north with 27 DI in reserve. The Nationalists could exploit the Saragossa Highway and railroad for supplies, but the defenders' logistics were hampered by the lack of roads and the wintery conditions, leaving them short of food and ammunition. The attack began on January 17 after a powerful artillery and air preparation. Then Aranda attacked on a 10km front with Galera sweeping through the Celadas Heights within an hour while Bautista moved upon El Muleton.[21] During the next two days Aranda pushed eastward with Bautista taking El Muleton on January 17 after a noon attack. The crisis forced Barcelona, which had wanted the campaign to be a totally Hispanic operation, to commit the International Brigades of Walter's 35 DI to join Modesto's 47 DI and ten batteries in a 10km defensive arc north of Teruel. But Galera pushed it back to take the last height dominating the lower Alfambra during a day in which Nationalist airmen flew 400 sorties and dropped 120 tonnes of bombs.

By January 20 the Nationalists had reached the Alfambra, and by taking the new cemetery a couple of kilometers from Teruel they controlled the upper Turia. They also threatened the enemy salient in the Sierra Palomera, although the success was costly, with Galera alone suffering 4,300 casualties, including 405 dead, about half the divisional strength. Yet Nationalist morale remained high, unlike that of their enemies, and when Nieto, on January 20, was ordered to regain the new cemetery his 84 BM mutinied, having earlier lost a quarter of its men in action. The brigade commander Major Benjamín Iseli Andrés quickly court-martialed some 115 mutineers and executed 53, including three sergeants.[22]

Meanwhile, Dávila, worried about the vulnerability of his communications, warned Yagüe on January 13 to secure the vital highway and railroad as he prepared to push deeper into the lower Alfambra Valley. The following day he published plans to envelop Teruel, but on January 19 Franco ordered an offensive against the Sierra Palomera salient to the town of Alfambra. This was briefly compromised on January 25 when Balibrea's XIII CE launched a three-day attack from the salient to cut the highway using the reinforced 27 DI, underlining Dávila's concerns about his communications. Alerted by a deserter, Barrón's strongpoints around Singra stopped Balibrea, while a diversionary attack from February 3 by 54 DI against Varela's 81st Division in the Turia Valley was also defeated.[23]

Dávila's plans were hindered but on February 2 he ordered a double envelopment of the salient in two days' time supported by 320 guns. Yagüe would attack in the north with four divisions (1st, 4th, 5th, and 82nd) and their breakthrough would be exploited by Monasterio's Cavalry Division and

Lieutenant Colonel Pedro Peñarredonda's mobile brigade, while Aranda would strike from the west with three divisions (85th, 83rd, and 84th).

Balibrea held the salient with 42, 39, and 66 DI on a 70km front with two brigades in reserve, but the Republican command was surprised by the rapid delivery of the blow. It also faced a self-made distraction, for also on February 2 Rojo issued a directive which called not only for the execution of Plan "P" but also simultaneous operations to take Cordoba in Andalusia, reduce the Jarama salient, and either take Saragossa or bring it under artillery fire.[24] It was an astonishing flight of fancy, utterly beyond the Republic's resources and it is difficult to understand whether he was desperate or suffering a surfeit of optimism. Supporting the Teruel front was a severe strain involving 1,353 trains in support from December 6 through February 28, yet just before the campaign ended Rojo teletyped Prieto: "Our problem, as I am tired of repeating, is tragically simple: material, material, material, everything comes down to this. If we had only a half or one third of what the enemy has, our victory would soon be assured."[25]

On February 1 the Communists had a fright when Hernández Saravia arrived at Modesto's command post and without explanation ordered him to report immediately to General Toribo Sanchez Cabrera at the Defense Ministry. The Communists feared Prieto intended to dismiss Modesto who found excuses to remain at his post until the Nationalist offensive on February 5. A later conversation with Rojo indicated that he had been summoned to discuss participation in the Estremadura offensive.[26]

The weather remained bitterly cold, keeping the ground hard while creating mists and fogs which, with problems assembling and supplying Yagüe, caused the attack to be postponed for 24 hours, allowing deserters to alert the defenders. On the morning of February 5 Nationalist batteries lashed the defenses for two hours while German and Italian bombers added their loads. The latter were responsible for a friendly fire incident upon Yagüe's troops, inflicting 500 casualties, including 156 dead. But he still moved off on time and rapidly advanced 10km to clear the way for Monasterio.[27]

The following day Monasterio's 3,000 horsemen, paced by the 5th Division, swept down behind the Sierra Palomera through Argente and Visiedo to cut the main road into the salient from Perales de Alfambra, then linked up with Aranda to isolate the sierra. After leaving a screening detachment, Monasterio rode southeast to take Alfambra on February 7, as many defenders sought only flight or surrender. It was the only pure cavalry action of the war in a millennium-long tradition that faded from European history within a decade. The cavalry were supported by air power which assumed many of its traditional

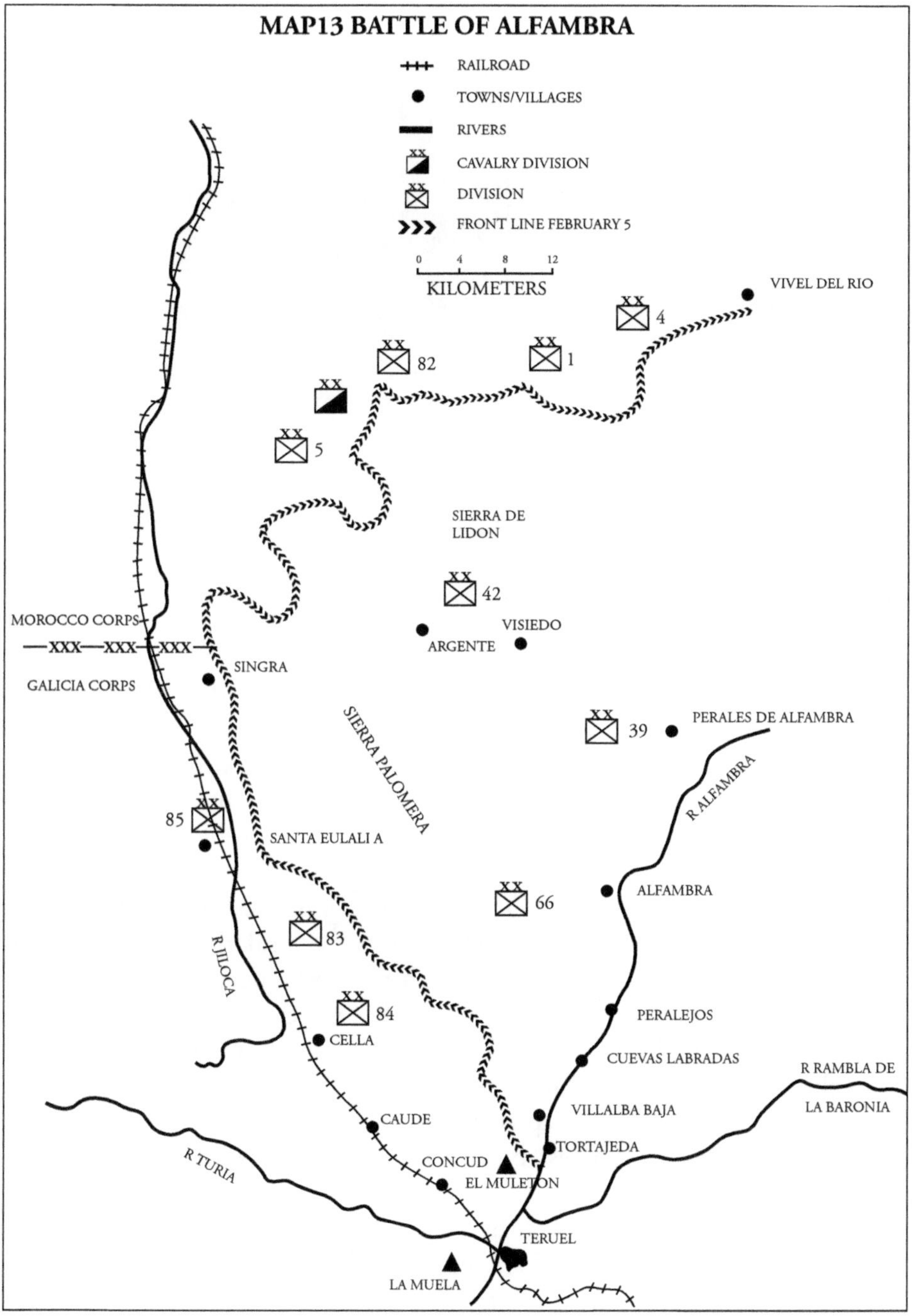
MAP13 BATTLE OF ALFAMBRA
RAILROAD
TOWNS/VILLAGES
RIVERS
CAVALRY DIVISION
DIVISION
FRONT LINE FEBRUARY 5
0 4 8 12
KILOMETERS
VIVEL DEL RIO
4
82
1
5
SIERRA DE LIDON
42
MOROCCO CORPS
GALICIA CORPS
VISIEDO
ARGENTE
SINGRA
SIERRA PALOMERA
39
PERALES DE ALFAMBRA
R ALFAMBRA
85
SANTA EULALI A
66
ALFAMBRA
83
R JILOCA
84
CELLA
PERALEJOS
CUEVAS LABRADAS
R RAMBLA DE LA BARONIA
VILLALBA BAJA
CAUDE
TORTAJEDA
R TURIA
CONCUD
EL MULETON
TERUEL
LA MUELA

Colonel José Monasterio's cavalry move up for what was to be the last major cavalry action in western Europe. Their success in the Alfambra campaign owed much to the fact the defenders were weak and overstretched. (Photo by José Demaría "Campúa")

roles, such as interdicting communications and striking the defenders' attempts at rallying. The Condor Legion's fighter bombers alone flew up to six sorties a day in this role while the Italians, who had dropped a maximum 19.5 tonnes of bombs on December 27, peaked at 233 sorties on January 17.[28] To the north the remainder of Yagüe's men steadily overcame stubborn resistance to reach the Alfambra.

In the center of the storm 42 DI was virtually annihilated and the flanking 27 and 39 DIs had to retreat quickly to avoid a similar fate, while 66 DI manfully held the shoulders of the breech as Hernández Saravia sent in 19 DI in a vain bid to plug the gap. By the end of the day Rojo had abandoned all hope of saving the salient and focused upon salvaging what he could from the wreck, throwing three pontoon bridges across the river to aid the withdrawal. As resistance collapsed the thrusting Yagüe occupied Perales de Alfambra on February 7 and established a bridgehead around Tortajeda, south of Villalba Baja.

Aranda's secondary role saw the 83rd Division deliver the main blow, breaking through on February 5 and entering the southern Sierra Palomera to envelop the massif from the south and link up with Monasterio. On its right the 84th Division consolidated the Nationalist grip on the southern part of the salient. By February 8 Yagüe and Aranda had extended Nationalist control to 800 square kilometers of territory on the Alfambra's western bank along most of its course in an advance of some 30km. The damage to the Republican army was profound, with some 15,000 casualties including nearly 4,400 dead, and 8,235 prisoners, the weakened defenders now facing the prospect of losing Teruel as Dávila prepared to exploit his commanding position.

To meet the new threat the Reserve Army was reactivated on February 9 in the Alfambra Valley under Menéndez, whose corps was given to Lieutenant Colonel Francisco Galán.[29] Menéndez, aged 46, was an infantry officer who had been a classmate of Franco. In the Rif War he played an important role as a cartographer and remained in the army when the Republic was established. He became President Azana's military advisor and organized the Presidential Guard, which he commanded while helping to plan the Brunete offensive. He was rewarded with a corps command and promoted to colonel on December 24, 1937, becoming a brigadier general on August 16, 1938. He now had XXI CE (70, 27 DI), XIII CE (39, 19, 25 DI) and V CE (35, 47 DI) while the Levante Army defended Teruel with XX CE with 66, 67, 46 DI with XIX CE (40, 41, 64 DI).

The canny Dávila was determined to exploit the success as soon as possible and at midnight on February 10/11 he ordered Aranda to strike across the lower Alfambra, secure the Sierra Gordo on the opposite side, then advance south across the Rambla de la Baronia (Rambla) to envelop Teruel.[30] Barrón would push out of the Tortajeda bridgehead, shielded by Galera, advance 5km eastward, then swing south across the Sagunto Highway. The 83rd and 150th Divisions, supported by a cavalry brigade and 60 tanks, would cross the Alfambra to take the Sierra Gordo, supported by a 1st Division task force, including two of Monasterio's cavalry brigades. Meanwhile Varela would press Teruel from the west with the 81st Division, while his 61st Division crossed the Turia Valley below Teruel. There would be the usual heavy artillery support, including Martinez de Campos's artillery train with 300 guns. Facing the juggernaut was Hernández Saravia with Galán's XX CE, including Campesino's 46 DI in Teruel, while Colonel Joaquín Vidal's XIX CE was south of the city. Artillery support for the defenders was poor and many of the divisions were under strength, having been battered in weeks of fighting. D-Day was set for February 13 but bad weather caused its postponement to February 17 which dawned with fog that did not lift until late morning, so H-Hour was reset for 11:00.

Barrón crossed the swollen river to penetrate 3km, supported by Galera who established the defensive flank.[31] But the 150th Division coming down

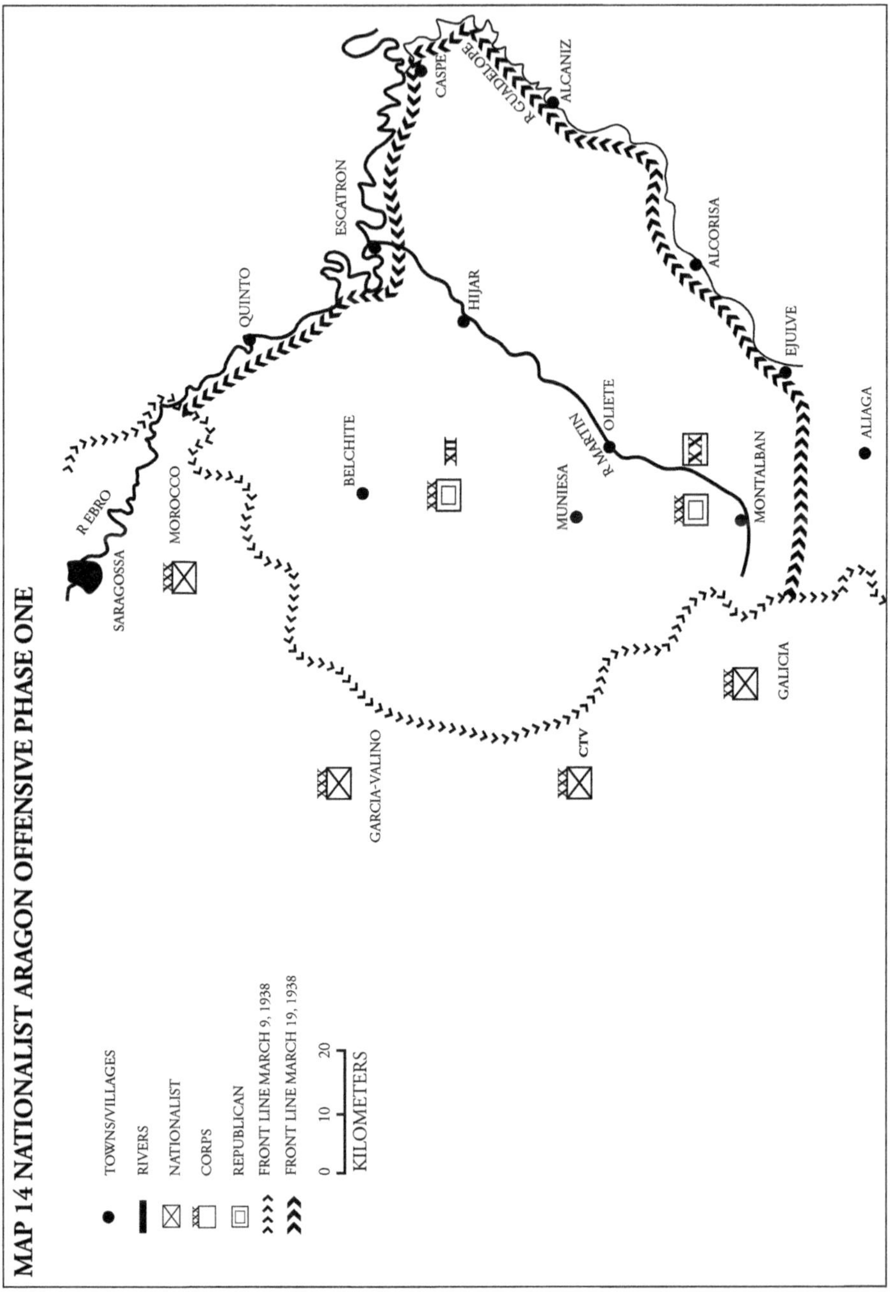

MAP 14 NATIONALIST ARAGON OFFENSIVE PHASE ONE

from El Muleton encountered fierce resistance from Major Fulgencio González Gómez's 67 DI and was unable to reach the Sierra Gordo until dusk, although Galán's response was delayed and ineffective.

The next day Galera, paced by the 83rd Division, drove south and crossed the Rambla to take Valdecebro on February 19, threatening the Sagunto Highway and railroad. In a desperate effort to hold the enemy Galán was withdrawn and Modesto (11, 46, 47 DI) faced the road roller coming south while Ibarrola with three divisions (25, 28, 66 DI) deployed on the northern and eastern faces of the growing Nationalist salient. During February 18 the 1st Division assaulted the old cemetery but it was two days before they drove out Campesino, while part of the division crossed the Rambla with 83rd Division to take the heights dominating Teruel from the north as the 84th Division cut the Sagunto Highway. Simultaneously Varela's 61st Division struck from La Muela and forced its way across the Turia to link up with Aranda a kilometer outside Teruel, trapping Campesino and 14,500 men.

The following day the 1st Division began to force its way into the city as Aranda and Varela struck into the Turia Valley to regain most of the ground lost in December. Bowing to the inevitable, Hernández Saravia ordered a withdrawal while Modesto was ordered on February 22 to relieve Campesino, only to learn, as his men assembled, that Campesino had broken out in a tank. He loudly complained that Lister and Modesto had abandoned him, both responding to the accusations with contempt.[32] The remainder of Campesino's men surrendered Teruel at 08:00 with some 2,000–3,000 of Major Pedro Mateo Merino's 101 BM being captured.

Teruel cost the Nationalists 43,800 casualties, 9,500 in the enemy offensive and the remainder in relief operations, including 17,100 reported sick, while the Republicans suffered 54,000.[33] A quarter of the tanks (24) were lost while 63 required major overhaul, leaving only 17 operational.[34] It was the material losses that proved so debilitating, including 80 guns, 227 automatic weapons, and 3,080 rifles, as well as some 50 aircraft, compared with 21 Nationalist. The loss of 34 fighters to enemy action and 42 in accidents caused the disbandment of two fighter squadrons.[35] The Republican commanders comforted themselves that the enemy had suffered just as severely, and this was true of some units, with 5th Division alone suffering 8,655 including 984 dead, or almost the whole division. But the Nationalists rapidly rotated units, allowing even the most battered to recover while Republican formations, such as 64 DI, spent the whole battle in the line.

The performance of both armies, now a year old, reflected the perennial weaknesses of the prewar Spanish Army. Republican combined-arms coordination remained poor, with tanks often left fighting alone. Rojo also complained to Prieto in February about the absence of the FARE despite incessant enemy air attacks, but when Prieto asked whether or not his staff had a senior air force officer Rojo replied he did not know and had only unofficial communications with an air force commander.[36] The Levante Army's Communist commissar noted that its chief of staff, Lieutenant Colonel Eduardo Sáenz Aranaz, rarely visited the front and that Fernández-Heredia was "inefficient." It is worth noting that Sáenz Aranaz, a Socialist, was the only trained staff officer in the Levante Army and probably had little time to leave his headquarters.[37]

Many of these problems were shared with the Nationalist Army. A gunner noted that Nationalist infantry expected the artillery to crush the enemy and were unwilling to advance under fire or fight at close quarters. Kindélan complained that many field commanders were sitting on their hands and devoid of initiative, often stopping at the first hurdle. He claimed that both Dávila and Vigón had a low opinion of most of their divisional commanders, while Vigón was especially critical of the corps commanders whom, he claimed, were ignorant of the tactical situation. The problem was exacerbated by poor communications networks between and within corps and divisions.[38]

The Aragon Offensive: Phases One and Two

On February 24 Franco hosted a briefing in which Vigón presented Barosso's plan, based upon the Fall 1937 concept, for a three-phase advance westward into Aragon and Catalonia. The first phase was a 125km front attack south of the Ebro where the enemy salient bulged out west of Belchite, and would involve a 65km advance to the River Guadalope, which joins the Ebro at Caspe. The broad valley of the Ebro was an undulating plain and, despite being cut by ravines, the open ground made possible rapid movement, although the southern edge of the advance would be through sierras in terrain over 800m. There were no significant disagreements and Dávila promptly ordered the operation to commence within a fortnight, on March 8. From February 21 through March 20 the Nationalists ran 1,811 military trains into the new front but delays in assembling men and supplies led to a 24-hour postponement.[39]

Dávila had 14 divisions and a cavalry division with some 160,000 men, 160 tanks and 600 guns organized into corps under (north-to-south) Yagüe, Berti, and Aranda.[40] There were 350 aircraft, with the Condor Legion supporting Yagüe while Berti had the Aviazione Legionaria and Aranda the BAH. The corps would separately strike along the great curve of the Belchite salient, reach the Martin, then converge around Alcaniz, with García-Valiño's Task Force, including 2,500 cavalry, covering the gap between Yagüe and Berti.

Although Yagüe cleared potential Republican sympathizers from every front-line village, Barcelona noted the increased activity, but Rojo believed it would take Franco two months to make up the losses of men and material at Teruel. For the Republic the replacement of the equipment was the most pressing problem due to a tightening air and naval blockade which meant that arms and ammunition were shipped to French depots.

Rojo remained uncertain of enemy intentions and concluded that there were three offensive options: around Teruel, at Guadalajara, or toward the sea, possibly from Teruel. Units were instructed to "hold until relieved" which was easier said than done, for in the Belchite salient, held by Pozas's Eastern Army with some 150 guns (including antitank), the defenses were often little more than observation posts and foxholes with the men living in nearby villages. However, in the Ebro Valley were three positions in a 20km belt to Quinto, with shallow trenches and wispy barbed-wire barriers and the rear positions were rudimentary at best.[41]

Within the Belchite salient was Colonel Pedro Sánchez Plaza's XII CE holding an 80km front with three divisions and one 50km from the front in reserve. To the south, facing Aranda, was Major Juan Perea's XXI Corps of Menéndez's Reserve Army with three divisions. Together they had some 70,000 men and 75 guns, while to the south, watching Teruel like a hawk, was Hernández Saravia's Levante Army with Colonel José Gallego's XIII CE, Vidal's XIX CE, Fernández-Heredia's XVIII CE and Ibarrola's XXII CE, with a dozen divisions and 135 guns, although these were initially spectators of the debacle.[42]

Table 5.3: Nationalist forces at the beginning of the Aragon offensive

Corps	Commander	Divisions
Morocco	Yagüe	5, 13, 15
CTV	Berti	Littorio, XXIII de Marzo, Flechas
Liaison Task Force	García-Valiño	1, 105, Cavalry
Galicia	Aranda	4, 82, 83, 84, 108

Table 5.4: Republican forces at the beginning of the Aragon offensive

Army	Corps	Commander	Divisions
Eastern	XII	Sánchez Plaza	24, 30, 35, 40
Reserve	XXI	Perea	27, 34, 70

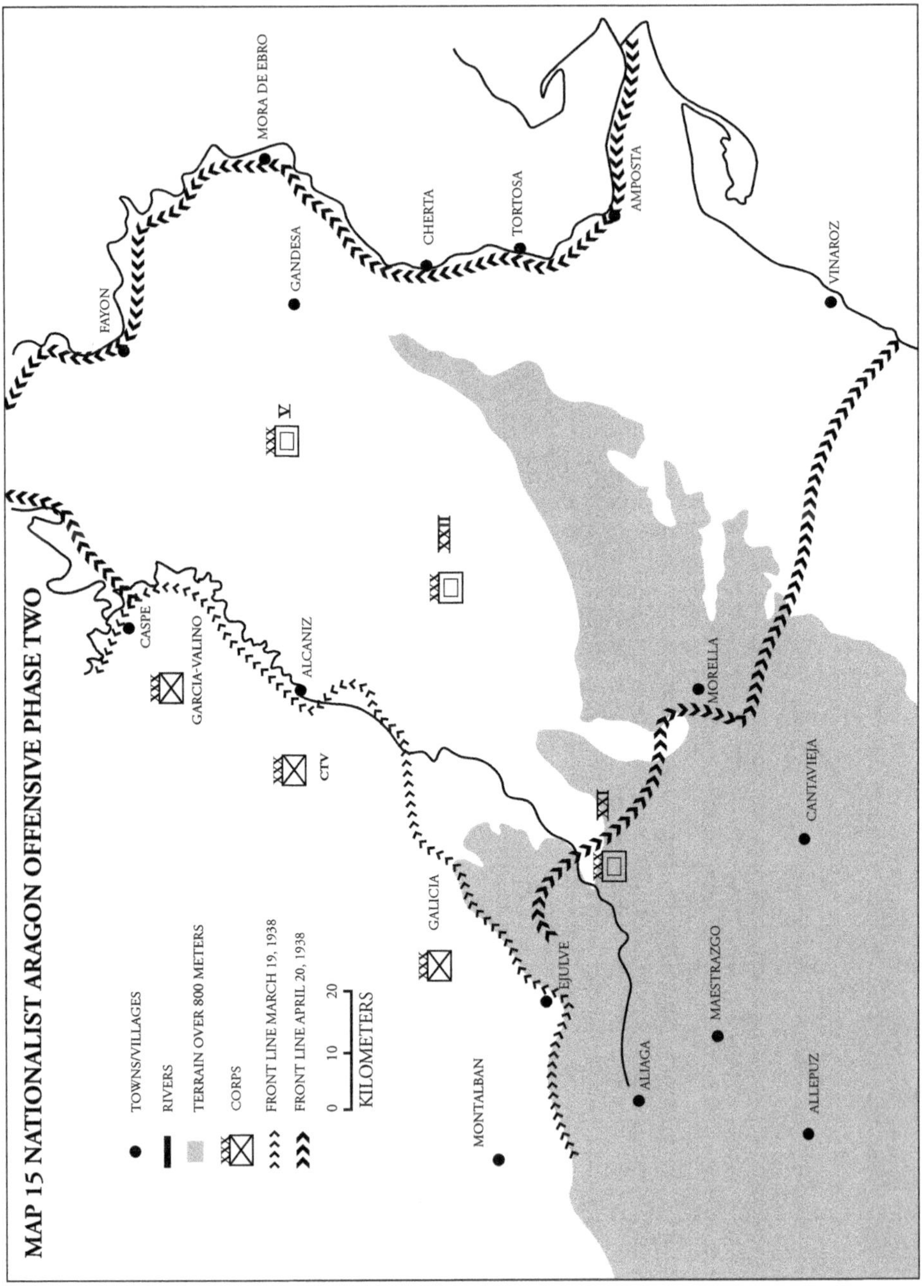

MAP 15 NATIONALIST ARAGON OFFENSIVE PHASE TWO

Franco and his staff study maps as they plan for the March 1938 offensive in Aragon. This was originally planned for late 1937 but because it was impossible to prepare the Nationalist Army in time Franco opted for a renewed offensive on the Madrid front. To preempt it, the Republic launched an offensive at Teruel which so weakened its forces that the enemy crushed them during the spring and early summer of 1938. (Photo by José Demaría "Campúa")

Widely dispersed, Nationalist infantry advance during the early morning at the beginning of the 1938 Aragon offensive. (Photo by José Demaría "Campúa")

The Nationalist batteries opened fire at 06:30 March 9 while bombers made up to three sorties and fighters struck the trenches to crush Sánchez Plaza's 24 DI. This allowed Yagüe to feed 5th Division through the gap in trucks supported by 30 tanks and two Condor Legion 88mm batteries.[43] In a 36km dash they overran the second line during the afternoon to take the ruined town of Belchite, then reached the Ebro opposite Escatron on March 12. Behind them marched the infantry companies behind battle banners and carrying stretcher poles, which made their columns look like ships running before a storm.[44]

Sánchez Plaza was quickly replaced by an Asturian officer, Lieutenant Colonel Claudio Martín, but he could not prevent the corps fleeing across the Ebro to find brief sanctuary. It was deactivated on March 13 and its headquarters became the Independent North Ebro Task Force (Agrupación Autónoma del Norte del Ebro) on March 17 to prop up the defense of the Ebro. Hernández Saravia rushed Fernández-Heredia's and Ibarrola's corps to the shattered front, the former holding the south bank of the Ebro while the latter moved into Perea's right to hold the Martin as half a dozen divisions and Perea's two reserve brigades tried to plug the gap. When Martín's corps was driven across the Ebro on March 11, Fernández-Heredia was sucked into the vacuum but with only Walter's 35 DI and the month-old 72 DI, whose headquarters was promptly overrun, he failed to delay Yagüe, who swatted off counterattacks to take Hijar on March 13.

This threatened the key road junction of Caspe where Walter and the divisional-sized Task Force Reyes dug in to form what Rojo hoped would become the western anchor of a new defensive position and the jump-off point for a counteroffensive. Modesto was ordered north on March 13 to stop Berti by holding the Guadalope around Alcaniz, which Italian bombers wrecked on the second day of the offensive. Berti had struck 30 DI on March 9 but, despite a three-hour bombardment, Perea's men resisted stubbornly and were not overcome until their flank was exposed by Sánchez Plaza's collapse. The gap was exploited by Babini with 55 AFVs and the Flechas Negras who cut the Belchite road at Muniesa the following day to reach the Martin at Oliete.[45] Berti then reinforced Babini with an *ad hoc* regimental-sized motorized battle group which on March 14 launched a surprise attack to take Alcaniz.

That same day Yagüe pushed toward Caspe but without German air support, which Volkmann cancelled in a moment of pique over the Spanish general's "indecisiveness."[46] The undaunted Morocco Corps pressed on to take Caspe on March 17 after a bitter two-day battle in which Walter was lucky to avoid capture. The Nationalist success was not universal, for Aranda, despite having 40 tanks, initially failed to break through despite using every gun and bomber. Only on March 12 did he succeed, but Perea slowly swung back his right, fighting a tenacious defense of Montalban and Alcorisa before losing both by March 15.

Franco was ecstatic at the progress and on March 15 issued General Instruction #2 to exploit the success along two axes. Action "A" (Accion "A") continued the drive south of the Ebro to reach the sea and isolate Catalonia. Action "B" was to be a complementary operation north of the Ebro advancing to the Cinca and, if possible, to the Segre as a jump-off point for a push deeper into Catalonia. Franco also warned the other Nationalist armies to be ready to exploit enemy signs of retreat or weakness. Dávila was also warned to be ready to drive from Teruel to Sagunto, taking first Morella then Cantavieja. Tellingly Franco ordered battalions and brigades to follow the *Instrucciones para el combate de las pequenas unidades de infanteria* (*Combat instructions for small infantry units*) and exploit fleeting opportunities to advance, maintain contact with the enemy, and establish bridgeheads.[47] By March 17 the Nationalists, who claimed 1,000 prisoners, had reached the Guadalope, having seized 7,000 square kilometers in eight days and were ready to push eastward to the sea and south into the heights of the Maestrazgo.

There was chaos behind the Republican lines, with units that tried to make a stand often facing not the enemy but a torrent of exhausted men throwing away weapons and equipment to speed their flight, ignoring officers with drawn pistols.[48] One commentator noted: "The panic occurred almost simultaneously throughout one Army Corps and spread like a contagion through the other."[49] Men passed overturned or shot-up trucks, sometimes with a dead driver, and through the abandoned detritus of a demoralized army, including ammunition boxes (some full), rifles, gas mask containers, and greatcoats.

The perennial desertion problem grew worse, many Anarchists fleeing to their homes, driven by a variety by factors including shortages of food, clothing, and arms. The Defense Ministry created regrouping centers (*centros de recuperación de personal*) and some men voluntarily returned to the front. Once there, many non-Communist units complained that the Communists creamed off the best of everything or deliberately deprived them of both supplies and support as retreat fueled political paranoia. Yet the Communists also had a deserter problem, leading some commanders, such as Lister, to shoot officers for abandoning their positions which had often been outflanked.[50] There were bitter disputes within Communist ranks, with comrades denouncing each other as well as blaming traitors and Trotskyists for the collapse of the supply organization, while there were also calls to dismiss International Brigade commanders including Walter.[51] The logistics problem was exacerbated by the slow reaction to the crisis of the main Republican railroad, the MZA, which ran 235 military trains from March 1 through March 12 and 290 from then to March 27, or 145 a week. From then until July 24 it would run 1,898, or about 112 a week.[52]

Republican losses were so heavy that on March 11 commanders and commissars toured camps, hospitals, and rest homes seeking replacements while local authorities combed out those in reserved occupations. For a week there was a pause as the Nationalists prepared for Action "B," while on March 19 Dávila issued orders for Phase Two of Action "A" along the lower Ebro through Gandesa and Mora de Ebro and then to the sea to isolate Catalonia, with bridgeheads across the Ebro for a future offensive.[53] With Yagüe committed to Action "B" García-Valiño would now secure the left along the Ebro Valley.

Berti on his right would drive eastward to help secure the Ebro bend around Gandesa while Aranda pushed in a westerly direction to secure the Morella gap as the springboard to the sea. The advance would be through terrain over 800m high, rising in the south up to 1,500m, but the route to the coast was barred by similar-sized massifs running northeast to southwest, apart from the gap south of Morella. They faced Modesto, Ibarrola, and Perea with 13 divisions, including three *ad hoc* formations created from brigades of the Andalusian, Estremadura, and Levante Armies, as well as a division-sized Coast Defense Task Force at the mouth of the Ebro.

García-Valiño and Berti struck V CE on March 26 but required four days' bitter fighting with constant maneuvering and powerful air support to break through, and it was Berti's move to isolate him from the south which caused Modesto to retreat. García-Valiño then made a daring 20km night march to envelop Gandesa on April 3 and reach the Ebro within the bend. Such was the confusion that 100 British troops from 15 BI were captured after marching up to what they thought were friendly tanks, while elsewhere fleeing Republican troops accidentally joined Nationalist columns.[54] Modesto withdrew in good order either down river or across the bridges which were blown up at the last minute to deny the Nationalists a bridgehead. Modesto now replaced Martín as commander of the Ebro Task Force defending the whole lower river and was replaced by Lister.[55]

On March 30 Dávila ordered Aranda and Varela to advance into the Maestrazgo at Allepuz.[56] Aranda had already broken through on March 24, climbing eastward out of the Guadalope Valley along the tributaries. On April 3 the Nationalists got their first view of the Mediterranean, and two days later Alonso Vega's 4th Division took Morella, opening the way to the sea. To support them, and shield Berti's right, García-Valiño's 1st Division switched flanks and became Aranda's spearhead, pushing along the road and through the pass to take Cherta (Xert) on the edge of the coastal lowlands on April 14.

In the race for the sea Aranda was clearly ahead of Berti who encountered enemy reinforcements, including Major Manuel Tagüeña's 3 DI, brought up from Madrid by truck. Tagüeña had spent childhood summers in the area and exploited that knowledge to delay Berti's advance. He later observed that the International Brigades who made up two of Modesto's three divisions on his right had "completely lost all capacity to fight."[57]

Glory-hunting Berti asked Franco to rein in Aranda and give the Italians the privilege of reaching the sea first, but received very short thrift.[58] Instead Berti drove down the Ebro to take Amposta on April 18 and Tortosa's southern suburbs the next day, giving the Nationalists control of the whole southern bank of the Ebro. On his right Alonso Vega, facing dwindling resistance, reached the sea at Vinaroz on April 15, although the enemy retreated in good order, losing only 45 automatic weapons and 100 rifles. Aranda's advance pushed Gallego's, Perea's, and Ibarrola's corps southward in a line hinged upon Aliaga. The performance of Perea led to his promotion on March 30 to command of the Eastern Army as a colonel and he was replaced by the Basque Communist Lieutenant Colonel Manuel Cristobal. Pozas became Military Commander of Girona, then Figueras, and after the war went into exile in Mexico.

The Republican armies had taken a terrible beating south of the Ebro, with 25,500 casualties including 6,000 dead by April 1 while 35,900 men entered prison camps. Also lost were 29 tanks, 110 guns, 274 automatic weapons, and 15,000 rifles. Incomplete figures put Nationalist casualties to mid-April at about 13,500 including some 1,600 dead, while the Italians suffered 3,225 casualties. The equivalent of ten Republican divisions were destroyed or wrecked but the exhausted Condor Legion withdrew for a brief rest.

When the Republic was split Negrín and Rojo assumed command in Catalonia while on April 16 Miaja was appointed commander of the Central-Southern Zone Armies Task Force (Agrupación de Ejércitos de la Zona Centro-Sur) which included the Levante Army (XII, XIX CE) and the Reserve Army (XXI, XXII CE) each with six divisions, as well as an Operational Level reserve of nine divisions (XVI, XVII, XX CE). On May 1 he had 491,511 men and 457 guns while Perea had 197,618 men and 261 guns.[59] On June 2 the forces in Catalonia became the Eastern Army Group (Grupo de Ejercitos de la Región Oriental—GERO) while Miaja's became the Central Army Group (Grupo de Ejercitos de la Región Central—GERC).

The Nationalist success encouraged the Fascist-supporting prophet of armored warfare, General John Fuller, to include the Aragon offensive in

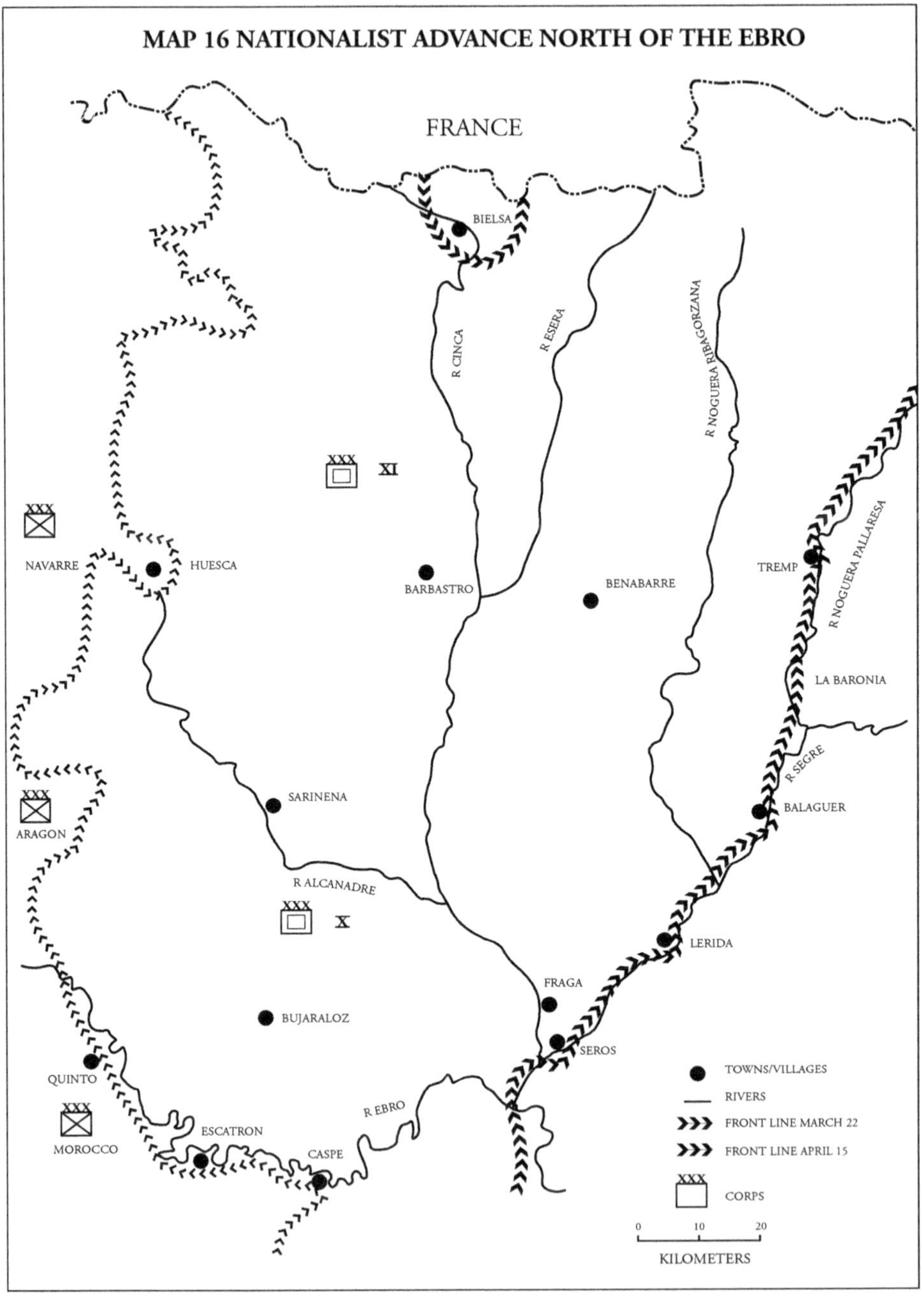
MAP 16 NATIONALIST ADVANCE NORTH OF THE EBRO
FRANCE
BIELSA
R CINCA
R ESERA
R NOGUERA RIBAGORZANA
XI
NAVARRE
HUESCA
BARBASTRO
BENABARRE
TREMP
R NOGUERA PALLARESA
LA BARONIA
R SEGRE
SARINENA
BALAGUER
ARAGON
R ALCANADRE
X
LERIDA
FRAGA
BUJARALOZ
SEROS
QUINTO
R EBRO
MOROCCO
ESCATRON
CASPE
TOWNS/VILLAGES
RIVERS
FRONT LINE MARCH 22
FRONT LINE APRIL 15
CORPS
0 10 20
KILOMETERS

the first edition of his *Decisive Battles of the Western World and their Influence upon History*. In reality these were conventional campaigns in which artillery conquered the ground, and while radio-controlled, motorized groups with air support did exploit the success, their accompanying advances were limited to a few tens of kilometers while tanks were used in conventional infantry-support/mechanized cavalry roles. The offensive also highlighted the logistics problems of rapid advances, and while the Nationalists generally succeeded in supplying their forces, their troops sometimes had to dig up potatoes and onions from peasant vegetable gardens to survive.[60] Similar logistics problems would have a major impact upon Anglo-American strategy in western Europe during 1944.

Two British views of the Nationalist Army at this period came from Lieutenant Colonel A. F. G. Renton, who visited the front in May, and the assistant military attaché in Paris, Major C. A. de Linde, who visited Vinaroz the day after it fell. Renton commented favorably upon the Nationalists' motorization and the good condition of horses and mules while noting that columns of no more than 20 trucks moved at 40mph (65km/h). He claimed that mechanization, which he defined as fighting by AFVs, was regarded as a complete failure, with tanks suffering heavy casualties due to antitank weapons and unsuitable ground.[61] Linde was astonished that the Republicans did nothing to cut the Vinaroz corridor and noted that the roads were lined with numerous broken-down, wrecked, and abandoned vehicles.[62]

The Aragon Offensive north of the Ebro

While the Nationalists consolidated their hold on the Ebro west of the Guadalope, preparations began to strike north of the Ebro. There Pozas's X (Gallo) and XI (Major Bartolomé Muntané) CE had been milked to help prop up the Ebro front, leaving Muntané with two reserve brigades, although the lower Segre was held by Martín's Independent North Ebro Task Force with nine brigades including two of 26 DI.[63] The sole Operational Level reserve for these 35,000 men was 30 DI at Lerida (now Lleida) with some defensive works along the Cinca.[64]

Two days after Franco issued Instruction # 2, Dávila produced an outline plan for Action "B" with a detailed version on March 20.[65] This involved a general advance eastward by some 65,000 men to the line of the River Esera and then the Noguera Pallaresa and lower Segre. Three corps, each of four divisions, were to be used. Solchaga's Navarre Corps with 25 tanks and 70 guns would advance from either side of Huesca supported on his right by Moscardó's Aragon Corps and 60 guns, but in a master stroke possibly suggested by himself, Yagüe's Morocco Corps with 20 tanks and 80 guns would strike across the Ebro to compromise the Segre defenses.[66] He would have the easier task traveling across a broad, relatively flat river valley, while the others would have to fight their way through a series of heights exceeding 400m which ran east-to-west in the north but north-to-south along most of the front, separated by river valleys which provided further barriers.

From March 22 Solchaga, supported by the Condor Legion at Vigón's personal request, and Moscardó, advanced slowly across a succession of well-defended heights in poor visibility with frequent rain, sleet, snow, and even a thunderstorm. Progress was slow at first but then picked up pace as the defenders' retreat became increasingly disorganized. Solchaga advanced some 12km in the first two days then, on March 26, reached and crossed the River Alcanadre to take Barbastro on the Cinca by March 28 before throwing a bridgehead across the river.[67]

The Republicans opened sluice gates upriver to sweep away his pontoon bridges but until they were replaced the bridgehead held out with artillery support, allowing Solchaga to drive eastward to take Benabarre on April 2. Moscardó's advance kept pace, Huesca was finally relieved by March 25, and on March 27 he took Sarinena on the lower Alcanadre. From his bridgehead he advanced upon Balaguer, which fell on April 6 after being bombed by 100 aircraft, and then Marzo's 54th Division exploited an intact bridge to establish a 4km-deep enclave. Muntané was relieved by Francisco Galán on April 4, probably due to promotion.

Table 5.5: Nationalist forces in offensive north of the Ebro

Corps	Division	Commander
Navarre (Solchaga)	3	Iruretagoyena
	61	Garcia Navarro
	62	Sagardía
	63	Tella
Aragon (Moscardó)	51	Urrutia
	53	Sueiro
	54	Marzo
	55	Arados
Morocco	5	Bautista
	13	Barrón
	15	Garcia-Escámez
	150	Muñoz Grandes

While Republican propaganda made much of Nationalist motorization, the infantry assembling for an advance in the Aragon were supported by packhorses or mules. (Photo by José Demaría "Campúa")

Colonel Juan Yagüe's advance across the Ebro in March 1938 undermined the Republican defense north of the river. In addition to pontoon bridges, the Morocco Corps' engineers also provided ferries. (Photo by José Demaría "Campúa")

Table 5.6: Republican forces in offensive north of the Ebro

Corps	Division	Commander
XIII (Gallego)	25	Eusebio Sanz
	28	Jover
	39	Alba

The capture of Barbastro pushed 43 DI on Gallo's right against the Pyrenees as Solchaga crossed the Noguera-Ribagorzana to take Tremp on April 7, creating a 8km bridgehead to the east and a 2km one at La Baronia, some 20km to the south. He then pushed up the Noguera-Pallaresa to take Sort on April 11, giving the Nationalists total control of Catalonia's plants which produced a third of the country's hydro-electric power, driving Gallo's new right, 31 DI, across the French frontier by April 20.

The 43 DI's original commander, Lieutenant Colonel José Escassi, fled across the border and was replaced by the energetic militia officer Major Antonio "The Dodger" ("El Esquinazao") Beltrán who had 7,000 men and four guns around Bielsa.[68] Sagardía's 62nd Division pushed from the west as Iruretagoyena's 3rd Division squeezed Beltrán from the west, but he skillfully exploited the terrain in a stubborn but ultimately inevitable retreat. Despite bad weather Iruretagoyena and Sagardía pushed him into the Pyrenean valleys and on June 16 he crossed into France, where 6,000 of his men opted for repatriation into the Republic.

The greatest success came on the right where Yagüe would boldly establish a bridgehead with a pontoon bridge across the Ebro a kilometer north of Quinto, link up with Moscardó, and advance toward the lower Segre. Barrón's 13th Division quietly sent two battalions across the river on the evening of March 22 to infiltrate 26 DI positions as work began on the bridge, which allowed the rest of the division to flow across with armor. It was followed by 150th Division, then the mobile brigade to cover Barrón's left, Yagüe maintaining control by telephone, with radio as a backup.

The weakened 26 DI resisted stoutly but within 24 hours Yagüe's corps was across the river in a 10km-deep bridgehead despite air attacks in which the Republicans suffered heavy losses. Yagüe pushed up the road to Lerida, spearheaded by Bautista's motorized 5th Division, which advanced 40km toward Bujaraloz, which it occupied on March 25 to meet Moscardó. This preempted Martín's containment efforts and he rapidly retreated, allowing Yagüe by noon on March 26 to reached Fraga's outskirts, overrunning one of the two defending brigades to establish a bridgehead across the Cinca. Below

Lerida Cathedral the Catalan government had established a chemical weapons plant but production may not have begun.[69]

Dávila gave Yagüe his head to reach the lower Segre as Martín brought up three divisions to stop him. Lerida, a key communications center, was shielded by Campesino's 46 DI, whose 6,882 men, dozen tanks, and 60 guns briefly slowed the advance as Yagüe outstripped his supply lines and mopped up. He soon recovered and Barrón entered Lerida on April 3 to secure it the following day, taking 7,000 prisoners and six guns. Simultaneously Yagüe pushed down the Segre and 20km south of the city established a 2km bridgehead at Seros. The effort of holding Lerida exhausted Campesino who fell ill on April 4 and was sent to hospital.[70]

By now the Nationalists were exhausted, while the defense was strengthened by Perea's appointment to command the Eastern Army.[71] On April 19 he reorganized his 130,500-strong command into two six-division task forces whose boundary was near the confluence of the Noguera Ribagorzana and the Segre: the Northern (Lieutenant Colonel Javier Linares) consisting of X and XI CE with 18 batteries and the Southern (Lieutenant Colonel Antonio Cordón) consisting of two *ad hoc* corps "A" and "B", later XVIII and XII CE, with 19 batteries. Yet he was still licking his wounds, and while Nationalist casualties were under 6,500, plus 1,000 sick, the Republicans had lost about 8,900 plus 18,000 prisoners, 29 tanks, 64 guns, 235 machine guns, and 14,874 rifles.[72]

As a boy soldier Perea, now aged 48, served in Morocco and earned a commission but his Republican beliefs saw him jailed and cashiered during the dictatorship of General Miguel Primo de Rivera.[73] Under the Republic he regained his commission but promptly retired only to rally at the time of the uprising, then led an Anarchist column with some success. He rose rapidly and was given XXI CE in October 1937 and with his new command was promoted to lieutenant general. He was a tall, slim man with a healthy complexion and succeeded owing to competence and his skillful use of limited resources, rarely making requests which he knew his superiors could not meet.

As he rebuilt his forces Rojo demanded on April 10 counteroffensives to retake Tremp and Balaguer, but the Catalonian troops were exhausted and Perea did not issue his orders until May 7. A Radio Barcelona appeal on April 5 for 100,000 volunteers fell upon deaf ears, but conscription of 30/40-year-olds of the 1915 and 1926–29 classes, and 17/19-year-olds of the 1941 class, the last nicknamed the Baby-Bottle Class (*La Quinta del Biberón*), helped fill the ranks with officers provided by schools, hospitals, dissolved units, and even some who had escaped from the Asturias.[74] Equipped with the weapons arriving from France, they were committed to an offensive to relieve enemy pressure in the Levante. The bridgeheads would be attacked by 14 divisions, 50 tanks, 90 guns, and 100 aircraft: X CE (Sort), XI CE (Tremp), XVIII CE (Balaguer), and XII CE (Seros) and, hopefully, to regain the line of the Noguera-Pallaresa and possibly even the Cinca.

The offensive began on May 22 with the attackers trying, but often failing, to infiltrate the enemy positions so that almost everywhere Perea was repulsed with heavy losses. At Balaguer responsibility was transferred within a few days to Modesto's Ebro Task Force using V and XV CE with little effect, the task force being renamed Ebro Army on May 29. Modesto renewed his assault on June 22 but all the attacks failed.[75] Perea was the Communists' scapegoat for poor planning but he blamed inadequate resources, the failure of infiltration tactics, and claimed that the enemy were forewarned. The losses, possibly 30,000 including 3,000 prisoners, reflected poor troop training, especially among the "Baby-Bottle" boys, for whom it was a massacre of the innocents.

Meanwhile the succession of defeats made Prieto so pessimistic that Negrín took over the Defense Ministry and pledged to continue the war. On March 9 the Anschluss crisis began and three days later Austria was absorbed into the Third Reich at bayonet point in the face of token protests from Britain and France. The next day the kaleidoscope of French domestic politics turned again and returned Socialist Leon Blum to power, leading Negrín to fly to Paris on March 12 to seek military support.[76] He requested that five French divisions and 150 aircraft be sent to Spain but the French Army depended upon integrated active and reserve units, and mobilizing the latter posed insurmountable problems. When the Permanent Committee of National Defense (Comité permanent de la défense nationale) discussed intervention, it noted that there was no plan for mobilizing forces around the Spanish frontier and a covering force alone would mean mobilizing a million men.

However, Paris did agree to reopen the border, closed in January, to release stockpiles of weapons in French ports. From March 17 a flood of equipment entered Catalonia, and by the time the frontier was closed again on June 12 some 19,000–25,000 tonnes of weapons, ammunition spares, and supplies including nearly 190 combat aircraft (127 Russian) and bridging equipment entered Spain.[77] If all the accumulated Russian, Czech, and Polish shipments crossed the border then the Republic received some 25 tanks, 500 guns, 5,000 automatic weapons, and 140,000 rifles while the French provided 100 guns and 200 antitank weapons.[78] From March 13 through June 19 the Republican railroads ran 831 trains carrying material, much of this from across the border.[79]

The Aerial Sword

Nationalist air power played a major role and demonstrated the vulnerability of contemporary defensive concepts, as it began the takeover of the cavalry's role which would be completed by mechanized forces. The Great War had showed that air power was essential to Tactical Level operations and had potential at higher levels, but the quantum leap in postwar technology demonstrated air power was now significant at the Operational Level.[80]

After Berlin and Rome sent reinforcements (36 Bf 109 in April and July as well as 26 Italian bombers in July), Nationalist air strength was maintained at a nominal 350 aircraft.[81] Intensive air operations proved a force multiplier, with the Condor Legion ground-attack aircraft flying up to five sorties a day and the bombers three. The Italians flew 3,350 sorties (700 bombers dropping 600 tonnes) from March 9 through March 31, 2,548 (363 bombers/225 tonnes) in April, and 2,207 (534 bombers/409 tonnes) in May.

The bombers were especially formidable, providing tremendous destructive power against defenses that received 210 tonnes of bombs on March 9, and also against communications. On March 14 the center of Alcaniz was wrecked by 14 Italian S.79s which dropped 11 tonnes of bombs while even the lumbering He 59 seaplane could carry a tonne of bombs. Railroads were vulnerable and while breaks in the line could be repaired within five hours, traffic was still disrupted, making it difficult for defenders to assemble reserves to seal any breakthrough. In Catalonia between 5 and 12 percent of all stations were hit, while in the Northern network four viaducts and 34 bridges needed to be repaired or replaced, most due to bomb damage.[82] The aerial disruption of communications undermined the traditional defensive doctrine; indeed two years later Sperrle, the Condor Legion's first commander, would shield the Wehrmacht's open southern flank as it drove for the Channel.[83] It is worth noting that between March 9 and July 25 the Nationalists lost only ten bombers, one to a night fighter and the remainder to antiaircraft artillery.

Their work was complemented by six ground-attack squadrons, usually equipped with biplane fighters, while Volkmann also had a Stuka flight.[84] Forward air support was also aided by creating temporary airfields behind the front line. Using light bombs and machine guns, Nationalist "chains" (*cadenzas*) lashed not only enemy defenses but increasingly communications. Targets included troops, either on the move or assembling, and vehicles, further disrupting the flow of supplies. Fighter pilots also joined attacks against road traffic, dubbed by the Condor Legion "louse hunts" and on March 23 the ace Captain Angel Salas with two companions destroyed a five-vehicle convoy

MAP 17 LEVANTE CAMPAIGN

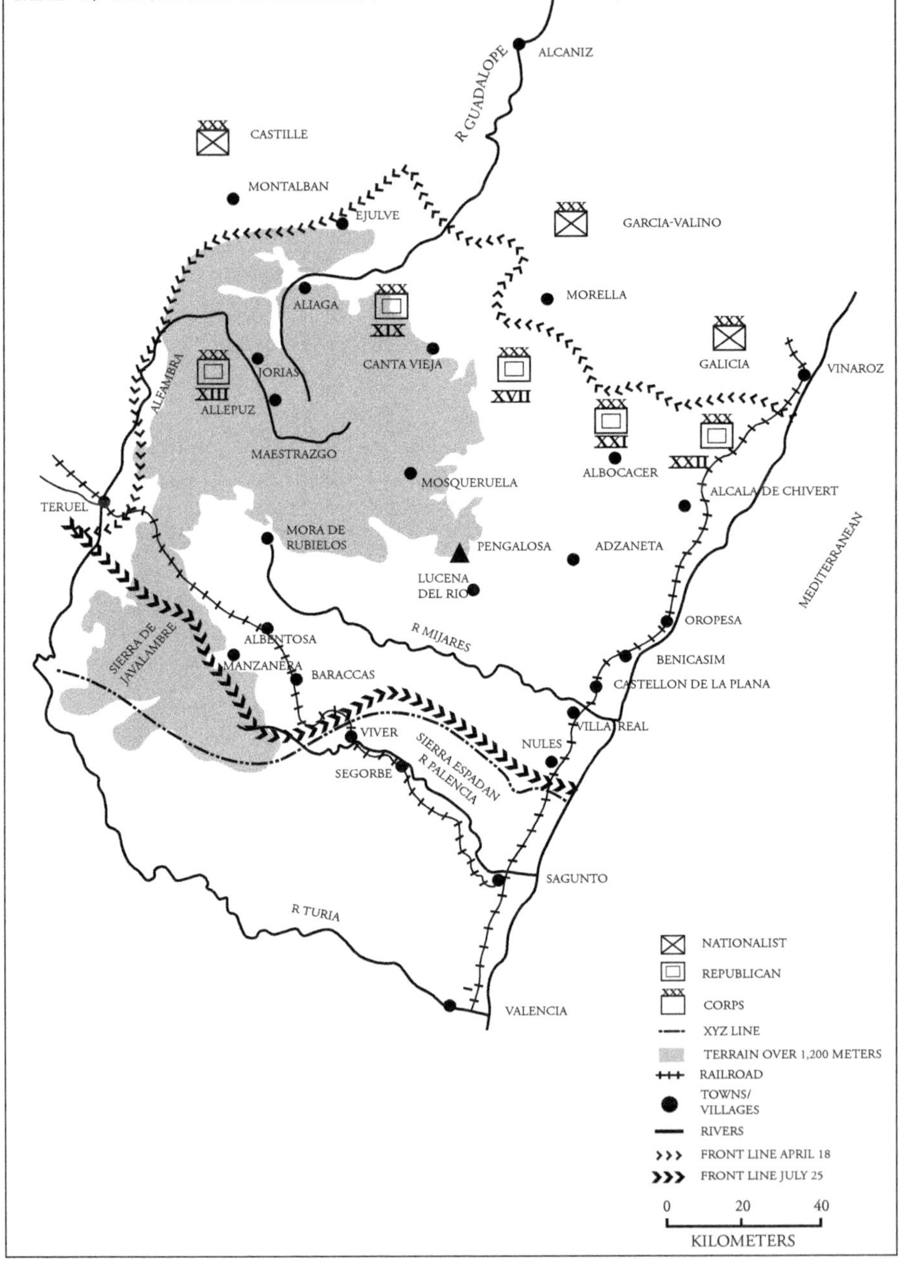

attempting to convey a battery to safety.[85] The Condor Legion He 51s, which often spent only 15 minutes over the target, also dropped primitive napalm bombs from converted fuel drop tanks, while the Stukas' 500kg bomb proved equally effective. However, the Stuka pilots were still honing their skills and in March twice failed to drop a bridge across the Ebro at Sastago, leaving it to K/88 … which also failed!

Such attacks were hazardous, exposing pilots to ground fire which accounted for many of the 64 Nationalist aircraft lost from March 9 through July 25; indeed on June 8 the Condor Legion stood down its He 51 squadrons which soon received Bf 109 fighters.[86] Many fighters were lost in air superiority battles in which the Nationalists generally had the upper hand; yet the FARE remained a formidable opponent and on June 3 nine bombers struck the Condor Legion forward command post. The Republicans came to call their air force "The Rainbow" because it always appeared after the storm had passed, yet on March 11 alone it flew 155 fighter sorties.[87] According to the DCA on the Palencia River front from July 13 through July 25 the Nationalists flew 2,007 sorties and the FARE only 226.[88]

As the Soviet element was reduced, two FARE fighter squadrons were disbanded, but during March the arrival of 210 Spanish pilots from Russia with new aircraft allowed them to be reactivated. Spares remained a problem and by May 21 there were only 43 serviceable Rata fighters, while the enemy's rapid advance meant that many aircraft were abandoned, accounting for half the 58 aircraft lost in March and April.[89] Actual losses during June and July were 62 aircraft, including 18 in accidents.[90] When the Republic was split in two, so was the fighter force, while the shortage of strike aircraft meant that in July 1938 the lumbering R-5 and R-Z biplanes were increasingly used for harassing attacks at night, forcing the Condor Legion to create a night fighter flight (*Kette*).

The Levante Campaign

When Franco met German intelligence chief Rear Admiral Wilhelm Canaris on April 4, he was euphoric and even spoke about withdrawing the Condor Legion, but what next?[91] He was reluctant to push further into Catalonia and wanted to strike south into the Levante, despite the opposition of his staff and Kindélan. There were two potential reasons: possible French military intervention if Italian troops appeared on the frontier, and fear of a prolonged war of attrition against Catalonian nationalists and Anarchists strengthened by

Table 5.7: Nationalist forces for Levante offensive

Corps	Commander	Divisions
Castile	Varela	5, 81, 82, 85, 108
Galicia	Aranda	4, 55, 83, 84
CTV	Berti	Littorio, XXIII de Marzo, Flechas, 15
Liaison Task Force	García-Valiño	1 (plus 55 in May)

Table 5.8: Republican forces in Levante offensive, mid-April 1938

Army	Corps	Commander	Divisions
Levante	XIII	Gallego	25, 28, 39
(Hernández)	XIX	Vidal	40, 64, 66
Reserve	XXI	Cristóbal	6, 22, 70
(Menéndez)	XXII	Ibarrola	19, 41, 47

Table 5.9: Republican forces in Levante offensive, mid-May 1938

Army	Corps	Commander	Divisions
Levante	XIII	Gallego	25, 28, 40
(Hernández)	XIX	Vidal	A, 19, 52
Reserve	XX	Durán	49, 50, 68
(Menéndez)	XXI	Cristóbal	E, 70
	XXII	Ibarrola	6, 41
	Reserve		48

Table 5.10: Levante Army order of battle, July 1938

Corps	Commander	Divisions	
		July 4	July 21
XIX	Vidal	5, 64, 66	5, 64, 66
XVI	Palacios	39, 48	39, 48, 52
XIII	Gallego	28, 65	28, 54, 61
XVII	García Vallejo	19, 25, 40	19, 25, 40
XXI	Galán	52, 68	10, 15, 50
XX	Durán	49, 53	6, 29, 53
XXII	Ibarrola	47, 70	47, 67, 70
"A"	Güemes	10, 15, 50	merged with XXI
"B"	Romero	54	merged with XIII
Reserve		41	

new war material. Even success brought the prospect of a debilitating guerrilla war in the occupied territory.[92]

Until late May, as his troops advanced southward from the Vinaroz Corridor, Franco continued to waver between Barcelona and Valencia, but the latter was the central region's prime port and a vital agricultural and industrial area. He may also have been influenced by the unrestrained optimism of Aranda and Varela, the latter anxious to strike out from Teruel, who knew the defenders had received little of the largesse crossing the French border. Moreover, prolonged operations would consume GERC's resources, thus undermining the long-term defense of the region.

Since April 10 Rojo had also been considering his options and optimistically believed that an enemy drive into the Levante provided an opportunity to regain the strategic initiative, if he could get the chess pieces in place.[93] Cutting the Vinaroz Corridor might weaken Franco's strategic reserve, while striking westward in both Catalonia and Estremadura were gambles. Thus he opted for a composite plan, striking westward in Catalonia and north in the Levante. He proposed a counteroffensive around Morella to Menéndez and Hernández Saravia on April 30 but unrelenting Nationalist pressure dashed his hopes.

South of the Ebro, the Republic occupied a huge salient stretching some 190km from Teruel to Montalban and then down to the coast south of Vinaroz. Its foundation was the formidable Maestrazgo, framed by the River Guadalope in the north, the Mijares in the south, and the Alfambra in the west, with the most important town being Cantavieja. The Maestrazgo consisted of a maze of sierras from 480 to 1,800m with deep gorges and pine- or maple-forested slopes, but with few good roads, mostly carved into hillsides. This region of arid hills, whose highest point was the 1,831m Penagolosa in the east, was notorious for short, hot summers and extreme seasonal changes, with snow and sleet encountered as late as May, turning rivers into torrents. It is regarded as one of the most inhospitable areas of the country in contrast to the fertile coastal plain with vineyards, olive groves, and fields of cereals.

Between the massif and the coast were a series of north–south sierras leading down to the Mijares. There were few roads here, the most important following the Alfambra and Mijares valleys through Allepuz to Mora de Rubielos, with a west-to-east route from Teruel through Allepuz to Cantavieja. East of Teruel ran the highway and railroad through Albentosa, Viver, and Segorbe to Sagunto, crossing the Palencia, while to the east of the Maestrazgo lay lower ground with sierras running north-to-south, but between the Mijares and Palencia lay the east–west heights of the Sierra Espadan.

Hernández Saravia's 33,500-man Levante Army held the Aliaga salient, which included the Maestrazgo and the upper Guadalope Valley, while Menéndez's 62,300-man Reserve Army held the line to the coast. The salient, which was on the army's eastern boundary, was the foundation for the proposed Morella counteroffensive. Both army commanders were pessimistic about their prospects, leading Menéndez on April 16 to order work on a new line using 12 engineer battalions.[94] On the western and northern sides of the salient were three divisions of Gallego's XIII CE facing Varela's five divisions and a cavalry brigade, while Aranda in the east had four divisions. The Levante campaign would see Aranda pushing slowly down the coast while Varela and García-Valiño on the right exploited the valleys to open fissures, undermining Republican defensive systems which were then abandoned. This strategy continued until mid-June.[95]

On the morning of April 18 Aranda attacked, only to encounter fierce resistance in the heights dominating the coastal road to Alcala de Chivert (Alcala). Then a fierce storm swept in from the west on April 26, further slowing progress despite support from Condor Legion Stukas and 88mm guns, delaying Alcala's fall until May 5. This storm originated in the Maestrazgo and also disrupted Varela's April 23 assault on the northwestern face of the Aliaga salient using 5th and 82nd Divisions supported by 13 batteries. Their short 75-minute bombardment surprised Gallego as 108th Division struck along the northern bank of the Guadalope. Aliaga fell on the second day but resistance stiffened with strong air support as Varela pushed into the upper Alfambra and Guadalope. The storm grew in intensity from April 25 but Jorcas, at the head of the Alfambra, was taken on April 27. Torrential rain and hail now washed away major operations until early May but the Nationalists had taken a third of the Maestrazgo, including the whole of the northern bank of the Guadalope, which together with Aranda's advance exposed the defenders, forcing them to evacuate the salient.

Yet the line still bulged, and to buttress it, work began from April 25 upon the Levante Line, some 20–35km to the south between the Turia and the sea at Oropesa, the trace being agreed by Miaja on April 28. But on May 3 another system was proposed further south and a commission under Colonel Tomás Ardid, who had commanded the Engineer Corps at the outbreak of war, began detailed planning. Work started on the Levante Line in the southern Maestrazgo, the coastal sierras, and the heights facing Teruel, with the secondary XYZ Line, covering the approaches to Valencia north of the River Palencia in the Sierra de Javalambre, while an unnamed third system arched around Valencia.[96]

From May 4 onward the Levante Line was compromised as Varela struck into the Maestrazgo along two axes: westward from the Alfambra Valley by 15th, 81st and 85th Divisions and south along the river valleys by the 5th, 82nd and 108th Divisions. The eastern flank was sheltered by García-Valiño, reinforced by an infantry brigade, while Aranda was to advance upon Castellon de la Plana (Castellon). Varela faced Hernández Saravia with Gallego's XIII CE in the west and Vidal's XIX CE in the east while Menéndez held the line to the sea with Lieutenant Colonel Carlos García Vallejo's XVII CE, Cristobal's XXI CE, and Ibarrola's XXII CE, the defenders having 14 divisions and 200 guns.

The western advance made slow progress, delayed by torrential rain and swollen rivers, which would wash out the offensive by May 18, but on May 12 Varela did take Allepuz. García-Valiño captured Cantavieja, having penetrated deep into the salient to take Mosqueruela on May 17, pushing back Hernández Saravia to expose Menéndez's left and fatally compromise the Levante Line. On May 10, Miaja's chief of staff, Manuel Matallana, warned: "We need to take urgent decisions to prevent a possible enemy advance which might endanger the Sagunto region."

Despite their successes both Aranda and Varela faced criticism from the GHQ representatives at corps headquarters, Majors Rufino Beltrán and Gonzalo Méndez Parada, as well as Kindélan over the perennial leadership problems.[97] While persistent bad weather and tenacious defense by a strong enemy were recognized as slowing the advance southward, the generals were also criticized for their subordinates' propensity for frontal assaults and the usual absence of maneuver, Kindélan being especially critical in a letter to Franco of May 22. But the corps commanders themselves were also aware of problems. Aranda noted that in the 4th Division Alonso Vega had to act as brigade commander due to poor leadership, while Varela's progress was hindered as much by his divisional commanders' sloth and blinkered attitudes as the weather.[98] The GHQ representatives also complained that batteries were blazing away without concern for resupply, although the support services were functioning well despite trying conditions.

Franco was again wavering over the ultimate objective, with his staff pushing for Barcelona because, as Vigón said, while Catalonia was a military objective, Valencia was only an economic one.[99] Throughout late May and into mid-June there were disputes within the Nationalist command about strategy. On May 18 Franco acknowledged the need to strike into Catalonia to dam the flood of arms coming across the border with France, yet also recognized that pressure had to be maintained upon the southern part of the Republic to keep the enemy off balance. He aimed to find a defensive line in the Levante which would allow him to create sufficient reserves to strike both in Catalonia and in the south.

Kindélan appears to have been the strongest advocate for closing down the Levante offensive and renewing attacks into Catalonia but this weakened his friendship with Franco. On May 22 he argued that it was pointless continuing the advance upon Valencia, which was becoming a battle of attrition, while the enemy in Catalonia recovered. He suggested ending the Valencia advance at the Mijares Valley so that Aranda and Varela could provide forces for a 20-division offensive into Catalonia. Franco's response is not recorded but was obviously negative. Nearly a month later, on June 18, Vigón supported the idea of closing down the Levante offensive and added: "The unanimous opinion within the Army is for an operation against Catalonia."[100]

Franco's decision to continue the southern advance reflected raised hopes as Dávila decided to exploit improved weather. On May 23 he ordered Aranda to advance upon Castellon, for which two two-division task forces were activated under Alonso Vega in the east and Martín Alonso in the west, the former to strike Cristóbal, while the latter outflanked Ibarrola. García-Valiño, reinforced by the Flechas Negras and a brigade each of infantry and cavalry, would shield them from Gallego.

Aranda attacked on May 26 supported by 100 guns but Alonso Vega made slow progress until García-Valiño pushed southeast to take the key communications nodes of Adzaneta on June 8 and Lucena del Cid on June 12. Alonso Vega's advance accelerated and he pushed back Cristóbal while Martín Alonso made steady progress down the coast. Although facing envelopment Menéndez was slow to react due to Miaja's decision to establish a unitary command within the Levante. On June 1 Hernández Saravia was sent north to command GERO and his Levante Army was absorbed by Menéndez's Reserve Army, forcing Menéndez to spend precious time acquainting himself with his new command. It was only on June 10 that he ordered a withdrawal to the Mijares, dooming the Levante Line and forcing an exposed Ibarrola to fight a desperate rearguard action to safety.

Everything now depended upon the XYZ Line and, luckily for the Republicans, rain again slowed Nationalist progress, forcing them to build tracks to move their artillery, but Martín Alonso still took both Oropesa and Benicasim on June 12. Nor did it stop Alonso Vega in a bold move reaching the Mijares within 24 hours to establish a bridgehead at Villarreal on June 13 as Martín Alonso neared the outskirts of Castellon. Major Valeriano Marquina's 6 DI withdrew into the city, intending to draw the enemy into debilitating street battles, but their resolution faltered as they faced isolation. When Martín Alonso entered Castellon the following day the defenders fled south and the

Nationalists established more bridgeheads across the Miajes. Aranda wished to extend his bridgeheads to Nules but as he advanced upon the town he was ordered to stop, possibly for fear it would become too exposed.

Enemy pressure led Miaja's engineer commander on May 8 to urge a start on the XYZ Line and this began in the coastal section. The task was assigned to 5,500 engineers and fortification battalions reinforced by civilians and 2,000 prisoners, a total of 14,000 men. By June 10 it was beginning to take shape with 14 "resistance centers" and a total of 23 sub-sectors.[101] Another 6,000 civilians together with support troops were mobilized to create defenses along the Miajes and also to work on the XYZ Line, and by June 29 it was reported that the Turia Valley and Viver defenses were complete while those on the coast were usable, being occupied from June 15 by Colonel Ernesto Güemes's Cuerpo "A".

Inland, Varela was plagued with rain that turned the roads into swamps and rivers swollen to bursting point, so that, after advancing 12km eastward, he halted at the end of May. Nevertheless, the latest advance had netted the Nationalists 6,000 prisoners and put them on the borders of the Levante with jump-off points for a new advance south once they had received supplies and replacements, for many battalions were at half strength. During most of June Varela crept forward along the Sagunto Highway and toward Mora de Rubielos, pushing back Colonel Miguel Palacios's XVI CE and Gallego, but by June 24 he was only another 12km east of his start line. García-Valiño and Aranda ironed out some enemy salients, then defeated Ibarrola's counterattack upon the Mijares bridgehead on June 15. Three days later Aranda began expanding the bridgehead which was 15km deep and 35km wide by the end of the month. The Republicans were left with another great salient from Mora de Rubielos to the Sierra de Espadan with better observation posts and the advantage of interior lines of communication.

Franco now strengthened the Nationalist right and brought Berti into the line south of Varela, while on June 25 former Navarre Corps commander, 56-year-old Brigadier General Solchaga, was given the newly activated Turia Corps on Berti's right. Solchaga was born into a Navarrese, Carlist military family which made him an ideal leader for Navarrese units. Two days later Franco issued his orders from "Terminus," with the first phase to reach the line of the River Palencia and from there the Nationalist line would swing like a door hinged on Segorbe to cut the Madrid–Valencia Highway. Success seemed assured, for intelligence claimed that the defenders included newly organized units with little training and few vehicles, restricting their mobility.

Varela, Berti, and Solchaga with a dozen divisions would sweep eastward along the axis of the Mijares, the Italians and Turia Corps pushing back Vidal, Gallego, and Palacios to take Segorbe and isolate Vallejo in the tip of the salient around Mora de Rubielos. The envelopment would be achieved aided by García-Valiño, with the equivalent of two divisions plus the Flechas Negras, striking southwest. Meanwhile Aranda with five divisions would push down from the north to take the Sierra de Espadan and Nules. The offensive committed 150,000 men (227 battalions and 20 squadrons) and 645 guns (possibly including antitank and antiaircraft).[102]

In addition to the corps in the west, Menéndez had Gallego and Ibarrola in the east. Uniquely, he possessed an Operational Level reserve occupying the XYZ Line: Durán's XX CE and Güemes's Cuerpo A in the Sierra Espadan with five divisions, while Romero's Cuerpo B held the south bank of the Palencia with two divisions.[103] In all Menéndez had 120,000 men (220 battalions), 200 guns, and 128 aircraft but lacked artillery ammunition for counter-battery work and believed the main blow would be on the coast. He also expected a blow in the west around Sarrion and had built a system between there and the Sierra de Javalambre held by Gallego with strongpoints built behind. Rojo was confident in the defenses and informed Negrín that preparations would continue for an offensive across the Ebro.

Aranda struck first on June 30 and despite Ibarrola's fierce resistance broke through to take Nules on July 8 after a five-hour bombardment, but was unable to exploit this success along the coast or into the eastern Sierra Espadan because of the XYZ Line. García-Valiño had more success, aided by Nationalist pressure from the west upon the Mora de Rubeilos salient, but his progress was slow and Vallejo was able to withdraw in good order to occupy the XYZ Line between the Sierra Espadan and the Palencia around July 17.

The 115km line stretched from the Turia to the sea, mostly in good defensive terrain. The positions incorporated the latest concepts of distributed positions and, just like the Siegfriedstellung of 1917, trenches were to ease troop movements around the battlefield. There was usually only a single trench line, although on the coast there were two about 20–50m apart with wire entanglements up to 2m deep, some 15–20m from the forward positions. The defense was based upon mutually supporting, platoon strongpoints using automatic weapons, with some positions designed to take the enemy in the flank. Trenches and saps led to scattered firing points, some in fox holes, some in bunkers or pillboxes either of reinforced concrete or timber covered with logs, earth, and sandbags. Under bombardment the reserves used shelters, often log-like, brick structures, on reverse slopes. The platoon positions were integrated into company and battalion strongpoints and batteries had plotted potential assembly areas.

The offensive in the west began on July 2 but Berti was unable to break through until July 13, and three days elapsed before he pushed Gallego out of Albentosa, as blazing woods and bombs created a plume of smoke which darkened the sky. On his right Solchaga took Manzanera on July 14, then Baraccas on July 18. With the fall of Sarrion on July 14 and Mora de Rubielos two days later the Republicans now withdrew into the XYZ Line and the Nationalists prepared for a set-piece attack. Their growing casualties led Kindélan to beg Franco to break off the attack but, having recently received 6,000 Italian replacements, the caudillo refused.

Berti, supported by 300 guns, would deliver the main blow in the Palencia Valley, where the XYZ Line crossed the river around Viver. He struck on July 21, but rather than exploit weak points discovered by Italian airmen, the Nationalists made a frontal attack upon the whole line and every assault was mown down.[104] Assaults continued in vain through July 23, and the following day the Nationalists began to regroup their artillery for a new attack, Italian batteries actually beginning corrective fire on July 25 when news arrived that the enemy had launched an offensive across the Ebro. Orders soon arrived to transfer men and guns north to meet the new crisis. It is claimed that the Nationalists suffered 15,000 casualties assaulting the XYZ Line while the defenders suffered only 5,000, but the Nationalist figure probably relates to the entire Levante campaign.[105] The Nationalist Legion tank battalion lost 26 tanks and suffered 259 casualties.

The truth was that after a 100km advance the Nationalists had exhausted both men and material.[106] The offensives were driven by Franco's obsession with political status, compounded by a possible failure of intelligence to determine details of the XYZ Line and clumsy command arrangements. Defense Minister Dávila was also controlling a huge front, for Franco neglected to establish a separate Army of the Levante until the end of the year.

Notes

1 See Martinez, *Zaragoza*, pp. 37–56; Salas, *Army*, vol. 3, pp. 1765–1771; Thomas, p. 239.

2 For Teruel the best account is Martinez, *Teruel*. For operations up to the great blizzard, see pp. 35–161 and for the counteroffensives, pp. 163–228. Arminan, *Bajo el cielo de Levante*, pp. 16–175 (hereafter Arminan). For operations during the blizzard see Arminan, pp. 27–175, for the counteroffensive, pp. 99–101, 111–115; Alonso, *La batalla de Teruel* (hereafter Alonso). Planning and operations to the blizzard, pp. 47–51, 54–58, 62–139. Nationalist counteroffensive, pp. 140–173; Rafael Casa de la Vega, *Alfambra* (hereafter Casa-Vega). First phase, pp. 13–26; counteroffensive, pp. 27–263; Dávila, *Batalla en los campos de Teruel* (hereafter Dávila). This has detailed accounts of conferences. Planning and operations to blizzard, pp. 11–136; counteroffensive, pp. 137–204. See also Alcofar, *Air*, pp. 273–283; Arias, pp. 228–236; *Aznar*, pp. 535–584; Beevor, pp. 313–322; Cardona, pp. 215–226; Bollati and Del Bono, *Dalla liberazione di Gijon alla vittoria*, pp. 17–33 (hereafter Bollati and Del Bono); Engel, *Operations*, pp. 189–211; García-Valiño, *Guerra de Liberacion*, pp. 161–185, 185–222

(hereafter García-Valiño); Hildago, pp. 175–178; Hills, pp. 169–172; Lister, pp. 171–187; Lojendio, pp. 359–395; Kowalsky, ch. 15; Manca, pp. 257–309; Martínez and Martínez, pp. 239–261; Modesto, pp. 138–153; Murias, pp. 190–192; Perea, pp. 212–241; Permuy, pp. 63–64; Proctor, pp. 171–186; Ries and Ring, pp. 110–127; Rojo, *Heroica*, pp. 131–146; Saiz, vol. 2, pp. 627–654; Salas, *Air*, pp. 288–307; Salas, *Army*, vol. 3 pp. 2169–2260; Vidal, pp. 307–325; Thomas, pp. 788–794; Håkan site.

3 See Arce, pp. 253–262.
4 Arminan, p. 63.
5 The 61st, 62nd, and 82nd Divisions arrived on December 21, and the 54th Division on December 24. They would be followed by the 1st Division on December 27 and both the 150th and 13th Divisions the following day, the last going into army reserve.
6 Arminan, pp. 75–76.
7 The Italians had 164 aircraft on December 19.
8 Thomas, p. 794.
9 The 52nd Division was reorganized in March under Cremades. Delgado Serrano would command the 82nd Division until the end of the war and was promoted brigadier general on May 17, 1938.
10 Lister, pp. 172–173.
11 Arce, pp. 285–287. See also Garriga, *El General Juan Yagüe.*
12 From January 2 through January 3 his corps batteries fired 205 x 77mm, 250 x 105mm, and 942 x 155mm rounds.
13 Also on December 31 three British journalists covering the Nationalist operations died after a shell landed near their automobile. The survivor, Kim Philby, had a minor wound for which he was personally decorated by Franco. Philby was one of the Soviet Union's most successful spies.
14 Cayón Garcia/Muñoz Rubio, *Railway*, table 9.
15 There were 3,000 cases of frostbite in García-Valiño's division alone.
16 For a description of conditions see Baxell, pp. 281–282.
17 During the retreat from Catalonia, Rey d'Harcourt and the Bishop, with 42 other prisoners including 21 Italians and a German, were shot by their guards at Girona en route to the French border on February 7, 1939. Barba appears to have survived the war.
18 Arminan, pp. 119–121.
19 For details of Nationalist counteroffensive plans see Engel, *Operations*, pp. 195–207; Martinez, *Teruel*, pp. 174–175.
20 The Castile Corps' batteries fired 117,445 shells from December 29 through February 23.
21 From January 17 through January 19 the corps batteries expended 36 x 77mm, 500 x 105mm, and 1,855 x 155mm rounds.
22 The brigade had had four commanders in eight months. Republican morale was uneven, with numerous desertions and executions, including six "agitators" after a panicky retreat, according to Rojo on December 31. He urged unit commanders to follow this example. Alpert, p. 169.
23 Múgica had been replaced by Colonel Luis Ollo on January 12 after being injured in an accident. For this offensive see Casa-Vega, pp. 125–143.
24 Martinez, *Teruel*, pp. 186–187.
25 Alpert, p. 240; Cayón Garcia/Muñoz Rubio, *Railway*, table 9.
26 Modesto, pp. 144–145, 148.
27 For the cavalry operation see Casa-Vega, pp. 243–262. Before the war Monasterio praised mechanization. Herrero Perez, pp. 291–292.
28 UKNA HW 21/4.
29 Galán had escaped from the northern enclave in November.

30 Engel, *Operations*, pp. 202–206; Martinez, *Teruel*, pp. 193–196. Aranda had difficulty assembling men and supplies, the latter including 2 million cartridges and 7,000 mortar bombs.
31 The day saw the first mission of three Ju-87A-1 Condor Legion dive bombers (Sturtzkampffugzeuge-Stuka) but they attacked the wrong target and missed. Ring and Ries, pp. 123, 127. Nine German dive bombers were sent to Spain by January 1937 but were not used operationally, although Hs-123A were used for close-air support. Howson, *Air*, pp. 172, 186–187, 211–212.
32 Lister, p. 182; Modesto, p. 151.
33 Martinez, *Teruel*, p. 227.
34 Kowalsky, ch. 15; Zaloga, *Soviet*. The Nationalists, who lost 16 tanks, reported capturing 22. Martinez, *Teruel*, p. 228.
35 Saiz, vol. 2, p. 653; Salas, *Air*, p. 303. The Nationalists claimed the destruction of 92 aircraft.
36 Alpert, p. 236. Salas, *Army*, vol. 4, pp. 3058–3069.
37 In March 1938 he became the Estremadura Army chief of staff. Alpert, p. 188.
38 Herrero Perez, pp. 304–305, 309–310.
39 Garcia Lomas, p. 156.
40 Martinez, pp. 32–35, says 750 guns. My figure is based upon batteries. Within the CTV Frusci commanded the MSVN division and Roatta the Hispano-Italian, while there was an Armored Group (Raggruppamento Carristi) under Colonel Valentin Babini.
41 Martinez, *La Llegada al Mar*, pp. 26–27 (hereafter Martinez, *Mar*).
42 Menéndez's reserve, V CE, also faced Teruel.
43 On March 10 the German 88mm guns fought a duel with an antiaircraft battery. Ries and Ring, p. 134.
44 For operations south of the Ebro see Alcofar, *Air*, pp. 264–273, 283–292; Alcofar, *CTV*, pp. 147–148; Arminan, pp. 176–198; Aznar, pp. 603–638; Ballester, *La Batalla del Ebro*, pp. 25–27, 35–44 (hereafter Ballester); Beevor, pp. 323–327; Belforte, *Guerra civile in Spagna; La campagna dei Volontari italiani e la Vittoria di Franco*, pp. 12–45 (hereafter Belforte, *Vittoria*); Bollati and Del Bono, pp. 35–53; Cardona, pp. 229–234, 235–236; Engel, *Operations*, pp. 213–220, 231–238; Galdón, *La batalla por Valencia*, pp. 17–33 (hereafter Galdón); García-Valiño, pp. 59–95; Hills, p. 172; Kindélan, pp. 119–136; Lister, pp. 189–199; Lojendio, pp. 441–460; Martinez, *Mar*, pp. 23–68, 139–179; Martinez, *La Ofensiva Sobre Valencia*, pp. 13, 24 (hereafter Martinez, *Valencia*); Martínez and Martínez, pp. 265–271, 274–277; Manca, pp. 313–374; Modesto, pp. 156–169; Murias, pp. 138–149; Perea, pp. 241–263; Permuy, pp. 75; Rojo, *Heroica*, pp. 150–151; Saiz, vol. 2, pp. 678–687, 694–709; Salas, *Air*, pp. 312–315, 317; Salas, *Army*, vol. 3, pp. 2261–2405, 2273–2274; Thomas, pp. 79–800, 802–803; Vidal, pp. 330–333; Voltas, vol. 3, pp. 97–101, 103–105, 108. Armiñan, *Bajo el cielo de Levante*, has interesting background to the Galicia Corps operations.
45 Babini would lose nine AFVs by early April.
46 Ries and Ring, p. 141.
47 Martinez, *Mar*, pp. 71–72; Martinez, *Valencia*, p. 37, Anexo 1 and 2.
48 Matthews, pp. 309–313.
49 Quoted by Engel, *Operations*, p. 219.
50 Alpert, pp. 169–171.
51 Beevor, pp. 324–326.
52 Cayón Garcia/Muñoz Rubio, *Railway*, table 9.
53 Engel, *Operations*, p. 231.
54 Matthews, pp. 314–316.
55 Martín assumed command of the new Cuerpo "B" which became the reformed XII CE later under Major Etelvino Vega.

56 Martinez, *Valencia*, p. 37.
57 Tagüeña, p. 107.
58 Ries and Ring, pp. 153–154.
59 Payne, *The Spanish Revolution*, p. 350, quoting *Katalonskaya Operatsiya.*
60 Matthews, pp. 109–110.
61 From March 1 through April 21 the Nationalist armored corps suffered 121 casualties, including 43 drivers, and the 1st Group lost 15 tanks, including six T-26s. Salas, *Intervencion*, Anexo 8.
62 UKNA WO 106/1583 & 1588. See Harvey's article on British views.
63 Muntané had commanded a unit in the African colony of Ifni at the beginning of the war. He reached the Republic through French Morocco and would end the war as the Eastern Army's Operations Officer.
64 See Martinez, *Zaragoza*, pp. 29–32.
65 Martinez, *Mar*, pp. 71–72, Anexo 4; Engel, *Operations*, pp. 221–226.
66 Moscardó's 55th Division was a brigade-sized static formation. Yagüe also had Major Alfredo Jurado's reinforced cavalry brigade.
67 For operations north of the Ebro, see Arias, pp. 241–243; Aznar, pp. 641–653, 791–795; Ballester, pp. 28–30; Beevor, pp. 326, 347; Cardona, pp. 234, 237–238; Engel, *Operations*, pp. 221–229, 271–289; Lojendio, pp. 460–479; Martinez, *Mar*, pp. 69–137; Martinez, *La Batalla del Ebro*, pp. 25–58, 282–293 (hereafter Martinez, *Ebro*); Martínez and Martínez, pp. 271–274, 283–285; Mezquida, *La Batalla del Segre*, pp. 11–70 (hereafter Mezquida); Modesto, pp. 172–175; Perea, pp. 267–310; Permuy, pp. 75–76; Rojo, *Heroica*, pp. 151–154; Saiz, vol. 2, pp. 691–694; Salas, *Air*, pp. 315, 317; Thomas, pp. 800–802, 831; Vidal, pp. 333–335; Voltas, vol. 3, pp. 101–103, 160–167.
68 Dodger was a family nickname. Thomas, p. 818 and n.1.
69 The death blow to Catalonian chemical weapons plans came on July 15, 1938, when Francisco Sánchez Mur, a 37-year-old chemist directing the programme, was arrested and accused of both being a Trotskyist and sabotaging chemical weapons production. Armas, pp. 528–529.
70 Martinez, *Zaragoza*, p. 92. His malady is unclear.
71 Perea, p. 267; Salas, *Army*, vol. 3 p. 3179.
72 On April 19 Yagüe criticized the Nationalists' allies in a speech to fellow Falangists but he was briefly relieved for criticizing Franco's decision not to strike into Catalonia. Thomas, pp. 819–822.
73 Salas, *Army*, p. 334; Zaragoza, pp. 288–289.
74 Alpert, p. 157; Martinez, *Valencia*, pp. 28–32.
75 Mezquida, pp. 85–123; Modesto, pp. 173–175; Perea, pp. 298–305.
76 For the French reaction see Beevor, pp. 335–336; Doughty, pp. 38–39; Thomas, pp. 804–806, 823.
77 Howson, *Arms*, pp. 239–240. He claims under 18,500 tonnes and the French 25,000 tonnes, but the latter includes engineering equipment.
78 Salas, *Army*, vol. 4, Cuadro 50–54. Moscow sent 152 aircraft, 25 tanks, 469 guns, 4,910 machine guns, and 125,050 rifles to Spain from December 14, 1937 through August 11, 1938. Kowalsky, table IV-3.
79 Cayón Garcia/Muñoz Rubio, *Railway*, table 9.
80 For air operations from March to July April see Galdón, pp. 216–219; Murias, pp. 192–193; Proctor, pp. 187–203, 205–219; Ries and Ring, pp. 127–178; Salas, *Air*, pp. 318–328, 334–349. See also articles by Ghergo Guerra aerea nei deli di Spagna and Pedriali L'Aviazione Legionaria nel Levanto e sull'Ebro. For operations during 1918 see Hooton, *War Over the Trenches*, pp. 196–267. UK NA HW 21/2. Imperial War Museum Ger/Misc/MCR/19/1A.

81 The Italians' reported strength on March 7 was 156, including 42 bombers, while on March 11 the Condor Legion had 33 serviceable He 111. From Majorca 20 Italian bombers and ten German He-59 seaplanes struck ports and coastal railroads. The German reconnaissance squadron also acted as bombers.
82 Cayón Garcia/Muñoz Rubio, *Railway*, pp. 21n.46, 22n.47.
83 Hooton, *Phoenix*, pp. 251, 253.
84 The Italians flew 301 ground-attack sorties from March 9 through April 15.
85 Salas ended the war with 16 victories and was credited with another seven over Russia in 1941.
86 The Italians lost 30 aircraft.
87 Permuy, p. 75.
88 Galdón, p. 217.
89 Republican losses from March 9 through to July 25 were reported as 212 aircraft but the figure was perhaps about 120.
90 Salas, *Army*, vol. IV, p. 3302.
91 Canaris was promoted on April 1.
92 Martinez, *Valencia*, pp. 13–18. See also Beevor, p. 324.
93 Martinez, *Valencia*, pp. 33–34.
94 Salas, *Army*, vol. 3, pp. 2391–92, 3179.
95 For the Levante offensive see Alcofar, *Air*, pp. 292–298; Alcofar, *CTV*, pp. 163–165, 292–298; Arias, pp. 243–250; Arminan, pp. 199–436; Aznar, pp. 653–736; Ballester, pp. 30–34; Beevor, pp. 345–347; Levante Belforte, *Vittoria*, pp. 49–58, 61–67, 73–87; Bollati and Del Bono, pp. 73–99; Cardona, pp. 246–248; Coverdale, p. 356; Engel, *Operations*, pp. 239–257; Galdón, pp. 53–68, 72–87, 90–102, 107–113, 134–156, 160–180, 184–195, 198–209, 213–216, 220–229; García-Valiño, pp. 97–129, 131–160; Hildago, pp. 179–182; Hills, p. 172; Lojendio, pp. 479–526; Martinez, *Valencia*, pp. 158–183; Manca, pp. 377–413; Martínez and Martínez, pp. 280–283, 285–287; Modesto, pp. 177–181; Muria, pp. 149–153; Permuy, pp. 76; Rojo, *Heroica*, pp. 155–162, 168–169; Saiz, vol. 2, pp. 722–750; Salas, *Air*, pp. 332–334 and air operations pp. 334–349; Sole and Villarroya, pp. 198–207; Thomas, pp. 818–819, 830–831; Vidal, pp. 335–342; Voltas, vol. 3, pp. 158–159.
96 Martinez, *Valencia*, Map 7. The XYZ designation indicated it was the ultimate defense.
97 Engel, *Operations*, pp. 244–245; Martinez, *Valencia*, pp. 82n.70, 96–98, Anexo 6.
98 Herrero Perez, p. 310.
99 Martinez, *Valencia*, pp. 13–24.
100 For the discussions see Martinez, *Valencia*, pp. 95–96; Kindélan, pp. 128–135.
101 For the XYZ Line see Martinez, *Valencia*, pp. 155–156. See also the websites Linea XYZ and Linea Defensive XYZ. The first has a very detailed article in Catalan with excellent illustrations produced for the Grup d'Estudis de la Batalla del Llevant de l'Associació Les Muntanyes de la Guerra de la Vall d'Uixó.
102 The Cavalry Division was sent south and replaced along the Ebro by the new 50th Division.
103 Durán relieved Galán on April 4.
104 Belforte, *Vittoria*, p. 82.
105 García-Valiño suffered 2,528 casualties and Berti 1,845, half of them Italian.
106 García-Valiño, p. 160.

CHAPTER 6

The Last Acts: Ebro and Catalonia

The Battle of the Ebro

Planning for the Republican Ebro offensive had its origins in Rojo's April efforts to regain the strategic initiative, and efforts redoubled as the enemy neared Valencia and Europe seemed to drift toward war. The Anschluss crisis rang alarm bells in chancelleries, which grew louder during the summer as Hitler began denouncing the alleged harassment of ethnic Germans in Czechoslovakia, which had a pact with France, and it was clear that Spain would be on the Allied side if a European war erupted.[1]

Negrín wanted an offensive in Catalonia to show solidarity with France, which would restore supplies across the border and also relieve pressure upon Valencia. An outline plan published on June 5 envisaged the destruction of the Vinaroz Corridor from north and south, but the need to defend Valencia and reorganize the forces in Catalonia meant that a month later this was scaled back to an attack across the Ebro. Rojo easily convinced Negrín and on July 24 the Premier pushed through the War Council's approval by stating that Valencia would be lost without an offensive. Yet this was a gamble, the last throw of the dice, and failure would weaken the forces in Catalonia, inviting their total destruction, as did the alternative of a purely passive defense.

The Matarrana, which joins the Ebro near Fayon, was the northern boundary and below it the Ebro circles eastward around 300–400m of high ground in a 32km bend to the River Canaletas near Benifallet, the southern boundary, before meandering 40km to the sea through a narrow gorge south of Cherta (also Xerta). The river around the Gandesa bend is about 100–150m wide, 5m deep (2m in the fords), and flows at a rate of 1–2m per second.

Within the bend sierras run east-northeast to west-southwest, with the main massifs split by the valley of the River Sec. The northern massif consists in the east of the Sierra de Fatarella, whose highest peaks are 563.5m and 552m, and

Table 6.1: Republican forces in battle of Ebro

Corps	Divisions	Commander	Notes
V (Lister)	11	Joaquin Rodriguez	
	27	Marcelino Usatorre	Arrived Aug 6
	43	Antonio Beltrán	
	45	Hans Luis Rivas	Hans to Sept 23, then Rivas
	46	Domiciano Leal Vicente López	Leal to Sept 23, then López
XV (Tagüeña)	3	Esteban Cabezos	
	16	Manuel Mora	
	35	Pedro Mateo Merino	
	42	Manuel Álvarez Antonio Ortiz	Álvarez to Nov 13, then Ortiz
	44	Ramón Pastor	Arrived Sept 10
	60	Manuel Ferrándiz	Arrived Aug 5

Table 6.2: Nationalist forces in battle of Ebro

Corps	Divisions	Commander	Notes
Morocco (Yagüe)	4	Camilo Alonso Vega	Arrived July 26
	13	Fernando Barrón	Withdrawn Oct 15
	50	Luis Campos-Guereta Manuel Coco	Campos to Aug 17, then Coco
	82	Francisco Delgado Serrano	Arrived July 28
	102	Antonio Castejón	Arrived July 28
	105	Natalio López Bravo	Not in Gandesa bend
	150	Agustin Muñoz Grandes	Arrived July 26
	152	Ricardo Rada	Arrived July 26
Maestrazgo (García-Valiño)	1	Mohammed Ben Mizzian	Arrived Sept 1
	53	Álvaro Sueiro	Arrived Sept 16
	74	Pablo Arias	Arrived July 28
	84	Alfredo Galera	Arrived July 26

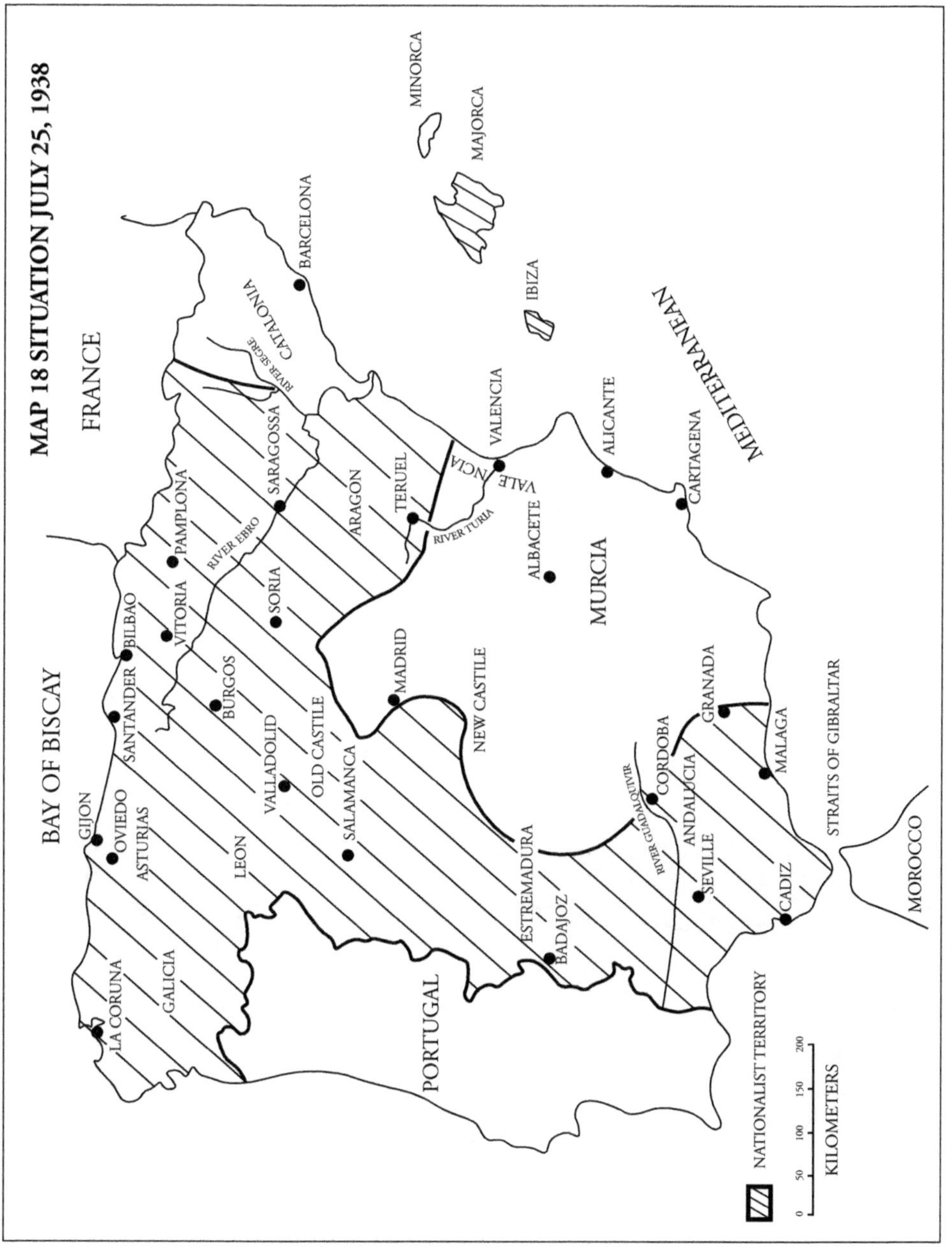
MAP 18 SITUATION JULY 25, 1938
FRANCE
BAY OF BISCAY
GIJON
OVIEDO
ASTURIAS
SANTANDER
BILBAO
VITORIA
PAMPLONA
BURGOS
SORIA
SARAGOSSA
RIVER EBRO
RIVER SEGRE
CATALONIA
BARCELONA
MINORCA
MAJORCA
IBIZA
ARAGON
TERUEL
RIVER TURIA
VALENCIA
VALE NCIA
ALICANTE
CARTAGENA
MEDITERRANEAN
ALBACETE
MURCIA
MADRID
NEW CASTILE
OLD CASTILE
VALLADOLID
SALAMANCA
LEON
GALICIA
LA CORUNA
PORTUGAL
ESTREMADURA
BADAJOZ
CORDOBA
RIVER GUADALQUIVIR
ANDALUCIA
SEVILLE
GRANADA
MALAGA
CADIZ
STRAITS OF GIBRALTAR
MOROCCO
NATIONALIST TERRITORY
0 50 100 150 200
KILOMETERS

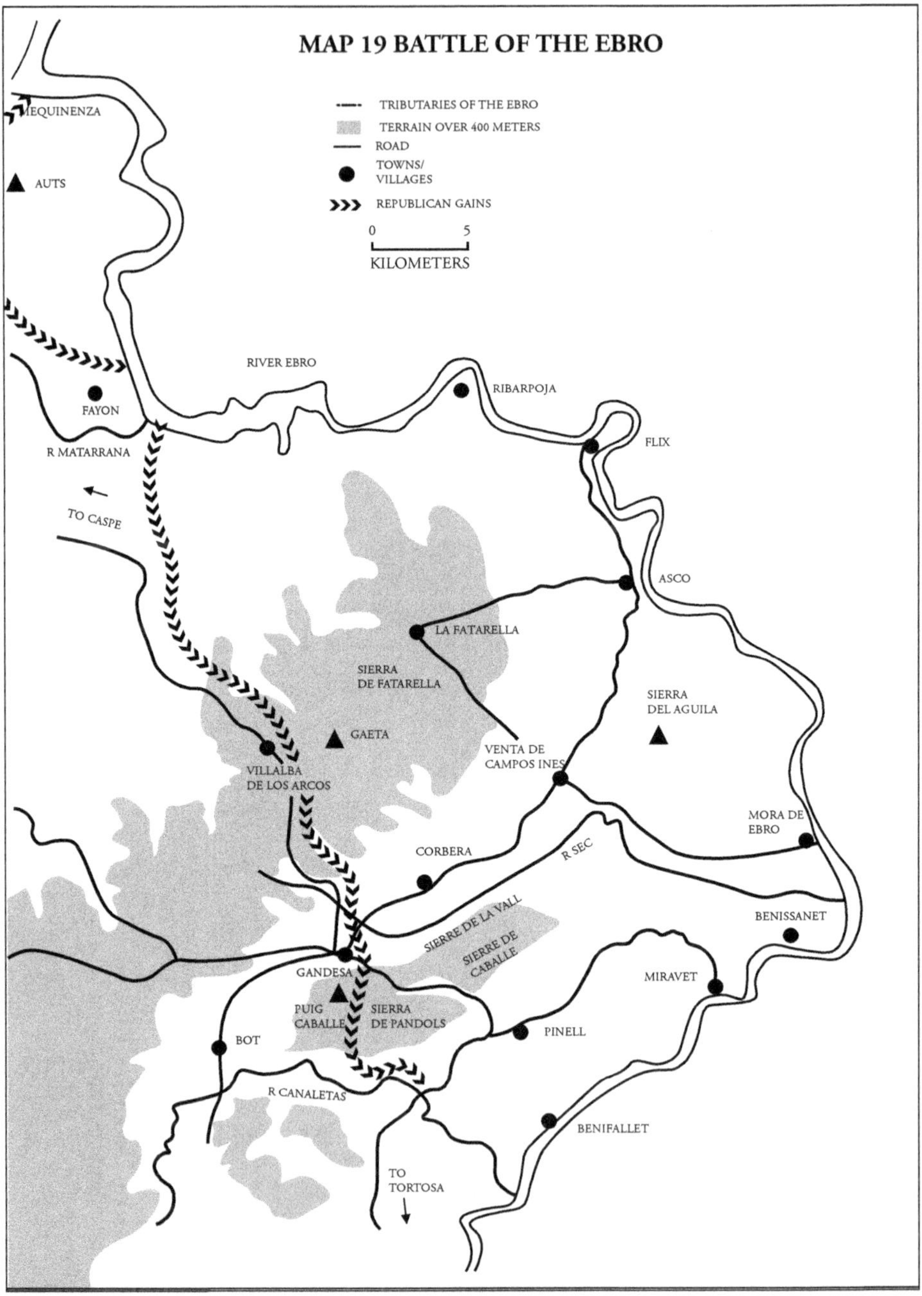
MAP 19 BATTLE OF THE EBRO
TRIBUTARIES OF THE EBRO
TERRAIN OVER 400 METERS
ROAD
TOWNS/ VILLAGES
REPUBLICAN GAINS
0 5
KILOMETERS
MEQUINENZA
AUTS
RIVER EBRO
RIBARPOJA
FAYON
R MATARRANA
FLIX
TO CASPE
ASCO
LA FATARELLA
SIERRA DE FATARELLA
SIERRA DEL AGUILA
GAETA
VENTA DE CAMPOS INES
VILLALBA DE LOS ARCOS
MORA DE EBRO
CORBERA
R SEC
BENISSANET
SIERRE DE LA VALL
SIERRE DE CABALLE
GANDESA
MIRAVET
PUIG CABALLE
SIERRA DE PANDOLS
PINELL
BOT
R CANALETAS
BENIFALLET
TO TORTOSA

in the west is Mount Gaeta (548m). To the south are the Sierra de Caballs (or Cavalls), up to 659m, overlooking its northern outcrop, including the 363m Sierra de la Vall de la Torre (Sierra de la Vall), running northeast beside the Sec toward Venta de Camposines (Camposines) and separated from it by a shallow valley. To the east are some low hills, the most prominent of which is the 487m Sierra del Aguila. To the west of it are the blue slate mountains of the 705.5m Sierra de Pandols while the 709m Puig Caballe overlooks Gandesa from the south. The rugged terrain of this area features steep slopes with olive groves, hazelnut, and almond trees.

Along the Ebro, weaving through olive groves and orchards, ran a hard-topped road, another of which extended 20km up the Sec Valley through fig and olive trees as well as vineyards to Gandesa. This was a town of 3,400 people lying like a spider in the web of the local road system going north through Villalba de los Arcos (Villalba) to Caspe, east through Camposines to Asco and Mora de Ebro and south to Tortosa and around the Sierra de Pandols to Pinell de Brai (Pinell). Most were tracks suitable only for infantry and pack animals, but lower down the Sec Valley a road which could be used by vehicles ran north from Camposines to Fatarella.

Planning and Execution

While Rojo was in the Superior War School before the Civil War, he held an exercise involving crossing the Ebro, although the influence of that upon the new offensive is uncertain. As early as April 20, just after being driven across the river, Modesto had begun planning a cross-river counterattack, while both the general staff and the reactivated XV CE holding the bank opposite the Gandesa bend also examined the possibilities.[2] On May 7 members of the 13 BI swam the river to demonstrate a crossing was feasible and the information was fed upward, leading to a conference later in the month. This led to intensified reconnaissance from observation posts and scouts while Comint monitored enemy radio signals, the data coordinated by Republican Intelligence and a Russian officer, Colonel "Tumanov."[3]

This confirmed that the lower Ebro was lightly held by Yagüe's Morocco Corps with Colonel Luis Campos-Guereta's 50th Division, activated in May, and Colonel Natalio López Bravo's 105th Divisions, while in reserve were II Brigade (Colonel Carlos Rubio) of Barrón's 13th Division and two Cavalry Division battalions, some 22,000 men and nine batteries. Campos-Guereta was a cavalryman who had 11 battalions and seven batteries (20 guns) split into two sectors and whose boundary was the Sec. The headquarters of Lieutenant

Colonel José Peñarredonda's I Brigade were in Pinell, while Lieutenant Colonel Eduardo Capablanca's II Brigade had headquarters in Fatarella.[4] Capablanca had four battalions along the river and two in reserve while Peñarredonda had four battalions along the river and three in reserve. López Bravo, also a brigade commander at Teruel, had 12 infantry battalions with two cavalry battalions and six batteries with his I Brigade (three battalions) and II Brigade (six battalions). Barrón's brigade had 11 battalions and six batteries as well as a machine-gun battalion, with the equivalent of two battalions around Gandesa and another two opposite Amposta.

The defense of Catalonia and the Levante absorbed the Republican staff during May and June, so detailed planning of the Ebro offensive began only in mid-June. Rojo's return to the project may have been influenced by Negrín's view of the international situation, and his strategy was based upon the Ebro Army's hammer coordinating with the Levante Army's anvil. He hoped to strain the Nationalist Army to allow the launch of his long-hoped-for Estremadura offensive.

Preparations accelerated in late June, and soon after the fall of Castellon, Modesto was secretly flown south to coordinate operations with Menéndez and Miaja.[5] But Menéndez was facing strong pressure, and while Miaja and his chief of staff Mantallana admitted they could assemble a three-corps task force to support the Ebro Army, they needed at least a fortnight's notice. As planning was still under way Modesto was unable to indicate when the offensive would begin and failed to get a firm commitment of support although the others agreed not to leave him in the lurch. Since Menéndez's chief of staff, Lieutenant Colonel Frederico de la Iglesia, was a personal friend, this had to be sufficient.

Modesto's planning role appears to have been limited, with most of the work apparently performed by his chief of staff Colonel José Sánchez Rodriguez. It was certainly the latter who went to Rojo's home in Madrid at the end of the month with Lister for briefings by both Rojo and operations chief Lieutenant Colonel Rámon Ruiz-Fornells, first chief of staff of XVIII CE.[6] Although an attack across the Segre was an option the consensus was to strike across the Ebro because it directly threatened the enemy rear. Rojo assured the attendees that he would have no problem selling the concept to the government and on July 16 he issued an outline directive for establishing the Gandesa bridgehead, briefed the Ebro Army's leadership two days later, and issued detailed orders on July 22.

Modesto's Communist-dominated Ebro Army had 80,000 men, 151 guns (51 batteries, nine from Eastern Army), and 62 tanks to support three corps:

Lister's V CE and Tagüeña's XV CE with José del Barrio's XVIII CE in reserve, giving a total of ten divisions.[7] Later the Eastern Army's XII CE under Vega was added to Modesto's right with 20 guns. On July 22 Campesino reported sick, so a furiously skeptical Lister sent him for medical treatment in Barcelona, then assigned 46 DI to Major Domiciano Leal.[8] Modesto's command post was established at Espluga de Francoli at 21:00 on July 24 with D-Day set for 00:15 the following day.

The 31-year-old Lister was a stonemason who spent his teens in Cuba before returning to Spain where he joined the Communist Party.[9] In 1934 he went to the Soviet Union where he worked on the Moscow Metro before joining the Frunze Military Academy for junior officers, then a mechanized corps. He returned to Spain in 1935 and during the war rose steadily through his competence as much as his political position. He was a warm-hearted man with a strong sense of friendship, ready to support any propaganda activity. He was also a good orator. He could be harsh but if he liked someone was willing to tolerate their mistakes.

Physics graduate Tagüeña, at 25 the youngest corps commander in the army, earned his degree at Madrid University where he also studied mathematics and joined the Socialist Youth.[10] After the uprising he led a militia column and in November 1936 joined the Communist Party, rising steadily to the rank of colonel and was assigned XV CE. He would serve in the Red Army and became divisional chief of staff, later advisor, to the Yugoslav and Czech armies. In the mid-1950s he abandoned Communism and went to Mexico where he worked in a pharmaceutical laboratory and died in 1971.

As usual the Republic would rely upon surprise and infiltration to penetrate the defenses, and Modesto urged his subordinates to advance as rapidly as possible. Tagüeña would strike the northern side of the bend while Lister would strike the southern side with the Gandesa–Mora de Ebro road as the boundary to the River Canaletas. They would advance upon Gandesa and secure the town and the surrounding heights. There would be two diversionary operations, by Tagüeña's 42 DI under Major Manuel Álvarez, north of the bend against Campos-Guereta's left, and at the mouth of the Ebro by a brigade striking from Amposta. The ambitious Rojo hoped to use motorized columns during a third phase to exploit the success, roll up López Bravo's line, and reach Vinaroz. While the Republican command was certain of Tactical success the shortage of reserves in Catalonia meant exploiting this at the Operational and Strategic Levels and depended upon the Central Zone attracting the enemy.

The most serious hurdle was simply assembling strong forces west of the Ebro, with serious doubts among the Republican Army leadership about their prospects. The last pontoon bridge in Catalonia was destroyed by the enemy at Amposta on April 18, and while some replacements were imported the workshops of the Inspector General of Engineers had to fabricate much equipment. It provided eight 150m pontoon bridges, five foot bridges on cork floats (*pasarelas*), three steel and two wooden bridges, the last for heavy loads, and three ferries which could carry 30 tonnes.[11] Some 200 boats, some inflatable, imported from France, each carrying up to seven to 20 men, were provided for the assault force, who were trained to embark and disembark rapidly, but a number of commando-type troops would swim the river.

From July 18 the divisions and their supporting engineers began covertly to survey their crossing points. At night they assembled equipment near the shrub-covered river bank in well-camouflaged positions, although the noise of the vehicles bringing it echoed across the water off the hills and ravines. On July 19 Rojo was surprised to receive a visit from the Soviet staff advisor, Colonel "Maximov," who had previously approved the offensive but now advised abandoning it. After informing Negrín, Rojo ignored the advice, which indicated the limitations of Soviet influence.[12] That same day Modesto informed his subordinates that the crossing would begin at midnight on July 23, and from the night of July 21/22 the troops assembled using vehicles without lights despite the numerous curves in the road winding down the slopes. By midnight on July 23/24 the riflemen and engineers were in position, only to learn that there was to be a 24-hour postponement because the gunners had failed to meet the deadline, which raised tension.

Across the river, fears of Republican activity seemed to fade with every kilometer from the bank to create a situation similar to the Ardennes offensive more than six years later. Ungria's SIPM provided detailed warnings from June 11 while Yagüe's divisions began hearing rumors from July 3 and noted both troop movements and the assembly of crossing equipment. By July 20 SIPM had submitted more than a score of reports while the presence of Lister's and Campesino's divisions were confirmed on July 5.[13] German and Italian air reconnaissance also detected signs of the buildup but warnings foreign or domestic were swamped by other reports coming over a 1,750km front and mixed with GHQ complacency.

Yagüe failed to alert his troops, whose defenses consisted of fortified riverside towns with camouflaged positions and observation posts covering wired potential landing points. On July 13 Yagüe belatedly demanded the construction of concrete blockhouses but nothing was done, and on July 24/25, the Feast of St James, the patron saint of Spain, Republican assault troops entered the Ebro on a clear, moonless night from just after midnight.

Swimmers carrying grenades neutralized the defense of the main crossing points and were quickly followed by boatloads of assault troops who achieved surprise. Any serious resistance was quickly suppressed by fire across the river, the troops pushing inland leaving follow-on forces to mop up, but resistance increased as the sun rose. Tagüeña, scheduled to be supported by a cavalry regiment, four tank and four armored car companies, was to take the northern half of the bend and Gandesa, while Lister, who was to have a couple of tank and three armored car companies, had a secondary initial role securing Tagüeña's left and supporting the assault upon Gandesa, but would then drive down from the Ebro to Vinaroz.

The defense was in chaos during the morning as Campos-Guereta telephoned his scattered units, with some calls unanswered and contact with others lost after claims that they had nothing to report. At least three of the riverside battalions were mauled and their remnants were pushed westward, so by evening Campos-Guereta held only Fayon and Mora de Ebro, the latter falling the following morning. Meanwhile, Tagüeña pushed through the northern massif and along the Sec Valley to take both Camposines and brigade commander Peñarredonda in the morning, while La Fatarella and Corbera fell during the evening, the loot including a pontoon bridge. By dusk he was on the outskirts of Gandesa while Lister moved into the southern massif, destroying reserves that were attempting to close the crossings, cutting the Gandesa–Pinell road and securing the flank along the Canaletas.

Tagüeña wanted to push into Gandesa using his reserve division but Rojo vetoed this for fear that its crossing would aggravate growing congestion at the crossing points. The corps' first echelon infantry had crossed by the late morning and were then followed by the second echelons, but dispatching the armor, artillery, and trucks proved more difficult. The 1.2m-wide *pasarelas* were easy to deploy, taking only two hours, but could be used only by infantry. An attempt by cavalry to lead their horses across one near Ribarroja saw several of them fall off and drown while bombing scared the remainder. After the *pasarelas* were deployed work began assembling two pontoon bridges with a capacity of 4.5 tonnes and 60 vehicles an hour, then two ferries which took 30 minutes to cross. Ultimately, everything depended upon erecting the wooden and steel bridges which could take 10 tonnes and 25 tonnes respectively, and by the end of the day one of each had been completed.[14]

But the crossings soon came under air attack which exacerbated traffic congestion on the eastern bank while the wooden bridge at Asco was damaged when a truck hit a stanchion. The problems were compounded during July 25 when the Nationalists opened locks upstream, with flood water sweeping away some *pasarelas* and damaging both pontoon bridges and ferries. When this was repeated from August 19 through August 21 three bridges were damaged. The combination of problems restricted the movement of heavy equipment and it was only on July 27 that three tanks, 28 armored cars, and some corps artillery crossed.

The first reports reached Yagüe at 02:25, Dávila at 04:50, and Vigón at 06:20, with the two local commanders reacting quickly. By 09:30 they were dispatching reinforcements which by mid-morning were marching to the sound of the guns; Yagüe calmly used them to plug gaps while regrouping forces north and south of the bridgehead to seal it off.[15] Meanwhile the surviving defenders fell back upon Gandesa, whose defense was assigned to Barrón, while just after midday Franco demanded Campos-Guereta hold Fayon as the northern anchor of a line through to Cherta.

But much of this line was already compromised and then Franco, in one of his periodic flights of fancy, suggested the enemy be allowed to make a deep penetration westward which would then be enveloped. He was quickly persuaded that a conventional defense would be more effective but he still wanted major counterattacks when the infantry were guaranteed air and artillery superiority. In fact few commanders seemed enthusiastic about fighting a prolonged battle on the Ebro and preferred an offensive around Lerida, which Yagüe had first proposed in April. Dávila agreed and felt it would keep the enemy in Catalonia off-balance and ease the capture of Valencia. Vigón, Kindélan, Aranda, and Solchaga all opposed a stand on the Ebro, but Franco apparently said he could not understand their arguments and ignored them.[16]

While artillery batteries under Martinez de Campos were rolling north from the Levante together with the Condor Legion's 88mm guns on July 29, there was no wholesale stripping of that front, as Franco's and Dávila's staffs calmly pulled the hard centers from the candy box. The remainder of Barrón's division was immediately deployed and from July 26 through July 28 Nationalists received six divisions from the Segre, Levante, and even Estremadura fronts. Aranda's men were transported 160km at the rate of 40 trains a day while some had to travel 300km with 20–30 trains a day. Once detrained, the men had to march under a blazing sun to the battlefield and many suffered heatstroke. The FARE made no effort to interdict this vital rail traffic which faced only the occasional interference from the Republican Navy shelling the coastal railroad. Within 24 hours four battalions were propping up the battered remnants of Campos-Guereta's division and dozens more followed but became mixed up in response to the numerous minor crises, with the front not secure until early August.

Heavily loaded pack horses or mules were a major feature of the Nationalist logistical organization. (Photo by José Demaría "Campúa")

Having crushed the wire defenses, these Nationalist PzKpfw I or Negrillo tanks have covered the infantry and now prepare to advance on the main Republican positions. The Negrillo was the backbone of the Nationalist tank force and was usually operated by Spanish troops, although German instructors of Gruppe Imker sometimes participated in actions and five would be killed during 1937. (Photo by José Demaría "Campúa")

One of three Ju-87A dive-bombers or Stukas delivered to Spain in 1938, from the Luftwaffe's StG 163 which also provided aircrew. A single Ju-87A, together with seven other dive-bombers, was delivered during the New Year of 1936/1937 but not used. Their initial operations proved a disappointment but experience brought improved performance and when Richthofen returned to Spain at the end of 1938 five Ju-87Bs had arrived to replace the other aircraft. Richthofen and the Ju-87B would be synonymous with the Wehrmacht's victories in 1939–42, yet he had wished to abandon dive-bomber development.

The defense of Fayon thwarted Republican attempts to extend the bridgehead north of the bend, although a brigade of 42 DI penetrated 15km and took a battery of 150mm howitzers north of the town. It was eventually stopped by a Foreign Legion bandera after the Republic had taken a 60-square-kilometer bridgehead separated from the main force by a narrow corridor around Fayon. This was always regarded as a diversionary operation together with the Amposta bridgehead plan which aimed to aid the planned advance upon Vinaroz. Launched by the Franco-Belgian 14 BI supported by 45 elderly coast-defense guns, it proved a disastrous failure against an alert defense that isolated, then annihilated the vanguard and slaughtered reinforcements. López Bravo suffered 200 casualties while the attackers' losses were four times that number.[17]

The shortage of heavy weapons and supplies inevitably slowed the Republican advance on the second day and proved an insurmountable hurdle for Tagüeña as he tried to take Gandesa but faced strong resistance around Villalba, which acted as a breakwater when Major Esteban Cabezos's 3 DI tried to outflank Gandesa from the north. The later assistance of Major Manuel Mora's 16 DI failed to improve the situation while the international brigades of Major Pedro Mateo Merino's 35 DI encountered fierce resistance in the Sec Valley as they tried to storm Gandesa.

To ease command Dávila split the Ebro front into four sectors on July 27: Fayon under Lieutenant Colonel Gonzalo de la Lombana with 3½ battalions, the left under Brigadier General Francisco Delgado Serrano with 102nd and 82nd Divisions, the center under Barrón with 13th and 74th Divisions together with a cavalry brigade, and the right under Alonso Vega with 4th and 84th Divisions. López Bravo's 105th Division continued to hold the lower Ebro. It was Barrón who was under the greatest pressure but, exploiting defenses built by the civilian population and reinforced by six battalions of Colonel Pablo Arias's 74th Division, he kept the enemy 2km outside the town. Lister made better progress and secured half of the Sierra de Pandols but not the Puig de Aliga, which overlooked Gandesa and dominated the pass carrying the Gandesa–Pinell road, while the Nationalists also held the Puig de Caballe.

From July 27 reinforcements had halted the Republican advance as the front became increasingly stabilized, but the numerous crises meant that battalions were mixed together almost randomly and the threat did not cease until early August. Meanwhile Lister tried to outflank Gandesa from the south, striking at Bot, while the Nationalists launched counterattacks at Puig de Aliga. On July 29 Rojo wrote to his friend Matallana, "The Ebro front is almost paralyzed" but the next day Modesto, who may not have appreciated his men's exhaustion, launched a final all-out assault. Deploying the equivalent of six divisions with 22 tanks and 72 guns, he made little progress in five days of bitter fighting which saw every meter of ground contested while Nationalist counterattacks eroded Republican strength.

By August 3 Modesto had suffered 12,000 casualties and taken 4,000 prisoners but he realized that his men could do no more and went on the defensive, his successful crossing earning him promotion to colonel on August 26. But, as critics had feared, support and supply problems meant that he failed to exploit the success at the Operational or Strategic Level. Diversionary operations from the central zone were essential but the Levante front was itself exhausted and incapable of an offensive to reach the Ebro front 100km away. GERC made token attacks to relieve pressure but during the summer faced a Nationalist offensive in the Estremadura which gained some ground and weakened the central zone.[18] The Republicans now faced a battle of material as the Nationalists ran 2,979 military trains from July 25 through September 15 alone, moving up to 3,000 tonnes a day to the Ebro front. The Republicans, who halted all civil rail traffic from July 25 through August 29, would run 3,737 military trains, mostly in support of their forces on the Ebro, from start to finish.[19]

The Counteroffensive

The Republican front consisted of two salients and Franco was determined to regain prestige by retaking the Gandesa bend. As early as July 29 Yagüe proposed an attack down the Sec Valley, but Vigón was brought in to restore the caudillo's prestige, establishing a local command post upon the 482m Col de Moro on the Alcolea del Pinar–Tarragona road. The first order of business was to tidy the battlefield by eliminating the bridgehead north of Fayon.[20]

Roughly half-way between Mezquinenza and Fayon was Mount Auts, a ridge peaking at 434m, dominating open grassland and scrub with shallow ravines marking dry watercourses and now defended by Álvarez's 42 DI whose three brigades were supported by cavalry. Delgado Serrano's 82nd Division was to destroy the bridgehead, supported by four battalions of 4th Division, a tank company, 24 batteries (70 guns), and an 88mm battery. Delgado Serrano organized his division into three regimental battle groups (*Agrupaciones*) each assigned its own axis: one in the north fighting its way along the bank, the central force with tanks striking through the heights of Mount Auts, while the southern force pushed along the road to Fayon.

The assault force assembled before dawn on August 6, and at 06:00 a three-hour bombardment began, the Italians dropping 80 tonnes of bombs. When the bombardment lifted the infantry moved forward, closely supported by mortars and machine guns to outflank centers of resistance whose numbers declined during the day as the defenders fled for the safety of the *pasarela*. By the morning of August 7 the bridgehead had been crushed and of 9,500 defenders some 3,500 were casualties, including 1,300 prisoners. The Nationalists, who suffered 1,400 casualties, could now focus upon a single front and had captured a considerable amount of equipment, including five antitank guns, 56 machine guns, and 1,600 rifles. But it was clear that they needed more artillery and on August 8 Franco requested guns from the CTV who provided 134, with 24 antiaircraft guns, under their own commander.[21] Meanwhile, the Republic dispatched the 27 and 60 DIs under Majors Marcelino Usatorre and Manuel Ferrándiz to buttress Tagüeña.

There were now substantial resources to clear the Gandesa bend with the 150th and 84th Divisions on the northern and southern flanks, then from north-to-south the 50th, 102nd, 74th, 13th, 82nd, and 4th Divisions.[22] Yagüe was ordered to regain the Sierra de Pandols, held by Lister, to expose the southern Sierra de Caballs and the upper Canaletas Valley which ran south of the jump-off point. The task was assigned to Alonso Vega's 4th Division and Colonel Alfredo Galera's 84th Division supported by 26 batteries (80 guns) plus three batteries of 88mm.[23] Alonso Vega was to advance up the Bot–Gandesa road at night, although it was overlooked by the enemy positions, then strike into the Sierra about halfway along, supported by Galera on his right.

Major Joaquín Rodríguez's 11 DI held the Sierra de Pandols with excellent observation posts but he could do little to improve the defenses, for the rocky terrain meant that only the shallowest trenches could be dug and even these barely protected a prone man. The defenders here, and in the other sierras, would more often rely upon saggers (stone breastworks) although numerous caves were used as dugouts. Most of the ravines into the heights were turned into killing grounds with wire and machine-gun cross-fire and there was support from Leal in the Canaletas Valley.

The attack began after a three-hour bombardment from 07:00 on August 10, and with 75mm guns firing 120 rounds an hour, 105mm howitzers firing 90 and 155mm howitzers 40/45 an hour some 9,000 tonnes of shells blasted the defenses which were also bombed by all three air forces, generating rock fragments as deadly as shell splinters. The stress of surviving this and later bombardments was such that men clamped their teeth on small bits of board tied around their necks.

The battle was fought in conditions of scorching heat (up to 30°C), similar to those experienced the previous year on the Castilian plains around Brunete, dehydrating the men who received little food and less water, making them vulnerable to dysentery and typhus. The last was due to the lice that plagued the men together with flies, scabies, and rats. Alonso Vega secured much of the sierra the following day but Lister's watchwords were "vigilance, fortification and resistance." He demanded: "If anyone loses an inch of ground he must retake it at the head of his men or be executed," and this was no idle threat. Sergeants were ordered to shoot officers who tried to withdraw without written orders. In numerous counterattacks battalions evaporated as the fighting reached an unprecedented intensity, with peaks changing hands up to seven times a day and the wounded often left in no-man's land.

Rodriguez suffered 2,500 casualties including two brigade commanders and 570 prisoners but on the night of August 13/14 he was relieved by Mateo Merino who quickly lost half the 15 BI and a quarter of 11 BI while Lister was down to two dozen guns. Yet Alonso Vega was left in an exposed salient unable to take the northern and eastern heights and on August 14 he too abandoned the attack, which had cost 3,800 casualties, including 413 dead. To the south Galera was able to exploit his neighbor's success and push a kilometer further down the Canaletas but Lister held the Sierra almost to the end of the battle.

For Dávila the grim battle for the Sierra de Pandols was overshadowed by the destruction of the Fayon bridgehead. Even generals have an off-day and for him it was August 17, 1938, for he underestimated the enemy as he prepared to retake the Gandesa bridgehead by an attack at Villalba.[24]

A breakthrough here would be the first stage, followed by the capture in rapid succession of Mounta Gaeta and the Sierra de Fatarella, then an advance down the Sec Valley. The surfeit of optimism was due to Dávila's belief that the enemy had little artillery support and were unable to replace their heavy losses. The task was assigned to Delgado Serrano's 82nd Division and Arias's 74th Division, with Colonel Antonio Castejón's 102nd Division on their left and Barrón's division in the Sec Valley. There would be considerable fire support with 60 batteries (180 guns) and three antiaircraft batteries providing a three-hour preparation, while bombers would strike ravines concealing enemy reserves.

They would attack up gentle slopes covered with ilex trees aided by an extensive defensive system featuring deep trenches with rock-covered logs. Tagüeña had three divisions in line under former militia majors: (north to south) Ferrándiz, Cabezos, and Mora, with Usatorre in the Sec Valley, but they had only 50 guns. Tagüeña was warned by Rojo on August 18 that he faced an attack but had little time to improve his defenses.

Under Franco's gaze Arias began a preliminary attack southeast of Villalba on the morning of August 19 with the main effort the following day by Delgado Serrano with strong artillery preparation which cut Tagüeña's telephone lines for up to 38 hours. Initially the infantry were successful and Delgado Serrano broke through to take several hills but at great cost, one Requete battalion being almost wiped out. The main blow fell upon Cabezos who was severely tried and had to be supported by Mora, but both fought tenaciously and the Nationalist armor had to run the gauntlet of field and antitank artillery augmented by fire from camouflaged dug-in T-26s while Molotov Cocktails were thrown from foxholes.

Delgado Serrano succeeded in outflanking the defenses, forcing Tagüeña to abandon Mount Gaeta and his former headquarters, which was in Nationalist hands by August 23, but four Republican sapper battalions created a new defensive line. Arias took most of the heights dominating Corbera from the north but by then the attackers were exhausted, having suffered 5,000 casualties, including 1,000 dead, and advanced 3km on a 7km front to create another salient exposed to enemy fire. Tagüeña had suffered 8,000 casualties including 2,000 dead and nearly 2,200 prisoners including nearly 300 deserters. During this battle the Stukas were used for Tactical air support, striking gun positions around Corbera and interdicted the rear from August 19 through August 23, flying 29 sorties and dropping 14.5 tonnes of bombs.[25]

If Franco had a change of heart about battling for the Gandesa bend it was too late as he was now a prisoner of his earlier decisions.[26] He had sufficient artillery and support services while the Republicans had only 120 guns due to maintenance problems and they were short of ammunition. The Nationalists rationalized command and control by bringing in García-Valiño's Maestrazgo Corps headquarters for operations south of the Sec, leaving Yagüe responsible for the northern sector. With his broad confident grin, 39-year-old García-Valiño came from a military family and was a brilliant student who became a leading light among the younger generation of Franco's generals. He distinguished himself in Morocco, became a staff officer in 1935 but was not involved in plots against the Republic, and when the uprising began he was vacationing on the Basque coast. He quickly joined the rebels to command a brigade, then a division, and he continued to hold high military and political office until he retired in 1964.

Against this background a new plan was drafted and presented on August 31, with Dávila providing Tactical command while the Generalissimo was metaphorically looking over his shoulder. Belatedly it was recognized that the Sierra de Caballs was the key to retaking the bridgehead, so this would be the prime objective, but first the Sierra de la Vall had to be taken as a jump-off point for the capture of the Caballs, which would then be followed by an advance down the valley to Camposines.

Dávila remained convinced that enemy morale was low and decided to strike east of Gandesa into the Sierra de la Vall with Colonel Mohamed ben Mizzian's 1st Division, which would then advance along the heights to Camposines.[27] In the Sec Valley García-Valiño would push down the river to reach the Fatarella–Camposines road using Barrón supported by the Legion Tank Battalion. North of the river Yagüe would support Barrón by advancing along two diverging axes each with a tank company: Brigadier General Ricardo Rada's 152nd Division would strike eastward from Mount Gaeta to take the heights east of the Fatarella–Camposines road while on his right Alonso Vega would sweep down on Corbera, then consolidate his hold on the northern Sec Valley.

Franco's Master Gunner, Martinez de Campos, had 67 batteries (220 guns) augmented by nine antiaircraft batteries and would earn the nickname "The Optimist" (La Esperanza) because of his confidence in his gunners.[28] Given the international situation, few shells could be expected either from Germany or Italy and it appears that Franco placed greater reliance upon domestic sources by severely restricting consumption elsewhere. The attack would strike right down the Republican corps boundary in the valley with Tagüeña facing Yagüe, with Cabezos, Hans with 45 DI and Mora, while Lister had Usatorre and Leal facing García-Valiño.

Aided by 27 bombers whose 60 fighter escorts repulsed attacks by 52 fighters, García-Valiño struck Usatorre on a 2km front northwest of Corbera from September 3 but encountered stubborn resistance. Eventually pressure from Barrón in the west and Alonso Vega from the northwest pushed back 27 DI with heavy losses, forcing Lister to send Rodriguez to support him as Modesto demanded "resist without giving a meter." However, the Nationalists took Corbera at 07:00 the following day after a four-hour bombardment but, thanks to Tagüeña's commitment of Mateo Merino and artillery crossfire from the heights, progress down the Sec slowed.

To reduce losses the Nationalist infantry now attacked only after prolonged bombardments, sometimes up to five hours, to create "an inferno of fire and explosions" which cut Tagüeña's line 83 times.[29] García-Valiño had 43 tanks but they were vulnerable because the narrow tracks through the heights forced them to drive in single file. Thoma and the tank commander

Lieutenant Colonel José Pujales wanted to withdraw them from the battlefield but Franco refused.[30] Despite ground-attack aircraft supporting the infantry, fierce counterattacks slowed the advance and one supported by 22 tanks and every available gun finally halted the Nationalists on September 7, although bloody fighting continued until September 10. On the flanks Rada made little progress, following a series of bloody frontal attacks, but Mizzian pushed slowly along the Sierra de la Vall despite stubborn resistance by Beltran's newly arrived 43 DI and on September 6 reached the valley which divided it from the Sierra de Caballs.

The Nationalists had advanced 5km down the valley at a cost of 7,000 casualties, 5,100 in Maestrazgo Corps, and had a jump-off point to strike the Sierra de Caballs, but all the captured ground was under enemy observation. The defenders suffered 12,000 casualties with Modesto facing a serious desertion problem, so each corps created a punishment company while sometimes machine guns were set up to kill retreating soldiers.[31]

Dávila recognized that he must extend his grip on the Sierra de Fatarella and the Sec Valley to create more space for the artillery before striking into the Sierra de Caballs. On the afternoon of September 17 he ordered García-Valiño, supported by 61 batteries, to strike toward Camposines and its vital crossroads. This time Barrón, with a tank company, would push along the northern bank and into hills which dominated the middle of the valley while Mizzian paced him in the Sierra de la Vall using two battle groups each supported by a tank company, but first he transferred the remainder of the sierra to Arias.

Barrón faced Mateo Marino and Hans whose Brigadistas restricted his advance on the first day to a kilometer despite the usual heavy air and artillery bombardment, although he did establish a foothold in the northern hills. During the next two days he extended his hold but by then exhaustion caused him to be relieved by Alonso Vega who completed taking the high ground on the left by September 27. By contrast Mizzian made painfully slow progress across the smoke-obscured high ground. A storm which raged from September 23 brought the Nationalist advance to a halt until October 1. The brief lull saw the Brigadistas withdrawn and replaced by Álvarez and Leal, but the latter was killed by a sniper on September 23 while scouting. Campesino wanted his division back but Lister selected Major Vicente López Tovar and in later confirming this decision, a board of inquiry correctly concluded that Campesino was unfit to command in every sense of the word.[32]

The Nationalist renewed their advance from October 1 and completed the occupation of the Sierra de la Vall on October 4, by which time Alonso Vega could interdict the La Fatarella–Camposines road with artillery fire. Barrón and Mizzian, who had suffered 4,612 casualties (about half the division), were relieved by Delgado Serrano and Brigadier General Álvaro Sueiro's 53rd Division, Barrón's division being the only Nationalist formation withdrawn during the battle. Delgado Serrano pushed on from October 7 through October 12 to take a hill overlooking the Fatrella–Camposines road from the west, while Mizzian took heights which overlooked the town from the south. But by October 14 both sides were exhausted with low morale, the Nationalists having suffered some 23,000 casualties, including 19,000 by García-Valiño, although he took 4,900 prisoners. Yet the Nationalists had achieved their objective, having driven a 5km wedge down the Sec Valley between Modesto and Tagüeña, and their guns could now engage the whole length of the Sierra de Caballs and the remainder of the Sierra de Faterella.

Death from the Skies

During August and September Europe seemed on the verge of a new war, which was only averted by the signing of the Munich Treaty on September 30, an event influenced by the weakness of Anglo-French air power, especially in the face of German bombers.[33] Air power also contributed significantly to the Nationalist Ebro victory.[34] When the crossing began the Nationalists had some 325 aircraft and the Republic about 300, with strong concentrations on the Levante front, leaving barely 50 FARE fighters and ground-attack aircraft in Catalonia.[35] Six German and Italian fighter squadrons were based on the south bank of the Ebro, and 17 squadrons were within operating range of the Ebro Valley.

Kindélan was ordered to "destroy and disorganize the [enemy] deployment, cut their communications with the rearguard and weaken his penetrative capacity."[36] The Condor Legion's reconnaissance aircraft located most of the crossing points by mid-morning on July 26, the first aircraft dropping a report to the Italian base at Caspe which led Italian bombers to start attacking the crossings from 09:00. During the day there were some 45 German and Italian bombing sorties, the latter cutting the high-capacity bridge at Ginnestar, forcing traffic to divert to Flix and Mora del Ebro, while Italian fighters strafed the crossings. For two days the defense of the bridges relied upon six heavy (76.2mm), four medium (40mm), and 16 light (20mm) antiaircraft batteries together with a dozen quad-machine guns. They shot down few aircraft but damaged many, seven German on August 3, to force the bombers from 3,000–4,000m to 6,000m which reduced accuracy.

Six bridges were damaged on July 26, Italian dive bombers cutting the Asco bridge, and the Italians alone dropping 61 tonnes of bombs to hinder the passage of armor and corps artillery. The scale of the attack was maintained with 28 Italian attacks from August 1 through August 10, while in the first three days of August alone the Italians dropped 128 tonnes of bombs on the crossings, forcing the Republicans to become more active at night while daytime crossings were made as rapidly as possible.

It became a battle of wills between the airmen and the Republican engineers who learned to submerge footbridges to make them invisible from the air. Damaged bridges were rapidly repaired, then hit again: on August 8 the Flix bridge was hit by eight Italian bombers, repaired in eight hours, then hit again by 14 S.79s. The Italians calculated that their medium bombers needed 600 bombs to hit a bridge, but their dive bombers hit the Flix bridges from August 12 through August 18 with 36 bombs. The intensity of the effort may be judged from German records which show that their bomber and reconnaissance squadrons flew 1,858 strike sorties over the bridgehead from July 25 through August 30, usually against the crossings, and dropped 1,870 tonnes of bombs. The reconnaissance squadron reverted to its traditional role from August 14, while Stukas flew another 229 sorties and dropped more than 103 tonnes of bombs, although by September only two were serviceable.[37]

The Italian bombers actually resumed operations over the Levante on July 27 but then they and the Spanish began to transfer squadrons northward and the last big air battle over the Levante was that day. The Germans were already close to the battlefield and Volkmann moved his command post on the afternoon of July 25 from Benicarlo near Yagüe's headquarters in Caspe.

Modesto, presumably on the basis of ground observer reports, claimed that the enemy flew 4,129 sorties from July 25 through August 25, including 2,408 by bomber.[38] By contrast he lacked air support for the vital first three days of the offensive, possibly because FARE leaders felt that their forces were too weak. The first operation, by Rasantes and Delfin ground-attack aircraft, was on July 27 with two aircraft lost, while the first fighters appeared only two days later, probably from the Barcelona air shield. Even before the crossing Rojo told his friend Matallana that he was worried about air support and soon complained indignantly to FARE operations chief Colonel Joaquin Martinez Visiedo about its failure to support the crossing, leading to Visiedo's replacement on September 1.[39] Only from July 30 were reinforcements sent north, initially 12 Ratas and 14 Katiuskas, joined by a Chato squadron and three more of Ratas over the next week, but total Republican air strength was only 200 aircraft including 120 fighters. The arrival from Russia of 100 fighters and 24 Katiuskas in July and August allowed the FARE to add another Rata squadron in Catalonia, but one was sent to Estremadura from September 2, leaving only 90–110 supporting the Ebro front. During August the FARE lost 25 aircraft, six in accidents, mostly on the Ebro.[40]

Republican fighters flew sweeps of 30–40 aircraft and from August 1 became involved in swirling dogfights of 80–90 fighters. The more experienced Nationalist pilots established air superiority and by late October the FARE had only 91 fighters and 24 bombers in Catalonia. Apart from fighter sweeps it contributed little in the way of Tactical Level air support, although from late August the Chatos were sometimes used for ground-attack missions. Direct support operations, such as tactical reconnaissance, continued until the end of September, possibly involving some 300 sorties, while the bombers staged weak Operational Level attacks mostly upon airfields and communications. Modesto had wanted to bomb Gandesa in late July but Visiedo vetoed the idea, and while his replacement, Colonel Andreas García Lacalle, agreed with Modesto, there was no significant change. In part this was due to the departure of Russian aircrew due to the international agreement to withdraw foreign volunteers, bomber crews in September, then the fighter pilots, which severely weakened the FARE.

Not only did Nationalist airmen strike the crossings but Spanish and Italian squadrons also provided considerable Tactical Level air support. From mid-August Italian bombers focused upon this and in September dropped hundreds of tonnes on sierras to interdict the enemy rear. The Condor Legion's contribution was more limited, flying 33 bomber sorties (16.5 tonnes of bombs) during the Sierra de Pandols attack and 38 bomber sorties (69 tonnes) during the Villalba offensive.[41]

The international agreement also saw the withdrawal of Italian airmen, with seven squadrons disbanded and their aircraft transferred to the Spanish. German air strength was also reduced and, with prospects of a European war following the Sudetenland crisis, Berlin ordered Volkmann to return 246 of his most experienced aircrew including half his fighter and bomber pilots who were replaced by Spaniards to make up a third of the German squadrons' aircrew.[42] Volkmann's constant stream of pessimistic reports and demands for men and equipment irritated Berlin and he became increasingly querulous during the Ebro campaign, leading to his recall to Germany and leaving his chief of staff, Major Hermann Plocher, in command from November 13.

The withdrawal of so many veteran airmen, together with poor weather during late September and early October, saw a decline in Nationalist air operations, although attacks continued. When the weather improved Nationalist air activity surged from October 19 until the end of the campaign and decimated the FARE. A Nationalist press bulletin of November 16 claimed the confirmed destruction of 242 aircraft including 206 fighters and 17 bombers and the probable destruction of another 94 including 84 fighters. A more conservative and probably more accurate figure was 81 aircraft (75 fighters and eight bombers), with 59 Republican pilots killed or missing.[43] Republican air strength in Catalonia fell from 177 aircraft, of which 144 were serviceable, including 86 fighters and 18 bombers, to 161 by October 1 with 135 serviceable, including 91 fighters and 8 bombers.[44]

The Nationalists are reported to have flown 19,535 sorties and dropped 4,256 tonnes of bombs in an air campaign which never saw their airmen seriously challenged. Losses were relatively light at 43 aircraft shot down or damaged beyond repair (nine Italian, ten German, and 24 Spanish) while about 30 pilots were killed.[45]

The Final Push

By October the weather was changing, with storms and torrential rain from October 20 and later light falls of snow while mist hindered air support, so the rapid elimination of the Gandesa bridgehead was a matter of urgency. Franco and his commanders discussed the issue on October 23 and agreed it was essential to take the Sierra de Caballs.[46] Dávila issued his orders on the evening of October 26, with García-Valiño to launch the main blow on the Sierra de Caballs in an "energetic attack" from the Sec Valley. The main blow would be through the center of the sierra with Mizzian and Delgado Serrano jumping off from just east of Corbera while Arias would strike from the Sierra de Pandols supported by Galera on his right. They would converge upon Pinell and from there push on to the Ebro. All were reinforced: Aria with a tank company, two 65mm batteries each for Mizzian and Delgado Serrano who received mortar companies, while Galera was given three battalions, six heavy batteries, and a mortar company. Artillery support involved a complex fire plan upon coordinated objectives and organized by Martinez de Campos with 68 batteries (200 guns).

There would be no dodging the main blow for Beltran holding the line with López on his left and Major Ramón Pastor's 44 DI on his right. In the Ebro Valley were Rodríguez and 45 DI, now under Major Luis Rivas, reorganized following the withdrawal of the International Brigades. Battalions augmented most of the divisions which were supported by 134 guns, with Lister having 23 batteries and Tagüeña 32, augmented by three antitank batteries.[47] With dwindling air support the bridgehead relied increasingly upon antiaircraft artillery.

The spectacular three-hour artillery preparation began at 08:30 on October 30 and the Republican line disappeared under fire from guns of all calibers, followed by 200 bombers covered by 150 fighters and infantry heavy weapons.[48] Mizzian had moved into his jump-off positions the previous day and now infiltrated the shattered defenses by means of small teams, with many defenders still cowering in their dugouts. By 17:00 he had almost all the key heights while the defenders had suffered 3,000 casualties, one brigade losing 70 percent of its men, as the Nationalists took 700 prisoners.

The following day Mizzian continued his advance and by dusk had advanced 8km beyond the Sierra and into the Ebro Valley to threaten the Pinell–Miravet road which Rodríguez and two brigades were hastily sent to shield. On Mizzian's left, Delgado Serrano pushed along the Sierra de Caballs to secure almost all the eastern heights while on Mizzian's right Arias and Galera advanced up to 4km to secure the western Sierra de Caballs as well as most of the Sierra de Pandols while Rivas was brought forward. Despite all Lister's efforts the Nationalist advance was irresistible and his front was split when Arias took Pinell on November 3 while Mizzian pushed on to the Ebro between Miravet and Benifalet. Bowing to the inevitable, Lister withdrew his southern brigades in good order by dawn on November 4 as Arias and Galera also reached the river, and by November 7 the whole of the southern part of the bend was in Nationalist hands.

That day Modesto ordered Tagüeña, who returned to the front on November 2, to assume command of the northern elements of Lister's corps to simplify command and control. As a professional courtesy Tagüeña immediately went to Lister's command post at Mora del Ebro to inform him personally. Lister recrossed the river that night with the remainder of the defenders leaving Beltran retreating northward. Also on November 7 Yagüe began pressing the rump of the bridgehead from the west while García-Valiño completed the capture of the Sierra de Caballs and pressed on to take Mora de Ebro. Tagüeña had fortified the Sierra de Aguila but on November 8 it fell to García-Valiño who cut the Camposines–Mora de Ebro road the following day and by November 9 was enveloping Camposines which fell to Delgado Serrano on November 11. During the fighting Álvarez, a former Asturian fisherman, was killed by a shell and replaced by Major Antonio Ortiz. Tagüeña recognized that his men could do no more and from November 9 began hastily withdrawing his artillery across the Ebro, so by the next day only six Republican batteries remained on the west bank of the river.

In a desperate attempt to divert the enemy Modesto went north to organize an attack upon the Segre, leaving Tagüeña, assisted by a Soviet General

"Zaponov," to command a fighting withdrawal from the bridgehead covered by Ortiz.[49] The Segre offensive was launched on November 7 simultaneously with a Levante Army's coastal attack but neither diverted the enemy.

During the afternoon of November 12 Dávila issued his final orders of the campaign. García-Valiño would be the hammer and Yagüe the anvil, the Maestrazgo Corps sweeping north up the Ebro Valley with (west-to-east) Delgado Serrano and Mizzian, while Galera was in reserve together with the Legion Tank Battalion, and Sueiro garrisoned the river bank behind them. Meanwhile, the Moroccan Corps would push eastward through the Sierra de Fatarella, led by Alonso Vega, then, supported by Rada and Coco, swing northward to secure the Ebro south of Fayon. Delgado Serrano and Mizzian would be supported by two tank companies, 11 batteries from Galera and Sueiro, and 24 from the corps. Tagüeña had Mateo Merino north of the sierra, Cabezos within it, while Pastor, reinforced by two brigades, held the Sec Valley, but during the night of November 11/12 Ortiz and Beltran were withdrawn.

The Nationalist advance ground on remorselessly against an enemy more interested in retreating than resisting, despite Modesto's demands. Yagüe overcame defenses within the sierra, to take Fatarella on November 14, two days after García-Valiño cut the Camposines–Asco road, then entered Asco the following day and Flix on November 16. On the night of November 15–16 Tagüeña and his command staff sadly crossed the Ebro followed by Mateo Merino. After six tanks came across the Flix bridge it was blown up at 16:30 on November 16, leaving just three footbridges for the retreating troops. Luckily heavy mist allowed them to cross safely, which boosted morale and rendered superfluous the arrangements to cover the retreat with 40 fighters. The final push cost García-Valiño some 4,800 casualties, including 400 dead, and he took 6,100 prisoners together with five tanks, 200 machine guns, and 3,000 rifles.

So ended the battle of the Ebro, the bloodiest battle of the war with 126,000 casualties, the Republican government's gamble failing at a cost of some 70,000 casualties including 19,400 prisoners, with the Nationalists claiming to have buried 13,275 bodies. The Nationalists suffered 56,957 casualties, including 4,007 dead and 15,238 sick, but the figure appears to exclude some 4,000 prisoners, while a third of the casualties (17,837) were suffered by Alonso Vega and Mizzian.[50] The Nationalists mitigated these losses by rotating and withdrawing battalions to ensure that they were never burned out. They proclaimed the capture of 17 tanks (another 18 were destroyed), 14 guns, 45 mortars, 394 automatic weapons, 24,114 rifles, and some 5,000 tonnes of rifle ammunition.

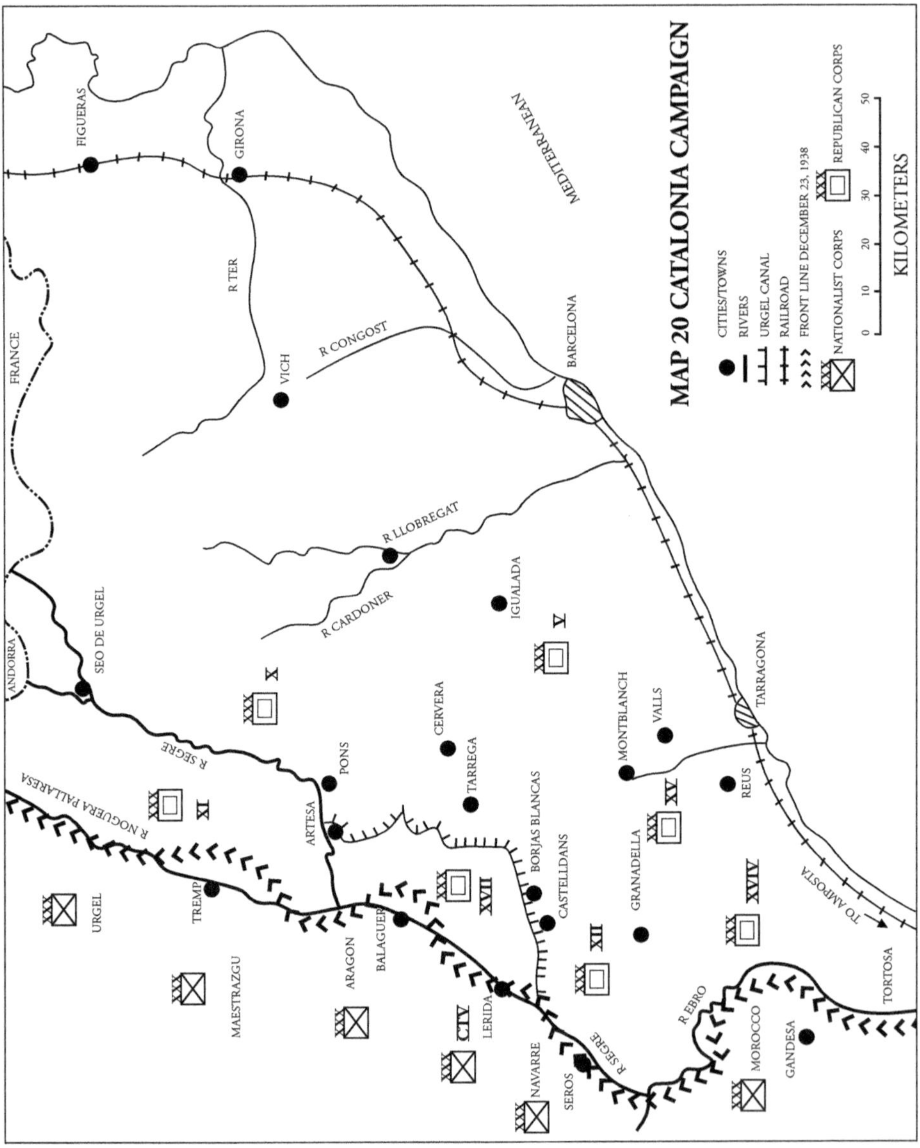
MAP 20 CATALONIA CAMPAIGN
CITIES/TOWNS
RIVERS
URGEL CANAL
RAILROAD
FRONT LINE DECEMBER 23, 1938
NATIONALIST CORPS
REPUBLICAN CORPS
0 10 20 30 40 50
KILOMETERS
FRANCE
ANDORRA
FIGUERAS
GIRONA
R TER
VICH
R CONGOST
BARCELONA
MEDITERRANEAN
R LLOBREGAT
R CARDONER
IGUALADA
SEO DE URGEL
R SEGRE
PONS
ARTESA
CERVERA
TARREGA
BORJAS BLANCAS
CASTELLDANS
MONTBLANCH
VALLS
TARRAGONA
REUS
GRANADELLA
TO AMPOSTA
TORTOSA
R EBRO
GANDESA
MOROCCO
SEROS
NAVARRE
LERIDA
CTV
ARAGON
BALAGUER
MAESTRAZGU
URGEL
TREMP
R NOGUERA PALLARESA
X
V
IX
XVIII
XV
XII
XXIV

Much of this was the manna that came across the French border, and its loss, together with thousands of veterans, compromised the defense of Catalonia. The whole Republican Army which had 176 tanks in May had only 126 by December, although the number of armored cars rose from 285 to 291. Nationalist armor also suffered its heaviest losses of the war: 28 tanks lost and 286 casualties including 35 dead.[51] With the threat of a European war now receding Franco could be certain that his allies would not only replace his limited material losses but provide new weapons to augment captured weapons and supply the expanded Nationalist Army.[52]

The Catalonian Campaign

Franco's options were again to strike toward Barcelona or Valencia but the choice was now clear. GERO had been fatally weakened on the Ebro and the Munich Agreement meant that there would be no European war in the immediate future, so no prospect of French intervention. The conquest of Catalonia's industries would have strong strategic benefits and bases there would strengthen the blockade.

Table 6.3: Nationalist forces in Catalonia offensive

Corps	Division
Urgel (Muñoz Grandes)	61, 62, 63, 150
Aragon (Moscardo)	40, 51, 53, 54, Brigade/1 Cavalry
Maestrazgo (García-Valiño)	1, 82, 84
Navarre (Solchaga)	4, 5, 12, 1 Cavalry (-)
CTV (Gambara)	Littorio, Flechas Negras, Flechas Azules, Flechas Verdes
Morocco (Yagüe)	13, 50, 105

Table 6.4: Republican forces in Catalonia offensive

Army	Corps	Division
Eastern (Perea)	X (Jover)	30, 31, 34
	XI (Galán)	26, 32, 55
	XVIII (Barrio)	27, 60, 72
Ebro (Modesto)	XII (Vega)	16, 44, 56
	XV (Tagüeña)	3, 35, 42
	XXIV (Buxó)	24, 43
Army Group	V (Lister)	11, 45, 46

Franco began regrouping his forces on November 19 using 1,950 trains.[53] To help Dávila and Vigón focus upon what would be the former's final campaign Franco activated the Army of the Levante front under Orgaz. Dávila's orders, published on November 26, were simply to gut Perea's army group in a few days of "determined and energetic action." Franco had wanted to keep the Italians in reserve but Gambara persuaded him, or twisted his arm, to give the CTV a major role.

Catalonia is bounded in the north by the Andorra and French frontiers and in the east by the Mediterranean, much of the terrain being more than 400m high, often pierced by narrow river valleys. North of a line roughly from Tremp to Girona, the heights tend to run east–west, cut by rivers, and were largely manned by each side's division-sized Pyrenean Task Force. To the south brooding sierras and massifs restricted movement to the northeast and along the coastal plain. Only the Urgel Plain west of the lower Segre provides relatively open ground, while barriers to an advance upon Barcelona include the Segre's tributary, the Noguera Pallaresa, together with a man-made irrigation waterway, the Urgel Canal (Canal d'Urgel) built in the 19th century, and zigzagging some 245km from the Segre, northeast of Artesa de Segre (Artesa), to just south of Lerida, irrigating some 70,000 hectares. To the east there were only two significant river barriers: the Llobregat, fed by the Cardoner, running northwest to southeast with Barcelona near its mouth, and the Ter running west to east with Girona standing mid-way.

There was little in the way of lateral communication, with the most extensive road network being southeast of the Segre and north of the Ebro, south of the Lerida–Tarrega–Cervera–Igualada–Barcelona Highway with a railroad running to the north. There was also the coastal highway, with neighboring railroad, from Amposta through Tarragona, Barcelona, Girona, and Figueras to the border, but Dávila's planning was clearly constrained by geography.

Dávila's Urgel (Muñoz Grandes), Aragon (Moscardó), Maestrazgo (García-Valiño), and Navarre Corps (Solchaga), together with Gambara's CTV, had 17 divisions (230,000 men) and would strike out of the western bridgeheads. They would roll up Perea's line from north to south to establish a bridgehead bounded by the Segre and the Urgel Canal and meet between Tarrega and Borjas Blancas. Then Yagüe's Morocco Corps would cross the Ebro with three divisions and 40,000 men. Beyond that Dávila opted to keep his options open.

Muñoz Grandes, who would celebrate his 43rd birthday the day after Barcelona fell, was an old friend of Franco, born into a humble family and had distinguished himself during the Rif War.[54] He was a liberal and a Republican who helped to create the Asaltos but at the time of the uprising was in prison accused of plotting against the state. In March 1937 he escaped and was rapidly promoted to brigadier general and given the Urgel Corps. He would continue fighting "the Reds" in Russia, commanding the Spanish Blue Division from 1942 to 1943, and would later serve as defense minister.

Dávila was confident of success, for, as he noted in his instructions, the Ebro campaign had destroyed the best enemy divisions and depleted their reserves, making it unlikely that they could stage a prolonged resistance. He had a total of 332,750 men, of whom 270,000 were in the combat units, including 61,550 in the CTV, of whom 28,000 were Italian.[55] His material support was more than adequate, with 135 tanks, 864 guns (640 Spanish), augmented by 102 antitank and 48 heavy antiaircraft guns.[56] He could also count upon 368 aircraft including 80 of the Condor Legion now under Richthofen, who returned to Spain, possibly at Franco's request, on November 30 and assumed command the next day.[57]

The offensive was scheduled for December 10, and to oversee it Franco moved his headquarters to Pedrola Castle, north of Lerida, but torrential rain washed away Nationalist hopes, forcing Dávila to redraft his instructions on December 11.[58] The offensive was further delayed until December 15 in the hopes of better flying weather but these hopes were dashed, and with river levels rising it was again postponed until December 23. This raised tensions in GHQ where fears grew that the army might become involved in prolonged fighting, with Barcelona becoming the new Madrid.

The defense of the 400km front was under Hernández Saravia's 220,000-man GERO, whose western front was held by Perea's Eastern Army with ten divisions while nine divisions of Modesto's Ebro Army held the lower Segre and the Ebro. By combing out rear services and drafting raw recruits, the two armies had received 20,000 replacements but Perea still had only 90,000 men and Modesto 80,000 with understrength units of semi-trained men.[59] The army group reserves consisted of Lister's V CE with 22,000 men between Valls and Barcelona, and to help respond to the anticipated blow all civilian rail traffic ceased.[60]

There were shortages not only in manpower but also equipment, whose replacement was impossible now that the French frontier was closed, and Modesto was lucky to receive 100 machine guns while Perea reported he lacked 12 antitank batteries, 460 machine guns, 300 automatic rifles, and 9,000 rifles.[61] The army group had only 173 guns, many with worn-out barrels, as well as 100 antitank guns and 40 tanks—little wonder that morale was as low as the ammunition stocks.[62] Brigades were down to 20 automatic weapons and 1,000 rifles against establishments of 80 and 1,850 respectively, while the army group had only 5,000 automatic weapons and 125,000 rifles.

The defense had also been undermined when the government dispatched 35 fighters to the central zone, leaving 54 operational in Catalonia, the squadrons having a strong complement of inexperienced pilots.[63]

The transfer of aircraft was to support the resuscitated Plan "P" which Rojo hoped to launch as a diversion in the Estremadura, but GERC commander Miaja did not wish to waste scarce resources on what he regarded as a fool's errand. Rojo hoped that Franco would take several months to recover, possibly until the spring, but Republican intelligence soon reported signs that the enemy would soon strike into Catalonia and he deduced that the main blow would be from the west.[64] Early in December army and corps commanders were briefed about potential threats and the planned response, while on December 5 Rojo sought, and received, Negrín's permission to execute Plan "P," the orders being radioed that night.

The defenses of Catalonia anticipated holding the enemy on the Noguera Pallaresa, the lower Segre, and the Ebro in Line 1 (Linea 1 or L-1) for several days, then gradually withdrawing 15–30km over a 10–12-day period to L-2. L-1 had been built by divisions and a few engineer battalions but was up to 10km deep and in the south consisted of a double line but was weaker on the Ebro Army sector.[65] Although there were several hundreds of kilometers of trenches, they consisted mostly of strongpoints and resistance centers, some of which could survive 100kg bombs. Within Perea's sector there were 2,188 automatic weapon positions, 310 shelters, and 115km of wire. L-1 ran along the upper Segre, then down the River Francoli, which runs into the sea near Tarragona, with a switch-line extension through Pobla de Granadella (Granadella) facing the lower Segre and the Ebro.

Lieutenant Colonel Gregorio Jover's X CE was holding L-2 along the Segre with 31,000 men while Tagüeña's XV CE with 21,000 men held the switch line. The Republicans hoped that the exhausted enemy would be held on L-2. They even dared to hope that Lister and Tagüeña might be able to counterattack the exposed enemy. If L-2 was pierced there were plans for an L-3 behind it, together with the Llobregat-based L-4, an L-5 covering Girona and an L-6 covering Figueras, but these positions had barely been surveyed. The only fortifications behind L-2 was an east–west line 40km northwest of Barcelona and bisected by L-4, and rudimentary defenses south of Vich on each side of the River Congost.

Artillery preparation began around 08:00 on December 23 and Muñoz Grandes led the assault on the left breaking out of the Tremp bridgehead with a single division, but he was closely followed by García-Valiño and Moscardó.[66] Together they pushed back Perea's right toward the Segre, then split, forcing Jover northward and Galán's XI CE eastward. Low cloud and sleet on the first day grounded aircraft until noon and in the following days the advance would continue through rain, sleet, snow, and fog.

García-Valiño was first to the Segre on December 25 but Galán prevented Muñoz Grandes from reaching the river until December 28 as Moscardó erupted from the Balaguer bridgehead. Moscardó used most of his troops to drive into Galán's left to help García-Valiño pierce L-2, but fierce resistance from Barrio's XVIII CE meant that they did not take the key communications town of Artesa until January 3. Seven days later, despite fog, Moscardó established his own bridgehead across the Segre which allowed Sueiro's 53rd Division to cross the Urgel Canal and sweep down its eastern bank pushing back Barrio who still retained his stretch of the Segre until January 6.

Meanwhile Moscardó sent Marzo's 54th Division south to cut the Lerida–Tarragona road and take the eastern bank of the Urgel Canal. Progress was slow, with Barrio again proving a stubborn defender, and this helped to expose Gambara's northern flank. He and Solchaga, supported by 300 guns, had broken out of the Seros bridgehead in the early afternoon of December 23 to maul Vega on Modesto's right. Vega, whose headquarters were in Castelldans, 30km from the front, did not learn of the breakthrough for two hours and was then desperately trying to catch up. By the end of the day the Nationalists here had advanced 8km on a 10km front and had taken 2,000 prisoners. But Lister and Tagüeña both resisted stubbornly, and on the morning of December 24 the former struck Gambara's left supported by every available Republican airplane, which helped him regain some ground. Two days later, as Italian bombers dropped 51 tonnes on Lister's positions, the Littorio counterattacked, determined to show that, despite a popular Spanish song (see Chapter 1), they had not only trucks but also balls and slowly pushed back the Republicans.

This action showed that, despite the weather, air power continued to play an important role in the victory, with Italian bombers beginning an interdiction campaign on November 20 while fighters staged sweeps destroying many of the 34 FARE aircraft lost during December.[67] The Condor Legion was boosted by the arrival of 40 Bf 109E with 20mm cannon to replace Bf 109 B/C which were given to the Spanish together with 13 He 112 to form two squadrons. Despite the weather the Condor Legion's fighters flew up to six sorties a day and on January 27 alone dropped 29 tonnes of bombs. A week later they struck Figueras rail station four times but within a week Richthofen had only 61 serviceable aircraft. On February 3 all Republican aircraft which could not fly within 48 hours were ordered destroyed while the remaining 43 aircraft, including 14 fighters, flew to France where they were assembled at Toulouse.

On the ground Solchaga made steady progress on Gambara's right, reaching the confluence of the Segre and the Ebro on December 24, allowing the 5th and 12th Divisions, under Bautista and Asensio, to advance along the northern bank of the Ebro. Gambara's Spanish divisions were fighting with an intensity unexpected by the defenders and penetrated L-2 near Granadella, undermining Hernández Saravia's whole defensive concept. He ordered Modesto to launch an immediate counterattack with Lister and Tagüeña from Borjas Blancas and Granadella respectively to recover the Segre defenses. But assembling the troops required transport of which there was desperate shortage, and although each corps quickly dispatched a division eastward, the remainder did not arrive until the morning of December 25. Fog and snow grounded the airmen as the counterattack slowed Solchaga and Gambara, but the former took Granadella on December 28. Optimistically Hernández Saravia hoped to launch a counteroffensive but he lacked men and equipment, and soon informed the government that he had only 17,000 rifles left. Rojo toyed with the idea of shipping men from Valencia but the blockade made this impossible.

By New Year's Day L-2 was completely compromised and Republican resistance was weakening. Another breakthrough on January 3 saw Gambara take Castelldans the next day, Lister's headquarters staff having to fight off an enemy probe, while on January 5 Borjas Blancas fell and with it the last remnant of L-1. The news got worse, for the same day saw Yagüe begin to cross the swollen Ebro at the Gandesa bend, brushing aside resistance by Colonel Mariano Buxó's XXIV CE, and by January 6 the defenders, having committed all their reserves, were on the verge of collapse. The advances of Solchaga and Gambara, who was injured about this time, threatened to isolate most of Barrio's XVIII CE, forcing it into a hasty retreat.[68] Meanwhile, Marzo steadily pushed southward to link up with Gambara just east of Lerida on January 9. The only fly in the ointment was Richthofen playing armchair general and loudly complaining to Franco, Dávila, and Vigón about Spanish military leaders and threatening to withhold support.[69]

By now the Nationalists had driven a 45km salient between Perea and Modesto and their advance began to accelerate; indeed even the Condor Legion's motorized 88mm batteries were unable to keep pace. Despite snow, sleet, and rain, Gambarra pushed eastward to take Montblanch on January 11, and Hernandez Saravia ordered Buxó to abandon the Ebro estuary, which opened the door for Yagüe to take Tortosa and Reus on January 13. The following day Solchaga took Valls and headed for Tarragona in a vain bid to isolate Buxó. Solchaga and Gambarra had now advanced some 70–80km on a 40km front, while the Nationalist left had advanced some 30km on a

60km front with resistance generally weakening with every pace eastward. Gambara's motorized troops now pushed past the last organized defenses and the whole Nationalist front was swinging northward like a door hinged on the Tremp bridgehead.

By January 11 the Republic had lost 70,000 men, including 23,000 prisoners, GERO was exhausted and barely capable of defense, while the demoralized men thought only of retreat, many deserting to their homes, and despite desperate rearguard actions the barely manned L-3 was overrun.[70] There was a brief moment of hope when Plan "P" was finally executed but quickly held and brought no relief. However, the French did reopen the frontier but only 30 fighters, 14 guns, three antitank guns, 2,700 automatic weapons, and 35,000 rifles actually reached Hernández Saravia's men.[71]

Tarragona fell to Yagüe as the Republicans were like flotsam on the incoming tide. On the Nationalist left, Muñoz Grandes began to take the door off its hinges, striking Jover to take Pons on January 18, then slowly pushing X CE up the western bank of the Segre toward Andorra. Within a fortnight the Nationalist bulldozer was nearing Barcelona with Yagüe on the coast and Gambarra and Solchaga inland. García-Valiño pushed eastward to take the vital communications hub of Manresa, 40km northwest of Barcelona, on January 24, and that day Solchaga and Gambara reached the Llobregat, the foundation of L-4 and Barcelona's last hope.

Perea tried to hold the line but Modesto fell back and on January 25 Solchaga crossed the river. The growing confusion meant that the city itself was only lightly held by elements of Beltran's 43 DI, Buxó's corps, and the equivalent of five battalions, mostly lightly armed police. Any hopes of emulating the defense of Madrid by mobilizing the population collapsed under the burden of falling morale following the undermining of Catalan nationalism and Communist machinations against the Trotskyists and Anarchists.

The city was occupied amid light resistance during January 26 and much of the population fled northward following the bickering government which moved to Girona. No preparations had been made and everything disintegrated into anarchy as the Condor Legion ignored Franco's wishes and attacked refugees. Hernández Saravia became the scapegoat for Barcelona's fall and on January 27 was dismissed for "defeatism," but allegedly because he wanted Perea to replace Modesto. He was replaced by Jurado, who was powerless to influence events, and the Republican retreat continued, with counterattacks growing weaker because of the enemy's numerical superiority.

With the fall of Barcelona and the occupation of the Llobregat/Cardoner lines, the advance slowed owing to a combination of exhaustion, heavy rain, and sleet, and did not pick up pace until January 31. Now Yagüe on the coast pushed back Barrio and Tagüeña while on his flank Solchaga advanced through the high ground defended by Lister and Vega who were little more than breakwaters, withdrawing as the troops on their left were pushed northward. The CTV remained behind for fear that a diplomatic crisis might follow the arrival of Italian troops on France's southern frontier.

The Nationalists remorselessly pushed Modesto northward and the Communists decided in a meeting held on the night of February 3/4 to hold Girona and the River Ter, but when Lister returned to his headquarters he learned that the enemy were penetrating the defenses. Despite everything Modesto held on until February 6, by which time a threat was developing from the west where Muñoz Grandes had advanced along the Segre, isolating Jover and taking Seo de Urgel on February 5. García-Valiño and Moscardó switched places, with the latter helping Muñoz Grandez to drive back Galán while the former pushed Barrio out of Vich at the beginning of February.

Although Paris had permitted Spanish civilian refugees to enter the country from the night of January 27/28, they held back the troops, including 10,000 wounded, until February 5. On February 4 Rojo ordered another withdrawal and four days later bowed to the inevitable and ordered his men across the French border. Covered by Perea in the west, the Republican bridgehead slowly collapsed like a leaky balloon. Girona fell on February 5, followed by Figueras on February 8, and during the next two days the Nationalist corps swept up to the frontier in sequence, like a curtain sweeping across a stage to end the drama of the Catalonia campaign. By then some 63,000 troops were in French internment camps, having dumped 1,000 automatic weapons and 30,000 rifles, but the French also took 100 Nationalist airmen including 30 Italians and ten Germans.[72]

The final campaign had cost the Nationalists some 40,000 casualties and 16 aircraft, most in the fighting to mid-January, during which the CTV lost 2,700, of whom 1,110 were Italian. The defenders probably suffered some 80,000 casualties, with some 52,000 taken prisoner and up to 20,000 deserting.[73] The campaign cost Franco 13 tanks and 102 tank crew, including 16 dead, but only 29 casualties were in Russos.[74] Just after the campaign the Nationalists claimed the capture of 150 guns, 3,000 automatic weapons, as well as 262 locomotive and 1,000 rail wagons. The victory in Catalonia was Dávila's swansong, for the Army of the North was promptly disbanded and the architect of Franco's most important victories focused upon his duties as defense minister, then other high military and political offices, where he proved honest, unlike some of his colleagues, and in 1949 was briefly head of government.

The Republic's Last Days

Negrín would not read the writing on the wall and was determined to fight, but increasing numbers of politicians and soldiers recognized that this was their death warrant. With desperate optimism he sought a negotiated end to the conflict based upon conditions of continued democratic government and no reprisals. Franco, like the Allies in World War II, demanded unconditional surrender and the irresistible force shattered the immovable object. Negrín hoped to erode Nationalist resolution with a prolonged defense, but his military leaders, as well as the rank and file, while still committed to the ideals of the Republic, were unwilling to be sacrificed upon the altar of his diplomacy.

Many of the senior commanders who crossed into France, including Rojo, despaired of the future and effectively resigned their commissions. Only a few Communist commanders were in favor of prolonged resistance, while Miaja blew hot and cold on the issue. Prolonged resistance depended upon new supplies of weapons and in October 1938 Negrín told a British diplomat that Republican Spain needed 400 aircraft, 200 tanks, 1,500 guns, 12,000 machine guns, and 500,000 rifles.[75]

On November 11 FARE commander Hidalgo de Cisneros presented Stalin with a request for 410 combat aircraft, 250 tanks, 2,150 guns, 10,000 automatic weapons, and 400,000 rifles at a cost of $103 million but there was less than $100 million of Spanish gold left in Russian vaults.[76] There was some grumbling by Soviet Defense Minister Voroshilov, but Stalin eventually authorized seven shipments from Murmansk to France between December 15 and February 15, including 168 aircraft, 40 tanks, 199 guns, 300 antitank guns, 4,000 automatic weapons, 40,000 rifles, and 3,000 tonnes of ammunition.[77] While much of this weaponry was second hand, at least Stalin had helped while Paris ignored Negrín's request on January 7 for 2,000 machine guns and 100,000 rifles. A little of this Soviet largesse reached the retreating Republican troops in Catalonia but most remained in French depots until the end of the war, when it appears to have been returned to the Soviet Union. There was simply no way of transporting it through the Nationalist air–sea blockade, while the French lacked the political will to dispatch it.

With the Munich agreement and the loss of Catalonia, the defeat of the Spanish Republic was only a matter of time and Franco began to concentrate his forces for the final campaign.[78] The regrouping involved 4,003 trains in February and March, including 1,528 for troops.[79] In addition to Orgaz's Army of the Levante with Aranda's, Varela's, Moscardó's, and Muñoz Grandes' corps, Saliquet's Army of the Center had the Madrid and Toledo Corps augmented by García-Valiño's, Solchaga's, and Gambara's corps, while the four corps of Queipo de Llano's Army of the South were augmented by Yagüe's. With 600,000 men in 56 divisions supported by 2,500 guns, 600 armored fighting vehicles, and some 500 aircraft, this overwhelming numerical and qualitative strength made victory inevitable.

Miaja had only 490,000 men in 49 understrength divisions supported by 50 tanks, 450 guns, and 164 aircraft, and in their desperation many of his subordinates fell into the trap of self-delusion.[80] They convinced themselves that they could negotiate a surrender on favorable terms with their brother officers on the other side but would first need to overcome the perceived obstacle of Communist opposition. Led by Central Army commander Casado, a friend of Barrón, they mobilized the anti-Communists, so that a military uprising not only marked the beginning of the Spanish Civil War but also its end. Their resolve was strengthened when Negrín met his military commanders at Los Llanos airfield near Albacete on February 16 and ignored most of the generals who were calling for peace and advocated continuing resistance, despite admitting the failure of efforts to negotiate a peaceful end to the conflict.[81]

As insurance Modesto was appointed Central Army commander on March 2 but three days later Casado's uprising began and at the cost of some 800 casualties by March 11 the plotters were in control and authorized the immediate surrender of the last 59 combat aircraft.[82] But the negotiations proved fruitless and the Nationalists broke them off on March 25. The next day Franco ordered his troops to advance and most of the Republicans simply fled homewards. Many Republican leaders fled, including Modesto, Casado, and Menéndez, the latter pair making for Great Britain.[83] On March 31 the last Republican tricolor came down. Informed of victory by an aide, Franco did not look up and merely replied "Very good, many thanks."

Generally Franco observed his one concession to Casado of sparing officers who surrendered, but they served jail terms appropriate to their "crimes" or "malice" (*malicia*). But those who had played a role in the deaths of their comrades were executed, as were those with a left-wing track record. Some officers had their death sentences commuted but all lost pensions and had to forge new careers.[84]

The Lessons

Military observers from Europe and the United States watched the conflict with interest, but events in Spain had little influence upon European military thought.[85] Military orthodoxy was unchallenged and armies continued to believe in the supremacy of defensive power and the continued reign of artillery as queen of the battlefield; indeed Nationalist archives claim that all 126 Spanish-operated tanks destroyed during the war, including 80 Negrillos, were lost to artillery or antitank fire.[86] It is also worth noting that this would be the last conflict that used large quantities of traditional shrapnel shells, which showered pellets over a small area. They were replaced by the new generation of high-explosive shells introduced at the end of the Great War, which created a cloud of splinters over a wider area.

The Young Turks of the German Panzerwaffe saw little of relevance in the Spanish conflict apart from minor tactical lessons, and within six months these modern Luthers began demonstrating the irrelevance of the Holy Writ of conventional military doctrine. Yet the Civil War did stimulate a revolution in tank design, for it confirmed Russian fears about their vulnerability not only to antitank guns but also to field artillery. This led to the "gun proof" T-34 and the KV-1 tanks with superior armor and more powerful guns, as part of a philosophy that remains relevant to the present day. On a more humane note, the war did stimulate advances in battlefield medical treatment and the use of blood transfusions.

The conflict convinced air force commanders that the new generation of bombers could operate without escort, a philosophy that continued until the disastrous Eighth US Air Force Schweinfurt raids in the Fall of 1943. Such threats could be matched only by the new generation of heavily armed, high-speed interceptors, and dogfighters quickly disappeared from the skies. Attacks upon Republican cities also raised doubts about the effectiveness of strategic bombing, as the civilian population endured them with considerable equanimity rather than panicking as was anticipated.

At the Tactical and Operational Level the Civil War confirmed the value of the fighter-bomber in particular and air power in general, although the Soviet Union opted to pursue a dedicated ground-attack aircraft which became the famed Ilyushin Il-2. Nationalist air power was able to disrupt enemy rail and road communications and thus prove a major hurdle for defenders trying to plug gaps in their line. Richthofen would develop the idea so that radio-equipped forward controllers would be able to control ground-attack aircraft to aid the panzer divisions, and over the next three years he would be the spearhead of Nazi conquest. The most significant development, however, was fighter tactics based upon pairs of aircraft rather than cumbersome trios.

The Nationalists' victory was due to their more effective use of resources. Moreover the Nationalist army, though deeply flawed, was generally of a higher quality than its enemy, with professional soldiers playing a key role in decision-making. By contrast Republican decision-making was bedeviled by political factions and poorer use of resources, while the presence of foreign troops on both sides had a marginal effect upon the progress of the war or its outcome.

Even as the Republic was in its dying throes Germany reneged on the Munich agreement and occupied Prague, lighting the fuse for World War II, which started five months later. To the profound disappointment of his German and Italian allies Franco adopted a policy of benevolent neutrality due to a mixture of economic exhaustion, his pragmatic caution, and the determination of many of his generals that Spain should not fight the Allies. However, they themselves became involved in a fierce dispute with the Falange about restoring the monarchy, which saw several imprisoned.

The monarchy was not restored until after Franco's death but the constitutional struggle between Centrists and the centrifugal effects of regional autonomy continue, as demonstrated by the issue of Catalonian independence which has provided a background to the writing of this book.

Notes

1 Franco's concern led him to begin fortifying both the French and Moroccan frontiers using 20,000 prisoners. Thomas, p. 848.

2 XV CE was reactivated on April 16, 1938.

3 For Republican preparations and their offensive see Aznar, pp. 737–790; Ballester, pp. 59–61; Beevor, pp. 349–354; Cabrera, *Del Ebro a Gandesa*, pp. 9–23, 91–166, 187–290 (hereafter Cabrera); Cardona, pp. 251–268; Cervello and Agudo, *La Batalla del Ebro*, pp. 285–290 (hereafter Cervello and Agudo); Engel, *Operations*, pp. 311–319; Henry, *The Ebro 1938*, pp. 27–50 (hereafter Henry); Kindélan, pp. 139–170; Lojendio, pp. 395–438; Lister, pp. 201–209; Martinez, *Ebro*, pp. 68–163; Martínez and Martínez, pp. 289–306; Modesto, pp. 177–179, 184–199; Reverte, *La batalla del Ebro*, pp. 19–31, 36–44,. 47–72, 77–149 (hereafter Reverte, *Ebro*); Rojo, *Heroica*, pp. 165–178; Salas, *Air*, pp. 356–357; Tagüeña, pp. 139, 142–153; Thomas, pp. 835, 837–842; Torres, *La batalla del Ebro*, pp. 43–90, 105–122 (hereafter Torres); Vidal, pp. 351–360; Voltas, vol. 3, pp. 168–177, 180–187, 196–197; Hughes article *The European Aldershot*.

4 Based upon Engel, *Divisions*, p. 85, amended by Martinez Bande. Peñarredonda should not be confused with Colonel Pedro Peñarredonda who had led a mobile brigade some months earlier.

5 He was flown by in the FARE commander's personal transport. Modesto, p. 177.

6 This is based upon Lister and it suggests that neither Modesto nor Tagüeña was present. Significantly there appears to have been no GERO presence. Lister, p. 205.

7 All levels of command down to division were led by Communists together with 25 of the 27 brigades. Thomas, p. 825.

8 Lister, p. 223; Tagüeña, p. 167; Zaragoza, p. 92.

9 Buckley, p. 370; Tagüeña, p. 187; Thomas, p. 836; Zaragoza, pp. 112–133.

10 Thomas, p. 837n.1; Zaragoza, pp. 190–217.

11 For bridge details see Martinez, *Ebro*, p. 93n.114.
12 Alpert, pp. 230–231; Rojo, *Vicente Rojo*, pp. 222–223.
13 For warnings see Martinez, *Ebro*, pp. 73–79; Salgado-Araujo, *Mi vida junto a Franco*, pp. 262–263 262–263.
14 For bridges see Tagüeña, pp. 163–164.
15 See Morocco Corps war diary. Martinez, *Ebro*, Appendix 2.
16 Cardona, p. 273.
17 For the International Brigades see Robert Cole's article in Cervello and Agudo, pp. 243–255.
18 For operations in the Central zone see Martinez, *La Batalla de Pozoblanco y el Cierre de la Bolsa de Merida*. See also Aznar, pp. 795–801; Beevor, p. 347; Engel, *Operations*, pp. 259–270; Lojendio, pp. 526–535; Martinez, *Ebro*, pp. 274–282; Martínez and Martínez, pp. 328–329, 338–342; Saiz, vol. 2, pp. 754–762; Salas, *Air*, pp. 349–355; Vidal, pp. 342–344.
19 Cayón Garcia/Muñoz Rubio, *Railways*, pp. 10, 18–19, table 9; Garcia Lomas, pp. 157–158.
20 For the Nationalist counteroffensive see Alcofar, *Air*, pp. 154–163; Beevor, pp. 354–359; Cabrera, pp. 293–312, 315–350, 357–411, 419–508, 527–618, 621–673, 683–727; Cardona, pp. 269–275, 277–289, 290–299; Cervello and Agudo, pp. 290–300; Engel, *Operations*, pp. 319–361; García-Valiño, pp. 223–236, 236–280; Henry, pp. 56–85; Lister, pp. 209–225; Manca, pp. 413–429; Martinez, *Ebro*, pp. 167–269; Martínez and Martínez, pp. 306–307, 309–323; Mezquida, *La Batalla del Ebro*, pp. 157–171 (hereafter Mezquida); Modesto, pp. 200–230, 237–243; Reverte, *Ebro*, pp. 150–572; Rojo, *Heroica*, pp. 181–195; Salas, *Air*, pp. 357–359; Tagüeña, pp. 154–160, 162–168, 170–175; Thomas, pp. 842–844, 852, 854–855; Torres, pp. 123–234; Vidal, pp. 360–373.
21 Alcofar, *CTV*, pp. 165–166; Coverdale, p. 358.
22 From August 17 the 50th Division was under Colonel Manuel Coco, Campos-Guereta having been cashiered.
23 Galera in 1956 would be the last commander of the Spanish Army in Morocco.
24 Engel, *Operations*, p. 326.
25 IWM Ger/Misc/MCR/19 (1A).
26 Cardona, p. 288.
27 Known to the Spanish as Ben Mizzian, he was the only Moroccan officer to command a Nationalist division. He had fought alongside the Spanish in the Rif War and become a friend of Franco, whose life he was reported to have saved. He left the Spanish Army in 1957, became Morocco's defense minister and in 1970 the only field marshal in the Moroccan Army.
28 Reverte, *Ebro*, p. 478.
29 Tagüeña, p. 163.
30 Herrero Perez, p. 339; Salas, *Intervencion*, p. 553.
31 Alpert, p. 171.
32 Lister, pp. 223–225; Zaragoza, p. 92.
33 For the crisis see Beevor, pp. 340, 360–368; Cardona, pp. 289–290; Hooton, *Phoenix*, p. 164; Martinez, *Ebro*, pp. 218–222; Thomas, pp. 844, 848–851. The British had only 84 modern fighters and the French 23.
34 For air operations see Arias, pp. 251–259; Alcofar, *Air*, pp. 300–324; Henry, pp. 51–56; Hildago, pp. 182–189; Ries and Ring, pp. 178–200; Salas, *Air*, pp. 359–395; Ghergo, *Guerra Aerea nei deli di Spagna*, pp. 89–90; Modesto, p. 218; Muria, pp. 193–196; Permuy, pp. 76–77; Proctor, pp. 221–236; Saiz, vol. 3, pp. 777–835; Torres, pp. 90–104. Pedriali article, *L'Aviazione Legionaria nel Levante e sull'Ebro*, pp. 91–93; IWM Ger/Misc/MCR/19 (1A); Håkon site.

35 The Italians had 140, the Germans 80, and the Nationalists 105, 115 bombers, and 150 fighters. The Republicans had 40 bombers and 140 fighters and two of their Rata squadrons were still Russian-manned. Based upon Pedriali, p. 93.
36 Kindélan, p. 151.
37 IWM Ger/Misc/MCR/19 (1A).
38 Modesto, p. 218.
39 Alpert, p. 309. Visiedo, a qualified pilot and observer, clearly had a narrow, conservative view of air power. See Axis History Forum, "Colonel Visiedo" for March 25, 2018.
40 Salas, *Army*, vol. IV, p. 3302.
41 IWM Ger/Misc/MCR/19 (1A).
42 Hooton, *Phoenix*, p. 141. In late autumn 1938 the Germans had 45 serviceable Bf 109s.
43 In October the FARE lost 19 fighters including six in accidents. Saiz, vol. 3, p. 833.
44 Permuy, p. 77.
45 Casualties based upon Håkon, Pedriali, Ries and Ring, and Salas.
46 Martinez, *Ebro*, pp. 246–247.
47 Tagüeña went to Madrid on October 25 to attend a Young Socialists' meeting and was temporarily replaced by his chief of staff, Major Manuel Martinez. Tagüeña, pp. 168–170.
48 From now until the end of the battle the Nationalists expended 8,000 tonnes of shells and 9,000 tonnes of bombs. Mezquida, p. 139. By comparison, during the first stage of the 3rd battle of Ypres 1,295 British guns fired 2,766,824 rounds or 85,396 tons from June 25 through August 31, 1917.
49 "Zapanov" was chosen because he was apparently visiting the front.
50 Salas, *Army*, vol. IV, p. 3303.
51 Salas, *Intervencion*, p. 552.
52 In October Franco told Germany that victory would be assured through the delivery of 100 field guns, 2,000 automatic weapons, and 50,000 rifles in December. Thomas, p. 850.
53 Garcia Lomas, p. 158.
54 Arce, pp. 291–293.
55 Martinez Bande, *La Campaña de Cataluña*, pp. 28–29 (hereafter Martinez, *Catalonia*).
56 Italy's industrial limitations meant that some CTV batteries were under strength with 224 barrels compared with 289 in the middle of the year, while at 58 AFVs, tank strength was almost half the establishment of 91. Based on Armas, p. 229; Salas, *Intervencion*, p. 554.
57 Aircraft figure based upon an inventory of December 23. Salas, *Air*, pp. 402–403 and Appendix 8. The Italians provided 136 aircraft.
58 Engel, *Operations*, p. 364.
59 Lister, pp. 239–240. Martinez claims that there were 300,000 but this may include police. Lister's corps replaced only half its losses.
60 Cayón Garcia/Muñoz Rubio, *Railway*, pp. 18–19.
61 On December 1 he had 54,455 rifles, 1,320 automatic rifles, 941 machine guns, and 144 guns. Salas, *Army*, vol. 4, p. 3312.
62 Alpert, p. 239; Armas, pp. 277–278; Rojo, *Alerta*, Appendix 2; Salas, *Army*, vol. 4, pp. 3354–55.
63 Permuy, p. 77.
64 See Rojo, *Alerta*, pp. 44–53, 64–72, Appendix 1.
65 For details see Perea, pp. 428–431.
66 For the Catalonia campaign see Martinez, *Catalonia*, and Rojo, *Alerta*. For the background see pp. 13–53; for the break-through, pp. 55–92 and the following operations, pp. 96–216; also Martinez, *Ultimos*, pp. 39–49, 51–68. See also Alcofar, *CTV*, pp. 175–180; Arias, pp. 261–269;

Aznar, pp. 804–838; Beevor, pp. 371–383; Belforte, *Vittoria*, pp. 125–141; Bollati and Del Bono, pp. 161–185, 197–213; Cardona, pp. 317–321, 322–325, 327–331; Coverdale, pp. 377–381; Engel, *Operations*, pp. 363–380; Hildago, pp. 191–194; Hills, p. 172; Lister, pp. 231–242; Lojendio, pp. 535–597; Martínez and Martínez, pp. 329–338, 343–344; Mezquida, pp. 173–184; Modesto, pp. 252–259, 264–274; Muria, pp. 161–166, 196–198; Perea, pp. 417–519; Tagüeña, pp. 178–188, 190–198; Thomas, pp. 867–880; Vidal, pp. 381–390. For air operations see Alcofar, *Air*, pp. 324–334; Permuy, pp. 77–78; Proctor, pp. 237–247; Ries and Ring, pp. 201–217; Rojo, *Alerta*, pp. 78–154; Saiz, vol. 3, pp. 837–890; Salas, *Air*, pp. 401–412; Ghergo article, p. 90, Pedriali, *Battaglie Aeree per la Catalogna*, pp. 76–81; Hårkon site.

67 Permuy, p. 78.

68 Gambara remained at his headquarters until the end of the campaign.

69 Richthofen would display similar petulance at Stalingrad in 1942.

70 For Republican casualties see Lister, p. 235.

71 Arms from Howson, *Arms*, p. 301. For the Estremadura offensive see Beevor, pp. 372, 376; Cardona, pp. 321–322, 325–326; Engel, *Operations*, pp. 381–386; Martinez, *Ultimos*, pp. 49–51; Martínez and Martínez, pp. 307–308; Modesto, pp. 261–263; Rojo, pp. 80–85; Saiz, vol. 3, pp. 891–906; Salas, *Air*, pp. 413–419; Thomas, p. 871. The Nationalists considered transferring aircraft from Catalonia to meet the threat but then decided it was unnecessary. Ries and Ring, p. 207.

72 Lister, p. 240.

73 Alcofar, pp. 179–180. The Italians reported firing 450,000 shells and taking 16,500 prisoners. Rodrigo, p. 392.

74 Salas, *Intervencion*, Anexo 8.

75 Alpert, p. 239. Beevor, p. 239, quoting FO 371, W14601/29/41 of October 31, 1938.

76 Beevor, p. 4448n6, based upon Ricardo Miralles, *Juan Negrín: La Republica en Guerra* (Madrid, 2003), p. 303.

77 Armas, p. 62; Howson, *Arms*, p. 301; Kowalsky, ch. 10; Thomas, p. 869.

78 Salas, *Air*, pp. 419–422.

79 Garcia Lomas, p. 159.

80 Matallana claimed the army group had 80 tanks, 800 guns, and 350,000 rifles. Alpert, p. 239.

81 For the final days of the Republic the most detailed description is Preston, *The Last Days of the Spanish Republic*, although it provides little information on the military situation and takes a jaundiced view of the Republic's military leaders, while Rodriguez, *El final de la Guerra civil*, looks at Miaja's role. See also Alcofar, *Air*, pp. 335–339; Alcofar, *CTV*, pp. 181–183; Aznar, pp. 839–847; Beevor, pp. 387–397; Lojendio, pp. 597–609; Martinez, *Ultimos*, pp. 78–294; Rojo, *Alerta*, pp. 158–175; Thomas, pp. 884–915.

82 Another 47 had flown to North Africa. Ghergo, p. 90; Salas, *Air*, p. 425. Francisco Galán, the new commander of the Cartagena naval base, fought the rebels but later joined the fleet when it fled to Tunis.

83 Menéndez later moved to Latin America.

84 Alpert, pp. 294–302.

85 For US reports see Cortada, *Modern Warfare in Spain*.

86 Salas, *Intercencion*, Anexo 8; Zaloga, *Tanks*, p. 44, claims that there were tank-versus-tank actions but, if so, these probably involved dug-in Republican tanks essentially acting as antitank guns.

Bibliography

Books

Academy of Sciences of the USSR. *International Solidarity with the Spanish Republic 1936–1939* (Moscow: Progress Publishers, 1976)

Alcofar Nassaes, José Luis (pseudo. José Luis Infiesta). *C. T. V. Los Legionarios Italianos en la Guerra Civil Española 1936–1939* (Barcelona: Dopesa, 1972)

Alcofar Nassaes José Luis. *La Aviación Legionaria en la Guerra Española* (Barcelona: Editorial Euros, 1975)

Alcofar Nassaes, Jose Luis. *Los Asesores Sovieticos en la Guerra Civil Española* (Barcelona: Dopesa, 1978)

Alcofar Nassaes José Luis. *Spansky* (Barcelona: Dopesa, 1973)

Alonso, Pedro Luis. *La Batalla de Teruel* (Barcelona: Editorial Bruguera, 1975)

Alpert, Michael. *The Republican Army in the Spanish Civil War 1936–1939* (Cambridge: Cambridge University Press, 2013)

Álvarez, Santiago. *Historia Política y Militar de la Brigadas Internacionales* (Madrid: Compañía Literaria, 1996)

Andrew, Christopher M. *Defend the Realm: The Authorised History of MI5* (London: Random House, 2010)

Aragon Gomez, Bartolome. *Con Intendencia Militar de las Gloriosas Brigadas Navarras* (Madrid: Imprenta del Patronato de Huerfanos de Intendencia e Intervencion Militares, 1940)

Arce, Carlos de. *Los Generales de Franco* (Barcelona: ATE, 1984)

Armiñán Odriozola, Lide. *Bajo el Cielo de Levante: La Ruta del Cuerpo de Ejército de Galicia* (Madrid, 1940)

Arias Ramos, Raul. *La Legion Condor en la Guerra Civil: El apoyo military aleman a Franco* (Madrid: Esfera de los Libros, 2003)

Aznar, Manuel. *Historia Militar de la Guerra España* (Madrid: Ediciones Idea, 1940)

Balfour, Sebastian. *Deadly Embrace: Morocco and the Road to the Spanish Civil War* (Oxford: Oxford University Press, 2002)

Ballester Escalas, Rafael. *La Batalla del Ebro* (Barcelona: Bruguera, 1975)

Baxell, Richard. *Unlikely Warriors: The British in the Spanish Civil War and the Struggle against Fascism* (London: Aurum Press, 2012)

Beevor, Antony. *The Battle for Spain: The Spanish Civil War 1936–1939* (London: Weidenfeld & Nicolson, 2006)

Beevor, Anthony. *D-Day: The Battle for Normandy* (London: Penguin Books, 2010)

Belforte, Francesco. *La Guerra Civile in Spagna; La campagna dei Volontari italiani dale Baleari a Teruel* (Milan: Istituto per gli Studi di Politica Internazionale, 1939)

Belforte, Francesco. *La Guerra Civile in Spagna; La campagna dei Volontari italiani e la Vittoria di Franco* (Milan: Istituto per gli Studi di Politica Internazionale, 1939)

Blanco Escolá, Carlos. *Franco y Rojo: Dos generals para dos Españas* (Barcelona: Editorial Labor, 1993)
Blas. Juan Antonio de. *La guerra civil en Asturias* (Gijon: Ediciones Júcar, 1986)
Bollati, Ambrogio and Giulio del Bono. *La Guerra di Spagna. Dalla liberazione di Gijon alla vittoria* (Turin: Giuli Einaudi, Editore, 1939)
Bond, Brian. *British Military Policy Between the Two World Wars* (Oxford: Clarendon, 1980)
Buckley, Henry. *The Life and Death of the Spanish Republic: A Witness to the Spanish Civil War* (London: I.B.Tauris, 2013, reprint)
Cabrera Castillo, Francisco. *Del Ebro a Gandesa: La Batalla del Ebro, Julio–Noviembre 1938* (Madrid: Almena, 2002)
Cappellano, Filippo and Pier Paolo Battistelli. *Italian Light Tanks, 1919–1945* (Oxford: Osprey Publishing, 2012)
Cardona, Gabriel. *Historia Militare de Una Guerra Civil: Estrategias y Tácticas de la Guerra de España* (Barcelona: Flor del Viento Ediciones, 2006)
Casas de la Vega, Rafael. *Brunete* (Madrid: Fermín Uriarte, 1968)
Casas de la Vega, Rafael. *Alfambra: La reconquista de Teruel* (Barcelona: Luis de Caralt Editor SA, 1976)
Castells, Andreu. *Las Brigadas Internacionales de la Guerra de España* (Barcelona: Editorial Ariel, 1974)
Cervelló, Josep Sánchez, Sebastion J. Agudo Blanco (eds.). *La Batalla del Ebro: Perspectivas y balance-Actas del Congreso Internacional sobre la Batalla del Ebro, 70 años después Congreso Internacional sobre la Batalla del Ebro, Mora de Ebro, 2008* (Tarragona: Arola Editors, 2011)
Colodny, Robert Garland. *The Struggle for Madrid: The Central Epic of the Spanish Conflict 1936–1937* (New Brunswick: Transaction Publishers, 2010, reprint)
Cortada, James W. and Stephen Ogden Fuqua. *Modern Warfare in Spain: American Military Observations on the Spanish Civil War 1936–1939* (Washington DC: Potomac Books, 2012)
Corum, James S. *The Luftwaffe: Creating the Operational Air War 1918–1940* (University Press of Kansas, 1997)
Coverdale, John F. *Italian Intervention in the Spanish Civil War* (Princeton: Princeton University Press, 1975)
Crociani, P. and Pier Paolo Battistelli. *Italian Blackshirt, 1935–1945* (Oxford: Osprey Publishing, 2013)
Dávila Jalón, Valentin. *Batalla en los campos de Teruel* (Madrid: Talleres, "prensa espanola," 1980)
Day, Peter. Franco's Friends: How British Intelligence Helped Bring Franco to Power in Spain (London: Biteback Publishing, 2011)
Delperrié de Bayac, Jacques. *Les Brigades Internationales* (Paris: Marabout, 1990)
Díez, Luis. *La Batalla del Jarama* (Barcelona: Oberón, c.2005)
Doughty, Robert Allen. *The Seeds of Disaster: The Development of French Army Doctrine 1919–1939* (Hamden, Connecticut: Archon Books, 1985)
Engel Masoliver, Carlos. *Historia de las Brigadas Mixtas del Ejército Popular de la Republica* (Madrid: Almena Ediciones, 1999)
Engel Masoliver, Carlos. *Historia de la divisions del Ejército Nacional* (Madrid: Almena, 2000)
Engel Masoliver, Carlos. *Estrategia y Táctica en la Guerra de España* (Madrid: Almena Ediciones, 2008)
Forsyth, Robert. *Aces of the Legion Condor* (Oxford: Osprey Publishing, 2012)
Galdón i Casanoves, Edelmir. *La batalla por Valencia, una Victoria defensive* (Publicacions de la Universitat de València (PUV), 2010)
García-Valiño, Rafael. *Guerra de Liberación Española. Campañas de Aragón y Maestrazgo, Batalla de Teruel, Batalla del Ebro 1938–1939* (Madrid: Imprenta Biosca, 1949)
Garriga, Ramón. *Guadalajara y sus consecuencias* (Madrid: G.del Toro, 1974)

Garriga, Ramón. *El General Juan Yague: Figura clave para conocer nuestra historia* (Barcelona: Planeta, 1985)

González Álvarez, Manuel. *Aspectos Militares de la Guerra Civil: La Actuation en Espana de la Legion Condor* (León: Universidad de León, Secretariado de Publicaciones, 2006)

Gudmundsson, Bruce I. *On Artillery* (Westport CT: Praeger Publishers, 1993)

Habeck, Mary R. *Storm of Steel: The Development of Armor Doctrine in Germany and the Soviet Union 1919–1939* (London: Cornell University Press, 2003)

Harris, John. *Men, Ideas and Tanks: British Military Thought and Armoured Forces 1903–1939* (Manchester: Manchester University Press, 1995)

Henry, Chris. *The Ebro 1938: Death Knell of the Republic* (Oxford: Osprey Publishing, 1999)

Hidalgo Salazar, Ramón. *La Ayuda Alemana a España* (Madrid: Liberia Editorial San Martin, 1975)

Hills, George. *The Battle for Madrid* (London: Vantage Books, 1976)

Hooton, E. R. *Phoenix Triumphant: The Rise and Rise of the Luftwaffe* (London: Arms and Armour Press, 1994)

Hooton, E. R. *Stalin's Claws: From the Purges to the Winter War. Red Army Operations before Barbarossa 1937–1941* (Pulborough: Tattered Flag Press, 2013)

Hooton, E. R. *War Over the Trenches: Air Power and the Western Front Campaigns 1916–1918* (Hersham: Midland Publishing, 2010)

Hooton, E. R. *War Over the Steppes: The Air Campaigns on the Eastern Front 1941–1945* (Oxford: Osprey Publishing, 2016)

Howson, Gerald. *Aircraft of the Spanish Civil War* (London: Putnam Aeronautical Books, 1990)

Howson, Gerald. *Arms for Spain: The Untold Story of the Spanish Civil War* (London: John Murray, 1998)

Jensen, Geoffrey. *Franco: Soldier, Commander, Dictator* (Washington DC: Potomac Books, 2005)

Johnston, Verle Bryant. *Legions of Babel: The International Brigades in the Spanish Civil War* (Pennsylvania State University Press, 1967)

Keene. Judith. *Fighting for Franco: International Volunteers in Nationalist Spain during the Spanish Civil War 1936–1939* (London: Leicester University Press, 2001)

Kindelán Duany, Alfredo. *Mis Cuadernos de Guerra* (Barcelona: Editorial Planeta, 1982)

Kowalsky, Daniel. *Stalin and the Spanish Civil War* (Columbia University Press 2004), downloaded from (www) Gutenberg-e.org/kod01

Lefebvre, Michel and Skoutelsky, Rèmi. *Las Brigadas Internacionales* (Barcelona: Imágenes recuperadas, 2003)

Lister, Enrique. *Nuestra Guerra: Aportaciones para una Historia de la Guerra Nacional Revolucionaria del Pueblo Español 1936–1939* (Paris: Coleccion Ebro, 1966)

Lloyd, Nick. *Passchendaele: A New History* (London: Viking, Penguin Random House, 2017)

Logoluso, Alfredo. *Fiat CR.32 Aces of the Spanish Civil War* (Oxford: Osprey Publishing, 2013)

Lojendio, Luis María de. *Operaciones militares de la Guerra de España 1936–1939* (Barcelona: Montaner y Simon SA, 1940)

López-Fernández, Antonio. *El General Miaja, Defensor de Madrid* (Madrid: G.del Toro, 1975)

López-Muñiz, Teniente Coronel Gregorio. *La Batalla de Madrid* (Madrid: Impresa F. G. Vicente, 1943)

Maiolo, Joe. *Cry Havoc: The Arms Race and the Second World War 1931–1941* (London: John Murray, 2010)

Manca di Mores, Ettore. *L'Impiego dell'Artiglieria Italiana nella Guerra di Spagna, maggio 1937, novembre 1938* (Rome: Tipografiaregionale, 1941)

Manrique García, José María, and Lucas Molina Franco. *Las armas de la Guerra Civil Española:*

El primer studio global y sistemático del armament empleado por ambos contendientes (Madrid: Esfera de loss Libros, 2006)

Martínez Bande, José Manuel. *La lucha en torno a Madrid en el invierno de 1936–1937* (Monografias de la Guerra de España No. 2) (Madrid: Libreria Editorial San Martin, 1984)

Martínez Bande, José Manuel. *Vizcaya* (Monografias de la Guerra de España No. 6) (Madrid: Librería Editorial San Martín, 1971)

Martínez Bande, José Manuel. *La ofensiva sobre Segovia y la batalla de Brunete* (Monografias de la Guerra de España No. 7) (Madrid: Libreria Editorial San Martín, 1972)

Martínez Bande, José Manuel. *El final del frente norte* (Monografias de la Guerra de España No. 8) (Madrid: Libreria Editorial San Martín, 1972)

Martínez Bande, José Manuel. *La gran ofensiva sobre Zaragoza* (Monografias de la Guerra de España No. 9) (Madrid: Libreria Editorial San Martín, 1973)

Martínez Bande, José Manuel. *La Batalla de Teruel* (Monografias de la Guerra de España No. 10) (Madrid: Librería Editorial San Martín, 1974)

Martínez Bande, José Manuel. *La llegada al Mar* (Monografias de la Guerra de España No. 11) (Madrid: Librería Editorial San Martín, 1975)

Martínez Bande, José Manuel. *La Ofensiva Sobre Valencia* (Monografias de la Guerra de España No. 12) (Madrid: Librería Editorial San Martín, 1977)

Martínez Bande, José Manuel. *La Batalla del Ebro* (Monografias de la Guerra de España No. 13) (Madrid: Librería Editorial San Martín, 1978)

Martínez Bande, José Manuel. *La Campaña de Cataluña* (Monografias de la Guerra de España No. 14) (Madrid: Librería Editorial San Martín, 1979)

Martínez Bande, José Manuel. *La batalla de Pozoblanco y el de la bolsa de Merida* (Monografias de la Guerra de España 15) (Madrid: Editorial San Martin, 1978)

Martínez Bande, José Manuel. *El Final de la Guerra Civil* (Monografias de la Guerra de España 17) (Madrid: Librería Editorial San Martín, 1979)

Martínez Bande, José Manuel. *La lucha por la victoria* (Monografias de la Guerra de España No. 18) (Madrid: Librería Editorial San Martín, 1980)

Martínez Bande, José Manuel. *Los cien ultimos dias de la Republica* (Barcelona: Luis de Caralt, 1973)

Martínez Bande, José Manuel. *Frente de Madrid* (Barcelona: Luis de Caralt Editor SA, 1976)

Martínez Paricio, Jesus Ignacio. *Los Papeles del General Vincente Rojo: Un military de la generación rota* (Madrid: Espasa Calpe, 1989)

Martínez Reverte, Jorge. *La Batalla del Ebro* (Barcelona: Crítica, c. 2003)

Martínez Reverte, Jorge. *La Batalla de Madrid* (Barcelona: Crítica, 2004)

Martínez Reverte, Jorge and Mario Martínez Zauner. *De Madrid al Ebro: Las grandes batallas de la Guerra civil* Española (Barcelona: Galaxia Gutenberg, 2016)

Matthews, James. *Reluctant Warriors: Republican Popular Army and Nationalist Army Conscripts in the Spanish Civil War 1936–1939* (Oxford Historical Monograph) (Oxford: Oxford University Press, 2011)

Meredith, Richard. *Phoenix: A Complete History of the Luftwaffe 1918–1945: Volume 2. The Genesis of Air Power 1935–1937* (Solihull: Helion & Company, 2017)

Meretskov, Kyril A. *Na Sluzhbe Narodoo (Serving the People)* (Moscow: Politizdat, 1968)

Mezquida y Gené, Luis María. *La Batalla del Ebro: Asedio y defensa de Gandesa en sus aspectos military, economic, demografico, y urbanisto* (Tarragona: Excma. Diputación Provincial de Tarragona, 1970)

Mezquida y Gené, Luis María. *La Battala del Segre: Repercusiones del Ebro en el oeste de Cataluña. Marcha por Aragón, Asedio y defensa de Lérida. Ataques a las Cabezas de Puente de Balaguer y Serós. Acción diversiva de Vilanova de la Barca y ofensiva del Bajo Segre* (Tarragona: Excma. Diputación Provincial de Tarragona, 1972)

Modesto Guilloto, Juan. *Soy del Quinto Regimento: Notas de la Guerra Española* (Paris: Editions de la Librairie du Globe, 1969)

Molina Franco, Lucas and Rafael A. *Permuy López. Importacíon de Armas en la Guerra Civil Española: Discrepancias historiográficas con Angel Viñas* (Valladolid Enero: Galland Editorial Books, 2017)

Murias, Carlos and Carlos Castañon, José María Manrique García. *Militares Italianos en la Guerra Civil Española: Italia, el fascism y los voluntaries en el conflict español* (Madrid: Esfera de los Libros, 2010)

Nesterenko, Ivan (ed.). *International Solidarity with the Spanish Republic 1936–1939 (Solidarnost' narodov s Ispanskoi respublikoi 1936–1939)* (Moscow: Progress Publishers, 1976)

Neulen, Hans (trans. Alex Vanags-Baginskis). *In the Skies of Europe: Air Forces Allied to the Luftwaffe 1939–1945* (Marlborough: The Crowood Press, 2000)

Parrish, Michael. *Sacrifice of the Generals: Soviet Senior Officer Losses 1939–1953* (Oxford: The Scarecrow Press Inc, 2004)

Payne, Stanley G. *The Spanish Revolution* (London: Weidenfeld & Nicolson, 1970)

Pedriali, Ferdinando. *Ali di Guerra sulla Spagna, 1936–1939* (Rome: IBN Editore, 2015)

Pedriali, Ferdinando. *Guerra di Spagna e aviazione italiana* (Rome: Ufficio Storico, Aeronautica Militare, 1992)

Perea Capolino, Juan. *Los Culpables: Recuerdos de la Guerra, 1936–1939* (Barcelona: Flor del Viento Ediciones, 2007)

Permuy López, Rafael A (trans. Juan Carlos Salgado). *Air War Over Spain: Aviators, Aircraft and Air Units of the Nationalist and Republican Air Forces 1936–1939* (Hersham: Classic, c. 2009)

Permuy López Rafael A (trans. Juan Carlos Salagdo). *Spanish Republican Aces* (Oxford: Osprey Publishing, 2012)

Preston, Paul. *The Spanish Holocaust: Inquisition and extermination in the Twentieth Century* (London: Harper Collins, 2012)

Preston, Paul. *The Last Days of the Spanish Republic* (London: William Collins, 2016)

Proctor Raymond L. *Hitler's Luftwaffe in the Spanish Civil War* (Wesport, Conn: Greenwood Press, 1983)

Reverte, Jorge Martínez. *La Batalla de Madrid* (Barcelona: Crítica, 2004)

Reverte, Jorge Martínez. *La batalla del Ebro* (Barcelona: Critica, 2003)

Ries, Karl and Ring, Hans (trans. David Johnston). *The Legion Condor: A History of the Luftwaffe in the Spanish Civil War 1936–1939* (West Chester, PA: Schiffer Military History, 1992)

Rodrigo, Javier. *La Guerra Fascista: Italia en la Guerra Civil Española 1936–1939* (Madrid: Alianza Editorial, 2016)

Rodriguez Miaja, Fernando. *El final de la Guerra civil: Al lado del General Miaja* (Madrid: Marcial Pons Historia, 2015)

Rojo, José Andrés. *Vicente Rojo: Retrato de un general republican* (Barcelona: Tusquets Editores, 2006)

Rojo Lluch, Vicente. *Alerta los Pueblos: Estudio politico-militar del period final de la Guerra española* (Buenos Aires: Aniceto López Editor, 1939)

Rojo Lluch, Vicente. *España Heroica: Diez bocetos de la Guerra Española* (Buenos Aires: Editorial Americalee, 1942)

Rojo Lluch, Vicente. *Historia de la Guerra Civil Española* (Barcelona: RBA Libros, 2010)

Rojo Lluch, Vicente. *General Vicente Rojo: Mi Verdad* (Saragossa: Mira Editores, 2014)

Romilly, Esmond. *Boadilla* (London: Hamish Hamilton, 1937)

Rotmistov, Aleksandr Ilyich. *Pod Nebom Ispanii (Under Spanish Skies)* (Moscow: Voenizdat, 1985)

Rust, William. *Britons in Spain: A History of the XVth International Brigade* (London: Lawrence and Wishart Ltd, 1939)

Sáiz Cidoncha, Carlos. *Aviació Republicana: Historia de la Fuerzas Aéreas de la Republica Española (1931–1939)* (Madrid: Almena Ediciones, 2006)

Salas Larrazabal, Jesus. *La guerra de España desde el aire* (Barcelona: Ediciones Ariel, 1972)
Salas Larrazabal, Jesus. *La Intervencion Extranjera en la Guerra de España* (Madrid: Editora Nacional, 1974)
Salas Larrazabal, Jesus. *Guernica* (Madrid: Ediciones RIALP, 1987)
Salas Larrazábal Ramón. *Historia de le Ejé*rcito Popular de la Republica (Madrid: Editora Nacional, c. 1973)
Salgado-Araujo, Francisco Franco. *Mi vida junto a Franco* (Barcelona: Editorial Planeta, 1977)
Sánchez Cervelló, Josep and Sebastián Agudo Blanco (eds.). *Las brigadas Internacionales: Nuevas perspectivas en la historiade la Guerra Civil y del exilio Congreso Internacional del Antifascismo Combatiente 2011* (Tarragona: Publicacions URV, 2015)
Shore, Christopher Francis. *Spanish Civil War Air Forces* (Oxford: Osprey Publishing, 1977)
Solé i Sabaté, Josep Maria and Joan Villarroya. *España en llamas: La Guerra Civil Desde el Aire* (Madrid: Ediciones Temas de Hoy, 2003)
Steer, G. L. *The Tree of Gernika: A Field Study of Modern War* (London: Hodder and Stoughton, 1938)
Stoker, Donald J. Jr and Grant, Jonathan A. (eds.). *Girding for Battle: The Arms Trade in a Global Perspective, 1815–1940* (London: Praeger, 2003)
Tagüeña Lacorte, Manuel. *Testimonio de Dos Guerras* (Barcelona: Planeta, 1978)
Thomas, Hugh. *The Spanish Civil War* (London: Penguin Books, 1990)
Thomas, Gordon and Max Morgan-Witts. *The Day Guernica Died* (London: Hodder & Stoughton, 1975)
Torres, Estanislau. *La Batalla del Ebro* (Barcelona: Editorial Nova Terra, 1974)
Vidal Manzanares, César. *La Guerra de Franco: Historia Militar de la Guerra Civil Española* (Barcelona: Planeta, 1996)
Voltas, Eduard (ed.). *La Guerra Civil a Catalunya. Vol. 1: Alçament military I primers mesos de Guerra; Vol. 2: Una revolució en plena Guerra; Vol. 3: Catalunya, centre neuralgic de la Guerra* (Barcelona: Edicions 62, 2004)
Voronov, Nikolai Nikolaevich. *Na Sluzhbe Voennoy (On Military Service)* (Moscow: Voenizdat, 1963)
Wais, Francisco. *Historia de los ferrocarriles espanoles* (Madrid: Editora Nacional, 2nd edition, 1974)
Zaloga, Steven J. *Spanish Civil War Tanks: The Proving Ground for Blitzkrieg* (Oxford: Osprey Publishing, 2010)
Zaloga, Steven J. *T-26 Light Tank: Backbone of the Red Army* (Oxford: Osprey Publishing, 2015)
Zaragoza, Cristóbal. *Ejercito popular y militares de la Republica 1936–1939* (Barcelona: Planeta, 1983)

Articles and Theses

Calvett Clarke III, J. "Italo-Soviet Military Co-operation in the 1930s," in Stoker and Grant (eds.). *Girding for Battle*, pp. 177–199
Candil, Antonio J. "Carros de Combate: Evolución, presente y future," *Isdefe*, Madrid (March 1999), pp. 84–94
Francisco Cayón Garcia and Miguel Muñoz Rubio. "Los Transportes y Las Comunicaciones Durante la Guerra Civil," (www) usc.es/estaticos/congresos/histec05/a2_cayon_munoz.pdf (also available through El Capitan forum.biblioteca online. Paper presented to VIII Congreso de la AEHE, Santiago de Compestela, 2005
Francisco Cayón Garcia and Miguel Muñoz Rubio. "El Ferrocarril como Sector Estratégico Durante la Guerra Civil Española: Reorganización, explotación y consecuensias," Working Paper 01/2006, Departamento de Análisis Económico, Teoria Económica e Historia Económica, Universidad Autonoma de Madrid, downloaded from http://ideas.repec.org/p/uam/wpapeh/200601.html

Daley, Dr John. "Soviet and German Advisors Put Doctrine to the Test: Tanks in the Siege of Madrid," *Armor*, Vol. 108 No. 2/3 (March–April, May–June 1999)

Garcia Lomas, José Maria. "La Explotación de Ferrocarriles Durante la Guerra de Liberación," *Revista de Obras Publica*, Numero Especial 1936–1939, Dedicado a la Guerra. Downloaded from http://ropdigital.ciccp.es/pdf/publico/1936/1936_1939_numeroespecial_14.pdf, or https://www. academia.edu

Ghergo, Giuseppe Federico. "Guerra aerea nei cieli di Spagna," *Revista Italiana Difesa*, January 1998

Harvey, A. D. "The Spanish Civil War as Seen by British Officers," *Royal United Services' Institute Journal*, August 1996, pp. 65–67

Herrero Perez, Jose Vicente."The Spanish Military and the Evolution of Warfare 1899–1939," (thesis, University of London, 2001)

Hughes, Dr Matthew. "The 'European Aldershot' for the Second World War? The Battle of the Ebro, 1938," *RUSI Journal*, December 2002, pp. 74–81

Matthews, J. "Our Red Soldiers: The Nationalist Army's Management of its Left-Wing Conscripts in the Spanish Civil War 1936–9," *Journal of Contemporary History*, Vol. 45 No. 2 (2010), pp. 344–63

Pedriali, Ferdinando. "Guadalajara, mito e realta: (1a parte). I precedenti della battaglia," *Revista Italiana Difesa*, December 1988, pp. 94–103.

Prediali, Ferdinando. "Guadalajara, mito e realta:(2a parte). La Controffensiva Repubblicana," *Revista Italiana Difesa*, January 1989, pp. 86–92.

Pedriali, Ferdinando. "Guadalajara, mito e realta," *Revista Italiana Difesa*, December 1988 and January 1989

Pedriali, Ferdinando. "L'Aviazione Legionaria nel Levante e sull'Ebro," *Revista Italiana Difesa*, October 2010

Pedriali, Ferdinando. "Battaglie aeree per la Catalogna," *Revista Italiana Difesa*, July 2011

Preston, Paul. "General Franco as a Military Leader," *Transactions of the Royal Historical Society, 6th series,* 1994

Rubio-Campillo, Xavier. "Combined Arms Warfare in the Spanish Civil War: The Assault on the Republican Defence Line at Fatarella Ridge," *Journal of Conflict Archaeology*, Vol. 10, Issue 1 (2015), p. 52

Serebryakov, A. G. "Brunetskaya Operatsiya Respublikanskoi Armii Ispanii (Operativno-Takticheskii Ocherk) (Brunete Operation in Republican Army Spain, Operational-Tactical Essay)" (Moscow: Voenizdat NKO, 1941)

Sullivan, Brian R. "Fascist Italy's Military Involvement in the Spanish Civil War," *Journal of Military History*, 59#4, 1995, pp. 697–727

Zaloga, Steven J. "Soviet Tank Operations in the Spanish Civil War," *Journal of Slavic Military Studies*, Vol. 12, No. 3 (September 1999)

UK National Archives

WO 106/1578/1579/1585. Reports of Major General Fuller on his Visit to Spain, March 1937, October 1937, April 1938

WO 106/1583. Some Impressions of the Nationalist Army (Lt Colonel A. F. G. Renton), May 1938

WO 106/1589. Visit by Brigadier General A. L. M Molesworth's Section to Army of Ebro

WO 106/1588. Visit of AMA (Assistant Military Attache) Paris to Nationalist Spain, April 1938. Major C. A. de Linde, written April 29

Imperial War Museum

Ger/Misc/MCR/19 (1A). Lagebericht Spanien an Juli 6 1938

Bundesarchiv, Militärarchiv

N671/1. Richthofen Tagesbuch
RL2/V. "Die kampfe in Norden"
RL7/57. "Unternehmen Ruegen"

Websites

Almenara, inici de la línia defensiva XYZ. Catàleg del Patrimoni Històric Militar de la Guerra Cinturon de Hierro, (www):elcorreo.com/vizcaya/prensa/20070211/vizcaya/cinturon-hierro_200070211.html.
Civil (1936–39) by Pere Hormigos i Sánchez, Miguel Sáez Landete, Antonio Sáez Landete, Pablo Ferrer Beltrán, Estel Bosó i Doménech, Carles Mallench Sanz for the Grup d'Estudis de la Batalla del Llevant de l'Associació Les Muntanyes de la Guerra de la Vall d'Uixó, (www):academia edu/4680710/Almenra_inici_defensiva_XYZ
Axis History Forum, Spanish Civil War and Legion Condor, https://forum.axishistory.com
Generals in World War II, (www):Generals.dk
el Gran Capitan, Foro de Historia Militar, (www):elgrancapitan.org/foro/Guerra Civil Española
Håkan's Aviation Page: Air War in the Spanish Civil War 1936–39, http://surfcity.kund.dalnet.se/scw.htm
Linea Defensiva XYZ, (www):senderosconhistoria.com/linea-defensiva-xyz-o-matallana. Linea XYZ (www):es.wikipedia.org/wiki/Linea_XYZ, academia edu/4680710/Almenra_inici_defensiva_XYZ, Linea XYZ
El Mazuco impossible defence, (www):Speleogroup.org/files/ElMazuco-impossible-defence
Republican artillery, (www):bhac.net/Republica/Fuerzas/Armas/Artilleria/ArtLinea/ArtLinea.htm
Sociedad Benéfica de Historiadores Aficionados y Creadores, (www):sbhac.net/Republica/Introduccion/Introduccion.htm
war heroes, (www):warheroes.ru
The Workers' and Peasants' Red Army (website of Aleksandr Kiyan), Dmity Churakov's Red Army Soldiers Repressed, sub site (www):rkka.ru

Index

General Index

Index of Personalities

Full Spanish names are given where known. Ranks are given generically i.e Lieutenant Colonel as Colonel and Brigadier or Lieutenant General as General. All are Spanish unless identified as foreign Brit = British, Fr = French, Ger = German, Hung = Hungarian, Ir = Irish, Ital = Italian, Rum = Rumanian, Sov = Soviet Union. No ranks given for foreign International Brigade officers.

Index of Formations